On the Path to the Place of Rest

On the Path to the Place of Rest

Demotic Graffiti Relating to the Ibis and Falcon Cult from the Spanish Mission at Dra Abu el-Naga^c (TT 11, TT 12, Tomb –399–, and Environs)

by

Christina Di Cerbo and Richard Jasnow

with contributions by

José M. Galán, Francisco Bosch-Puche, and Salima Ikram

LOCKWOOD PRESS
Atlanta, GA

On the Path to the Place of Rest

Demotic Graffiti Relating to the Ibis and Falcon Cult from the Spanish Mission at Dra Abu el-Naga^c (TT 11, TT 12, Tomb –399–, and Environs)

ISBN: 978-1-948488-41-9

Cover design by Susanne Wilhelm.

Library of Congress Cataloging-in-Publication Data

Names: Di Cerbo, Christina, editor. | Jasnow, Richard, editor. | Galán, José M., other. | Bosch-Puche, Francisco, other. | Ikram, Salima, other.

Title: On the path to the place of rest : demotic graffiti relating to the ibis and falcon cult from the Spanish mission at Dra Abu el-Naga' (TT 11, TT 12, tomb -399-, and environs) / by Christina Di Cerbo and Richard Jasnow ; with contributions by José M. Galán, Francisco Bosch-Puche, and Salima Ikram.

Description: Atlanta : Lockwood Press, 2021. | Includes bibliographical references and index.

Identifiers: LCCN 2021051271 (print) | LCCN 2021051272 (ebook) | ISBN 9781948488419 (cloth) | ISBN 9781948488426 (pdf)

Subjects: LCSH: Egyptian language--Demotic, ca. 650 B.C.-450 A.D.--Texts. | Dra Abu el-Naga Site (Thebes, Egypt)

Classification: LCC PJ1821.D73 O5 2021 (print) | LCC PJ1821.D73 (ebook) | DDC 493/.1--dc23/eng/20211115

LC record available at https://lccn.loc.gov/2021051271

LC ebook record available at https://lccn.loc.gov/2021051272

This paper meets the requirements of ANSI/NISO Z39.48-1992 (Permanence of Paper).

Dedicated to

Heinz-Josef Thissen
and
Eugene Cruz-Uribe

Lovers of demotic graffiti

Contents

Acknowledgments	ix
List of Figures	xi
List of Plates	xii
Abbreviations	xv
The Spanish Archaeological Mission to Dra Abu el-Naga[c] North: A Chronological Overview of the Site (*José M. Galán*)	1
The Archaeology of the Area: An Overview (*Francisco Bosch-Puche and Salima Ikram*)	17
Introductory Remarks and Overview of the Graffiti from the Spanish Mission at Dra Abu el-Naga[c]	37
Text Editions of Graffiti	69
1–44 Tomb of Djehuty (TT 11)	71
45–46 Tomb –399–	107
47–52 Tomb of Hery (TT 12)	109
53–61 Eastern Galleries	115
62–64 Upper Gallery	127
Appendix A: Graffiti Copied by Spiegelberg in a Tomb above Hery (TT 12) and "The Great Tomb of the Ibis and Hawks," Present Location Unknown	133
a. 65–66 Tomb above Hery (TT 12)	133
b. 67–88 "The Great Tomb of the Ibis and Hawks"	135
Appendix B: 89–92 Recently Discovered Graffiti in the Tomb of Hery (TT 12)	161
Appendix C: Additional Demotic Material Found by the Spanish Mission at Dra Abu el-Naga[c]	164
a. Ostraca	164
b. Mummy Bandages	173
Appendix D: Condition of the Individual Graffiti	175
Appendix E: Concordance of Graffiti Numbers Employed in This Volume with Those in the Editions of Spiegelberg and Vleeming	180
Glossary	181
Select Vocabulary	181
Personal Names	195
Titles	207
Deities	208

Glossary (cont.)
- Place Names 209
- Numerals 210
- Dates 212
- Greek Personal Names 212

Bibliography 213

General Index 225

Plates 233

Acknowledgments

We would like to express our gratitude to the entire team of the Spanish Mission to Dra Abu el-Nagaᶜ. Its conservation and restoration professionals deserve especial mention, since their hard and excellent work has proved essential in bringing the graffiti back to life. Most notably our thanks go to Nieves López Meijueiro, who carried out the cleaning of the walls of the tomb of Djehuty, and Miguel Ángel Navarro, responsible for the restoration of the tomb of Hery. The latter has also provided us with photographs of the graffiti on the north wall of the corridor of TT 12. We should also mention José (Pito) Latova, photographer of the mission in 2011–2018 and author of many of the images reproduced here, as well as the architect Juan Ivars, responsible for the plans, and Carmen Ruiz Sánchez de León for her assistance in the preparation of the figures that illustrate the contribution by Bosch-Puche and Ikram.

Di Cerbo and Jasnow are deeply grateful to Dr. José M. Galán for inviting them to work on these challenging, but fascinating demotic graffiti. He has been unfailingly enthusiastic and supportive of our study of the texts through the years. It has been a true pleasure to collaborate with him, Francisco Bosch-Puche, and Salima Ikram on this volume. Di Cerbo and Jasnow would also like to express their thanks to The Director of the Epigraphic Survey of the Oriental Institute of the University of Chicago, Dr. Raymond Johnson. Chicago House is naturally an ideal base from which to conduct such a field project, and Dr. Johnson, for his part, has always been extremely supportive of our demotic research in Luxor. The Department of Near Eastern Studies of Johns Hopkins University provides an ideal environment in which to pursue scholarship of the type represented in this volume. Jasnow would like to acknowledge a debt of gratitude to his fellow Egyptologist, Dr. Betsy Bryan, and the other members of the department, who have long labored to maintain a tradition of mutual respect and collegiality. We thank Billie Jean Collins, Susanne Wilhelm, and James Spinti of Lockwood Press for the great care and efficiency with which they have prepared the manuscript for publication.

Christina Di Cerbo
Richard Jasnow
José M. Galán
Francisco Bosch-Puche
Salima Ikram

List of Figures

Fig. 1. Plan of the Spanish Mission archaeological site at Dra Abu el-Naga^c North. 5
Fig. 2. Access to the Lower Gallery in the corridor of tomb –399–. 20
Fig. 3. Mud-brick staircase in the main shaft of tomb –399–, descending to the Lower Gallery. 21
Fig. 4. Bone deposit in burial chamber UE 230, with connection to burial chamber UE 235. 22
Fig. 5. Examples of bird mummies; the radiograph shows a falcon. 23
Fig. 6. Examples of raptor mummies. 24
Fig. 7. Examples of small packages with shrew/rodent and snake mummies. 25
Fig. 8. Example of bundle mummy containing broken parts of other mummies (top and bottom views). 26
Fig. 9. Example of ibis mummies stuck together. 26
Fig. 10. Ptolemaic container with painted plant decoration from chamber UE 225. 28
Fig. 11. Ptolemaic ovoid two-handled jar from chamber UE 230. 28
Fig. 12. Shrew and snake mummies from tomb above TT 11. 34
Fig. 13. Detail of Dra Abu el-Naga^c map. From Northampton, Spiegelberg, and Newberry, *Report on Some Excavations in the Theban Necropolis*, pl. 2. 38
Fig. 14. Plan of "The Great Tomb of the Ibis and Hawks." From Northampton, Spiegelberg, and Newberry, *Report on Some Excavations in the Theban Necropolis*, fig. 23 38
Fig. 15. S-wall of TT 12 vandalized by antiquity hunters. 39
Fig. 16. Conservator Nieves López Meijueiro cleaning area next to graffito 38 in TT 11 using a vibrating cutter with ultrasound. 40
Fig. 17. Animal mummies in the chambers at the foot of the staircase in tomb –399–. 43
Fig. 18. Suggested routes taken by the cult workers engaged in the interment of the ibis and falcon mummies. 49
Fig. 19. Staircase in tomb –399– with graff. 46. 51
Fig. 20. Graffiti 53 and 54 inscribed along the path leading to the "First Hall" and the staircase leading to the tombs of Baki and Ay. 51
Fig. 21. Graffiti 42 and 44 directing the cult workers from the main hallway to the staircase inside the chapel in TT 11. 52
Fig. 22. "First Hall" of the Eastern Galleries with graff. 55. 53

List of Plates

Plate 1. View of Dra Abu el-Naga[c] at the northern end of the Theban necropolis, on the West Bank of Luxor, opposite to Karnak temple on the East Bank. Photograph by J. Latova.
Plate 2. View of the archaeological site of the Spanish Mission, February 2018. Photograph by J. Latova.
Plate 3. a.–b. Photograph and drawing of stamped mud brick with a seal impression of Thoth. Drawing by P. Rodrígues Frade. Photograph by J. Latova.
Plate 4. Keyplan showing location of deposits of animal mummies and bones in tomb –399–, TT 12, Eastern Galleries, and tomb above TT 11.
Plate 5. Plan of TT 11, TT 12, tomb –399–, Upper Gallery, and Eastern Galleries.
Plate 6. Keyplan showing location of graffiti in TT 11, TT 12, tomb –399–, and Eastern Galleries.
Plate 7. Keyplan showing location of the graffiti containing distinctive architectural and directional terms (with demotic hand-copies).
Plate 8. Keyplan showing location of the graffiti containing distinctive architectural and directional terms (with translation of the demotic terms in pl. 7).
Plate 9. Keyplan of graffiti on N-wall in the tomb of Djehuty (TT 11). Photograph courtesy of J. M. Galán.
Plate 10. Keyplan of graffiti on S-wall in the tomb of Djehuty (TT 11). Photograph courtesy of J. M. Galán.
Plate 11. Graffito 1.
Plate 12. Graffiti 2 and 4.
Plate 13. a. Graffito 3; b. Graffito 5.
Plate 14. a. Graffito 6; b. Graffito 7.
Plate 15. Graffito 8.
Plate 16. a. Graffito 9; b. Graffito 10.
Plate 17. Graffiti 11 and 12.
Plate 18. Graffito 13.
Plate 19. Graffito 14.
Plate 20. a. Graffito 15; b. Graffito 16; c. Graffito 17.
Plate 21. Graffito 18.
Plate 22. Graffito 19.
Plate 23. a. Graffito 20; b. Graffito 21.
Plate 24. a. Graffito 22; b. Graffito 23.
Plate 25. Graffito 24.
Plate 26. a. Graffito 25; b. Graffito 26; c. Graffito 27.
Plate 27. a. Graffito 28; b. Graffito 29; c. Graffito 32.
Plate 28. Graffito 30.
Plate 29. Graffito 31.
Plate 30. Graffito 33.
Plate 31. Graffito 34.
Plate 32. Graffito 35.

Plate 33. Graffito 36.
Plate 34. Graffito 37.
Plate 35. a. Graffito 38; b. Graffito 39.
Plate 36. a. Graffito 40; b. Graffito 41.
Plate 37. a. Graffito 42; b. Graffito 43.
Plate 38. Graffito 44.
Plate 39. Graffito 45.
Plate 40. Keyplan of graffiti on S-wall in the tomb of Hery (TT 12). Drawing by G. Menéndez and J. M. Galán.
Plate 41. Detail of keyplan of graffiti on the W-section of the S-wall in the tomb of Hery (TT 12). Drawing by G. Menéndez and J. M. Galán.
a. W-section of S-wall at the time of Spiegelberg (ca. 1896) with graffiti 49 and 50.
b. W-section of S-wall in present time (2019) with graffiti 49 and 50.
Plate 42. a. Graffito 46; b. Graffito 48.
Plate 43. Graffito 47 (with DStretch images).
Plate 44. Graffito 49 in photograph and hand-copy with areas lost since the time of Spiegelberg indicated in gray.
Plate 45. Graffito 50.
Plate 46. Graffito 51.
Plate 47. Graffiti 89, 90, 91, and 92 in general photograph.
Plate 48. Graffiti 89 and 90.
Plate 49. a. Graffito 91; b. Graffito 92.
Plate 50. Graffito 52 (with DStretch images).
Plate 51. Graffito 53.
Plate 52. Graffito 54.
Plate 53. Graffito 55.
Plate 54. Graffito 56 (with DStretch image).
Plate 55. Graffito 57.
Plate 56. Graffito 58 (arrows indicate that the text continues around the corner or bend in the wall).
Plate 57. a. Graffito 59; b. Graffito 61.
Plate 58. Graffito 60.
Plate 59. Keyplan of graffiti in Upper Gallery.
Plate 60. a. Entrance to chambers H in Upper Gallery with graffito 62.
b. Chamber G in Upper Gallery with graffiti 63 and 64.
Plate 61. Graffito 62.
Plate 62. Graffito 63.
Plate 63. Chamber G in Upper Gallery with graffiti 64a–d.
Plate 64. Graffito 64a (with DStretch image).
Plate 65. Graffito 64b (with DStretch image).
Plate 66. Graffiti 64c and 64d with right side of graffito 64b.
Plate 67. a. Graffito 65 (Spiegelberg hand-copy); b. Graffito 66 (Spiegelberg hand-copy); c. Graffito 67 (Spiegelberg hand-copy).
Plate 68. a. Graffito 68 (Spiegelberg hand-copy); b. Graffito 69 (Spiegelberg hand-copy); c. Graffito 70 (Spiegelberg hand-copy).
Plate 69. a. Graffito 71 (Spiegelberg hand-copy); b. Graffito 72 (Spiegelberg hand-copy); c. Graffito 73 (Spiegelberg hand-copy).

Plate 70. a. Graffito 74 (Spiegelberg hand-copy); b. Graffito 75 (Spiegelberg hand-copy); c. Graffito 79 (Spiegelberg hand-copy).
Plate 71. Graffito 76 (Spiegelberg hand-copy).
Plate 72. Graffito 77 (Spiegelberg hand-copy).
Plate 73. a. Graffito 78 (Spiegelberg hand-copy); b. Graffito 80 (Spiegelberg hand-copy); c. Graffito 81 (Spiegelberg hand-copy).
Plate 74. a. Graffito 82 (Spiegelberg hand-copy); b. Graffito 83 (Spiegelberg hand-copy); c. Graffito 84 (Spiegelberg hand-copy).
Plate 75. Graffito 85 (Spiegelberg hand-copy).
Plate 76. a. Graffito 86 (Spiegelberg hand-copy); b. Graffito 87 (Spiegelberg hand-copy); c. Graffito 88 (Spiegelberg hand-copy).
Plate 77. a. Ostracon 1; b. Ostracon 2; c. Ostracon 4.
Plate 78. Ostracon 3.
Plate 79. a. Ostracon 5; b. Mummy Bandage 1.
Plate 80. Child mummy with Mummy Bandage 2.
a. Photograph of child mummy; b. detail of demotic inscription; c–d. DStretch images of demotic inscription; e. hand-copy of demotic inscription.

Abbreviations

GENERAL

BCE	Before Common Era
BM	British Museum, London
ca.	*circa*, approximately
circ. converter	circumstantial converter
cm	centimeter
cond.	conditional
cont.	continued
dem.	demonstrative
diss.	dissertation
E	East
EA	Egyptian Antiquity
e.g.	*exempli gratia*, for example
ed(s).	editor(s)
et al.	*et alii*, and others
fem.	feminine
fig(s).	figure(s)
graff.	graffito/graffiti
imperf. converter	imperfect converter
km	kilometer
m	meter
N	North
no(s).	number(s)
O.	ostracon
p(p).	page(s)
P.	papyrus
perf. part.	perfect participle
pers.	person
pers. comm.	personal communication
pl(s).	plate(s)
PN	Personal name
poss.	possessive
prep.	preposition
rel.	relative
S	South
SW	Southwest
TT	Theban tomb (tomb number)
vol(s).	volume(s)
W	West

SYMBOLS

[...]	missing signs and words
⸢...⸣	damaged signs and words
(...)	restored text for clarification
{...}	words regarded as superfluous
<...>	signs or words omitted by the ancient scribe
...	unread text
\.../	supra line
Ø	word too damaged for facsimile

BIBLIOGRAPHIC

ASAE	*Annales du Service des Antiquités de l'Égypte*. Cairo 1900–.
BdE	Bibliothèque d'Étude. Cairo, 1908–.
BES	*Bulletin of the Egyptological Seminar*. New York, 1979–.
BIFAO	*Bulletin de l'Institut français d'archéologie orientale au Caire*. Cairo, 1901–.
BMMA	*Bulletin of the Metropolitan Museum of Art*. New York, 1905–.
CDD	Johnson, J., ed. *The Demotic Dictionary of the Oriental Institute of the University of Chicago. 2001–.* https://oi.uchicago.edu/research/publications/demotic-dictionary-oriental-institute-university-chicago.
CENIM	Cahiers "Égypte Nilotique et Méditérranéenne." Montpellier, 2008–.
CH	Collectanea Hellenistica. Leuven, 1989–.
CNI	Carsten Niebuhr Institute. Copenhagen, 1986–.
Demot. Nb.	Lüddeckens, E. et al. *Demotisches Namenbuch*. Wiesbaden: Reichert, 1980–2000.
EA	*Egyptian Archaeology*. The Bulletin of the Egyptian Exploration Society. London, 1991–.
EES	Egypt Exploration Society.
Glossar	Erichsen, W. *Demotisches Glossar*. Copenhagen: Munksgaard, 1953.
JEA	*The Journal of Egyptian Archaeology*. London, 1914–.
LÄ	Helck, W., E. Otto, and W. Westendorf, eds. *Lexikon der Ägyptologie*. 7 vols. Wiesbaden: Harrassowitz, 1972–1992.
Leitz, LGG	Leitz, C. et al., eds. *Lexikon der ägyptischen Götter und Götterbezeichnungen*. 8 vols. OLA 110–16, 129. Leuven: Peeters, 2002–2003.
MÄS	Münchner Ägyptologische Studien. Berlin, Munich, 1962–.
MDAIK	*Mitteilungen des Deutschen Archäologischen Instituts, Abteilung Kairo*. Berlin, Wiesbaden, Mainz, 1930–.
MIFAO	Mémoires publiés par les membres de l'Institut français d'archéologie orientale du Caire. Paris, Cairo, 1902–.
MRE	*Monographies Reine Élisabeth.* Fondation égyptologique Reine Élisabeth. Brussels, 1971–.
OIP	Oriental Institute Publications. Chicago, 1924–.
OLA	Orientalia Lovaniensia Analecta. Leuven, 1975–.
PLBat	Papyrologica Lugduno-Batava. Leiden, 1941–.
PM 1^2/2	Porter, B., and R. L. B. Moss. *Topographical Bibliography of Ancient Egyptian Hieroglyphic Texts, Reliefs, and Paintings, Vol. 1: The Theban Necropolis, Part 2; Royal Tombs and Smaller Cemeteries.* 2nd ed. Oxford: Clarendon, 1964.

Ranke PN	Ranke, H. *Die ägyptischen Personennamen*. 3 vols. Glückstadt, 1935–1977.
RdE	*Revue d'égyptologie*. Cairo, Paris, 1933–.
SASAE	Supplément aux Annales du Service des Antiquités d'Égypte. Cairo, 1946–.
SDAIK	Sonderschrift des deutschen archäologischen Instituts, Abteilung Kairo. Cairo, 1975–.
SAOC	Studies in Ancient Oriental Civilization. Chicago, 1931–.
TT	Theban tomb.
UPZ	Wilcken, U. *Urkunden der Ptolemäerzeit (ältere Funde)*. 2 vols. Berlin, 1927–1957.
Wb.	Erman, A., and H. Grapow, eds. *Wörterbuch der ägyptischen Sprache*. 7 vols. plus 5 vols. Belegstellen. Berlin: Akademie Verlag, 1926–1963.
Wilson, *Lexikon*	Wilson, P. *A Ptolemaic Lexikon: A Lexicographical Study of the Texts in the Temple of Edfu*. OLA 78. Leuven: Peeters, 1997.
ZÄS	*Zeitschrift für ägyptische Sprache und Altertumskunde*. Leipzig, Berlin, 1861–.

The Spanish Archaeological Mission to Dra Abu el-Naga^c North: A Chronological Overview of the Site

José M. Galán

INTRODUCTION

Dra Abu el-Naga^c is the modern name given to the hill located at the northern end of the Theban necropolis, on the West Bank of Luxor (pl. 1). It rises parallel to the Nile at a distance of approximately two and a half kilometers and is located opposite the temple of Karnak. The hill is bisected by a short and narrow wadi that opens perpendicular to the riverbank, named wadi Sheikh el-Ateyat.[1] The northern half is only a few meters to the southwest from el-Tarif, an area that today is almost completely taken over by a modern village and its cemetery. However, in Egyptological literature, it is known for the Eleventh/early Twelfth Dynasty *saff* tombs located there. These were excavated by W. M. Flinders Petrie in the nineteenth century and by the German Archaeological Institute in the second half of the twentieth century.[2] Dra Abu el-Naga^c, on the other hand, is associated with the Seventeenth Dynasty, because the coffins and funerary equipment of some of the members of the royal family were found here by Auguste Mariette's men in the mid-nineteenth century, and because several royal mud-brick pyramids were located on the hillside, according to Papyrus Abbott.[3]

Reality, however, is more complex than this, and the chronological labels applied to geographical areas are generally oversimplifications that often lead to misunderstandings. The modern names used to refer to the different areas into which the ancient necropolis is presently divided distort the unity with which it probably was perceived and used through ancient times, despite its size, covering approximately 3.5 × 2 kilometers. Moreover, modern paved roads trace artificial divisions and create, in the mind of the contemporary observer, segregated areas where before there were only footpaths that did not arouse a sense of division or give rise to different territorial identities. This is the case between the modern areas of Dra Abu el-Naga^c North and el-Tarif, or between these two and the plain where the temples of Amenhotep I and Ahmes-Nefertari (known as *Men-iset*) were supposedly located.[4]

---

1 G. Miniaci, "The Necropolis of Dra Abu el-Naga," in *Seven Seasons at Dra Abu el-Naga: The Tomb of Huy (TT 14); Preliminary Results*, ed. M. Betrò, P. del Vesco, and G. Miniaci, Progetti: Documenti per l'archeologia egiziana 3 (Pisa: Pisa University Press, 2009), 14–33; Miniaci, *Rishi Coffins and the Funerary Culture of Second Intermediate Period Egypt*, GHP Egyptology 17 (London: Golden House, 2011), 50–54.

2 W. M. F. Petrie and J. H. Walker, *Qurneh*, British School of Archaeology in Egypt 16 (London: School of Archaeology; Quaritch, 1909), 1–6; Di. Arnold, *Grabung im Asasif 1963–1970: Das Grab des Jnj-jtj.f; Die Architectur*, Archäologische Veröffentlichungen 4 (Mainz: von Zabern, 1971); Arnold, *Gräber des Alten und Mittleren Reiches in El-Tarif*, Archäologische Veröffentlichungen 17 (Mainz: von Zabern, 1976). See also R. Soliman, *Old and Middle Kingdom Theban Tombs* (London: Golden House, 2009), 29–40.

3 S. Birch, *Select Papyri in the Hieratic Character from the Collection of the British Museum* (London: Woodfall & Kinder, 1860), vol. 2, pl. 3; T. E. Peet, *The Great Tomb-Robberies of the Twentieth Egyptian Dynasty: Being a Critical Study, with Translations and Commentaries, of the Papyri in Which These are Recorded* (Oxford: Oxford University Press, 1930), pl. 2; H. Winlock, "The Tombs of the Kings of the Seventeenth Dynasty at Thebes," *JEA* 10 (1924): 217–77.

4 See the map in Marquis of Northampton, W. Spiegelberg, and P. Newberry, *Report on Some Excavations in the Theban Necropolis during the Winter 1898–9* (London: Constable, 1908), pl. 2; D. Polz, *Der Beginn des Neuen Reiches: Zur Vorgeschichte einer Zeitenwende*, SDAIK 31 (Berlin: de Gruyter, 2007), 172–97, pls. 26–27; D. Polz et al., "Topographical Archaeology in

If the broad area used as a necropolis on the Theban West Bank did not have sharp inner divisions due to the rugged terrain relief, or because a particular ideological/symbolic meaning was assigned to a specific area, it may be assumed that the choice of a spot for a tomb and/or a chapel was not conditioned by the era in which the deceased was buried. Then, why are certain areas still associated with specific periods or even dynasties and vice versa?

Probably, one of the reasons for it goes back to the early days of Egyptology, when kings, queens, and members of the royal family attracted most of the attention and the history of ancient Egypt was reconstructed around them. By extension, archaeology in its early days focused on the presence of royal monuments or royal building and decorative programs in the description and understanding of excavated sites. An early example of this may be found in the guide to the ancient monuments of Egypt that was published in 1869 for the guests to the official opening ceremony of the Suez Canal, where Dra Abu el-Nagaᶜ is described only in regard to the royal monuments and pieces of royal funerary equipment discovered there.[5]

Old descriptions still influence current assessments of a site, and this is in part due to the fact that recent excavations in the Theban necropolis have not been able to reshape the traditional picture of an area whose use was chronologically divided, probably due to their more modest goals.[6] New materials that could become the basis for a more complex reinterpretation of a specific area, or of the necropolis as a whole, are relatively scarce. Archaeological investigations cover a very small portion of the necropolis area, and well-documented excavations constitute small islands of information in the midst of a sea of ignorance. Our archaeological picture is most probably distorted as there are no data from nearby unexcavated areas. Thus, any interpretation concerning the appearance of the Theban necropolis at any given time, how it was structured, organized, and used, will have to be considered a mere hypothesis, and unavoidably more questions will remain unanswered than solved.

It seems that in antiquity the Theban necropolis was considered a single unit, as attested by the fact that the most frequent terminology used refers to the whole area and not to specific divisions. Moreover, it seems that it was perceived and used as an open space, without a clearly defined perimeter.[7] It is significant that the terms used to refer to the necropolis, like *smyt* () or *ḏw* (), "(desert) mountain," or *ỉmnt.t* (), "west," were written with the mountain-sign as semantic determinative, which evokes an open area.[8] From the archaeological point of view, there are a number of burials that took place away from areas that were popularly trodden and visited in ancient times. These are not necessarily poor burials; on the contrary some of them, the better documented ones,

Dra' Abu el-Naga: Three Thousand Years of Cultural History," *MDAIK* 68 (2012): 123–27; U. Rummel, "Ramesside Tomb-Temples at Dra Abu el-Naga," *EA* 42 (2013): 14–17.

5 *Itinéraire des invités aux fêtes d'Inauguration du Canal de Suez qui séjournent au Caire et Font le voyage du Nil, publié par Ordre de S. A. Le Khédive* (Cairo: Mourès, 1869), 130–31.

6 For examples of old descriptions still influencing interpretations, see, e.g., E. Thomas, "The Royal Necropoleis of Thebes" (PhD diss., Princeton University, 1966), 3–4; Soliman, *Old and Middle Kingdom Theban Tombs*, 134–35, "What is certain is that the Dra Abu el-Naga hill across from Karnak is the burial site of the Seventeenth Dynasty kings."

7 The archaeological evidence does not always match the concept of "*terra sacra*," *tꜣ ḏsr*, as a segregated and defined area under divine jurisdiction (i.e., *ḫr.t-nṯr*); see *Wb.* 5:228, 6–14; J. Hoffmeier, *"Sacred" in the Vocabulary of Ancient Egypt: The Term DSR with Special Reference to Dynasties I–XX*, OBO 59 (Fribourg: Universitätsverlag; Göttingen: Vandenhoeck & Ruprecht, 1985).

8 Compare the terms *smy.t* (*Wb.* 3:444, 8–445, 14), *ḏw* (*Wb.* 5:542, 12), or *ỉmnt.t* (*Wb.* 1:86, 1–87, 13), with terms like *ḫft-ḥr-nb.s* 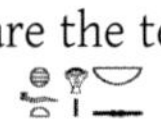 (*Wb.* 3:276, 8–9), with the rectangular enclosure *ḥw.t* 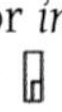 as semantic determinative. See Miniaci, *Rishi Coffins*, 52–54.

included what may be considered rich burial equipment.[9] It is true that these are only a few, but enough to suggest that it was probably not perceived as inappropriate, and apparently one could be buried almost anywhere without breaking an established rule. The search for burial places away from the nearby and traditional areas was also practiced by several kings and members of the royal family in the Eighteenth Dynasty.[10] The tomb for Hatshepsut as consort was built in the remote Wadi Sikket Taqa el-Zeid, one and a half kilometers southwest of the Valley of the Queens; and when she crowned herself king she chose the Valley of the Kings, then unoccupied and isolated. Later, Amenhotep III moved his tomb to the Western Valley.

On the other hand, some areas were nevertheless more in vogue than others at certain time periods, mostly influenced by the king's choice of a spot for his funerary monument. The royal family, courtiers, and high officials tended to group themselves near the king, as they did in life, in a manner not very different from the better-known arrangement of Old Kingdom mastabas in Giza and Saqqara, or the Middle Kingdom elite burials near the pyramids of their kings, as seen in Lisht and Dahshur.

In order to understand the choice of an exact place for a private burial near a royal funerary monument, it seems relevant to know what was there before, the surface irregularities of the area at that time, which monuments were standing, and among them, which were still in use and which were already abandoned. Indeed, for many sites these data are difficult to retrieve. Places are transformed with time and humans reinterpret the environment they live in by interacting and reacting to what was there before them.

On a smaller scale, many of the ancient monuments devoted to the worship of a god, to praise a king, or to honor the memory of a private individual and his family, were used beyond the time of their first builders/owners. Many of their structures and/or decoration were modified through time, reshaped, enhanced, and/or enlarged. In the process, in some cases the essence of the monument was maintained with only minor alterations, but in other cases its purpose and use evolved, and finally became quite different from the original one. Monuments, as well as the landscape, are in constant flux. For that matter, in order to understand them, their meaning, and use at a specific moment, it is advisable, among other strategies, to look back in time.

In the currently popular game of Sudoku, in order to reveal the unknown, that is, the value of a blank box, little progress will be obtained by staring at and scrutinizing the empty square, but the clue will be revealed by observing and analyzing the known/filled boxes around it, and deducing its value from them. In a similar way, in order to obtain a more profound understanding of the nature of a monument at a specific time, one of the strategies is to analyze its meaning and use before and after, and to observe the nature of the surrounding monuments and landscape. This is precisely the aim of the present introductory chapter.

---

9 Petrie, *Qurneh*, 6–10, pls. 22–29; Miniaci, *Rishi Coffins*, 65–66. An Eleventh/early Twelfth Dynasty coffin bought in Qena was supposedly found in the Farshut road, a wadi that runs parallel to the one leading to the Kings Valley to the north of the latter; see E. Brovarski, "Coffin of Menkabu," in *Mummies & Magic: The Funerary Arts of Ancient Egypt*, ed. S. D'Auria, P. Lacovara, and C. Roehrig (Boston: Museum of Fine Arts, 1988), 99–100, no. 31; Brovarski, "A Coffin from Farshût in the Museum of Fine Arts, Boston," in *Ancient Egyptian and Mediterranean Studies in Memory of William A. Ward*, ed. L. Lesko (Providence: Department of Egyptology, Brown University, 1998), 37–69. A prince called Amenemhat of the early Eighteenth Dynasty, who died when he was slightly over one year old, was reburied in the Third Intermediate period in the cliffs between the Deir el-Bahari *cachette* and the tomb of Meketra, left on the ground under a large flat stone; A. Lansing, "The Egyptian Expedition 1918–1920: I, Excavations at Thebes 1918–19," *BMMA* 15 (1920): 7–10, figs. 1, 4–6.

10 N. Strudwick and H. Strudwick, *Thebes in Egypt: A Guide to the Tombs and Temples of Ancient Egypt* (London: British Museum Press, 1999), 124–28.

THE SPANISH ARCHAEOLOGICAL CONCESSION AT DRA ABU EL-NAGAᶜ NORTH

The Spanish Mission working at Dra Abu el-Nagaᶜ North conducted its first archaeological campaign in January 2002, focusing on the rock-cut tomb-chapels of Djehuty (TT 11) and Hery (TT 12), of the early Eighteenth Dynasty (pls. 1–2).[11] The former was overseer of the treasury, overseer of works, and overseer of the cattle of Amun under the joint reign of Hatshepsut-Thutmose III, about 1470 BCE. The latter lived around fifty years earlier, around 1520 BCE, acting as overseer of the double granary of the king's mother and royal wife, Ahhotep. The two tomb-chapels were decorated in relief and they are relatively well preserved, despite having suffered from natural and human damage.

Between TT 11 and TT 12 lies a third tomb-chapel, which was numbered –399– by Friederike Kampp.[12] This one was originally plastered and painted, but the decoration is mostly lost and its owner remains unknown. Nevertheless, based on its layout and the traces of the decoration left, it can also be dated to the first half of the Eighteenth Dynasty. To the northeast of Hery's tomb-chapel there is a fourth one, which apparently was never decorated (fig. 1, no. 1).[13] The central corridors of these four tomb-chapels run parallel to one another, almost equidistant (separated by slightly over four meters) and hewn at the same level in the hillside.[14] Right above the latter, opened at a higher level in the slope, two other rock-cut tomb-chapels have been excavated and recorded. They are badly preserved, but it has been possible to identify their owners. One belonged to Baki, overseer of the cattle of Amun in the mid-Eighteenth Dynasty; the other one belonged to Ay, overseer of the weavers at the end of the Eighteenth Dynasty.

Having completed twenty campaigns of excavation in and around these Eighteenth Dynasty monuments, the evidence dating to the Eleventh/early Twelfth Dynasty at Dra Abu el-Nagaᶜ North has become more abundant and significant than expected. In 2007 and 2008 three rectangular wooden coffins dating to this time period were found 1.3 m below the floor of the open courtyard of the tomb-chapel of Djehuty.[15] One of them was left on the bedrock without any kind of protection, and only a few contemporary pottery vessels (one *hes*-vase and a couple of broken bowls) were found next to it, attesting to a modest libation and offering ritual. The body of a woman in her fifties was resting inside on her right side, facing east and only adorned by a faience necklace. The second coffin was found next to the first one, but in a very bad condition, with only the lower half partially preserved. The third was found pushed inside what looked like a narrow rock recess, which was then blocked by boulders. A mud libation tray had been left outside, to be used for the deceased (pl. 2 and fig. 1, no. 2). In this latter case, the coffin was painted in red with a polychrome inscription along the four sides and the lid. One of the three offering formulas included the name of the owner written at the

---

[11] See the website of the Spanish Mission to Dra Abu el-Nagaᶜ: https://proyectodjehuty.com/.

[12] F. Kampp, *Die thebanische Nekropole: Zum Wandel des Grabgedankens von der XVIII. bis zur XX. Dynastie; Teil 2*, Theben 13 (Mainz: von Zabern, 1996), 190–92, 769.

[13] This group of rock-cut tombs are oriented southeast–northwest, but given their layout perpendicular to the Nile River they were perceived and decorated as if they were oriented east–west.

[14] There is actually a fifth one to the northeast, which probably has to be dated to the reign of Amenhotep I, together with the fourth and Hery's tomb-chapel; see J. M. Galán, "The Tomb-Chapel of Hery (TT 12) in Context," in *Mural Decoration in the Theban New Kingdom Necropolis*, ed. B. Bryan and P. Dorman, SAOC (Chicago: Oriental Institute of the University of Chicago, in press); and see below n. 40.

[15] J. M. Galán, "Excavations at the Courtyard of the Tomb of Djehuty (TT 11)," in *Proceedings of the Tenth International Congress of Egyptologists: University of the Aegean, Rhodes, 22–29 May, 2008*, ed. P. Kousoulis and N. Lazaridis, OLA 241 (Leuven: Peeters, 2015), 207–20; Galán, "11th Dynasty Burials below Djehuty's Courtyard (TT 11) in Dra Abu el-Naga," *BES* 19: 331–46.

Fig. 1. Plan of the Spanish Mission archaeological site at Dra Abu el-Naga' North.

foot-end, Iqer, but with neither titles nor genealogical reference. Nevertheless, it may be dated to 2000 BCE, or a few years later. The body of a man in his late thirties was lying within, resting on his left side and facing east. His facial features are characteristic of a Nubian. Two self-bows and three curved staves were placed together with the body, while a bunch of five arrows were left outside, intentionally broken in half. Once the coffin was removed, it became clear that the rock recess was actually part of a contemporary unfinished rock-cut tomb. Probably due to an extraordinary heavy rain the rock lintel of the entrance collapsed and most of the interior was filled with debris. After an uncertain period of time the coffin was pushed inside in the only free space left between the debris and the ceiling.

A second rock-cut tomb of the Eleventh/early Twelfth Dynasty was found in 2014 around forty meters southeast (fig. 1, no. 3). Its entrance is still buried under ground, but we gained access inside through a hole in the burial chamber of a Seventeenth Dynasty funerary shaft that connects with the tomb's corridor. The latter is two meters in height, two meters in width, and must be almost thirty meters long (debris blocks the entrance also from inside). At the end of the corridor it makes a 50 degree turn to the right and becomes a sloping passage twenty meters long, which includes an antechamber and ends in the burial chamber. The tomb, which has not been excavated yet, was reused in the Seventeenth Dynasty (based on the pottery) as a mass grave to deposit almost a hundred individuals, most of them without a coffin, wrapped inside a reed mat, or just with a linen shroud and/or bandages. The bodies were dismembered by ancient robbers and the bones are scattered through the tomb, together with masses of linen and pottery.

The layout of this rock-cut Middle Kingdom tomb and the expected location of its entrance suggest a relationship with a tomb discovered and partially excavated by the German Archaeological Institute in 1995.[16] The two tombs are approximately twenty-five meters apart and, therefore, other contemporary tombs may be located in this area, with their entrances aligned and cut in the bedrock in the depression that is visible today near the modern road.

During the 2015 season, two other Eleventh/early Twelfth Dynasty rock-cut tombs were discovered, both filled with debris almost to the top. One of them has already been excavated (pl. 2 and fig. 1, no. 4). Its corridor is 3.05 m high, 1.90 m wide and almost 18 m long (its end is unfinished), with one burial chamber at each side.[17] The tomb was robbed, and later reused by several individuals of the first half of the Twenty-Second Dynasty, whose mummies were in turn stripped and dismembered. At the lower layer of the debris filling the corridor were remains of Eleventh/early Twelfth Dynasty funerary equipment that had been left by robbers. Lying on the rock floor there were fine quality marl clay vessels, fragments of paddle dolls, and clay libation trays.

Unfortunately, the identity of the initial owner(s) of the tomb remains unknown. Inside the eastern burial chamber, there were two large limestone blocks lying on the debris, one with a partially preserved incised royal cartouche, with the sign for Ra painted in red at the top; and the other block preserving the lower part of the falcon god Horus standing on a vertical rectangle, that is, a *serekh*, with the king's name inscribed in a missing block. These two blocks did not necessarily belong to the tomb, but they probably were part of a building somehow associated with a king and located in this area of the necropolis.

---

16 D. Polz et al., "Bericht über die 6., 7. und 8. Grabungskampagne in der Nekropole von Dra' Abu el-Naga/Theben-West," *MDAIK* 55 (1999): 370–402, pls. 56, 60–61; Polz et al., "Topographical Archaeology in Dra' Abu el-Naga," 116, 118–19.

17 The known Middle Kingdom rock-cut tombs in the Theban area do not seem to follow a fixed pattern; see Soliman, *Old and Middle Kingdom Theban Tombs*.

The two Middle Kingdom rock-cut tombs shared an open courtyard, with the facade and side-walls cut in the bedrock of the hillside, while leaving the entrance to the court wide open. At the southeast corner, in front of the excavated tomb, a small garden was built (pl. 2 and fig. 1, no. 6) over a 0.40 m layer of silt and sand that gradually accumulated over the rock floor, around 2000 BCE.[18] The structure, 3.0 x 2.2 m, was made of mud and mud bricks, it is 0.40 m high. There is a two-step staircase at its northwest side to facilitate watering and collecting in the center. The garden is divided into plots, most of them of 0.30 x 0.30 m, and from the botanical remains that have been retrieved and identified it can be deduced that it was used to provide the offering table with food and flowers, on a reduced scale, as a testimony of the deceased's desire to hold on to life.

The layout of these two rock-cut tombs sharing a courtyard (nos. 4–5), with their corridors almost parallel and oriented to the northwest, brings us back to the first four rock-cut tomb-chapels mentioned above, that of Djehuty (TT 11), Hery (TT 12), the one between these two (–399–), and the one to the northeast of Hery (fig. 1, no. 1). From the evidence now available, it seems that these were originally also Middle Kingdom tombs, which were taken over, enlarged, and three of them decorated by high officials of the early Eighteenth Dynasty. Middle Kingdom pottery was found smashed on the corridor's floor of the latter two tombs, and the layout and similarity in the measurements seem to relate these with the former two.[19]

Moreover, when excavating the shared open courtyard where the Middle Kingdom funerary garden is located in 2019, it was found that ancient robbers had opened a hole in the floor at the southwest corner, which connects with a side room at the northeast end of a *saff* tomb that remains completely buried (fig. 1, no. 7). The facade is 30.70 m wide and has ten pillars distributed along its breadth. It seems that the original plan was enlarged with five side rooms added to the northeast end, but the complete layout of the funerary monument cannot be precisely traced until it is excavated.

What seems clear is that this newly discovered *saff* tomb changes the perception of the landscape in this area of Dra Abu el-Nagaᶜ. First, the slope of the hillside descends deeper than expected, leaving the courtyard of the tomb-chapel of Djehuty not at the foothill, as it looked and was assumed when excavations started in 2002, but as an artificial terrace in the hillside.[20] The *saff* tomb is 5.40 m lower than the courtyard of Djehuty, and the entrance to the other large Middle Kingdom rock-cut tomb mentioned above (fig. 1, no. 3) is 6.65 m lower than Djehuty's. Second, a considerable number of large rock-cut Middle Kingdom tombs were built in the lower levels of the hillside, and not only higher up the hill.[21] This feature brings the appearance of Dra Abu el-Nagaᶜ North closer to that of el-Tarif, with

---

18 J. M. Galán and D. García, "Twelfth Dynasty Funerary Gardens in Thebes," *EA* 54 (2019): 4–8.

19 Galán, "The Tomb-Chapel of Hery (TT 12) in Context." On the reuse of Middle Kingdom corridor-tombs, see F. Kampp, "The Theban Necropolis: An Overview of Topography and Tomb Development from the Middle Kingdom to the Ramesside Period," in *The Theban Necropolis: Past, Present and Future*, ed. N. Strudwick and J. Taylor (London: British Museum Press, 2003), 3–7. See also E. Dziobek, "The Architectural Development of Theban Tombs in the Early Eighteenth Dynasty," in *Problems and Priorities in Egyptian Archaeology*, ed. J. Assmann and G. Burkard (London: Kegan Paul, 1987), 69; Polz, *Der Beginn des Neuen Reiche*, 279–302.

20 J. M. Galán, "The Tombs of Djehuty and Hery (TT 11–12) at Dra Abu el-Naga," in *Proceedings of the Ninth International Congress of Egyptologists: Grenoble, 6-12 Septembre 2004*, ed. J. Goyon and C. Cardin, 2 vols., OLA 150 (Leuven: Peeters, 2007), 777–87; Galán, "Early investigations in the Tomb-Chapel of Djehuty (TT 11)," in *Sitting beside Lepsius: Studies in Honour of Jaromir Malek at the Griffith Institute*, ed. D. Magee, J. Bourriau, and S. Quirke, OLA 185 (Leuven: Peeters, 2010), 155–81; Galán, "The Inscribed Burial Chamber of Djehuty (TT 11)," in *Creativity and Innovation in the Reign of Hatshepsut*, ed. J. M. Galán, B. Bryan, and P. Dorman, SAOC 69 (Chicago: Oriental Institute of the University of Chicago, 2014), 247–72.

21 See above nn. 15–16.

its *saff* tombs hewn at ground level.[22] Third, the number of Middle Kingdom tombs in this area of Dra Abu el-Nagaᶜ now becomes quite significant, which certainly must have encouraged, and at the same time conditioned, its occupation in later times. Although fragments of Old Kingdom pottery have recently been found, it seems that it was in the early Middle Kingdom when the first major rock-cut tombs were built and had a visual impact in the landscape.[23]

Between the end of the Middle Kingdom and the early Second Intermediate period, material evidence has been found indicating that this area of the necropolis was kept in use. However, the lack of architectural structures of considerable size probably had little relevance to the future use of the necropolis. A small chapel made of mud and mud bricks was recorded in the courtyard of the funerary garden, attached to the facade shared by the two Middle Kingdom rock-cut tombs. Inside there were three stelae and a faience necklace, with pottery scattered around it. [24]

In the Seventeenth Dynasty, according to Papyrus Abbott, several local kings chose the hill of Dra Abu el-Nagaᶜ to build their tombs.[25] Between 1857 and 1860, Mariette's men discovered the coffins of Kamose and the king's mother Ahhotep, as well as the obelisks and the tomb of Nubkheperra Intef in the northern half of the hill.[26] In 2001 the German Archaeological Institute discovered the base of the mud-brick pyramid of King Intef ninety meters northeast of the entrance to the tomb-chapel of Djehuty.[27] Furthermore, Spiegelberg and Newberry, in 1899, under the patronage of the fifth Marquis of Northampton, discovered the supposed location of his father's tomb, King Sobekemsaf (II), around sixty meters southwest.[28] According to Papyrus Abbott, the tomb of Sekhemra-Wepmaat Intef-aa must be located between these two, probably somewhere above the tomb-chapel of Djehuty. In fact, the German Archaeological Institute discovered part of the pyramidion of Sekhemra-Wepmaat Intef-aa.[29]

The pyramid of Nubkheperra Intef would have measured around 10 m in height. If the other two pyramids were of similar size, the area must have certainly drawn the attention of the passers-by around 1600 BCE, with three pyramids in a stretch of approximately 150 m. While the two other pyramids remain unlocated, what seems to be certain is that the royal family and courtiers associated with King Sobekemsaf and his two sons, Intef, were buried in this area of Dra Abu el-Nagaᶜ North. The mud-brick offering chapel and the funerary shaft of "the king's son Intefmose" is located 12 m southwest of the courtyard of Djehuty's tomb-chapel (pl. 2 and fig. 1, no. 8). Five fragmentary inscriptions

---

22 See above n. 2.

23 As an example of Old Kingdom pottery, during the 2020 archaeological season fragments of a "Meidum bowl," among others, were found smashed on the bedrock to the east of the Middle Kingdom courtyard with the funerary garden.

24 See also D. Polz, ed., *Für die Ewigkeit Geschaffen: Die Särge des Imeni und der Geheset* (Mainz: von Zabern, 2007).

25 See above n. 3.

26 Miniaci, "Necropolis of Dra Abu el-Naga," 36–43; Miniaci, *Rishi Coffins*, 54–56; J. M. Galán, "Ahmose(-Sapair) in Dra Abu el-Naga North," *JEA* 103 (2018): 181–83.

27 D. Polz and A. Seiler, *Die Pyramidenanlage des Königs Nub-Cheper-Re Intef in Dra Abu el-Naga: Ein Vorbericht*, SDAIK 24 (Mainz: von Zabern, 2003); Polz, *Der Beginn des Neuen Reiches*, 115–38; Polz, "New Archaeological Data from Dra' Abu el-Naga and Their Historical Implications," in *The Second Intermediate Period (Thirteenth–Seventeenth Dynasties): Current Research, Future Prospects*, ed. M. Marée, OLA 192 (Leuven: Peeters, 2010), 345–50.

28 Northampton, Spiegelberg, and Newberry, *Report on Some Excavations in the Theban Necropolis*, 14–15.

29 Polz and Seiler, *Die Pyramidenanlage des Königs Nub-Cheper-Re Intef*; Polz, *Der Beginn des Neuen Reiches*, 115–38; Polz, "New Archaeological Data from Dra' Abu el-Naga," 345–50; Galán, "Ahmose(-Sapair)," 179–201.

bearing his name have been found in the area, but it is through a limestone mummy-form figure (*shabti*?) that he may be associated with Sobekemsaf.[30]

Somewhere in this area, Spiegelberg and Newberry found a fragment of a small limestone obelisk and a stick-*shabti* mentioning "the king's son Ahmose-Sapair." Inside an offering chapel (pl. 2 and fig. 1, no. 9) very close to the left sidewall of Djehuty's courtyard, the Spanish Mission found a piece of "*daiu*-linen for Ahmose-Sapair"; and close to a third offering chapel located in front of the courtyard's entrance (fig. 1, no. 10) there was a stick-*shabti* inscribed with an offering formula "for the *ka* of Ahmose-Sapair." This evidence seems to support the hypothesis that prince Ahmose-Sapair was honored and received a posthumous cult in this area of Dra Abu el-Nagaᶜ.[31]

Twelve other stick-*shabtis* have been found in the area bearing the name Ahmose, one of them with the title "king's son." A reference to another "king's son" was found written on a coffin fragment inside a funerary shaft (pl. 2 and fig. 1, no. 11), but unfortunately the name was too faded to decipher. In another shaft (no. 12), a scarab was found belonging to a "son of the king of Upper and Lower Egypt."[32] Finally, a man in his mid-to-late-forties called Neb, whose administrative office and/or relationship with the royal family is unknown, was buried (no. 13) in a skilfully carved and painted *rishi*-coffin, which has decorative patterns in common with the coffin of King Nubkheperra Intef.[33]

There is a fourth Seventeenth Dynasty mud-brick offering chapel in the area west of the open courtyard of Djehuty's tomb-chapel (pl. 2 and fig. 1, no. 14). It was enlarged soon after it was built, turning it into the largest one documented until now, and showing that its owner was still honored years after his burial. The chapel is associated with the most elaborate and largest funerary shaft among the twenty others that have been excavated in this area.[34] In the northwestern half of the area, in the free space left between the offering chapels and shafts, covering almost three hundred square meters, a pottery deposit of around three thousand vessels accumulated at the end of the Seventeenth and/or beginning of the Eighteenth Dynasty.[35] The vessels were carefully placed on the ground as offerings, some of them preserving botanical remains, which seems to indicate that one or more structures in the area were considered worthy of receiving cult and expressions of devotion for some time. Since the excavations have not continued higher up the hill, it is difficult to identify with certainty which monument could have prompted the offerings. It could have been one of the mud-brick chapels mentioned above, or a royal pyramid located higher up the hill. It also could have been the case that it was not a specific structure, but that it was a broad area that was considered sacred. This interpretation may help to explain the number of coffins that were left on the ground without

---

30 The figure bears a statement mentioning a royal favor granted to the king's son Intefmose by King Sobekemsaf; see F. Borrego, "New Evidence on the King's Son Intefmose from Dra Abu el-Naga: A Preliminary Report," in *Proceedings of the XI International Congress of Egyptologists*, ed. G. Rosati and M. Guidotti, Archaeopress Egyptology 19 (Oxford: Archaeopress, 2017), 53–58.

31 Galán, "Ahmose(-Sapair)," 179–201.

32 Galán, "Ahmose(-Sapair)," 199–200; J. M. Galán and Z. Barahona, "Looking at a Robbed 17th Dynasty Funerary Shaft," in *Second Intermediate Period Assemblages: The Building Blocks of Local Relative Sequences of Material Culture*, ed. B. Bader (Vienna: Österreichische Akademie der Wissenschaften, in press).

33 J. M. Galán and A. Jiménez-Higueras, "Three Burials of the Seventeenth Dynasty in Dra Abu el-Naga," in *The World of Middle Kingdom Egypt (2000–1550 BC): Contributions on Archaeology, Art, Religion, and Written Sources*, ed. G. Miniaci and W. Grajetzki, Middle Kingdom Studies 1 (London: Golden House, 2015), 110–11.

34 L. Díaz-Iglesias Llanos, "Glimpses of the First Owners of a Reused Burial: Fragments of a Shroud with Book of the Dead Spells from Dra Abu el-Naga North," *BIFAO* 118 (2018): 83–126.

35 E. de Gregorio, "Votive Pottery Deposits Found by the Spanish Mission at Dra Abu el-Naga," in *Proceedings of the XI International Congress of Egyptologists*, ed. G. Rosati and M. Guidotti, 166–71.

any protection above them and not associated with any particular structure. Several Middle Kingdom burials (mentioned above) and, during the Seventeenth Dynasty, at least three coffins of infants were carefully placed on the ground near the area occupied by the offering vessels.[36]

All the funerary shafts that have been excavated were robbed in antiquity and filled again with sand and stones, in some cases more than once. A wide variety of material culture was retrieved, mixed in with the debris. Most of it is of funerary nature, but not exclusively so. While it is difficult to be sure that the objects, most of them in a fragmentary state, were originally placed inside the shaft where they were found, they can at least be ascribed to this area. If this is so, it may be significant to point out the number of stone fragments that have been found with a royal name inscribed on them. Two have already been mentioned above, which were found inside the rock-cut tomb associated with the funerary garden (fig. 1, no. 4). King (Montuhotep II) Nebhepetra is attested in three cases. In one of them he is shown praising the god Ptah, and in another he is the recipient of the praises made by the king's son Intefmose, his counterpart in the mirror scene being the goddess "Hathor, chief of the desert mountain" (*smy.t*, i.e., the necropolis). King Kheper[ka]ra (Sesostris I) is depicted burning incense in front of the god Anubis.[37] Finally, the cartouche of King Sobekem[saf] is partially preserved on a small sandstone fragment opposite the name of the god Ptah. These pieces of evidence, meager, few, and fragmentary as they might be, can be interpreted as the remnants of some kind of royal cult in the area, which may correspond well with the deposit of offering vessels mentioned above. But this is just a mere hypothesis.

The twenty-one funerary shafts dating to the Seventeenth Dynasty that have been recorded until now were cut in the free space left by the Eleventh/Twelfth Dynasty rock-cut tombs. The underground layout of the older tombs was taken into account when cutting the new ones, in order to avoid hitting and breaking into them.[38] In this way the density of tombs in the area increased, if not in an orderly linear fashion, at least following a certain spatial logic.

A similar situation was probably faced by King Amenhotep I when he decided to follow the tradition and built his tomb in Dra Abu el-Naga^c North. He chose a spot above the mud-brick royal pyramids of the previous dynasty, while his memorial temple, probably for lack of space, was built away from it, in the valley.[39] His courtiers, in turn, looked for available spots down the hillside, but most of the area was already taken by the Eleventh/Twelfth Dynasty rock-cut tombs and the offering chapels and funerary shafts of the Seventeenth Dynasty. Some high officials at the beginning of the Eighteenth Dynasty decided then to take advantage of the existing rock-cut tombs that were left unfinished or had been abandoned and reused them for themselves. This seems to have been the case for Hery (TT 12) and others, among them most probably Kenres and Kares, whose stelae were found in this area by Urbain Bouriant in 1886.[40] This practice seems to have continued in the area at least until the joint reign of Hatshepsut-Thutmose III, as Djehuty apparently also reused a rock-cut Middle

36 Galán and Jiménez-Higueras, "Three Burials," 113–16.

37 See photograph in J. Geisbusch, "Digging Diary 2016," *EA* 49 (2016): 36.

38 The funerary shaft where the *rishi*-coffin of Neb was found (pl. 2 and fig. 1, no. 13) is shorter than the rest, only three meters deep, probably because the workmen knew that the eastern burial chamber of the Middle Kingdom rock-cut tomb (no. 4) was right below.

39 U. Rummel, "Ritual Space and Symbol of Power: Monumental Tomb Architecture in Thebes at the End of the New Kingdom," in *The Ramesside Period in Egypt: Studies into Cultural and Historical Processes of the 19th and 20th Dynasties; Proceedings of the International Symposium Held in Heidelberg, 5th to 7th June, 2015*, ed. S. Kubisch and U. Rummel, SDAIK 41 (Berlin: de Gruyter, 2018), 249–75.

40 Galán, "The Tomb-Chapel of Hery (TT 12) in Context."

Kingdom tomb.[41] Probably for different reasons the high officials buried in this area gave priority to the strategic location of their monuments and relegated to a secondary level other criteria such as tomb size.

The double tomb complex that Amenhotep I built for himself and his mother Ahmes-Nefertari (K93.11 and K93.12), with the pyramids of previous kings standing at its feet, accompanied by their relatives and courtiers further down, must have made this area a noble and prestigious site for burial. At the same time, the high density of tombs and their offering chapels would have generated a significant flow of people and the continuous performance of rituals and spontaneous demonstrations of piety. These considerations could have influenced Djehuty's preference for this area, instead of looking for a place in the hill of Sheikh Abd el-Qurna, Khokha, or the Assasif plain facing Deir el-Bahari, as did most of his colleagues in Hatshepsut's administration in Thebes.

Djehuty probably enlarged the corridor of an earlier Middle Kingdom rock-cut tomb and added a transverse hall. The decorative program of the walls of the innermost room of his monument shows a set of funerary rituals that have clear Middle Kingdom precedents.[42] There are hints that indicate that he probably visited the—at that time—renowned Middle Kingdom monuments in the Theban necropolis.[43] Having this in mind, the Middle Kingdom monuments of Dra Abu el-Naga^c North also could have played a role in Djehuty's decision to locate his tomb-chapel here. The funerary garden had been covered since the Thirteenth Dynasty, but at least the rock-cut tombs, although most of them already robbed and reused, were probably visible, and their facades and entrances probably preserved their original appearance, making of this area a "classical" milieu, ideal as a resting place for a person who valued the past.

During the second half of the Eighteenth Dynasty and the Ramesside period the hillside of Dra Abu el-Naga^c, north and south, was densely occupied. It has already been mentioned that to the northeast of that of Hery, but one level higher up the hill, were two rock-cut tomb-chapels, one belonging to the overseer of the cattle of Amun, Baki, and the other to the overseer of the weavers, Ay. One level above the latter, and a little to the west, an overseer of the weavers under Ramesses II, called Ramose, also built his tomb-chapel (pl. 2, no. 15).

In the Twenty-First and Twenty-Second Dynasties many of the funerary shafts and rock-cut tombs were reused. The material culture of this period that has been retrieved is abundant, particularly *shabtis* and coffin fragments. In the Twenty-First Dynasty, when the floor of the courtyard of Djehuty's tomb-chapel was already covered by 30 cm of sand and rubble, the wooden anthropomorphic coffin of a middle-aged woman was placed on the ground only nine meters away from the facade, its base fixed with mid-size limestones and without any protection above. It was carefully carved, but was left undecorated, with only a coat of whitewash. Twenty-four meters away from the facade, a group of two anthropomorphic coffins, a rectangular box for an infant and a fourth body

41 See above n. 19.

42 M. de Meyer and J. Serrano, "Cattle Feet in Funerary Rituals: a Diachronic View Combining Archaeology and Iconography," in *Old Kingdom Art and Archaeology 7: Proceedings of the International Conference; Università degli studi di Milano 3–7 July 2017*, ed. P. Piacentini and A. delli Castelli, 2 vols., Egyptian & Egyptological Documents, Archives, Libraries 6 (Milan: Pontremoli, 2018), 402–7, pls. 76–83; J. Serrano, "The Ritual of 'Encircling the Tomb' in the Funerary Monument of Djehuty (TT 11)," *ZÄS* 146 (2019): 209–23; A. Diego Espinel, "Killing the Nubian: A Study on a Neglected Ritual Depicted in Two Theban Tombs and Its Possible Relationship to Execration Rituals," in *A Closer Look at Execration Figures*, ed. C. Kühne and J. Quack, ZÄS Beihefte (Berlin: de Gruyter, in press).

43 C. Ragazzoli, "Lire, inscrire et survivre en Égypte ancienne: Les inscriptions de visiteurs du Nouvel Empire," in *Les Lieux de Savoir*, II: *Les mains de l'intellect*, ed. C. Jacob (Paris: Alben Michel, 2011), 290–311; Ragazzoli, *La grotte des scribes à Deir el-Bahari: La tombe MMA 504 et ses graffiti*, MIFAO 135 (Cairo: Institut français d'Archéologie orientale, 2017).

only wrapped in linen bandages were also left on the ground, but this time they were covered by a pile of debris including coffin wooden planks, relief fragments, canopic jars, and pottery.

At the beginning of the Twenty-Second Dynasty relatively well-positioned and wealthy priests of Amun were buried, reusing earlier tombs. In the Middle Kingdom rock-cut tomb that has the garden in front (pl. 2 and fig. 1, no. 4), six leather mummy-braces engraved with the figure of King Osorkon I offering to different gods were found, together with linen bandages and three inscribed shrouds, two of them decorated with the figure of Osiris and a third one with a deified Amenhotep I, which belonged to *wab*-priests, *lesonis*, and god's fathers of Amun.[44] The funerary shaft associated with the largest Seventeenth Dynasty mud-brick offering-chapel mentioned above (pl. 2 and fig. 1, no. 14) was chosen as the burial place for eight carefully painted cartonnage mummy cases, some of which belonged also to *wab*-priests of Amun.[45]

It is difficult to grasp the reasons and circumstances that motivated people to be buried in this area, either placing the coffins in the courtyard of a tomb-chapel or reusing an old funerary shaft. Many of the Middle Kingdom, Second Intermediate period, and New Kingdom monuments were still standing and accessible around 900 BCE, and it seems that the area still retained the religious and social appeal of earlier times.

Pottery fragments of the Late period are abundant throughout the site and are present in the refilling of every funerary shaft of the Seventeenth and Eighteenth Dynasties. Well-preserved mummification deposits of the seventh to sixth centuries BCE have also been found, consisting of large jars (among them the "sausage" type) filled with linen, together with natron linen bags.[46] In the tomb-chapel of Djehuty, at the left side of the transverse hall, a new funerary shaft was opened during the Twenty-Sixth Dynasty, around 600 BCE. Different from the earlier shafts, its mouth is almost square, 1.20 x 1.10 m. It is 5.40 m deep and has two burial chambers at the bottom; the first one to be opened is oriented to the northwest and the second to the northeast. Their layout is also almost square, their ceiling slightly vaulted, and they have square holes in the floor to fit in a canopic box; the first chamber has one and the second has two, and therefore at least three people were probably buried in this shaft tomb.

It is difficult to deduce the appearance of the inner part of Djehuty's tomb-chapel at that moment. Was it completely cleared? Was debris piled in one or more corners? Had fires already been lit inside and blackened the walls and ceiling? Had parts of the walls and ceiling collapsed already? In the second century BCE, when the demotic graffiti were written on the walls by the priests in charge of the deposition of animal mummies in this area of the hillside of Dra Abu el-Naga^{c}, the walls and ceiling of the tomb-chapel of Djehuty had been broken in various spots for some time.[47] It is difficult to be precise as to when this occurred, but the wall surface in the middle of the corridor was already eroded and the reliefs here almost completely worn out as a direct consequence of water running and wind blowing along the tomb-chapel, which came in through the breaks that were opened, two

44 F. Borrego, "Inscripciones e imágenes sobre textiles de la dinastía XXII de Dra Abu el-Naga (Proyecto Djehuty)," *Trabajos de Egiptología/Papers on Ancient Egypt* 10, in press.

45 Díaz-Iglesias Llanos, "Glimpses of the First Owners of a Reused Burial," 83–126.

46 M. López-Grande and E. de Gregorio, "Two Funerary Pottery Deposits at Dra Abu el-Naga," *Memnonia* 18 (2007): 145–56, pls. 31–55; S. Ikram and M. López-Grande, "Three Embalming Caches from Dra Abu el-Naga," *BIFAO* 111 (2011): 205–28.

47 See N. Strudwick, "Some Aspects of the Archaeology of the Theban Necropolis in the Ptolemaic and Roman Periods," in *The Theban Necropolis: Past, Present and Future*, ed. N. Strudwick and J. H. Taylor (London: British Museum Press, 2003), 172, pls. 93–94.

in the ceiling of the innermost room and one at each end of the transverse hall. The two breaks in the ceiling connect with two tomb-chapels located above, one level higher up the hillside, and the breaks in the transverse hall connect with another two tomb-chapels at both sides of Djehuty's monument, one of them being –399–.

The break that connects Djehuty's transverse hall with that of the tomb-chapel –399– supports the hypothesis that the connective openings were made before the second century BCE. The fragments of the inscription that was carved at this end of the transverse hall, which were found in the excavation outside and were relocated in the lacuna caused by the break, are in perfect condition, even preserving the red color inside the hieroglyphic signs of the text, while the rest of the inscription that remained in situ has suffered much from water and wind to the point that some sections are difficult to read.[48] This circumstance seems to imply that the break must have happened earlier.

The connecting breaks were intentional with the clear aim of generating a large, single space inside the mountain with the minimum effort. Not all of them were necessarily opened at the same time, but it seems that the idea behind it was to create an underground structure similar to a catacomb by breaking the 0.5/1 m-thick rock walls that separated the tombs-chapels from one another, in a horizontal level, but also vertically. Many of the funerary shafts inside the tomb-chapels were also connected, and new annex rooms and galleries were cut (see Bosch-Puche and Ikram, this volume).

It seems that by the second century BCE some of the entrances to the tomb-chapels that were reused as part of the catacomb were blocked from outside by debris, as was the case for Djehuty's, Hery's, and –399– tomb-chapels. The number of accesses to the catacomb was fewer than the tomb-chapels involved and, therefore, the inner connections between them were even more necessary. The connections are generally big enough for a standing person to go through easily (unlike most of the robbers' holes, through which one could only crawl). When two tomb-chapels with floors at a different height were connected, a staircase was either cut in the rock or built with mud bricks. Separating walls between two tomb-chapels were occasionally demolished to generate a broader room, as happened between the tomb-chapels of Baki and Ay, while new mud-brick walls were occasionally built to divide or segregate an area, as was done between the corridor and the innermost room of Hery's tomb-chapel.

The priests involved in the cult and deposition of the animal mummies, and other people who might have carried out other activities in this part of the catacomb, were not interested on the original decoration of the monuments they reused. They not only wrote graffiti on the decorated walls indiscriminately, but in some cases they covered the reliefs and inscriptions with plaster, mud, or even mud bricks, as happened to the biographical inscription that was carved at the entrance of the tomb-chapel of Baki. On the other hand, it seems that they did not randomly vandalize the monuments, nor did they act aggressively against the wall decoration, as occurred before when a *damnatio memoriae* raid was perpetrated against Djehuty and his relatives and later against the god Amun's name. They simply ignored it. It may be deduced, therefore, that the identity of the original owners of the monuments, the figurative themes represented, and the inscriptions carved on the walls played no significant role in the choice of the site for the development of the animal cult in the second century BCE.

Despite the fact that Djehuty's name was erased from every inscription of his memorial soon after he passed away, it seems that—for other reasons—the god Thoth/Djehuty was somehow asso-

48 A. Diego Espinel, "Practical Issues with the Epigraphic Restoration of a Biographical Inscription in the Tomb of Djehuty (TT 11), Dra Abu el-Naga," in *The Oxford Handbook of Egyptian Epigraphy and Palaeography*, ed. D. Laboury and V. Davies (Oxford: Oxford University Press, 2020), 450–62.

ciated with this area of Dra Abu el-Nagaᶜ in the Ptolemaic and Roman periods.[49] Aside from the animal mummies themselves, among which the ibises make up the highest numbers (see Bosch-Puche and Ikram, this volume), and the demotic graffiti, which were written by personnel of Thoth's cult, there is one archaeological find that may support this hypothesis.[50] It is a mud brick of extraordinary dimensions, 48 × 24 × 12 cm, with a large seal impression (ten by seven centimeters) without frame, depicting an ibis on a stand (pl. 3). It was found at the entrance of the tomb-chapel of Ay in a disturbed context that included numerous pottery sherds of the Roman period. Unfortunately, it is not clear what its use or significance might be.

FINAL REMARKS

It is not at all clear what could have boosted the development of the animal cult in this area of Dra Abu el-Nagaᶜ. There was probably more than one reason for it, related to its strategic location from a religious and sociopolitical point of view. The hill of Dra Abu el-Nagaᶜ rises on the West Bank right in front of Karnak temple on the east side, which makes of the former the symbolic counterpart of the religious cult and rituals of the latter in an east-west axis.[51] While the cult of Amun-Ra was still the dominant one in Karnak, other cults developed in the Late and Ptolemaic periods, like that of Osiris, Thoth, and the royal *ka*. Moreover, the processional way connecting Karnak temple with shrines and memorial royal temples on the West Bank probably had the hill of Dra Abu el-Nagaᶜ as a landmark.[52] Unfortunately, there is little physical and written evidence to support these suggestions, which are more the result of Egyptological reasoning.

The religious potency of the area could have increased due to the presence of royal monuments, such as the Seventeenth Dynasty pyramids and the double tomb of Amenhotep I and Ahmes-Nefertari, which were transformed in the Twentieth Dynasty by the high priests of Amun Ramessesnakht and his son Amenhotep into their tomb-chapels and a cult installation for the deified Amenhotep I and his mother.[53] Unfortunately, it is difficult to know how much of these structures was still visible and how they were perceived and understood in the second century BCE. It is likely that they were al-

49 The aggressors who erased Djehuty's name did not go down the funerary shaft and his name and that of his parents were preserved in the burial chamber; Galán, "Inscribed Burial Chamber of Djehuty," 247–52, 268.

50 S. Ikram and M. Spitzer, "The Cult of Horus and Thoth: A Study of Egyptian Animal Cults in Theban Tombs 11, 12, and -399-," in *Archaeozoology of Southwest Asia and Adjacent Areas XIII*, ed. J. Daujat, A. Hadjikoumis, and R. Berthon (Atlanta: Lockwood Press, in press).

51 U. Rummel, "Gräber, Feste, Prozessionen: Der Ritualraum Theben-West in der Ramessidenzeit," in *Nekropolen: Grab—Bild—Ritual; Beiträge des Zweiten Münchner Arbeitskreises Junge Aegyptologie (MAJA 2), 2. bis 4.12.2011*, ed. G. Neunert, K. Gabler, and A. Verbovsek (Wiesbaden: Harrassowitz, 2013), 207–32; On the distinct position opposite Karnak temple and the term "great forecourt of Amun" used to refer to this area, see Rummel, "Ritual Space and Symbol of Power," 257 n. 31.

52 On the establishment of the procession of the god Amun from Karnak to Deir el-Bahari beginning from the third part of the reign of Montuhotep II, and on the close ritual connection between the cult for Amun-Ra and the royal cult, see M. Ullmann, "Thebes: Origins of a Ritual Landscape," in *Sacred Space and Sacred Function in Ancient Thebes*, ed. P. Dorman and B. Bryan, SAOC 61 (Chicago: Oriental Institute of the University of Chicago, 2007), 3–26. See also M. Bietak, "La Belle Fête de la vallée: L'Asasif revisité," in *"Parcourir l'éternité": Hommages à Jean Yoyotte*, ed. C. Zivie-Coche and I. Guermeur, Bibliothèque de l'École des Hautes Études, Sciences religieuses 156 (Turnhout: Brepols, 2012), 135–63.

53 See above n. 39.

ready in ruins by then.[54] Nevertheless, the aura of this area of Dra Abu el-Naga^c North as a sacred place associated with the royal cult could have endured beyond the physical testimonies of a more glorious past.

In the ongoing excavations in the area assigned to the Spanish Mission, several inscribed relief fragments seem to indicate that there might have been some kind of cultic activity devoted to a selection of memorable kings, which would have necessitated one or more shrines or chapels. It seems that King Montuhotep (II) Nebhepetra, in particular, was worshiped in this area, at least until the Seventeenth Dynasty.[55] At that time and in the early Eighteenth Dynasty a deposit of around three thousand vessels was placed on the ground, which seems to reflect a perception and use of this area as if it had a holy character. It is difficult, however, to point out the specific target of the offerings.

The southern end of Dra Abu el-Naga^c North apparently started being chosen as a burial ground by the Theban elite in the Eleventh and early Twelfth Dynasty. They built large rock-cut tombs, some of them with a broad *saff*-facade. In a relatively short period of time, the density of tombs was quite high, and the appearance of the area must have been impressive. At this time, the ideal location for a private tomb was considered to be somewhere in the slopes at both sides of the valley leading to the cliffs of Deir el-Bahari, where Hathor's speos and the memorial monument and tomb of Montuhotep II were located. However, the location of Dra Abu el-Naga^c right in front of the temple of Amun-Ra in Karnak, which was enlarged by King Montuhotep, and probably in a privileged position in the processional way of the religious festival coming from Karnak, which was also fostered by Montuhotep, made of this particular area a strategic place to be buried. Since then, with its continuous use by royal and illustrious members of the Theban elite, the site only increased in its significance, which continued into the Ptolemaic period.

---

54 The Ramessesnakht and Amenhotep tomb-chapels were destroyed by the end of the New Kingdom, ca. 1080 BCE; Rummel, "Ritual Space and Symbol of Power," 249.

55 Galán and Jiménez-Higueras, "Three Burials," 107–8; D. Franke, "Die Stele des Jayseneb aus der Schachtanlage K01.12," in Polz and Seiler, *Die Pyramidenanlage*, 73–83, pl. 2; K. El-Enany, "Le saint thébain Montouhotep-Nebhépetrê," *BIFAO* 103 (2003): 167–90.

The Archaeology of the Area: An Overview

Francisco Bosch-Puche and Salima Ikram

INTRODUCTION

One of the particularities of some of the most important rock-cut tomb-chapels within the concession of the Spanish Mission to Dra Abu el-Naga^{c} (also known as the Djehuty Project) is their reuse—or change of use—in the Ptolemaic period for the interment of animal mummies. Animal cults, although extant in one way or the other throughout Egyptian history, proliferated from the Late period onward.[56] As far as is understood, there were two types of animals associated with the celebration of these cults: sacred animals and votive ones (or "unique" and "multiple" ones, to use the vocabulary of Alain Charron).[57] The former were a god's totemic animal, recognized by particular pelage or signs associated with its birth, revered as a manifestation of the god on earth, a receptacle for its spirit/*ba*. Upon its death it was mummified and buried with reverence, and the *ba* of the god migrated to the body of another animal, much as believed to be the case for the Dalai Lama.[58] The latter group consisted of animals that resembled the cult animal in phenotype, but had no ritual value until their death, mummification, and consecration as an offering, and finally interment in reused human tombs or newly hewn pits or galleries. These votive mummies are numbered in the millions at some sites.[59] Devotees presented such ex-votos in the hope of obtaining something in return, often the fulfillment of a wish as simple as enjoying a long life, being cured of a certain disease, success in some endeavour, or ensuring the eternal permanence of the names of the devotee and their relatives in the necropolis next to the god.[60] This area of the Theban necropolis contains the remains of mummified animals, mainly ibis and raptors, which we presume are votive mummies. However, some of the texts in the corpus seem also to point to the existence of sacred, individual animals—specifically an ibis being designated "foremost of Thebes" (notably in graff. 14 and 63), which is said to have been buried after "spending many years in the temple"—but no archaeological evidence supporting this other type of animal burial has so far been uncovered.

---

56 D. Kessler, "Tierkult," *LÄ* 6:cols. 571–87; A. Charron, "Massacres d'animaux à la Basse Epoque," *RdÉ* 41 (1990): 209–13; Charron, "Les animaux et le sacré dans l'Égypte tardive: Fonctions et signification" (PhD diss., EPHE, 1996); Charron, "Les animaux sacrés à l'époque ptolémaïque," in *La mort n'est pas une fin: Pratiques funéraires en Égypte d'Alexandre à Cléopâtre; Catalogue de l'exposition, 28 septembre 2002 > 5 janvier 2003, Musée de l'Arles antique*, ed. A. Charron (Arles: Musée de l'Arles antique, 2002), 173–214; S. Ikram, ed., *Divine Creatures: Animal Mummies in Ancient Egypt*, rev. ed. (Cairo: American University in Cairo Press, 2015).

57 Charron, "Massacres d'animaux," 209–13.

58 S. Ikram, "Divine Creatures: Animal Mummies," in Ikram, *Divine Creatures*, 1–15; Ikram, "Shedding New Light on Old Corpses: Developments in the Field of Animal Mummy Studies," in *Creatures of Earth, Water, and Sky: Essays on Animals in Ancient Egypt and Nubia*, ed. S. Porcier, S. Ikram, and S. Pasquali (Leiden: Sidestone Press, 2019), 179–91.

59 Charron, "Massacres d'animaux," 209–13; S. Ikram, "Speculations on the Role of Animal Cults in the Economy of Ancient Egypt," in *Apprivoiser le sauvage/Taming the Wild*, ed. M. Massiera, B. Mathieu, and F. Rouffet, CENIM 11 (Montpellier: Université Paul Valéry Montpellier 3, 2015), 211–28.

60 J. Ray, *The Archive of Ḥor*, EES Texts from Excavations 2 (London: Egypt Exploration Society, 1976); Ray, *Texts from the Baboon and Falcon Galleries: Demotic, Hieroglyphic and Greek Inscriptions from the Sacred Animal Necropolis, North Saqqara*, EES Texts from Excavations 15 (London: Egypt Exploration Society, 2011). See also references in n. 56.

We have excavated animal burials, or uncovered evidence related to the cult that developed around their deposition, in different areas of the Spanish Mission's concession. The core of the material is found within the group of the most important New Kingdom tomb-chapels of the concession, in the "street" of mausolea formed by the tomb of Djehuty (TT 11), the tomb known by the team as the "intermediate tomb" (Kampp no. –399–), the tomb of Hery (TT 12), and the recently discovered tombs of Baki and Ay, both located at a slightly higher level than the rest (approximately 2.5 m above).

The tomb-chapels were modified in the Ptolemaic period to accommodate the cult, with the dividing walls demolished to allow for the interconnection between the different monuments (fig. 18). Connections were also opened in their shafts and burial chambers to transform the interior of the hill into a catacomb. To bridge the height difference between levels and facilitate the circulation, either stairs were cut into the rock (fig. 21) or mud-brick staircases built (figs. 3, 19–20). In contrast with what is documented in other locations in Egypt, such as Saqqara or Tuna el-Gebel (sites where during the Late and Ptolemaic periods necropolises are created *ex novo* to accommodate thousands—and even millions—of votive animal mummies),[61] at Dra Abu el-Nagaᶜ a new use was given to the preexisting hypogea, which were drastically transformed.

Besides these physical changes in the plan/layout of the earlier monuments and the corpus of demotic graffiti in red ochre inscribed in the upper part of the hypogea that are being published here, a third set of evidence bearing witness of the change in use of the space are the hundreds of thousands of animal mummies that were deposited in the burial chambers and lower galleries. They are mainly birds, in the vast majority ibises, but also falcons and other birds of prey, as well as shrews, snakes, and a sprinkling of other species.[62]

The excavation and systematic study of the animal mummies started in 2013. The work is being carried out by a small team, led by the authors of this contribution, together with Megan Spitzer, ornithologist at the Smithsonian Institution, who studied a number of bone deposits for three seasons (2014–2016), and Neal Woodman, an expert on small mammals also at the Smithsonian Institution, who studied the mummies and bones of shrews and other small mammals during the 2018 season, and subsequently through images.[63] The main aim of this contribution is to offer an overview of eight years of archaeological work, and to present some preliminary results, in order to help contextualize the inscriptions that are the focus of this monograph. A full, extensive archaeological report/account is currently in preparation.

---

[61] Ikram, "Divine Creatures: Animal Mummies," 1–15; P. Nicholson, "The Sacred Animal Necropolis at North Saqqara, the Cults and Their Catacombs," in Ikram, *Divine Creatures*, 44–71; D. Kessler and Abd el H. Nur el-Din, "Tuna El-Gebel: Millions of Ibises and Other Animals," in Ikram, *Divine Creatures*, 120–63. It should be noted, however, that at Saqqara, e.g., at the Bubasteion, older tombs were repurposed for animal burials, in addition to new ones being cut for dogs, ibises, raptors, baboons, and cattle, in the area now known as the Sacred Animal Necropolis.

[62] Ikram and Spitzer, "Cult of Horus and Thoth."

[63] N. Woodman, C. Koch, and R. Hutterer, "Rediscovery of the Type Series of the Sacred Shrew, *Sorex religiosus* I. Geoffroy Saint-Hilaire, 1826, with Additional Notes on Mummified Shrews of Ancient Egypt (Mammalia: Soricidae)," *Zootaxa* 4341 (2017): 1–24; N. Woodman, A. T. Wilken, and S. Ikram, "See How They Ran: Morphological and Functional Aspects of Skeletons from Ancient Egyptian Shrew Mummies (Eulipotyphla: Soricidae: Crociduriane)," *Journal of Mammalogy* 100 (2019): 1199–210; N. Woodman and S. Ikram, "Ancient Egyptian Mummified Shrews (Eulipotyphla: Soricidae) and Mice (Rodentia: Muridae) from the Spanish Mission to Dra Abu el-Nagaʿ, Luxor, and Their Implications for Environmental Change in the Nile Valley during the Past Two Millennia," *Quaternary Research* 100 (2021): 21–31.

Evidence of the interment of animal mummies has been attested in different places of the Spanish Mission's concession; they all are relatively nearby, but not always obviously connected. Additional evidence comes from other areas in the vicinity and outside the limits of the concession, including Spiegelberg's "Great Tomb of the Ibis and Hawks" (location uncertain, but probably nearby), thus proving that we are actually dealing with only a fraction of a much larger—clearly spatially but perhaps also chronologically—Ptolemaic complex, with different sectors and/or catacombs. Without doubt, the main "street" of mausolea within the Spanish Mission's concession would have constituted a privileged section of this complex, with prominence given to the tomb-chapel of Djehuty (TT 11) (fig. 18). The monument not only contains the highest concentration of graffiti, but also seems to have served as the main access point for the complex. As the courtyards and entrances to the neighboring tombs (–399– and TT 12) were already sanded up at the time, a connection was opened from the transverse hall of TT 11 to that of tomb –399–, and another one from the latter to the corridor of TT 12, connecting the three and thus defining the main route of this section of the animal catacomb, which would have given access to a number of burial spaces for the animals. One of those burial spaces (not yet excavated) is located aboveground, accessible from the inner chapel of TT 11 at the end of its corridor, through a staircase carved into the rock (fig. 21). All the shafts in tomb –399– give access to underground chambers used for the internment of animal mummies. Curiously, although this is one of the monuments most extensively used for animal burials, it is striking that graffiti are totally absent in its upper part, unlike what is found in TT 11 and TT 12. Most certainly this is due to the fact that the walls have suffered massive degradation and erosion caused by fire and subsequent wind erosion, which also explains why almost no sign of its New Kingdom decoration has survived. The main route then follows the corridor of the tomb of Hery (TT 12), toward the interior of the mountain, at the end of which a mud-brick wall was built. This was probably used to seal the innermost room or chapel, which was also probably used as a burial space for the animal mummies. From this point the route makes a right turn to the east (ritual/ideological north) and splits. One path goes upward, accessed by a mud-brick staircase, to the tomb-chapels of Baki and Ay, and the other is on a slightly lower level, leading toward a series of underground spaces below those two tombs, referred to as the Eastern Galleries (fig. 20).

THE LOWER GALLERY (TOMB –399– AND TT 12)

For several seasons (2013–2016) the archaeological work concentrated on the burial chambers at the bottom of the main shafts of both the tomb-chapel of Hery (TT 12) and the intermediate tomb (–399–), which were connected most probably in the Ptolemaic period. The plan of the substructure is identical in both cases: a shaft opening on to a rectangular, bigger chamber to the north (ritual/ideological west) (UEs 225 and 240), and a quadrangular, smaller one to the south (ritual/ideological east) (UEs 230 and 235) (pl. 4). Access to this lower section of the animal catacomb is gained through an opening at the end of the corridor of tomb –399– (fig. 2).

The small shaft opens on to a space with a ramp, leading to a long, rectangular chamber whose floor is at a considerably lower level. This set of architectural elements, which seem to be a later alteration to provide the New Kingdom tomb with an additional burial space, underwent important remodeling in the Ptolemaic period. First, a flight of mud-brick stairs was constructed to bridge the distance between the access ramp and the floor of the chamber. Second, the eastern (ritual/ideological northern) end of the chamber was sealed with a mud-brick wall, thus defining a small space that was used for the interment of animal mummies (UE 255). Third, a connection with the inner, main shaft of the tomb was opened at the western (ritual/ideological southern) end. Fourth, two demotic

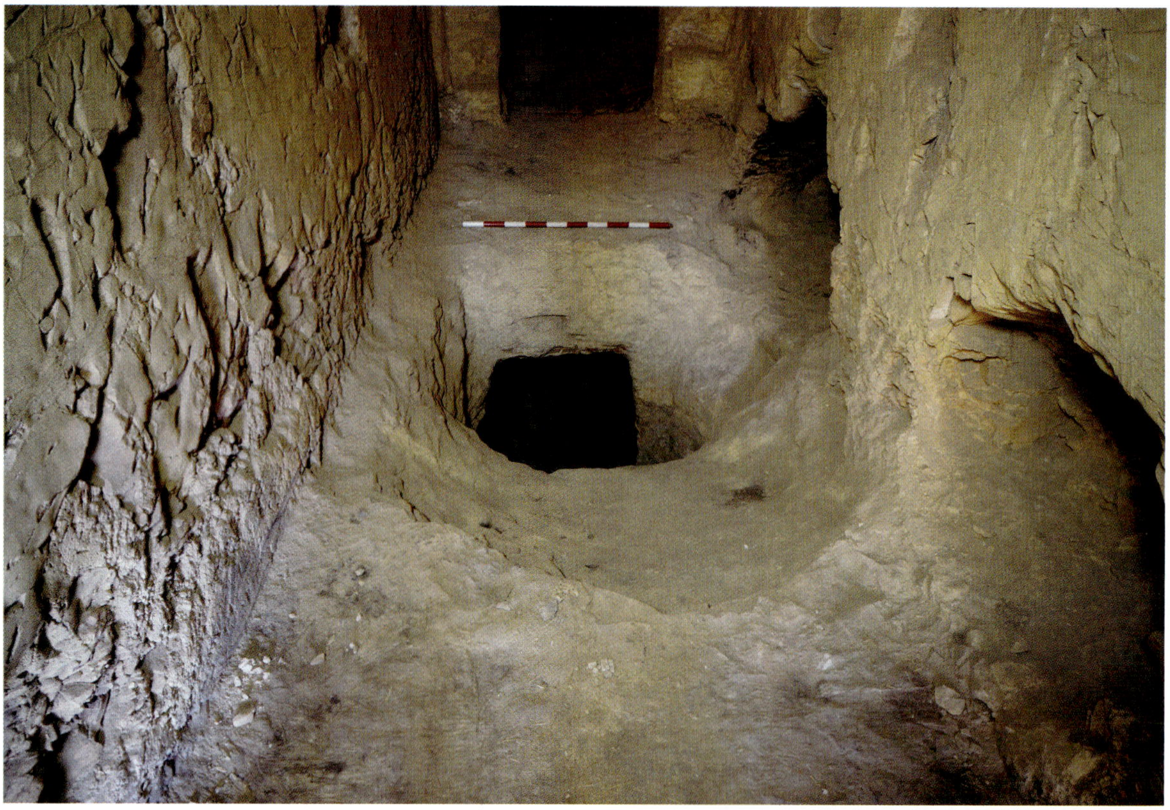

Fig. 2. Access to the Lower Gallery in the corridor of tomb –399–.

graffiti were inscribed on the walls (graff. 45 and 46). And finally, the inner shaft of the tomb was provided with an imposing, solid, mud-brick, six-step, straight staircase, which gave access to the lower chambers (figs. 3 and 19).

The two chambers on the northern side (UEs 225 and 240) were almost entirely filled with bundles of mummies (fig. 17), while the floor of the chambers on the southern side was completely covered with a reddish layer (up to 30 cm thick) of ash and calcined bones, many twisted from the heat—the result of a fire that had drastically destroyed their content (fig. 4).

During the first four seasons, we excavated both southern chambers entirely, while on the northern ones we just cleared the areas adjacent to the entrance to floor level, and examined the mummies, as well as making some spot checks (sondages) in different points and excavating test pits in the connection between the two chambers. An interesting discovery was that, under the mummy bundles, the floor of the northern chambers also had a bottom layer of ashes and crushed burnt bones, similar to what was found in the south, thus indicating that there had actually been a first internment of animal mummies in all four chambers, which had been totally destroyed by a fire, and a later, second internment that was made only in the northern ones.

We established that the types of mummies buried in those two phases were significantly different. Although only ashes and bones were left of the first internment, in two specific points we were able to document remains of carbonised mummies still in situ—in both cases in spaces that had been protected by fallen walls and where the oxygen must have been depleted. This showed us that the initial content of the chambers would have most likely been formed by individual mummies (and not bundles consisting of several mummies), mostly of ibises but also of raptors, which would have been deposited in an orderly and regular manner in rows, probably to make the most of the space,

Fig. 3. Mud-brick staircase in the main shaft of tomb –399–, descending to the Lower Gallery.

Fig. 4. Bone deposit in burial chamber UE 230, with connection to burial chamber UE 235.

and accompanied by small quadrangular/rectangular or circular/oval packages with mummified shrews/rodents and snakes, which would have been arranged to fill the empty spaces left by the larger mummies.

All the sediment in the southern chambers was collected, sieved, and sorted. We could establish that the majority of the bones were of ibis, mostly sacred ibis (*Threskiornis aethiopicus*), but also other species such as the glossy ibis (*Plegadis falcinellus*).[64] The next group in importance consisted of birds of prey, fundamentally different species of falcons and hawks, as well as vultures, and even some eagles and kites. Although the vast majority of bird bones belonged to adult animals, a remarkable percentage came from fledglings and juveniles.[65] This fact, together with the documentation of examples of healed fractures in leg bones mostly of adults—an indication that the birds would have survived despite walking with difficulty—as well as some evidence of infection, very similar to that observed nowadays in zoos, would suggest that at least the ibises, but also possibly some of the raptors, were either bred or kept in a controlled environment where they would have reproduced, thus providing the necessary number of individuals for the production of the large quantity of mummies required. Remains of shrews and different species of snakes were also retrieved.[66]

64 Ikram and Spitzer, "Cult of Horus and Thoth."

65 Graffiti 33 and 53 specifically mention "offspring," probably as a reference to young birds, and the latter also stresses the large quantities of animals being buried.

66 Ikram and Spitzer, "The Cult of Horus and Thoth."

Fig. 5. Examples of bird mummies; the radiograph shows a falcon.

Although most of these mummies were destroyed by fire, enough have been found in different parts of the concession to have an idea about their diversity, in terms of their appearance. The most common types are those of ibises (fig. 5), that were desiccated, coated in a dark resinous material and then were wrapped, using linen, thread, and sometimes linen string/rope for bulk, with a final outer wrapping to keep all the bandaging intact, thereby creating a typical ibis mummy teardrop shape. Some probably had plain outer wrappings, while others were more elaborately wrapped; there are examples of herringbone patterns, common in the Ptolemaic/Roman periods.

While raptors are also found in teardrop-shaped bundles (fig. 5, middle), they are more commonly found in a mummiform shape, with herringbone bandaging, and many with mud or cartonnage masks showing the face of a raptor, with a divine wig, making these manifestations of Horus or possibly even Re-Harakhte (fig. 6). A variant has the bird on its back, with a very long extension for the tail and feet, perhaps reflecting the length of the tail feathers.

Shrew/rodent and snake mummies tend to be wrapped in a similar manner (fig. 7): a small "nest" of cloth is made and the animal is nestled into it, after which it is wrapped up with bandages, thread, and then a plain, shroud-like piece of cloth is placed over it and secured around the perimeter with another folded linen bandage. The outermost linen wrapping on these round or square (and very occasionally, rectangular) bundles seems plain at first glance. However, under the perimeter bandage one can see that the original (fugitive) colors were pink/red or yellow, whose dye has faded. Thus, these small packets containing animals related to the solar cult were wrapped in colors associated with the sun. Unfortunately, thus far we have been unable to establish what dyes were used. Some larger, rectangular packages, often containing snakes, have elaborate coffered wrapping.

Fig. 6. Examples of raptor mummies.

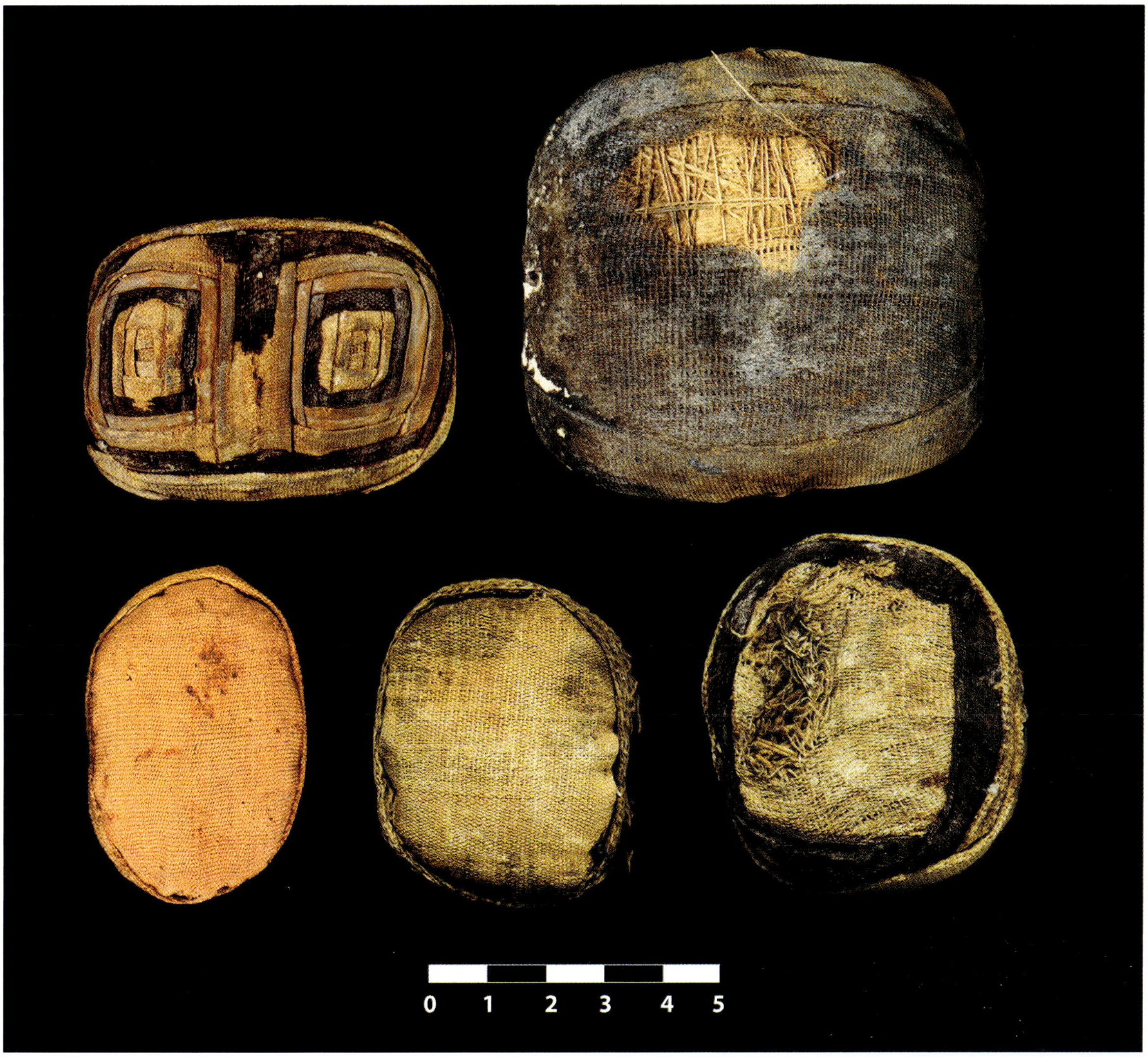

Fig. 7. Examples of small packages with shrew/rodent and snake mummies.

Thus, the animal mummies interred here were of the finest quality. Smudges of gold on a few of the bones might indicate that some of the animals were gilded, as is known from elsewhere,[67] or that the wrappings or cartonnage contained gold.

The mummy bundles belonging to the second phase, and almost completely filling the northern (ritual/ideological western) chambers, are very different (fig. 8). These are relatively large bundles, created by placing the blackened and broken up remains of bird (and, in a very few cases, snake and shrew) mummies in a large square cloth, which is then knotted together, crosswise. In many instances there is evidence that the linen was reused, as the pieces show hems, or joins. Some pieces are fringed, so it is clear that all sorts of linen from different sources were pressed into use. In some instances, when too many broken mummies have been placed on the cloth, another piece of linen is placed over the top so that the blackened mummies remain secure. Very often, linen bandages are

67 E.g., a gilded eagle in the Egyptian Museum in Cairo (CG 29681), unfortunately unprovenanced; see S. Ikram and N. Iskander, *Catalogue Général of Egyptian Antiquities in the Cairo Museum. Nos. 24048–24056; 29504–29903 (Selected); 51084–51101; 61089: Non-Human Mummies* (Cairo: Supreme Council of Antiquities, 2002), 12.

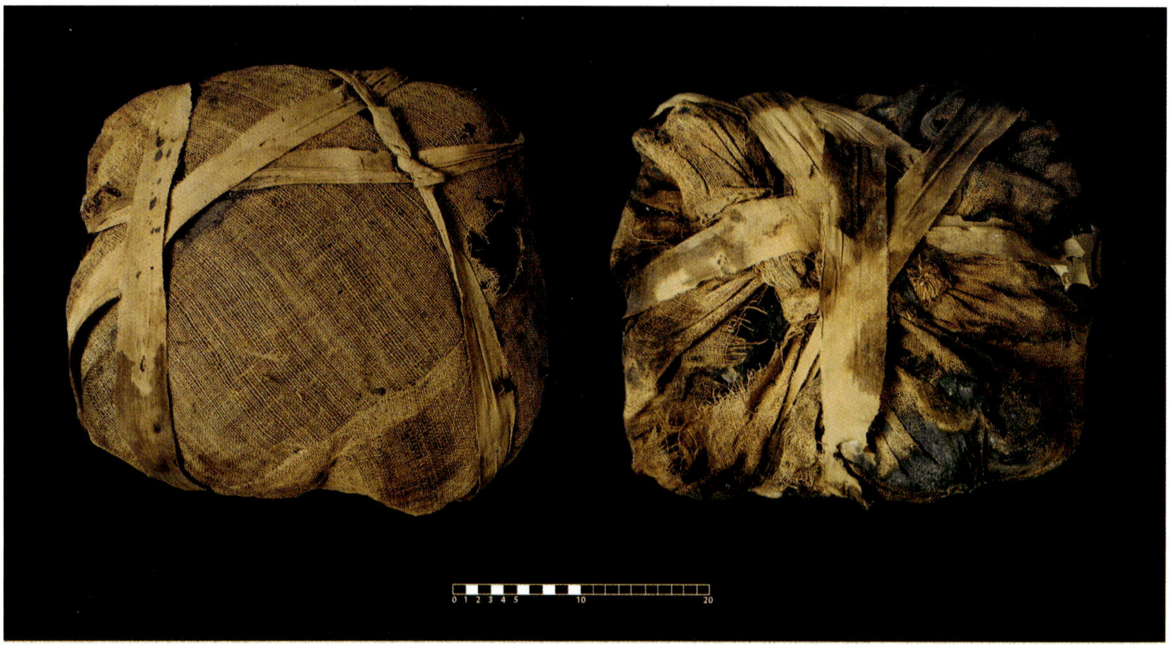

Fig. 8. Example of bundle mummy containing broken parts of other mummies (top and bottom views).

Fig. 9. Example of ibis mummies stuck together.

used to reinforce the packages, totally or partially wrapping them up. It seems that the blackened and broken mummies are from mummies that were exposed to fire and thus became black and brittle, and on occasion stuck together (fig. 9). Of course, some of the coloration is due to the original mummification materials (resins/oils/wax/possibly bitumen) that were used to create the bird mummies, but this would not account for the broken and, in some cases, slightly warped bones.

A smaller number of mummies were of individual birds, sometimes rewrapped. These mummies were reddish, as if they had started to burn, but had not carbonized. The smallest group of mummy bundles, also reddish, consisted of feathers, mud, straw, and detritus. These might be what are termed "false mummies," or the tidying up remnants of the birds that had been offered to the gods.[68] A few examples that are not reddish, and from other parts of the necropolis, also contained fragments of feathers, or the odd bone, or fur, thus creating a "false mummy." These mummy bundles appear to be pious reburials of mummies that had been damaged in a conflagration. Once again, ibises represent about 90 percent of the total, perhaps even more.

This secondary deposit seems rushed—the mummy bundles were not arranged in a specific way, but rather just tossed inside the rooms. It is also worth mentioning that no sealing walls were built in this second phase—the remains of the existing walls from the first phase stayed in place, and what open space in the doorways that remained was simply blocked with big stones from the main shafts of tomb -399- and TT 12, which at that time were both free of debris. The first internment, with its carefully placed mummies, could have been a single event or a series of them—if one were to take the model of the ibis or falcon galleries at Saqqara, the filling and sealing of a single chamber would be a unique event,[69] although this does not have to be the case at Dra Abu el-Nagaᶜ. The initial deposit, which could have been progressive, was made via tomb -399-, while the second reconsecration/re-use of the space after the fire seems to have been a single event, carried out hastily from two different flanks, with bundles being deposited from both the shafts in tomb -399- and TT 12.

This lower section of the animal catacomb has provided us with a number of other significant finds of contemporary date. One of these is a group of fragments of a large Ptolemaic container with painted plant decoration, recovered in Hery's northern (ritual/ideological western) chamber (UE 225) (fig. 10). It is a well-known type, of which almost identical parallels have been found, for example, in both living areas and the subterranean animal galleries at Tuna el-Gebel,[70] as well as in many other Theban tombs, such as that of Ibi (TT 36).[71] It dates to the end of the third to the second century BCE, thus matching the dates ascribed to the graffiti. From both northern chambers (UEs 225 and 240) come different fragments of a Ptolemaic globular four-handled jar with remains of ibis eggs,

---

[68] False, fake, and pseudo-mummies are all terms that have been used, over time, to describe mummy bundles that only contain part of the creature that they are thought to have been offered to, or, in some cases, consist of a body part of an entirely different animal, but wrapped and given as an offering. Explanations for this practice include: an insufficient supply of the requisite animal, so one creature is divided among several mummy packages; if a particular creature was unavailable, the priests wrapped something else in its form, and by means of the right incantations, transformed it into what it should be; these are the debris of mummification, and as these animals were consecrated to the gods, all portions must be placed in a sacred spot; these represent an effort on the part of the priests to cheat the donor (and the gods). For further discussion, including examples with human mummies, see Ikram, "Divine Creatures: Animal Mummies," 1–15; R. Germer, H. Kischekwitz, and M. Lüning, "Pseudo-Mumien der ägyptischen Sammlung Berlin," *SAK* 21 (1994): 81–94; L. McKnight et al., "The Pseudo-Mummies from Bolton Museum and Art Gallery, Great Britain," in *Mummies and Science—World Mummies Research: Proceedings of the VI World Congress on Mummy Studies; Teguise, Lanzarote, February 20th to 24th, 2007*, ed. P. Atoche Peña, C. Rodríguez Martín, and M. Ramírez Rodríguez (Santa Cruz de Tenerife: Academia Canaria de la Historia, 2008), 687–89.

[69] Nicholson, "Sacred Animal Necropolis at North Saqqara," 44–71.

[70] F. Steinmann, "Ein ptolemäerzeitlicher Gefäßtyp in Tuna el-Gebel," in *Kleine Götter—Große Götter: Festschrift für Dieter Kessler zum 65. Geburtstag*, ed. M. Flossmann-Schütze et al., Tuna el-Gebel 4 (Vaterstetten: Bose, 2013), 477–93.

[71] E. Graefe, *Das Grab des Ibi, Obervermögensverwalters der Gottesgemahlin des Amun (Thebanisches Grab Nr. 36): Beschreibung und Rekonstruktionsversuche des Oberbaus Funde aus dem Oberbau* (Brussels: Fondation Égyptologique Reine Élisabeth, 1990), 30, pls. 66–68. See also G. Schreiber, *Late Dynastic and Ptolemaic Painted Pottery from Thebes (4th-2nd c. BC)*, Dissertationes Pannonicae 3.6 (Budapest: Eötvös Lorand University, 2003), 46–48 ("Early" and "Advanced Floral Style A"), pls. 15–21, 24–26, 31.

Fig. 10. Ptolemaic container with painted plant decoration from chamber UE 225.

Fig. 11. Ptolemaic ovoid two-handled jar from chamber UE 230.

immersed in dark resin-like materials.[72] A similar ovoid two-handled jar, most probably of second century BCE date, was discovered, totally fragmented, in Hery's southern (ritual/ideological eastern) chamber (UE 230) (fig. 11).[73]

A significant collection of clay seal impressions has also been assembled. They have mostly been found in different spaces of tomb –399–, the majority in strata linked to the deposition of the animal mummies. Some present very simple marks, another bears a figurative depiction of the bust of a Greek/Hellenized Isis in profile, and a small group contains hieroglyphic inscriptions.[74]

ADDITIONAL ANIMAL BURIAL SPACES IN TOMB –399–

Part of the 2017 season was devoted to the excavation and study of the remaining underground spaces of tomb –399–. Accessible through a series of shafts in the transverse hall, those chambers are not at a particularly deep level. They were discovered during the 2008–2009 seasons, although their excavation was not carried out or completed then. The shaft on the eastern (ritual/ideological northern) end of the transverse hall is double: the southern section gives access to a small burial chamber to the east, which was yet to be excavated (UE 82K), and the northern one leads to an irregular double chamber to the north, already emptied when first discovered with the exception of a sort of niche or small room in its northwest corner (UE 82J) (pl. 4). With the excavation of those two small chambers and the analysis of the sediment they contained, we could confirm the reuse of the space in the Ptolemaic period for the interment of animal mummies and, here too, the destruction of the content by a fire. The small niche UE 82J was filled with light brown powder, burnt bones, and a few bits of stone. Once again, sacred ibises were the most abundant (of all ages, though no eggshells were noted), with a few glossy ibis being present. A few raptors (falcons primarily), at least two shrews, and at least one snake were also documented. Some unusual animal remains (for this site) were also found: elements from dogs, a cat, a fox, and a goat. It was unclear if these were part of the Ptolemaic deposit, remnants of earlier activities, or later intrusions. As regards chamber UE 82K, it is notable that the burnt materials included human as well as animal bones, suggesting that all species shared a tomb. Here too, the majority of animals were represented by sacred ibis of all ages, a few glossy ibis, shrew, and snake. Unfortunately, it is not possible to date the human remains from this area with any confidence. There are at least three explanations for this. The first: the area was initially carved for humans, and then they were pushed to one side and animals interred here. The second: the animals were buried here and later on, humans were put here, with the animals pushed aside. The third: the area was intended

72 J. Lauffray, *La chapelle d'Achôris à Karnak, Vol. 1: Les fouilles, l'architecture, le mobilier et l'anastylose* (Paris: Éditions Recherche sur les Civilisations, 1995), 99, 104, 101 fig. 50 [no. 73], pl. 17a (Ptolemaic period), and 106, 107 fig. 54 [no. 118] (Ptolemaic period); D. Aston, *Elephantine XIX: Pottery from the Late New Kingdom to the Early Ptolemaic Period*, Archäologische Veröffentlichungen 95 (Mainz: von Zabern, 1999), 319, pl. 107 [no. 2801] (third century BCE); G. Lecuyot and G. Pierrat-Bonnefois, "Corpus de la céramique de Tôd: Fouilles 1980–1983 et 1990," *Cahiers de la céramique égyptienne* 7 (2004): 145–209, esp. 175, pl. 9 [121] (two-handled example; 222–51 BCE); A. Wodzińska, *A Manual of Egyptian Pottery, Vol. 4: Ptolemaic Period—Modern*, AERA Field Manual Series 1 (Boston: Ancient Egypt Research Associates, 2010), 49 (Ptolemaic 64 = Lauffray no. 118).

73 For an almost identical example, see A. Masson, "Persian and Ptolemaic Ceramics from Karnak: Change and Continuity," *Cahiers de la céramique égyptienne* 9 (2011): 269–310, esp. 271, 291 fig. 3 (Ptolemaic period).

74 This set of seals is under study and will be published in the final archaeological report/account. It is possible that some of the individuals mentioned on the inscriptions correspond to or have links with some of the characters attested in the graffiti.

for both animals and the humans that were associated with their cult. Currently, we lean toward the second hypothesis, although this might change with further analyses and reflection.

When the western (ritual/ideological southern) shaft in the transverse hall was uncovered in 2009, it still contained the remains of a much-damaged Ptolemaic descending mud-brick staircase, which was dismantled for safety reasons. At the bottom of the shaft, an irregular underground chamber to the north (ritual/ideological west), with three distinct spaces, can be found (UE 260) (pl. 4). This chamber is almost completely filled with bundles of mummies. Although some spot checks were made all over the chamber, we just excavated a test pit in the area adjacent to the entrance in the shape of an inverted "L" in plan.[75] The floor was completely covered with halfa grass mats (*Desmostachya bipinnata* or *Imperata cylindrica*), which, at some points was deliberately attached to it with a thin mud mortar (*muna*), a clear indication of the care taken in preparing the space before the interment of the mummies. The mummy bundles were placed on top of these mats. The use of mats and mummies is paralleled by a deposit of dog mummies at the corner of Tetisheri's temple at Abydos, with mats forming the base and cover for a deposit of canine mummies.[76]

Most of the mummies in UE 260 were of the bundle type, each packet consisting of the remains of several mummies (many of the teardrop shape), burnt and damaged by fire. The majority were of ibis (both sacred and glossy, as well as juveniles and eggshells), but some anthropomorphic raptor mummies (falcons) were present, together with small packets of shrews and serpents. Some teardrop-shaped mummies that were not blackened seem to have been deposited here independently, without being part of a group, and, in a few cases it seems as if their enclosing shroud had rotted away. Clearly, they had been gathered up, restored, and reburied in connection with the second of the phases attested in the northern chambers of the lower section of the catacomb.

THE EASTERN GALLERIES

When Hery's innermost chamber was excavated in 2011–2012, the existence of a connection (UE 212) toward the east (ritual/ideological north) was discovered. This connection led to a large room at a higher level, which, once excavated, proved to be the remains of two further New Kingdom rock-cut tomb-chapels: the mausolea of Baki and Ay (fig. 1). Abundant material from the Roman period was uncovered there, including small vases, lamps, bronze bracelets, and a large group of amphorae and large containers. Those finds suggested that the current appearance of the place could be essentially due to its reuse in Roman and probably also later (Byzantine to modern) times, very likely as an industrial or living space. However, it is probable that, at least part of the destruction of the walls in both tombs to reconvert the space into a large, open hall had already taken place in the Ptolemaic period as part of the transformation of the area into an animal catacomb. The existence of a mud-brick staircase connecting the two levels certainly is in keeping with what is seen elsewhere in the animal necropolis.

Beside the staircase, the entrance to another space, crowned by an impressive demotic graffito (graff. 53), is found (pls. 4 and 6). Although, when first discovered, a number of human mummies

---

75 Actually, the very first discovery and exploration of this animal burial space occurred already in 2006, during the excavation of the tomb's exterior shaft. The shaft has two levels of burial chambers, and this space was accessed through a connection, probably a robber's hole, present in one of the corners of the north (ritual/ideological west) chamber in the upper level.

76 S. Ikram, personal experience in the field; S. Harvey, "Report on Abydos, Ahmose and Tetisheri Project, 2006–2007 Season," *ASAE* 82 (2008): 143–55.

lay scattered in the access area—evidence of some later use (possibly even the result of robbers' activities)—, several demotic graffiti—the one already mentioned above the entrance, but also others already visible inside (graff. 55, 57, 60)—indicated that this was the start of another section of the Ptolemaic complex, the beginning of a new gallery presumably running toward the interior of the hill to the east of Hery's tomb, below the tomb-chapels of Baki and Ay. This area, under extensive excavation since the second half of the 2017 season, has been called the Eastern Galleries.[77]

The entrance hall (UE 270) is, in fact, all that is left of a small chamber most probably linked to an initial phase in the development of TT 12.[78] The eastern wall of this space was demolished in the Ptolemaic period to create a connection (UE 275) to two empty spaces to the right. The first of the spaces, to the right (south) of UE 275, consists of a rectangular corridor of an earlier Middle Kingdom tomb (UE 276), parallel and very similar in plan to Hery's corridor, although a bit longer and at a slightly lower level. It runs below the tomb-chapel of Baki and its courtyard. The second space, in this case to the left (north) of UE 275, consists of a rectangular burial chamber (UE 277) deeper inside the mountain, which, although located below the innermost part of the tomb-chapel of Baki, belongs to the plan of the tomb-chapel of Ay and would have originally been accessed through its main shaft (UE 325). These two preexisting spaces of different dates would have been joined in the Ptolemaic period to create a much longer corridor with a south-north orientation, which was incorporated into the system of galleries that form the animal catacomb, as clearly witnessed by the group of graffiti written on its walls (graff. 56–60). The inscriptions recovered in all of this underground area (graff. 53–61) belong mostly to the directional/utilitarian group (pls. 7–8), providing instructions to the cult workers and helping them find their way in the maze of corridors. In this respect, it must be noted that they usually appear at every turn or are located on surfaces acting or serving as lintels or doorjambs.

This long corridor (formed then by UEs 275, 276, and 277) gives access to two distinct spaces—or series of spaces—further east. First, on the eastern wall of its southern stretch there is a connection (with graff. 56) to a large chamber opening at the end of another, very similar, rectangular corridor. These two architectural features belong to another adjacent Middle Kingdom tomb, located below the tomb-chapel of Ay and its courtyard and which would have originally formed part of the same "street" of tombs. This street seems to extend even further, as suggested by the existence of additional blocked connections to the east. It is filled with debris almost to its roof and is yet to be properly explored. From what is visible, it is evident that this much earlier monument was also later integrated into the animal catacomb, as confirmed by the discovery of another demotic inscription on one of its walls (graff. 61). Second, the northern stretch connects to the east with Ay's funerary shaft (UE 325), which in turn leads to a twin funerary chamber to the east (UE 326) and a series of lower chambers underneath (UEs 328 and 329), that are still being cleared. An oblique mud-brick wall was built to close the northern end of this stretch, thus defining a small chamber that was used for the deposition of animal mummies (pl. 4), although its contents were again destroyed by a fire.[79] Animal bones from here were, as usual, mainly of ibises, raptors of different varieties, and a few snakes and shrews; an inscribed seal impression related to the animal cult was also recovered from the sieving. Additionally, to make access from this point to the lower chambers easier, a solid, mud-brick, five-step, straight staircase was built at the bottom of Ay's funerary shaft. At the end of the 2020 season another shaft (UE 343) was found in the floor of UE 328. Yet to be excavated, this architectural element—probably

77 Or the Northern Galleries, if emphasis is placed on its ritual/ideological orientation.

78 Galán, "Tomb-Chapel of Hery (TT 12) in Context."

79 This corner or small chamber (UE 277B) was used as a burial space for animal mummies in the same way as UE 255 in tomb -399- (see above); in both instances, a dead corner was just filled with mummies and then walled up.

linked to the original layout of the tomb of Ay, or perhaps a later extension, still for a human burial—most probably leads to additional, deeper chambers, which almost certainly were also incorporated into this complex, labyrinthine, subterranean world created for the animal burials in the Ptolemaic period.

Apart from this series of alterations to the plans of these tombs, the graffiti, the bone deposit in UE 277, and the descending staircase, very little additional evidence related to the Ptolemaic activity in the area has so far been uncovered. The only exception is a small number of animal mummies, which were all recovered as part of later fills. Some of the mummies found here include teardrop-shaped ibis mummies and some raptor mummies, together with damaged remains of cartonnage masks for the latter. All those spaces were—and to a large extent still are—filled with debris almost up to the ceiling, and their excavation is revealing that the whole area was extensively reused in Late Ptolemaic, Roman, and Byzantine times. For example, a very significant number of Late Ptolemaic and Roman lamps were discovered lying on the floor of the long corridor, together with globular pots and unguent jars, some of which were Coptic in date, thus indicating that the place remained open and free of content for a prolonged period of time. The stratigraphy also shows that, later on, the space was used as a dump for human mummies, probably to clear space for habitation, or perhaps as a deposit for tomb robbers.

THE UPPER GALLERY

A few meters above the inner chamber of the tomb-chapel of Hery, the "Ramesside Chapel"—as it is known by the team—is located (pl. 2, no. 15). Discovered in 2009 and conserved in 2013, it is a small monument that belonged to an overseer of weavers named Ramose, who probably served under Ramesses II. Its excavation revealed that in one corner (southwest) there was a small deposit of teardrop-shaped, soot-blackened bird mummies, some wrapped in elaborate patterns (herringbone). It is not clear if these were deposited here by priests or robbers. It also became apparent that there was an access in its northern (ritual/ideological western) wall, still partially walled up, to what we now call the Upper Gallery. This penetrates some twenty meters inside the rock of the hill and is formed by more than half a dozen rooms, some of them with high ceilings and pillars (pls. 5 and 59). This area, like the others, is created by the linking together of a series of preexisting tombs in the Ptolemaic period for the deposition of animal mummies. The present access route through the weaver's tomb was probably not the original one used by the priests dealing with animal cults; it is more likely that the official access was through chamber G (pl. 60b), which contains the highest concentration of graffiti, namely five of the six documented in the entire space (graff. 63, 64a–d).

The remains of burnt as well as soot-impregnated mummies, some very elegantly wrapped in a herringbone pattern, as well as some burnt bones, were found in chamber H. The exterior of the chamber sported one of the best preserved and largest of the graffiti (graff. 62). Although much of the material within chamber H had burned, as had the other chambers in the Upper Gallery, the inscription had escaped as it probably had been covered by a sealing of some sort that only fell off after the fire had run its course (pl. 60a). A few bird bones were noted in chamber F, and it is possible that some mummies had been deposited there as well as in other chambers, but one cannot yet be sure about the scope of use for animal burials in this gallery. Although over the years we have explored the space at different occasions in order to map it properly, study the texts, sample the sediment, and analyze the pottery on surface, we have not been able to excavate or study the deposit due to safety issues. It is hoped that the progress of the excavation on the outside will bring other, more secure entrances to the gallery to light.

TOMB ABOVE TT 11

The last area to discuss is another mausoleum above the tomb-chapel of Djehuty, whose entrance hall overlaps and breaks part of the ceiling of the innermost chamber of TT 11 (pl. 4). Probably because of this miscalculation in the location and construction of the monument, its layout is unorthodox: instead of a second room aligned with the first one, a side room to the left of the entrance hall was opened. This side room has a shaft, probably dating to the Third Intermediate or Saite period, about 2 m deep and taken up to a large extent by another Ptolemaic mud-brick staircase—a solid, four-step, very steep, straight staircase. The shaft containing the staircase opened up to two chambers, one to the north (ritual/ideological west; UE 194A) and another to the south (ritual/ideological east; UE 194B). Discovered in 2016, those small chambers were explored in 2017 and entirely excavated in 2018.

The northern room had a thick layer (over 60 cm in some areas) of ash and burnt bones, many twisted from the heat, over the floor, yet again the result of a fire. The study of the sediment showed that the original deposit would have been probably formed by individual mummies, mainly ibises, but also raptors (fragments of burnt cartonnage masks were also found), together with shrews and snakes, although a number of other species were also recovered, including some crocodile remains (vertebrae and scutes). Oddly enough, some unburnt small shrew and snake packets, as well as a few teardrop-shaped ibis mummy packages, were also found placed on top of the ash and bone layer. These appear to be part of a reconsecration of the space, having been deposited after the devastation of the fire, similar to the reconsecration of UEs 225 and 240 in the Lower Gallery. It is possible that the priests felt that the incinerated remains were too burnt and friable to bundle up and rebury, but as these remains, and also the space, were sacred, they decided to stress the fact that the area was an active burial ground by placing fresh mummies on top of those that had been completely destroyed by fire.

The southern room showed no signs of burning, perhaps being sealed by debris that protected it from the fire. The floor had about 4–6 cm of dust accumulated, and a denser scattering of packages of shrews and snakes, certainly deposited at the same time as the ones placed above the burnt bones in the north chamber. A small, roughly rectangular depression just inside the door to the room was full of these small packets.

This tomb has provided us with the best and most numerous examples of shrew and snake mummies (fig. 12), many of which were x-rayed. Radiographs also revealed that a few of the packages actually contained mice instead of shrews. Indeed, some of the other areas had also yielded remains of mice (*Mus musculus*) and Nile rat (*Arvicanthis niloticus*). Quite probably, these animals came under the general idea of "shrew" and were used when shrews were scarce, or unavailable, as phenotypically these animals resembled one another.[80]

---

[80] For a discussion of shrews as nocturnal aspects of the sun god, see E. Brunner-Traut, "Spitzmaus und Ichneumon als Tiere des Sonnengottes," *Göttinger Vorträge vom Ägyptologischen Kolloquium der Akademie vom 25. und 26. August 1964. Nachrichten von der Akademie der Wissenschaften in Göttingen: Philologisch-Historische Klasse* 1965.7 (1965): 123–63; S. Ikram, "A Monument in Miniature: The Eternal Resting Place of a Shrew," in *Structure and Significance: Thoughts on Ancient Egyptian Architecture*, ed. P. Jánosi, Österreichische Akademie der Wissenschaften, Denkschriften der Gesamtakademie 33, Untersuchungen der Zweigstelle Kairo des Österreichischen Archäologischen Institutes 25 (Vienna: Österreichische Akademie der Wissenschaften, 2005), 335–40. For a slightly varying interpretation, see D. Kessler, "Spitzmaus und Ichneumon im Tierfriedhof von Tuna el-Gebel," *Bulletin of the Egyptian Museum* 4 (2007): 71–82. Also, for burials of other rodents with shrews, see A. Charron, "Les musaraignes d'Abou Rawash," *Égypte Afrique et Orient* 66 (2012): 3–14; Woodman and Ikram, "Ancient Egyptian Mummified Shrews."

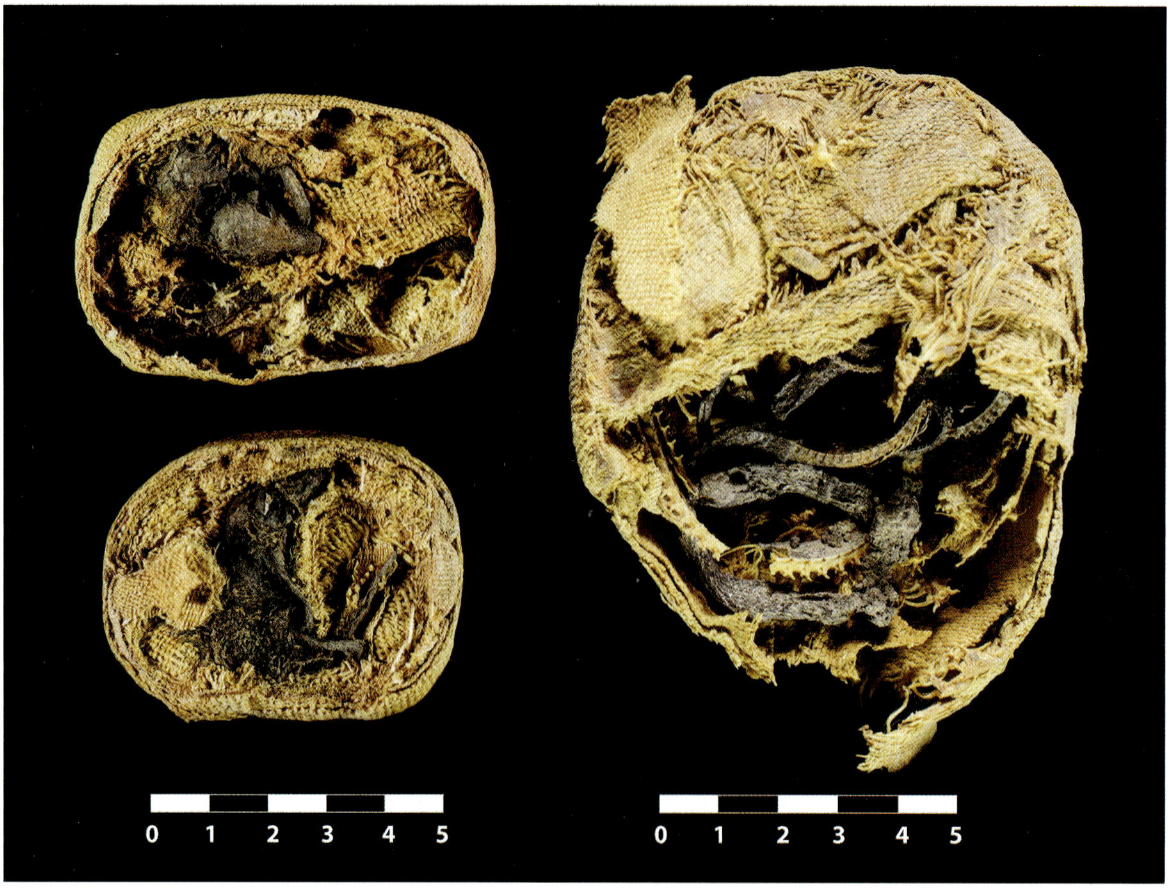

Fig. 12. Shrew and snake mummies from tomb above TT 11.

FINAL REMARKS

The many tombs for humans cut into the hillside of Dra Abu el-Naga[c] were repurposed in the Ptolemaic period for animal burials associated with animal cults, and their affiliated temples dedicated to Re/Horus and Thoth that were located somewhere in western Thebes. To make space for the deposition of thousands of animal mummies, the older tombs were joined together by breaking through walls of the chapels, as well as connecting existing subterranean chambers and creating new ones. Many of the chambers that were filled with animal mummies, consisting mainly of ibises, raptors, shrews, and snakes, were then sealed with mud-brick walls.

It is important to stress that evidence for fierce fires has been ubiquitously documented during these eight years of archaeological exploration, destroying mummies and blackening—in some instances, even calcining—the walls of burial chambers and tomb shafts. Evidence for burning has also been recorded in other animal mummy catacombs in Saqqara and elsewhere, with some being attributed to eighteenth and nineteenth century tourism. However, this does not seem to be the case here, as fires were explicitly mentioned in the graffiti that Spiegelberg recorded in "The Great Tomb of the Ibis and Hawks." In each section of the Ptolemaic animal complex that has been uncovered within the limits of the Spanish Mission's concession, proof of devastation by fire is coming to light, thus enabling us to establish links between the ancient texts and the archaeological evidence for the first time. Unfortunately, the inscriptions fail to elucidate the causes of those fires. Were they accidental, caused by careless use of lamps in the area, or due to spontaneous combustion of the mummies? However, they appear to be too numerous and occurred in spaces that are not physically connected, which suggests that they were intentional. Could they have been set by the cult workers themselves in order to free up space? Are they the result of the action of ancient tomb robbers looking for riches? Could they perhaps relate to a specific historical event, such as the so-called Great Revolt of the Egyptians (205–186 BCE) or one of the political conflicts that arose in the middle of the Ptolemaic Dynasty? Of course, any attempt to answer such questions is, for the time being, mere speculation, but this is one of the rare moments when texts and archaeological evidence combine to provide a fuller picture of the history of a site.

Introductory Remarks and Overview of the Graffiti from the Spanish Mission at Dra Abu el-Naga^{c}

In this volume we present the largely unpublished demotic graffiti chiefly from the tombs of Djehuty (TT 11) and Hery (TT 12) recovered by the Spanish Mission to Dra Abu el-Naga^{c} (pls. 1–2) under the direction of Prof. José M. Galán.[81] We also include two graffiti from the neighboring tomb -399-, and six graffiti from the Upper Gallery discovered by Galán higher up on the hill, as well as graffiti in the Eastern Galleries under the tombs of Baki and Ay. Plates 5 and 6 present keyplans displaying the locations of all these graffiti. We publish here as well five ostraca and two mummy bandage inscriptions.

The graffiti published by the young Wilhelm Spiegelberg from what he called "The Great Tomb of the Ibis and Hawks" and other localities in the area are closely related to those found by Galán.[82] We have therefore also incorporated those texts into this volume, although the location of this "Great Tomb" is nowadays unknown.[83] Since all these inscriptions were written by persons involved in the sacred animal cult in Dra Abu el-Naga^{c}, it is reasonable to present the new and previously published material together.[84]

Di Cerbo was able to photograph and record the graffiti in TT 11, TT 12, tomb -399-, and the Upper and Eastern Galleries on several occasions; Jasnow had the opportunity to visit the site in January 2019. Galán has kindly provided us with additional plans, images, and essential information.[85] On the basis of Di Cerbo's images we have prepared digital hand copies for the new graffiti, which are all written in red ochre.[86] As already mentioned, the location of "The Great Tomb of the Ibis and Hawks," probably situated near TT 141, is yet to be rediscovered; here we are dependent on Spiegelberg's editions.[87] While his hand copies and decipherments are masterly, corrections and alternative readings may be offered.[88]

---

81 The Spanish Mission has been working at the site since 2002. Detailed reports and information on the site are available on the Project website: https://proyectodjehuty.com/.

82 Northampton, Spiegelberg, and Newberry, *Report on Some Excavations in the Theban Necropolis*, 19–25 ("The Demotic Inscriptions"). See D. Kessler, *Die Oberbauten des Ibiotapheion von Tuna el-Gebel*, Tuna el-Gebel 3 (Haar: Brose, 2011), 186, for discussion of the Spiegelberg publication. S. Vleeming, *Demotic Graffiti and Other Short Texts Gathered from Many Publications (Short Texts III 1201-2350)*, Studia Demotica 12 (Leuven: Peeters, 2015), 121.

83 See now Vleeming, *Graffiti*, 114–37.

84 On the difficulty of distinguishing between sacred and votive animal mummies, see now Ikram, "Shedding New Light on Old Corpses," 172.

85 The keyplan of TT 12 is based on a drawing provided by Galán.

86 Here we would like to thank José Latova, mission photographer, for providing excellent infrared images and an overview image of TT 11 that has been used for the keyplan (pls. 9 and 10) published here. Salima Ikram also gave to us very useful preliminary documentation images taken in the course of the excavation. The facsimile of Mummy Bandage 1 is based on a photograph by Ikram.

87 "Cette tombe est située dans un ravin près de la tombe n° 141 (cf. PM $1^{2}/2$, p. 609)," M. Chauveau, "Un été 145: Post-scriptum," *BIFAO* 91 (1991), 129.

88 It must not be forgotten that Spiegelberg was working under quite primitive conditions. The tomb was unexcavated and he had certainly very poor lighting. Keeping this in mind, his editions are a remarkable achievement. A useful collection of corrections over the years to these texts is in A. den Brinker, B. Muhs, S. Vleeming, eds., *A Berichtigungsliste of Demotic Documents: Ostrakon Editions and Various Publications*, Studia Demotica 7b (Leuven: Peeters, 2005), 518–19.

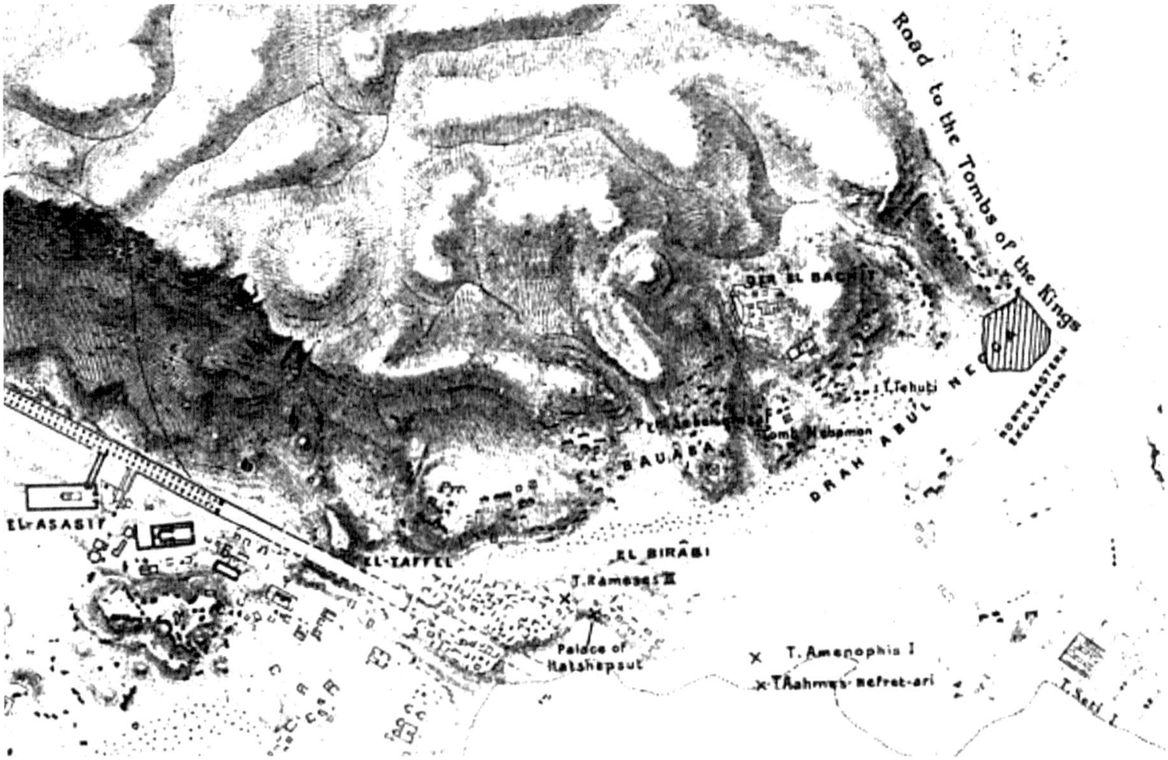

Fig. 13. Detail of Dra Abu el-Naga[c] map. From Northampton, Spiegelberg, and Newberry, *Report on Some Excavations in the Theban Necropolis*, pl. 2.

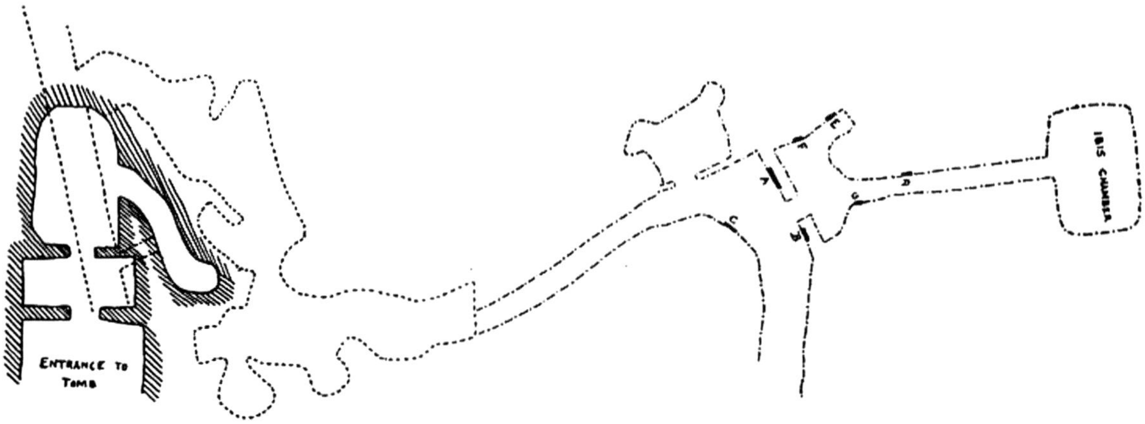

Fig. 14. Plan of "The Great Tomb of the Ibis and Hawks." From Northampton, Spiegelberg, and Newberry, *Report on Some Excavations in the Theban Necropolis*, fig. 23.

M. Chauveau has already reedited the historically significant "Great Tomb" graff. 14–15 (in Spiegelberg's numbering system; our graff. 80 and 81) in his analysis of the "year 145 B.C."[89] There are certainly differences between the graffiti of the "Great Tomb" and those in TT 11 and TT 12. The combination *Wsỉr pꜣ hb* and *Wsỉr pꜣ bik* is, for example, more frequently found in the "Great Tomb" ("Great Tomb" eight times; TT 11 twice). There is no apparent overlap in the individuals mentioned. Moreover, there are no directional texts in the "Great Tomb."

89 Chauveau, "Un été 145," 129–32, with reedition and discussion.

Fig. 15. S-wall of TT 12 vandalized by antiquity hunters.

Spiegelberg had concentrated on the graffiti from the "Great Tomb," but he did publish several inscriptions from TT 11 Djehuty (graff. 6, 7, 9, 14) and TT 12 Hery (graff. 48, 49, 50). He also edited two inscriptions "above the tomb of *Ḥrij*" (graff. 65–66).[90] In several cases, comparison of his copies with the present state of the graffiti reveals the extent of damage suffered by the tombs over the years.[91]

Given the many new graffiti, it was impractical to continue Spiegelberg's numbering system.[92] In this volume all the graffiti are therefore assigned a continuous catalogue number, while some graffiti receive an additional subdesignation. Every effort has been made to record all visible traces. Naturally, there may well have been more graffiti than can now be recovered. In tomb -399- the walls have suffered extreme erosion; almost no original decoration survives in its chapel. It is sometimes indeed impossible to distinguish one damaged graffito from another. The conservation program of the Spanish Mission has undoubtedly benefitted the graffiti immensely,[93] but many are beyond help.

We do not claim for our digital hand copies the level of accuracy attained by true facsimiles. The digital hand copies published here simply represent our best efforts at interpreting the demotic inscriptions; they are subjective drawings. Students of graffiti know well that producing a copy often

[90] This tomb has been rediscovered by L. Manniche, "A Report on Work Carried out at Dra^c Abu el-Naga^c," *ASAE* 72 (1992–1993): 49 and 52. See also Kampp, *Die thebanische Nekropole*, 695–96 (Grab-Nr. 141). We have not ourselves been able to collate the two inscriptions in this tomb, which are in any case outside of the Spanish concession.

[91] See, e.g., graff. 48 (TT 12/2). J. M. Galán and G. Menéndez, "The Funerary Banquet of Hery (TT 12), Robbed and Restored," *JEA* 97 (2011): 143–66.

[92] See the concordance of our catalogue numbers and the Spiegelberg numbers on p. 180.

[93] https://proyectodjehuty.com/report-campaign-2013/.

entails making painful choices from a myriad of possibilities; a sort of palaeographical triage.[94] In the case of these graffiti, discoloration through fire, erosion, clay concretions and tomb reuse, created a tremendous amount of epigraphic "static."[95] Unfortunately, since many of these graffiti are scarcely readable on even the best computer-enhanced photographic images, our colleagues will generally have to rely on our hand copies.

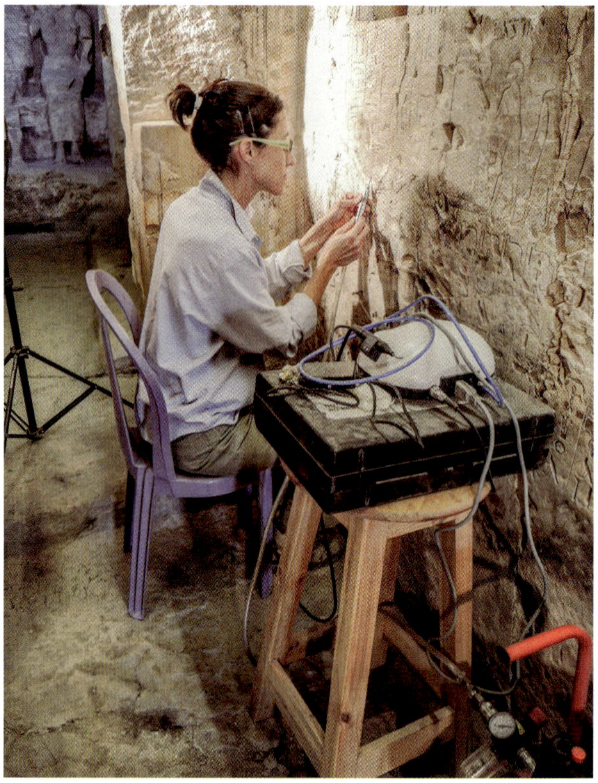

Fig. 16. Conservator Nieves López Meijueiro cleaning area next to graffito 38 in TT 11 using a vibrating cutter with ultrasound.

THE HISTORICAL BACKGROUND AND CHARACTER OF THE GRAFFITI

Spiegelberg's 1908 publication revealed most vividly the flourishing ibis and falcon cult at Dra Abu el-Naga^c from the Ptolemaic period.[96] The ancient writers designate these birds as the "Osiris ibis" and the "Osiris falcon."[97] The

[94] L. Prada and P. D. Wordsworth, "Evolving Epigraphic Standards in the Field: Documenting Late Period and Graeco-Roman Egyptian Graffiti through Photogrammetry at Elkab," in *The Materiality of Texts from Ancient Egypt: New Approaches to the Study of Textual Material from the Early Pharaonic to the Late Antique Period*, ed. F. Hoogendijk, A.J. Francisca, and S. van Gompel, PLBat 35 (Leiden: Brill, 2018), 76–93. There is much new insightful research on graffiti (both from Egypt and elsewhere); a fine example is C. Ragazzoli, "The Scribes' Cave: Graffiti and the Production of Social Space in Ancient Egypt circa 1500 BC." in *Scribbling Through History: Graffiti, Places and People from Antiquity to Modernity*, ed. C. Ragazzoli et al. (London: Bloomsbury, 2018), 23–36.

[95] https://proyectodjehuty.com/report-campaign-2013/.

[96] The topic of animal cults is, of course, immense, see in general Ikram, *Divine Creatures*; M. Fitzenreiter, ed., *Tierkulte im pharaonischen Ägypten und im Kulturvergleich*, Internet-Beiträge zur Ägyptologie und Sudanarchäologie 4 (Berlin: Golden House, 2005). On the ibis and falcon cult at Dra Abu el-Naga^c and elsewhere, see M. C. Flossmann-Schütze, "Études sur le cadre de vie d'une association religieuse dans l'Égypte gréco-romaine: L'exemple de Touna el-Gebel," in *Proceedings of the XI International Congress of Egyptologists*, ed. G. Rosati and M. Guidotti, 203–8; D. Kessler, *Die heiligen Tiere und der König: Beiträge zu Organisation, Kult und Theologie der spätzeitlichen Tierfriedhöfe*, Ägypten und Altes Testament 16 (Wiesbaden: Harrassowitz, 1989), 159–68; Kessler, "Ibis-Vögel mit Eigennamen: Tiere des Festes und des Orakels," in *Honi soit qui mal y pense: Studien zum pharaonischen, griechisch-römischen und spätantiken Ägypten zu Ehren von Heinz-Josef Thissen*, ed. H. Knuf, C. Leitz, and D. von Recklinghausen, OLA 194 (Leuven: Peeters, 2010), 261–72; Ray, *Texts from the Baboon and Falcon Galleries*, 341–42 ("concluding remarks on the cult of the Falcon"); Ray, *Archive of Ḥor*, 52–53, 72, 77, 83, 85, 105, 136–44; S. Cauville, "La Chapelle de Thoth-Ibis à Dendera édifiée sous Ptolémée Ier par Hor, scribe d'Amon-Re," *BIFAO* 89 (1989): 43–66. For a useful recent article on canine cults, see L. Rouvière, "Le culte des canidés dans la région de Hardaï/Cynopolis: Enquête épigraphique et archéologique," in *Géographie et archéologie de la religion égyptienne: Espaces cultuels et pratiques locales*, ed. C. Cassier, CENIM 17 (Montpellier: Université Paul Valéry, 2017), 109–28. See also the thesis of S. Wasef, "Ancient Egyptian Sacred Ibis Mummies: Evolutionary Mitogenomics Resolves the History of Ancient Farming" (PhD diss., Griffith University, 2016).

[97] See, e.g., Ray, *Texts from the Baboon and Falcon Galleries*, 246–47 and 286–87. The usual word in this corpus for "falcon" is *bi͗k*, but *ꜥḫm* occurs in Spiegelberg graffito "Great Tomb" 2, 2 (= graff. 68, 2 in this volume).

close relationship between these two entities is well expressed in a demotic inscription on a coffin in Berlin, where the deceased is addressed:

"You will go as a noble ibis and return as a divine falcon."[98]

In the past century much additional evidence for this cult at Thebes has naturally surfaced. Ptolemaic Theban demotic texts mention priests associated with the cult and other graffiti in the Theban hills allude to it as well.[99]

The more famous animal cults in Saqqara, Tuna el-Gebel, and elsewhere provide substantial information relevant to that at Dra Abu el-Nagaʿ.[100] As in Thebes, falcons and ibises were jointly buried, for example, in Saqqara and Tuna el-Gebel.[101]

The most distinctive title in the Dra Abu el-Nagaʿ graffiti, *wr Ḏḥwty*, "great one of Thoth," (e.g., graff. 53, 5 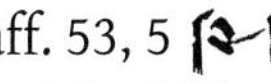), occurs at Saqqara and virtually all the other localities where the sacred bird cult flourished.[102] Indeed it was probably these "great ones of Thoth" who wrote most of the graffiti. Sue

---

98 M. Smith, *Traversing Eternity: Texts for the Afterlife from Ptolemaic and Roman Egypt* (Oxford: Oxford University Press, 2009), 578.

99 E.g., M. el-Amir, *A Family Archive from Thebes: Demotic Papyri in the Philadelphia and Cairo Museums from the Ptolemaic Period* (Cairo: General Organisation for Government Printing Offices, 1959), 67, notes that "in BM 10230 we find a priest and pastophoros of all title-deeds and leases of the resting place of the Ibis and Hawk which is in the Necropolis of Jeme"; "the silver price of the tomb-chapel of Psherchons the feeder (*trophos*) together with his people who rest therein with him, which is behind the way to the resting-place of the Ibis," 88; On P. BM 10230 and related documents, see especially P. Pestman, *Recueil de textes démotiques et bilingues*, 3 vols. (Leiden: Brill, 1977), 2:73–99. The individuals mentioned in those texts were almost certainly closely associated with the persons appearing in our graffiti. The ibis cult workers appear in the salt-tax documents published in W. Clarysse and D. Thompson, *Counting the People in Hellenistic Egypt: Population Registers (P. Count)*, 2 vols. (Cambridge: Cambridge University Press, 2006), 2:49 (Pachrates, a servant of the ibis, "is liable for the full [salt-tax] rate"), 55 (personnel of the Ibis-cult, and ibis buriers), 56 (a servant, *bꜣk*, of the ibis), 58 (ibis-breeders).

100 Ray comments on the differences between the ibis cults in Saqqara and Thebes, *Texts from the Baboon and Falcon Galleries*, 244. Also of interest are the texts from Ombos in F. Preisigke and W. Spiegelberg, *Die Prinz-Joachim-Ostraka: Griechische und demotische Beisetzungsurkunden für Ibis-und Falkenmumien aus Ombos*, Schriften der Wissenschaftlichen Gesellschaft in Strassburg 19 (Strassburg: Trübner, 1914); texts from Hermopolis: El-Hussein Omar M. Zaghloul, Frühdemotische Urkunden aus Hermupolis, Bulletin of the Center of Papyrological Studies 2 (Cairo: Ain Shams University- Center of Papyrological Studies, 1985), 14–19. The available evidence for the ibis and falcon cult in Ptolemaic Egypt is enormous, and much research remains to be done. A valuable recent contribution to the subject is F. Scalf, "Resurrecting an Ibis Cult: Demotic Votive Texts from the Oriental Institute Museum of the University of Chicago," in *Mélanges offerts à Ola el-Aguizy*, ed. F. Haikal, BdE 164 (Cairo: Institut français d'archéologie orientale, 2015), 361–88. See also A. Grimm, D. Kessler, and H. Meyer, *Der Obelisk des Antinoos: Eine kommentierte Edition* (Munich: Fink, 1994), 122–23. For a discussion of the animal cult at Abydos, see S. Ikram, "Animals in a Ritual Context at Abydos. A Synopsis," in *The Archaeology and Art of Ancient Egypt: Essays in Honor of David B. O'Connor*, ed. Z. Hawass and J. Richards, SASAE 36 (Cairo: Conseil Suprême des Antiquités de l'Egypte, 2007), 417–32.

101 Ray, *Texts from the Baboon and Falcon Galleries*, 320; Kessler, *Die heiligen Tiere und der König*, 118.

102 There is a considerable amount of literature on this title: Scalf, "Resurrecting an Ibis Cult," 369–70; M. Schentuleit, *Aus der Buchhaltung des Weinmagazins im Edfu-Tempel: Der demotische P. Carlsberg 409*, Carlsberg Papyri 9, CNI Publications 32 (Copenhagen: Museum Tusculanum Press, 2006), 53 and 181. She takes this to be the head of the Cult Association of Thoth, citing F. de Cenival, *Les associations religieuses en Égypte d'après les documents démotiques*, 2 vols., BdE 46 (Cairo: Institut français d'Archéologie orientale, 1972), 1:169–70. Schentuleit compares the *wr bik*, "great one of the falcon," and *pꜣ sp wr n pꜣ ʿ.wy*, which form part of the funerary procession for the deceased sacred falcon in P. Lille 29, lines 11–12, de Cenival, *Les associations religieuses*, I:6. On Stela BM EA 1325 (30 BCE) thirty-six men are mentioned as *nꜣ wr Ḏḥwty*, so that "possibly all members of a Cult-Association could be so-named." Schentuleit cites further Vleeming, *Graffiti*, no. 33; G. Vittmann, "Ein thebanischer Verpfründungsvertrag aus der Zeit Ptolemaios' III. Euergetes," *Enchoria* 10 (1980):

Davies has aptly described the *wr.w Ḏḥwty* as the "leaders of religious confraternities associated with these bird cults," adding "that one of their duties was that of receiving deliveries of bird mummies."[103]

Thoth was a significant deity on the West Bank of Thebes in the Ptolemaic period. The best witness for his prominence is the Temple of Thoth at Qasr el-Aguz just south of Medinet Habu, constructed in the reign of Ptolemy VIII Euergetes II.[104] Associated with this temple is the common Ptolemaic name *Ḏ-pꜣ-ḥr-hb*, "The Face-of-the-ibis-has-spoken," which has oracular implications.[105] It is safe to assume that Thoth was venerated in numerous other places in the West Bank apart from Qasr el-Aguz.[106]

DATING OF THE GRAFFITI

On the basis of the double-dated graffiti (graff. 80 and 81), which are securely placed in 145 BCE, Spiegelberg had already attributed the corpus of these texts to the second century BCE, commenting: "There can be little doubt that all the inscriptions are of nearly the same date."[107]

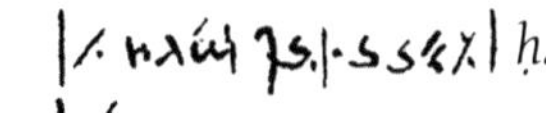 *ḥ.t-sp 36 ỉr ỉr ḥ.t-sp 25 ỉbt 3 šmw sw 11* (80, 3)

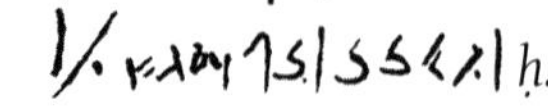 *ḥ.t-sp 36 ỉr ỉr ḥ.t-sp 25 ỉbt 3 šmw sw 11* (81, 5)

137; A. Farid, *Fünf demotische Stelen aus Berlin, Chicago, Durham, London und Oxford mit zwei demotischen Türinschriften aus Paris und einer Bibliographie der demotischen Inschriften* (Berlin: Achet, 1995), 56–58; Kessler, *Die heiligen Tiere und der König*, 162; J. Quaegebaeur, "La Désignation 'porteur(s) des dieux' et le culte des dieux-crocodiles dans les textes des époques tardives," in *Mélanges Adolphe Gutbub* (Montpellier: Publication de la Recherche-Université de Montpellier, 1984), 166; W. Clarysse and J. K. Winnicki in E. van 't Dack et al., *The Judean-Syrian-Egyptian Conflict of 103–101 B.C.: A Multilingual Dossier concerning a "War of Sceptres,"* Collectanea Hellenistica 1 (Brussels: Publikatie van het comité klassieke studies, subcomité hellenisme koninklijke Academie voor Wettenschappen, Letteren en schone Kunsten van België, 1989), 47; H. Smith, "The Saqqara Papyri: Oracle Questions, Pleas and Letters," in *Acts of the Seventh International Conference of Demotic Studies: Copenhagen, 23–27 August 1999*, ed. K. Ryholt, CNI Publications 27 (Copenhagen: Museum Tusculanum Press, 2002), 371. There is also a feminine counterpart, *tꜣ wr.t Ḏḥwty*, found in P. dém. Lille 98, dated to 245 BCE (from Ghoran); F. de Cenival, "Deux papyrus inédits de Lille avec une révision du P. dém. Lille 31," *Enchoria* 7 (1977): 22 and 34. See also J. Quack's comments on the possible title *ḥm*(?) *Ḏḥwty*, rendered by that scholar as "Diener(?) des Thoth"; "Eine weise Stimme der Autorität (Papyrus Amherst Eg. XLIII.1 rt.): Mit Anhängen über Abrechnungen (Papyrus Amherst Eg. XLIII.1 vs. Und XLIII.2)," in R. Jasnow and G. Widmer, eds., *Illuminating Osiris: Egyptological Studies in Honor of Mark Smith*, Material and Visual Culture of Ancient Egypt 2 (Atlanta: Lockwood Press, 2017), 315–16.

103 S. Davies, "The Organization, Administration and Functioning of the Sacred Animal Cults at North Saqqara as Revealed by the Demotic Papyri from the Site," in Ryholt, *Acts of the Seventh International Conference of Demotic Studies*, 80–81.

104 The walls of this interesting temple have been recently cleaned, M. Jenkins, "The 'Temple of Thot' on the West Bank at Luxor: Qasr el 'Aguz," *KMT* 21.4 (2010–2011): 50–61. On the temple, see D. Klotz, *Caesar in the City of Amun: Egyptian Temple Construction and Theology in Roman Thebes,* MRE 15 (Turnhout: Brepols, 2012), 215–17; C. Traunecker, "Le temple de Qasr el-Agouz dans la nécropole thébaine, ou Ptolémées et savants thébains," *Bulletin de la Société Française d'Égyptologie* 174 (2009): 29–69 (mention of the Dra Abu el-Nagaᶜ graffiti on 65); Kessler, *Die heiligen Tiere und der König*, 165 (on the association of Qasr el-Aguz and these graffiti); Y. Volokhine, "Le dieu Thot au Qasr el-Agouz *Ḏd-ḥr-pꜣ-hb, Ḏḥwty-stm*," *BIFAO* 102 (2002): 405–23. For remarks on the importance of Thoth in the West Bank of Thebes, see E. Laskowska-Kusztal, *Le sanctuaire ptolémaïque de Deir el-Bahari*, Deir el-Bahari 3 (Warsaw: PWN-Éditions scientifiques de Pologne, 1984), 126–27.

105 See Ray, *Texts from the Baboon and Falcon Galleries*, 17–18; K. Vandorpe, "City of Many a Gate, Harbour for Many a Rebel: Historical and Topographical Outline of Greco-Roman Thebes," in *Hundred-Gated Thebes: Acts of a Colloquium on Thebes and the Theban Area in the Graeco-Roman Period*, ed. S. Vleeming, PLBat 27 (Leiden: Brill, 1995), 229.

106 See Klotz, *Caesar in the City of Amun*, 215–17.

107 Northampton, Spiegelberg, and Newberry, *Report on Some Excavations in the Theban Necropolis*, 23.

Fig. 17. Animal mummies in the chambers at the foot of the staircase in tomb –399–.

While we see little reason to disagree with Spiegelberg, it is probably advisable to be open to the possibility that some graffiti are of earlier date in view of the ostraca discussed below. The few securely identified individuals mentioned in the corpus belong to a Theban family well attested in the later third and middle of the second centuries BCE.[108]

The writers of the graffiti often record regnal years, but unfortunately did not feel it necessary to mention specific rulers.

The following texts have regnal years:

10, 1	TT 11	*ḥ.t-sp 11.t*	"11"
13, 1	TT 11	*ḥ.t-sp 9.t*	"9"
14, 3	TT 11	*ḥ.t-sp 9 ỉbt 4 pr.t sw 19;*	"9"
14, 4	TT 11	*ḥ.t-sp 9 ỉbt 3 sw 11*	"9"
19, 6	TT 11	*ḥ.t-sp 20.t r ḥ.t-sp 21.t*	"20; 21"
21, 6	TT 11	*ḥ.t-sp 21.t(?) ỉbt 3 pr.t sw 11*	21(?)

[108] See the section on "Personal Names with Titles," on pp. 66–67.

24, 3	TT 11	*ḥ.t-sp 10.t(?) ỉbt 4 pr.t sw 11*	“10(?)”
30, 9	TT 11	*ḥ.t-sp 9.t(?) [...]*	“9(?)”
31, 3	TT 11	*ḥ.t-sp 5.t*	“5”
33a, 7	TT 11	*ḥ.t-sp 9 ỉbt 3(?)*	“9”
34, 2 34, 6	TT 11 TT 11	*ḥ.t-sp 9.t r ḥ.t-sp 10.t ;* *ḥ.t-sp 10.t(?) ... ỉbt 3(?) pr.t ...*	“9; 10”
37a, 1	TT 11	*ḥ.t-sp 10.t ỉbt 4 ... sw 11*	“10”
45, 1	tomb -399-	*ḥ.t-sp 20 ỉbt 4 pr.t sw 11*	“20”
47, 3	TT 12	*ḥ.t-sp 2.t ỉbt 3 [...]*	“2”
48, 7	TT 12	*ḥ.t-sp ...*	lost
62a, 1	Upper Gallery	*ḥ.t-sp 7 ỉbt 4 pr.t sw 11*	“7”
69, 2	“Great Tomb”	*ḥ.t-sp 5.t*	“5”
74, 5	“Great Tomb”	*ḥ.t-sp 5.t*	“5”
80, 3	“Great Tomb”	*ḥ.t-sp 36 ỉr ỉr ḥ.t-sp 25 ỉbt 3 šmw sw 11*	“36 = 25”
81, 5	“Great Tomb”	*ḥ.t-sp 36 ỉr ỉr ḥ.t-sp 25 ỉbt 3 šmw sw 11*	“36 = 25”
82, 7	“Great Tomb”	*ḥ.t-sp [...]*	lost
Ostracon 1, 2; Ostracon 1, 3	southwest of TT 11–12	*ỉbt 2 pr.t sw 6(?);* *ḥ.t-sp 34 ỉbt 4 pr.t sw 17*	“34”
Ostracon 2, 1	southwest of TT 11–12	(ετους) ε	“5”
Ostracon 5, 6	southwest of TT 11–12	*ḥ.t-sp 28 ỉbt 1 ꜣ[ẖ.t ...]*	“28”

The double dates in graff. 80 and 81 enabled Chauveau and Spiegelberg to date these to 145 BCE.[109] In graff. 19 and 45, the relatively high regnal years 20 and 21 appear. These may also refer to the reigns of Ptolemy VI (i.e., 162–161 BCE) or Ptolemy VIII (i.e., 151–150 BCE). Again, an attribution of the graffiti to the second century BCE is reasonable, although it is possible that some were inscribed already in the third century BCE.

Ostracon 1, 1 a “price of oil receipt,” which mentions an *ꜥ.wy ḥtp*, “place of rest,” 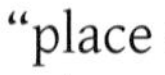 may be dated to 252/251 BCE.[110] This is one of five demotic and demotic–Greek ostraca discovered in the southwest of TT 11-12. The relationship of ostracon 1 to the graffiti corpus is therefore naturally uncertain. However, this ostracon is additional evidence for an active sacred animal cult at Dra Abu

109 Chauveau, “Un été 145,” 129.

110 We thank Brian Muhs for his comments on this ostracon.

el-Naga^{c} in the third century BCE. This third century BCE ostracon should perhaps be kept in mind when considering the possible dates of the graffiti corpus.

It is striking that ten texts specifically mention "day 11": graff. 14, 4; 21, 7; 24, 3; 37a, 1; 45, 1; 62a, 1; 63, 5; 64b, 6; 80, 3; 81, 5. It is therefore evident that the eleventh day of the month held a special significance for the cult of the ibis and the falcon. We have not, unfortunately, yet been able to determine more precisely the nature of this significance.

CONTENT OF GRAFFITI (SEE PLATES 7–8)

The graffiti fall broadly into at least three distinct types: (1) votive; (2) service and directional; (3) commemorative. Naturally, a given graffito may belong to more than one type. Although brief, the texts contain distinctive words or phrases that convey significant information about the cult activity, the physical environment, and the organization of the cult personnel. Plates 6–8 are key plans showing the location and type of graffiti in TT 11, TT 12, and the Eastern Galleries.

1. VOTIVE GRAFFITI

By votive graffiti we mean texts expressing notions of personal piety, that is, the writers hope to associate themselves with this sacred locality and the deities connected with it.[111] These votive graffiti are most often comprised of the "good name" or the "giving life" formulas.

a. "Good Name"

The cult workers were eager to memorialize themselves with the *rn nfr* formula so ubiquitous in temples such as Medinet Habu.[112] They wished their names to "remain" before the ibises and falcons embalmed and buried here. The basic idea may be expressed thus:

> "The good name of PN remains here before Osiris ibis and Osiris falcon for ever and ever."

This votive formula, which has numerous variants, is by far the most common in these graffiti: 1, 2, 6, 7, 8, 10, 11, 12, 13, 14, 15, 16, 18, 20, 22, 23, 24, 25, 28 *rn* , 29, 30, 31, 32 *rn*, 34, 35, 37a, 37b, 39, 41, 43 *rn*, 47, 48, 49, 50, 51, 62a, 64a, 64b, [67], 68, 72, 73, 77, 79, 80, 81, 82, 83, 84, 89.

b. "DN gives life to PN"

The more elaborate formula "DN gives life to PN" is only found in TT 11 (graff. 19, 1–2) and in the "Great Tomb" (graff. 74, 1–2):[113]

19, 1–2: *Wsỉr pꜣ hb Wsỉr pꜣ bỉk tỉ.t ꜥnḫ (n) PN* "Osiris the ibis (and) Osiris the falcon, give life (to) PN."

---

111 Useful is the overview of M. Luiselli, "Personal Piety," in UCLA Encyclopedia of Egyptology http://uee.cdh.ucla.edu/articles/personal_piety_(modern_theories_related_to).

112 On such formulas, see, e.g., S. Vleeming, *Some Coins of Artaxerxes and Other Short Texts in the Demotic Script Found on Various Objects and Gathered from Many Publications*, Studia Demotica 5 (Leuven: Peeters, 2001), 256; H.-J. Thissen, *Die demotischen Graffiti von Medinet Habu Zeugnisse zu Tempel und Kult im ptolemäischen Ägypten*, Demotische Studien 10 (Sommerhausen: Gisela Zauzich Verlag, 1989), 196–202.

113 For the formula, see, e.g., Vleeming, *Some Coins*, 250–53.

74, 1–2: *Wsir pꜣ hb Wsir pꜣ bik nꜣ ntr.w n pꜣ ꜥ.wy ḥtp tr=w ti.t ꜥnḫ (n) PN* "Osiris the ibis (and) Osiris the falcon (and) all the gods of the place of rest of the ibis give life (to) PN."

c. Invocation to the Ibis

There are notably few invocations or short hymns in this corpus. Again, in the "Great Tomb," there is one example of the optative formula *ꜥnḫ=k ꜥnḫ by=k* "May you live! May your ba live!" (graff. 68), which is apparently addressed to the ibis itself.[114]

68, 1–3: *ꜥnḫ=k ꜥnḫ by=k pꜣ hb pr-ꜥꜣ rpy=k rpy ꜣḥ=k Wsir pꜣ hb Wsir pꜣ bik Wsir pꜣ ꜥḫm Wsir Twtw(?) Wsir Ḥr nb Sḫm* "May you live! May your ba live! O ibis of pharaoh, may you be rejuvenated! "May your body be rejuvenated! O Osiris ibis, o Osiris falcon, o Osiris falcon, Osiris Tutu(?), Osiris Horus, Lord of Letopolis!"

2. SERVICE AND DIRECTIONAL GRAFFITI

More unusual and distinctive for this corpus are the service and directional graffiti. These contain advice or instructions to the readers, presumably the cult workers, with regard to the carrying out of their duties.

a. Service Texts Containing Advice or Instructions to the Cult Workers

The graffiti deal with several stages involved in the ibis and falcon burial cult. First of all, the tombs obviously had to be prepared to receive the mummies. Two graffiti at least appear to reflect this initial stage of preparation (graff. 65–66):

65, 1–4: *iw=f ḫpr iw wḫꜣ=w n ir(?) ꜥ.wy.w ḥtp ẖr pꜣ hb pꜣ bik my wn[=w] wꜥ myt my ir=w wpy.t nb* "If it happens that they have desired to make(?) places of rest for the ibis (and) the falcon, let [one] open a path, let one make all work."

66, 2–4: *iw=f ḫpr iw wḫꜣ=w [n ir] ꜥ.wy ḥtp [ẖr] pꜣ hb [pꜣ bik] ...* "If it happens that they have desired [to make] a place of rest [for] the ibis (and) [the falcon] ..."

These texts are significant since they document the early planning or preparatory stages for the burial of the sacred birds. The precise force of the phrase "let one open a path" (graff. 65) is not absolutely clear. Does this refer to clearing of the chambers and shafts (e.g., burial remains and other kinds of debris)? Moreover, the reuse of the New Kingdom tombs as "places of rest" for the sacred ibises and falcons certainly involved modification of the original structures (e.g., the breaking through of walls between tombs and the adding of staircases).[115]

---

114 On the *ꜥnḫ by* formula, see, e.g., S. Vleeming, *Demotic and Greek-Demotic Mummy Labels and Other Short Texts Gathered from Many Publications (Short Texts II 278-1200)*, 2 vols., Studia Demotica 9 (Leuven: Peeters, 2011), 2:789–802; C. Arlt, *Deine Seele möge leben für immer und ewig: Die demotischen Mumienschilder im British Museum*, Studia Demotica 10 (Leuven: Peeters, 2011), 110–15.

115 See, e.g., Strudwick, "Some Aspects," 167–88; S. Vleeming, "The Office of a Choachyte in the Theban Area," in Vleeming, *Hundred-Gated Thebes*, 250—51. See also the contributions of Galán, Bosch-Puche and Ikram in this volume. https://proyectodjehuty.com/report-campaign-2012/.

The official entitled the "great one of Thoth," who will be discussed in detail below, was evidently in charge of the entire ibis and falcon cult operation. One graffito specifically states that a "place of rest" is "in the hand of" a "great one of Thoth" (graff. 69, 1–2).

69, 1–2: *pꜣ ꜥ.wy ḥtp n pꜣ hb tr.t PN pꜣ wr Ḏḥwty* "The place of rest of the ibis is in the hand of PN, the great one of Thoth."

These responsible supervisors, presumably the "great ones of Thoth," were obviously concerned with the proper movement of ibis and falcon mummies through the tombs. The cult workers should not let the mummies sit for long in temporary locations; they should be brought to their destination as quickly as possible:

4, 1–4: *pꜣ rmt nb (n) pꜣ tꜣ nt iw=f (r) ꜥš nꜣy sẖ.w m-ir ti.t ti ḥtp ntr ty šꜥ-tw nꜣ ꜥ.wy.w ẖry.w ... wn(?)* "As for every man (in) the world who will read these writings, do not let a god be at rest here until the lower chambers ... open(?)."

58, 5: *m-ir ti.t ḥtp r pꜣy=w bnr* "Do not let rest here outside of them."

88, 3–4: *... qs.t m-ir ti.t ḥtp ntr ty šꜥ wꜥ wš ꜥšꜣy* "... burial. Do not let a god rest here for a long time."

It may be that the "great ones of Thoth" maintained records of the number of mummies being placed into the tomb:

76, 4–6: [...] *iy r nꜣy myt(?) šꜥ-tw=w sẖ(?)* "[...] to come to these paths(?) until they are recorded(?)."

These graffiti seldom provide details about the mummification process itself. However, two texts specifically emphasize the use of resin *sf* (graff. 54, 7 ; 76, 5). Graffito 76 also possibly mentions other elements of a suitable burial, such as a bouquet offering (graff. 76, 6):

54, 5–7: *pꜣ rmt nb nt iw=w (r) iy n-im=s ... my ir=f šw(?) r-r=w r qs=w sf ...* "As for every man who will come therein (the chapel?) .... Let him do right(?) to them (the ibises) so as to bury them (with) resin."

76, 5–6: *st wḫꜣ qs(.t) n sf wtḥ ꜥnḫ(?) r-hb=w* "They desire burial with resin [...] (of) anointing (or "refined resin"?),[116] (and) the bouquet(?)[117] that they sent."

The mummified animals themselves are interestingly qualified as *mqḥ*, "mourned" (graff. 55, 4 ; 57, 3 ; 76, 3).[118] A good example of *mqḥ* occurs in 55, 3–4 (TT 12):

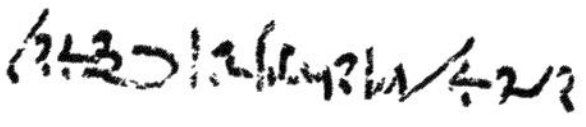 *nꜣ ꜣtr.w nꜣ ntr.w nt mqḥ* "the chapels of the gods who are mourned."

---

[116] *Sfy*, "Harz," *Wb.* 4:114, 18. On the use of resin in mummification, see, e.g., S. Ikram and A. Dodson, *The Mummy in Ancient Egypt: Equipping the Dead for Eternity* (London: Thames & Hudson, 1998), 116–17.

[117] Vases with bouquet remains have been recovered from this site, albeit of New Kingdom to Third Intermediate date, see M. López-Grande and E. de Gregorio, "Pottery Vases from a Deposit with Flower Bouquets Found at Dra Abu el-Naga," in Kousoulis and Lazaridis, *Proceedings of the Tenth International Congress of Egyptologists*, 305–18; A. Fahmy, J. M. Galán, and R. Hamdy, "A Deposit of Floral and Vegetative Bouquets at Dra Abu el-Naga (TT 11)," *BIFAO* 110 (2010): 73–89.

[118] *Mqḥ*, "betrübt sein," "Trauer," *Glossar*, 183.

The inscriptions several times call upon the cult workers to perform their duties in a conscientious and careful manner (graff. 54, 76, 85, 86):

86, x+9–11: *pꜣ rmt nb pꜣ tꜣ nt ỉw=f (r) gm nkt r tỉ.t wbꜣ=w r ẖ.ṱ=w r tꜣy=f gm my tỉ=f* "As for any man who will find a thing to give with regard to them ... according to his power, let him give (it)."

Significantly, the single example (graff. 85) of the well-known *h̭t*, "inspiration, curse" formula is simultaneously an admonition to the cult workers to perform their duties properly and possibly a commemoration of the writer's heroic exploits on the occasion of the fire in the "Great Tomb":[119]

85, 1–4: *pꜣ h̭ṱ n pꜣ hb pꜣ sẖ nb nt ỉw=f (r) ꜥš nꜣy sẖ(.w) my ỉr=f pꜣ bꜣk (n) pꜣ hb tꜣ ꜣtr ỉrm PN* "The inspiration of the ibis (for) every scribe who will read these writings. Let him do the work (of) the ibis in the chapel with PN."

The concerns about dereliction of duty found in this corpus remind one of the anxiety so vividly evident in the contemporary Ḥor archive.[120]

b. Directional Texts and Architectural Terms

Several graffiti clearly refer to the physical environment in which they are placed. The writers desired to label certain chambers or features so as to help the cult workers find their way within the tombs. The relationship between these directional graffiti and their location within the tombs is of exceptional interest. The keyplans of plates 7–8 show the placement of these directional graffiti within TT 11, tomb –399–, TT 12, and the Eastern Galleries. This type of graffito contains the architectural terms characteristic of the corpus. We discuss here the directional texts based on those architectural terms appearing in them. Naturally some texts occur under more than one rubric.

A series of graffiti (graff. 53–55, 57, 60) in the Eastern Galleries are virtually signposts for the cult workers.[121] The entire area here is so honeycombed with shafts and passages that the correct path was probably not always obvious to the workmen themselves. Figure 18 shows the possible routes taken by the cult workers engaged in interring the mummies. No graffito is preserved that confirms which entrance they used to enter the tomb. The high concentration of graffiti suggests that TT 11, which had the most accessible and spacious frontage, was the main entrance for these cult workers.

The directional graffiti are generally located at strategic points within the tombs so that the cult workers would have been guided to the places of burial.

Paths (my.t/myt)

The various paths leading to the chambers utilized in the cult are described by either the feminine *my.t*, "path, way" (graff. 33a, 1 ; 44, 1 ) or the masculine *myt*, "path" (55, 2 ; 57, 1 ; 60, 3 ; 65, 3 ; 86, x+5 ; 86, x+8).[122]

The writers wanted to provide the workers with information that would help them navigate confidently the labyrinth of chambers and shafts. Good examples of such directional texts are:

[119] For the *h̭t* formula, see, e.g., Ray, *Texts from the Baboon and Falcon Galleries*, 114.

[120] Most dramatically expressed in text 19 ("one god, one pot!"), Ray, *Archive of Ḥor*, 73–80.

[121] Eastern Galleries is a provisional designation for the series of connected underground spaces to the east of the concession that so far includes excavation units UEs 270, 275, 276, 277, 325, 326, 328, and 329.

[122] It is unclear to us whether the writers intended a distinction between the masculine and feminine words.

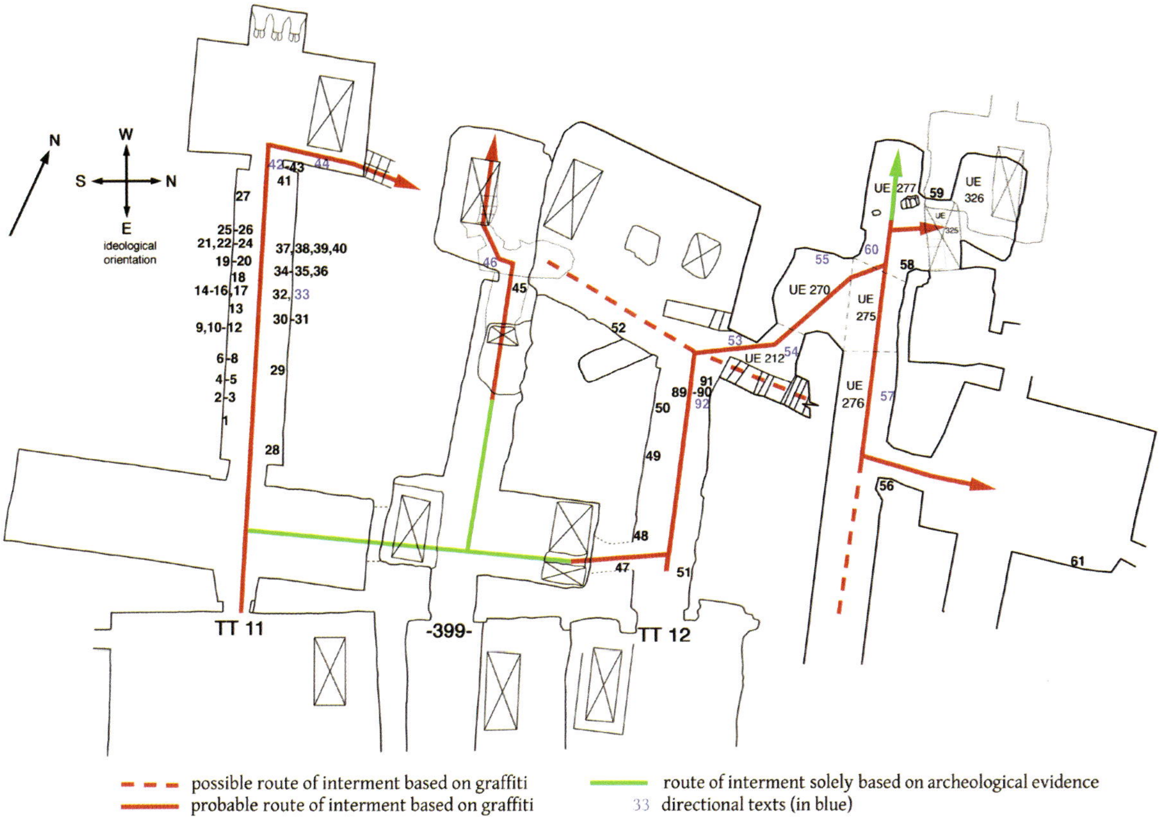

Fig. 18. Suggested routes taken by the cult workers engaged in the interment of the ibis and falcon mummies.

33a, 1–4: *tꜣ mi͗.t r hyn.w ꜥ.wy.w ḥtp r(?) pr i͗mnṱ n tꜣ ẖ.t mḥ-3.t ḏm r pḥ šꜥ rꜣ [r] tꜣ rnp.t pꜣ bnr nꜣy* "The path to some places of rest for/to(?) the west of the third group of offspring to arrive up to the entrance [for] the year outside of these (areas?)."

44, 1–3: *tꜣ mi͗.t r nꜣ ꜥ.wy.w ḥtp r ḥry ḥr pꜣ trt* " The path to the places of rest above upon the stairs." (the graffito is directly in front of the staircase)

46, 1: *pꜣ mꜣt (r-)ḥry(?)* "The path up(?)" (this graffito at the top of a staircase [figs. 3 and 19] may have signaled to the workmen who had just interred the mummies that this was the best way out)

60, 2–3: *my ṯꜣy=w nꜣ ntr.w tꜣ tꜣy ty pꜣ(?) myt r-r=s* "Let the gods be taken (there). This is here the(?) path to it (the chapel)."

65, 3–4: *my wn[=w] wꜥ myt my i͗r=w wpy.t nb* "Let [one] open a path (to a place of rest), let one make all work."

In the back of the tomb of Hery the path to the burial place takes a sharp turn. The entrance to the next chamber is rather hidden. Thus graff. 54 reassures the workman that he is on the right track (fig. 20):

54, 1: *pꜣ myt* "The path."

In one case the writer explicitly designates the hall as the way leading to the burial place:

55, 1–4: *tꜣ wsḫ mḥ-1.t tꜣ(?) tꜣy ty mtw=s tꜣ nt ṯ-myt (r) nꜣ ꜣtr.w nꜣ ntr.w nt mqḥ* "This is here the First Hall. It is the one that leads (to) the chapels of the gods who are mourned."

Sometimes, admittedly, it is difficult to understand why the writers decided to inscribe a directional graffito. Graffito 57, for example, is located in the middle of a corridor, where it would seem to have been obvious where a workman would have had to proceed:

57, 1–3: *pꜣ myt r-ẖn nꜣ ꜣtr.w nt ẖr nꜣ ntr.w nt mqḥ pꜣy pꜣy* "This is the path into the chapels that contain the gods who are mourned."

Graffito 86 describes a destructive fire in the tomb. In such circumstances it was undoubtedly difficult for the workers to identify the best path out:

86, x+4–9: *ỉr=n ḥꜣ=s(?) ỉw bn-pw=w <gm> myt r-r=s nꜣ-ꜥšꜣ pꜣ(?) ẖr[ẖr(?) ...] ỉw ḫpr=f n-ỉm=s n rn pꜣ tm gm myt r-ỉr=w r ḥr r-r=s* "We were before it(?), without <finding> a path to it. Abundant was the(?) de[struction(?) ...] that happened in it because of the not finding the path that they made before it."

Entrance/Door (rꜣ)

It must be emphasized that the area in the back of the tomb of Hery (TT 12) is particularly confusing, and that the directional graffiti are truly helpful.

When arriving at the "crossroad" in the back of the tomb of Hery (fig. 20), the workman could read in the very prominent graff. 53 that there was a doorway, which was not immediately obvious, leading to the burials below:

53, 1–2: *wn hyn.w ꜥ.wy ḥtp ẖry ty ṯ(?) pꜣy rꜣ r-[ẖ]n* "There are some (more) places of rest below here from(?) this entrance [in]side."

In the tomb of Djehuty (TT 11) graff. 33a apparently describes the spatial boundaries of the "places of rest." This text also mentions *rꜣ*, "entrance," but the reading of the entire sentence is unfortunately uncertain:

33a, 1–4: *tꜣ mỉ.t r hyn.w ꜥ.wy.w ḥtp r(?) pr ỉmnṯ n tꜣ ḫ.t mḥ-3.t ḏm r pḥ šꜥ rꜣ [r] tꜣ rnp.t pꜣ bnr nꜣy* "The path to some places of rest for/to(?) the west of the third group of offspring to arrive up to the entrance [for] the year outside of these (areas?)."

Stairway (trt/trtr)

The writers label the steps in the tombs as *trt/trtr*, "stairs" (graff. 42, 4 ; 44, 3 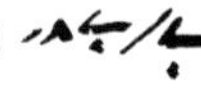; 87, 3 *trtr* ) (fig. 21).

Graffiti 42 and 44 in TT 11 are closely associated; they both refer to the same staircase. Graffito 42 is written in the doorway, while 44 is just around the corner, very close to the staircase:

42, 1–4: *wn ... qs(.t)(?) ꜥꜣ.t ḥtp ty ḥry n pꜣ trt ḥry(?)* "There are/is ... a great burial(?) (at) rest here above the stairs above(?)."

44, 1–3: *tꜣ mỉ.t r nꜣ ꜥ.wy.w ḥtp r ḥry ḥr pꜣ trt* "The path to the places of rest above upon the stairs."

Fig. 19. Staircase in tomb -399- with graff. 46.

Fig. 20. Graffiti 53 and 54 inscribed along the path leading to the "First Hall" and the staircase leading to the tombs of Baki and Ay.

In the still unlocated "Great Tomb" there were also obviously staircases:

87, 2–3: *k.t ꜥ.wy ḥtp ty(?) r-ḥry pꜣ trtr* "In another place of rest here(?) above the stairs."

Corridor, Row (of Connected Rooms)

In TT 12 graff. 92 (revealed in 2019) clearly designates the corridor in which it is placed as the *šym ꜥꜣ* 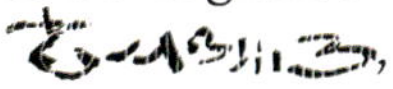, "great corridor." Can *pay* separate *šym* and *ꜥꜣ*? This architectual term is probably further qualified in the inscription as being "of the north" (*n pr mḥṯ*). Given that the focus of the falcon and ibis cult was in TT 11 and TT 12, the phrase "great corridor of the north" is fitting. *Šym* is the standard word in demotic for a "corridor" or "passage" *Glossar*, 486; *CDD Š*, 19, s.v. *šym*. Demotic *šym* is the masculine equivalent to the feminine *šmy.t*, found, for example, in Ptolemaic hieroglyphs, "corridor (in temple)," Wilson, *Lexikon*, 1009–10. As discussed in that entry in Wilson's *Lexikon*, the older related term, *šmmt*, is employed in hieratic ostraca to refer to "the main longitudinal passage or corridor" of a tomb. We have not found *šym* used elsewhere in demotic texts to label a tomb corridor.

Hall/Hallway (wsḫ.t)

A chamber below the tomb of Baki is the only one that receives the specific designation of *wsḫ.t*, "hall, hallway." Graffito 55, with its bright red ochre signs, is even now very prominently visible to anyone entering the chamber (fig. 22).

Fig. 21. Graffiti 42 and 44 directing the cult workers from the main hallway to the staircase inside the chapel in TT 11.

Interestingly, graff. 55, explicitly describes the chamber in which it is located as *tꜣ wsḫ.t mḥ-1.t*, "the First Hall." There is no evidence yet of a "Second Hall" in the graffiti, but excavations are continuing. Graffito 55 also reassures the visitor that he is on the path that leads to the chapels of the sacred birds:

55, 2–3: *tꜣ wsḫ mḥ-1.t tꜣ(?) tꜣy ty mtw=s tꜣ nt ṯ-myt (r) nꜣ ꜣtr.w nꜣ ntr.w nt mqḥ* "This is here the First Hall. It is the one that leads (to) the chapels of the gods who are mourned."

Area(?) of Ceremony (ẖ.t(?) tbtꜣ)

In graff. 86, 1 ("Great Tomb") we find a *ẖ.t(?) tbtꜣ*, "area(?) of ceremony," , which we understand as referring to a place for mummy preparation or ritual space.[123] However, the reading and translation are very tentative, particularly since we are dependent here on Spiegelberg's hand-copy:

86, 1–2: *tꜣy ẖ.t(?) tbtꜣ r-ẖry* "This area(?) of ceremony below."

Chapels (ꜣtr.t, ꜣtr.wt)

A rather rare demotic term employed in this corpus is the ancient word *ꜣtr*, "chapel" (from the older *itr.t*), which appears in graff. 60, 1 ; 71, 1 ; 85, 3 ; 55, 3 and 57, 2 .[124] *ꜣtr.t* may designate the ultimate burial place of the sacred ibises and falcons:

123 The interpretation depends on understanding *tbtꜣ* as "ceremony" or "ritual."

124 See *CDD ꜣ*, 108–9, s.v. *ꜣtr(.t)*, with references.

Fig. 22. "First Hall" of the Eastern Galleries with graff. 55.

55, 2–4: *mtw=s tꜣ nt ṯ-myt (r) nꜣ ꜣtr.w nꜣ ntr.w nt mqḥ* "It is the one that leads (to) the chapels of the gods who are mourned."

57, 1–3: *pꜣ myt r-ẖn nꜣ ꜣtr.w nt ẖr nꜣ ntr.w nt mqḥ pꜣy pꜣy* "This is the path into the chapels that contain the gods who are mourned."

60, 1–2: *tꜣ ꜣtr.t r ti͗.t ḥtp r-tbꜣ nꜣ mt.w i͗-i͗r ḫpr* "The chapel to cause to rest (the gods) on account of the things that happened."

71, 1–5: *tꜣy ꜣtr.t ḫpr hh n-i͗m=s* "As for this chapel, it happened that fire was in it."

85, 2–4: *my i͗r=f pꜣ bꜣk (n) pꜣ hb tꜣ ꜣtr* "Let him do the work (of) the ibis in the chapel."

Divine Chapel/Temple (i͗rpy/ḥ.t-ntr)

Graffiti 9, 14, 34, and 63 seem to commemorate the interment of an individual sacred ibis in the "place of rest." In these texts the ibis is said to be "caused to enter" the *i͗rpy* after "spending many years" in the *ḥ.t-ntr*. It is difficult to understand this striking statement as meaning anything other than that the *ḥ.t-ntr* denotes the location of the living quarters of the sacred ibis while the *i͗rpy* is used for the burial site, that is, the "place of rest."[125] Both *i͗rpy* and *ḥ.t-ntr* obviously mean "temple," but

[125] Graff. 21, 5 seems to have *ḥ.t-ntr* where one expects *i͗rpy*. However, the reading of that graffito is very insecure.

in order to distinguish the two terms in this corpus we render *ỉrpy* as "divine chapel" and *ḥ.t-nṯr* as "temple." These designations only appear in the tomb of Djehuty (TT 11) and the "Great Tomb," not in the tomb of Hery (TT 12) and the Eastern Galleries. The writers of the graffiti in the tomb of Hery (TT 12) and the Eastern Galleries only employ the term *ꜣtr.t*, "chapel," in place of *ỉrpy*. We have not found parallels to this usage elsewhere:

9, 4: … *ỉw=f ḥtp (n) ḥ.t-nṯr* "… he resting (in) the temple."

14, 1–3: *ꜥq=w Ḏḥwty ḫnṯ Wsr r pꜣ ỉrpy ḥ.t-sp 9 ỉbt 4 pr.t sw 19 m-sꜣ ỉr rnp.t ꜥšꜣy n ḥ.t-nṯr* "They caused to enter Thoth, foremost of Thebes, to the divine chapel (in) regnal year 9, fourth month of winter, day 19, after spending many years in the temple."

21, 5–6: *r ḥ.t-nṯr(?) … šꜥ ḏ.t* "to the temple (?) … forever"

34, 4–5: *ꜥq=w Ḏḥwty ḫnṯ Wsr … r [pꜣ] ỉrpy n Ḏḥwty m-sꜣ ỉr rnp.t ꜥšꜣ.w n ḥ.t-nṯr* "They caused to enter Thoth, foremost of Thebes … to [the] divine chapel of Thoth after spending many years in the temple."

63, 3–5: *ꜥq=w Ḏḥwty ḫnṯ Wsr r pꜣ ỉrpy m-sꜣ ỉr rnp.(w)t ꜥšꜣ n ḥ.t-nṯr* "They caused to enter (i.e., buried) Thoth, foremost one of Thebes, into the divine chapel after spending many years in the temple."

76, 2: *r ḥry r ỉrpy […]* "up to the divine chapel […]"

Place of Rest (ꜥ.wy ḥtp)

The burial location for the ibises and the falcons is the *ꜥ.wy ḥtp*, "place of rest."[126] This is, of course, a well-attested compound in demotic. As Ray has remarked: "the phrase *ꜥ.wy.w ḥtp* is regularly used as a description of the various sacred animal galleries."[127] It is to be expected, therefore, that *ꜥ.wy ḥtp* occurs frequently in this corpus, generally in close association with *pꜣ hb pꜣ bỉk*, "the ibis (and) the falcon" (with variants):

21, 1–3: *Wsỉr pꜣ hb Wsỉr pꜣ bỉk ꜥq=w n pꜣ ꜥ.wy ḥtp* "Osiris the ibis (and) Osiris the falcon, causing them to enter in the place of rest."

Occasionally *ꜥ.wy ḥtp* is qualified by an additional phrase or adverb:

53, 1: *ꜥ.wy ḥtp ḫry* "place of rest below"

65, 1–2: *ꜥ.wy.w ḥtp ḫr pꜣ hb pꜣ bỉk* "places of rest for the ibis (and) the falcon"

66, 3–4: *ꜥ.wy ḥtp [ḫr] pꜣ hb [pꜣ bỉk]* "place of rest [for] the ibis (and) the falcon"

In the "Great Tomb" graffiti a more elaborate variant appears:

67, 1: *Ḏḥwty nꜣ nṯr.w ꜥ.wy ḥtp n pꜣ hb pꜣ bỉk* "Thoth (and) the gods of the place of rest of the ibis (and) the falcon."

126 Schentuleit, *Aus der Buchhaltung des Weinmagazins im Edfu-Tempel*, 205, on the phrase *ꜥ.wy n ḥtp*, "Ruheplatz," as a possible designation of a temple; On *ꜥ.wy n ḥtp*, see Ray, *Archive of Ḥor*, 188; H. Smith, C. Andrews, and S. Davies, *The Sacred Animal Necropolis at North Saqqara: The Mother of Apis Inscriptions*, EES Texts from Excavations 14 (London: Egypt Exploration Society, 2011), 293; Kessler, *Die Oberbauten des Ibiotapheion von Tuna el-Gebel*, 6.

127 Ray, *Texts from the Baboon and Falcon Galleries*, 136.

67, 2: *Ḏḥwty nꜣ ntr.w pꜣ ʿ.wy ḥtp (n) pꜣ hb pꜣ bi͗k* "Thoth (and) the gods of the place of rest (of) the ibis (and) the falcon."

73, 2–4: *Wsi͗r pꜣ hb Wsi͗r pꜣ bi͗k nꜣ ntr.w pꜣ ʿ.wy ḥtp pꜣ hb* "Osiris the ibis (and) Osiris the falcon, the gods of the place of rest of the ibis."

74, 1–2: *Wsi͗r pꜣ hb Wsi͗r pꜣ bi͗k nꜣ ntr.w n pꜣ ʿ.wy ḥtp tr=w* "Osiris the ibis (and) Osiris the falcon (and) all the gods of the place of rest."

77, 1–2: *Wsi͗r pꜣ hb Wsi͗r pꜣ bi͗k nꜣ ntr.w pꜣ ʿ.wy ḥtp pꜣ hb* "Osiris the ibis (and) Osiris the falcon (and) the gods of the place of rest of the ibis."

80, 1–2: *Wsi͗r pꜣ hb Wsi͗r pꜣ bi͗k nꜣ ntr.w pꜣ ʿ.wy n ḥtp n pꜣ hb* "Osiris the ibis (and) Osiris the falcon (and) the gods of the place of rest of the ibis."

81, 2–3: *Wsi͗r pꜣ hb Wsi͗r pꜣ bi͗k nꜣ ntr.w n pꜣ ʿ.wy n ḥtp* "Osiris the ibis (and) Osiris the falcon (and) the gods of the place of rest of the ibis."

The *ʿ.wy ḥtp*, "place of rest," evidently had virtually the status of a temple in the eyes of the cult workers. They thus felt it appropriate to write *rn nfr* inscriptions eternally connecting themselves with the *ʿ.wy ḥtp* and the deities associated with the locality, that is, Thoth and the sacred animal mummies buried therein. Most of the writers do not have preserved titles (graff. 2, 16, 37a, 50, 67 (2x), 73, 77, 80, and 82), but at least two "great ones of Thoth" memorialize themselves in *rn nfr* inscriptions to the deities of the "place of rest" (graff. 30 and 81), as did four pastophoroi and their dependents (graff. 49):

49, 1–2: *pꜣ ʿ.wy ḥtp mn ty m-bꜣḥ pꜣ hb pꜣ bi͗k* "(The good name of the pastophoroi of) the place of rest remains here before the ibis (and) the falcon."

ʿ.wy ḥtp also appears in the following graffiti:

2, 3–4: *pꜣ hb pꜣ bi͗k ... ʿ.wy ḥtp* "The ibis (and) the falcon ... place of rest."

5, 7–8: *pꜣ hb pꜣ bi͗k(?) [...] pꜣ ʿ.wy ḥtp* "The ibis (and) the falcon(?) [...] the place of rest."

16, 2–3: *pꜣ rn nfr PN mn ty m-bꜣḥ ... ʿ.wy ḥtp* "The good name of PN remains here before ... place of rest."

30, 8: *... pꜣ ʿ.wy ḥtp* "... the place of rest ..."

37a, 4–5: *pꜣ hb pꜣ bi͗k ...ʿ.wy ḥtp* "The ibis (and) the falcon ... place of rest."

50, 3: *šms.w r pꜣ ʿ.wy (ḥtp)* "(Numerous were his) servants at the place (of rest)"

69, 1: *pꜣ ʿ.wy ḥtp n pꜣ hb* "the place of rest of the ibis"

82, 8: *n pꜣ rn pꜣ ʿ.wy ḥtp Ḏḥwty* "in/as the name of the place of rest of Thoth"

87, 2: *k.t ʿ.wy ḥtp* "another place of rest"

Chapel (kꜣ.t)

In graff. 54, 2, is found the word , which we have transliterated *kꜣ.t*, "chapel," and understood as a variant of *gꜣ.t*, "Kapelle," *Glossar*, 70. Unfortunately, the reading is not certain; an alternative transliteration is *ʿbꜣ.t*, "Kapelle," *Glossar*, 58.

3. *COMMEMORATIVE GRAFFITI*

A number of graffiti are commemorative in nature. The members of the ibis and falcon cult clearly wished to memorialize particularly important burials or events in their history.

a. Commemorative Texts concerning the Interment of Ibis Mummies

Graffiti 9, 3–4; 13, 1; 14, 1–2; 21, 3; 34, 4; 60, 1–2; and 63, 3–5 commemorate ibis burials. The key term here is *ꜥq*, used transitively, "to cause to enter" (i.e., "to bury, to inter").[128] In several cases, an ibis seems to be designated "foremost of Thebes." One wonders whether this would be the name of an individual bird holding a special place within the Theban ibis cult. Graffito 34, 4–5 describes this ibis as being buried in the *ỉrpy* of Thoth after "having spent many years" in the *ḥ.t-ntr*. Here *ỉrpy* seems to refer to the tomb of Djehuty itself, while *ḥ.t-ntr* would presumably stand for a local Theban temple of Thoth (Qasr el-Aguz?), in which precinct the ibis would have been kept. If the interpretation is correct, these descriptions certainly provide valuable new details about the organization of the ibis and falcon cult in the Theban area.[129] The commemorative graffiti are:

9, 3–4: *...ꜥq(?) ... Ḏḥwty ỉw=f ḥtp (n) ḥ.t-ntr* "... cause to enter(?)... Thoth ... he resting (in) the temple."

13, 1: *ꜥq=f Ḏḥwty ḥ.t-sp 9.t* "He caused to enter Thoth (in) regnal year 9." (This inscription has an abbreviated formula, but probably belongs to this group.)

14, 1–4: *ꜥq=w Ḏḥwty ḫnṯ Wsr r pꜣ ỉrpy ḥ.t-sp 9 ỉbt 4 pr.t sw 19 m-sꜣ ỉr rnp.t ꜥšꜣy n ḥ.t-ntr* "They caused to enter Thoth, foremost of Thebes, to the divine chapel in regnal year 9, fourth month of winter, day 19, after spending many years in the temple."

21, 1–5: *Wsỉr pꜣ hb Wsỉr pꜣ bik ꜥq=w n pꜣ ꜥ.wy ḥtp PN r ḥ.t-ntr(?) ...* "Osiris the ibis (and) Osiris the falcon, causing them to enter in the place of rest *PN* to the temple(?) ..."[130]

34, 4–5: *ꜥq=w Ḏḥwty ḫnṯ Wsr ... r [pꜣ] ỉrpy n Ḏḥwty m-sꜣ ỉr rnp.t ꜥšꜣ.w n ḥ.t-ntr ...* "They caused to enter Thoth, foremost of Thebes ... to [the] divine chapel of Thoth after spending many years in the temple ..."

60, 1–2: *tꜣ ꜣtr.t r tỉ.t ḥtp r-tbꜣ nꜣ mt.w ỉ-ỉr ḫpr my ṯꜣy=w nꜣ ntr.w* "The chapel to cause to rest (the gods) on account of the things that happened.[131] Let the gods be taken (there)."

63, 3–5: *ꜥq=w Ḏḥwty ḫnṯ Wsr r pꜣ ỉrpy m-sꜣ ỉr rnp.(w)t ꜥšꜣ n ḥ.t-ntr* "They caused to enter (i.e., buried) Thoth, foremost one of Thebes, into the divine chapel after spending many years in the temple."

Given that these commemorative texts seem to refer to the living birds, it is perhaps appropriate here to observe that the graffiti designate the ibises and falcons being brought to the tomb for burial as *ḏm*, "offspring" (graff. 33a, 2 ; 53, 3). This term suggests that these were young birds.

[128] Graff. 13, 1 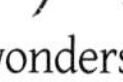; 14, 1 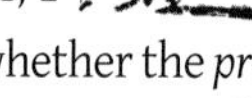; 21, 3 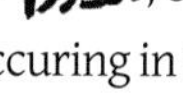; 34, 4 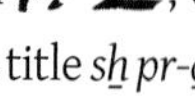; 63, 3 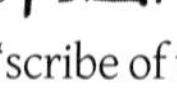.

[129] One also wonders whether the *pr-ḏ.t*, occuring in the title *sẖ pr-ḏ.t*, "scribe of the House-of-Eternity" (graff. 68, 3), refers to a specific Theban shrine or sacred precinct, see F. Colin "Un jeu de déterminatifs en démotique," *RdE* 65 (2014): 183.

[130] Elsewhere *ỉrpy* is used to denote the tomb. The reading of this graffito is very insecure.

[131] On this intriguing phrase, see the discussion in the text edition of graff. 60, 2 (a).

The writer of graff. 53, 3 proclaims that considerable numbers are being buried: *bn nꜣ-sbk=w in ḏm*, "they are not few, namely, the offspring."

b. Commemorative Text concerning the Fire in the Tombs

Such relatively brief demotic graffiti do not generally provide dramatic insight into historical events. Nevertheless, these texts occasionally offer details unusual in graffiti. Several inscriptions, for example, mention a disastrous fire in the "Great Tomb" (graff. 71, 2 ; 71, 5 ; 85, 6 ; 86, 3 ) and the steps apparently taken to combat it. Such fires in the tombs, full as they were with combustible mummies and material, were probably not uncommon.[132] They must have severely disrupted cult activity. One wonders whether the fire in the "Great Tomb" was the reason for the move to another burial location, namely, the area of TT 11 and TT 12. Of course, this is mere speculation. *Pꜣ-šr-Mn*, (son of) *Ḏḥwty-sḏm*, the most prominent "great one of Thoth" in this corpus, wrote these three graffiti.[133] He was himself apparently a witness and possibly led the effort to contain the fire.

The translations of the three graffiti are not always secure, but the gist of the texts seems clear:

71: commemoration of fire, records that the cult personnel attempted to persevere in their burial activities despite the danger:

71, 1–5: *tꜣy ꜣtr.t ḫpr hh n-im=s wḥm=w qs(.t) ʿq=w r pḥ r pꜣ mꜣ(?) n pꜣ hh ... iw=f ... [...]* "As for this chapel, it happened that fire was in it. They repeated burial. They entered so as to reach the place(?) of the fire ..., it being ... [...]."

85: commemoration of fire, records the actions of PN, "great one of Thoth," during the disaster:

85, 5–8: *PN r-ẖry [...]pr(?) ... hh [...] r ḥr=f iw bn-pw=f [wrr] r iy r-ḥry šʿ [...]* "PN was below [...]. Came out(?) ... fire [...] to his face. He did not [delay] to come up until [...]."

86: commemoration of fire, most extensive description of the fire in the "Great Tomb";[134] help apparently arrived too late to extinguish the fire:

86, 1 x+11: *tꜣy ẖ.t(?) tbtꜣ r ẖry ḫpr hh n im=s* (Presumably numerous lines lost) *ir-n ḥꜣ-s(?) bn-pw-w <gm> myt r-r=s nꜣ-ʿšꜣ pꜣ(?) ḫr[ḫr(?) ...] iw ḫpr=f n-im=s n rn pꜣ tm gm myt r-ir=w r ḥr r-r=s pꜣ rmt nb pꜣ tꜣ nt iw=f (r) gm nkt r ti.t wbꜣ=w r ẖ.ṱ=w r tꜣy=f gm my ti=*f "This area(?) of ceremony below. There happened a fire therein. (Presumably numerous lines lost) We were before it(?), without <finding> a path to it. Abundant was the(?) de[struction(?) ...] which happened in it because of the not finding the path that they made before it. As for any man who will do a thing to give with regard to them ... according to his power, let him give (it)."

Evidence of fire, with destruction of mummy deposits, has been archaeologically documented in tomb –399–, TT 12, the Upper Gallery, and the Eastern Galleries. None of the graffiti in these tombs clearly record a destructive fire, but graff. 60, 2 may refer obliquely to such an unfortunate event.[135]

---

[132] On the subject of fire in tombs see, e.g., D. M. Grimaldi and P. Meehan, "The Transformation of Theban Tomb 39 (TT39): A Contribution from a Conservation Viewpoint in Terms of Its History after Dynastic Occupation," in *Proceedings of the XI International Congress of Egyptologists*, ed. G. Rosati and M. Guidotti, 249–50.

[133] He appears in graff. 4, 4; 54, 7; 55, 4; 56, 3; 57, 4; 58, 6; 60, 4; 61, 2; 70, 4; 71, 10; 75, 5; 85, 4; 85, 12; 86, x+12; and 87, 5.

[134] "Great Tomb" 9, probably written by the same person, may also allude to the fire.

[135] See the contribution of Bosch-Puche and Ikram to this volume, pp. 19–20, 23, 26-27, 30–31, 33–35.

DEITIES MENTIONED IN THE GRAFFITI

The deities mentioned in the corpus are in general those expected in such an ibis and falcon cult functioning in Dra Abu el-Nagaᶜ.[136] The deceased ibises and falcons are generally described as *Wsỉr pꜣ hb*, "Osiris the ibis," and *Wsỉr pꜣ bỉk*, "Osiris the falcon." As mentioned above, graff. 9, 3–4; 13, 1; 14, 1–2; 21, 3; 34, 4; 60, 1–2; and 63, 3–5 commemorate the burial of "Thoth, foremost of Thebes." This epithet may designate a specific individual ibis, who would have played a particularly important role in the Theban cult. Apart from Thoth and Osiris, few other gods are mentioned. In graff. 7, 2 and 29, 4 the "House-of-Montu, lord of the land," is named. *Pr-Mnṱ*, "House-of-Montu," has been equated with El-Tod,[137] but, given the location of these graffiti in Dra Abu-el-Nagaᶜ, it may be better to identify this *Pr-Mnṱ* with the locality found in the demotic temple oaths sworn at Medinet Habu. These oaths not infrequently mention "Djeme in the House [*pr*]-of-Montu, lord of Medamud."[138] In both graff. 7, 2 and 29, 4 Montu receives the epithet *nb tꜣ*, "lord of the land." We have not found another example of this epithet in demotic texts. Montu is prominent in the demotic graffiti of Medinet Habu.[139] The Temple of Thoth at Qasr el-Aguz was considered to be in Djeme, that is, the precinct of Medinet Habu. One might therefore speculate that the "House-of-Montu, lord of the land," in graff. 7, 2 and 29, 4, refers to a Montu cult at Medinet Habu.[140] The more straightforward *Pr-ỉmn*, "House-of-Amun," is also attested in graff. 64d, 6. The rather elaborate votive graff. 68 in the "Great Tomb" addresses a series of ibis and falcon deities, namely, the *ᶜẖm*-falcon, Tutu, and Horus, Lord of Letopolis.[141] In mummy bandage 1, 1 (Khonsu) Neferhotep "gives life" to PN.

List of deities mentioned in the corpus:

1. *ᶜẖm*-falcon
   68, 2 *(Wsỉr)*

2. *Wsỉr* "Osiris"
   19, 1 *(pꜣ hb)*; 19, 1 *(pꜣ bỉk)*; 21, 1 *(pꜣ hb)*; 21, 2 *(pꜣ bỉk)*; 68, 2 *(pꜣ hb)*; 68, 2 *(pꜣ bỉk)*; 68, 2 *(pꜣ ᶜẖm)*; 68, 2 *(Twtw?)*; 68, 3 *(Ḥr nb Sḫm)*; 73, 2 *(pꜣ hb)*; 73, 3 *(pꜣ bỉk)*; 74, 1 *(pꜣ hb)*; 74, 1 *(pꜣ bỉk)*; 77, 1 *(pꜣ hb)*; 77, 2 *(pꜣ bỉk)*; *77, 5 (bỉk)*; 79, 3 *(pꜣ hb)*; 79, 3 *(pꜣ bỉk)*; 80, 1 *(pꜣ hb)*; 80, 2 *(pꜣ bỉk)*; 81, 2 *(pꜣ hb)*; 81, 2 *(pꜣ bỉk)*; 84, 2 *(pꜣ hb)*.

3. *Mnṱ* "Montu"
   7, 2 (Pr-*Mnṱ nb tꜣ)* ; 29, 4 *(Pr-Mnṱ nb tꜣ)*.

4. *Nfr-ḥtp* "Neferhotep" (epithet of Khonsu)
   Mummy bandage 1, 1.

---

136 We include also the deity named in mummy bandage 1.

137 J. Borghouts, "Month," *LÄ* 4:col. 200.

138 Borghouts, "Month," col. 202. See also D. Devauchelle, "Les serments à la porte de Djémé," *RdE* 48 (1997): 260–63.

139 Thissen, *Die demotischen Graffiti von Medinet Habu*, 192.

140 In C. Andrews, *Ptolemaic Legal Texts from the Theban Area*, Catalogue of Demotic Papyri in the British Museum 4 (London: British Museum, 1990), 102–3, there is a *wš pꜣ bỉk*, "feeder of the hawk," where Andrews remarks that it is difficult to know whether the sacred hawks are the counterparts of the local sacred ibises or "as sacred to the local god Monthu."

141 For Horus of Letopolis in demotic texts, see, e.g., R. Jasnow et al., *The Demotic and Hieratic Papyri in the Suzuki Collection of Tokai University* (Atlanta: Lockwood Press, 2016), 51; H. Smith and W. Tait, *Saqqara Demotic Papyri I*, EES Texts from Excavations 7 (London: Egypt Exploration Society, 1983), 39 and 55.

5. *Ḥr nb Sḫm* "Horus, Lord of Letopolis"
68, 3 *(Wsỉr).*

6.*Twtw* "Tutu"
68, 2 *(Wsỉr).*

7. *Ḏḥwty* (excluding the title *wr Ḏḥwty*) "Thoth"
9, 3; 12, 1; 13, 1; 14, 1 *(ḫnṯ Wsr)*; [14, 6]; 18, 4; 18, 6; 24, 6; 24, 7; 33a, 9; 34, 4 *(ḫnṯ Wsr)*; 34, 5; 62b, 1; 63, 3 *(ḫnṯ Wsr)*; 67, 1; 67, 2; 77, 6; 82, 8.

TITLES AND PROFESSIONS

The titles *wr Ḏḥwty*, "great one of Thoth" (graff. 4, 6; 7, 2 ; 8, 5; 9, 1; 18, 5; 19, 3–4; 29, 3; 30, 7; 33a, 6; 34, 1; 45, 4; 53, 5; 54, 8; 55, 5 ; 57, 5; 58, 7; 60, 5; 61, 3; 62a, 3; 64b, 3; 67, 1; 69, 2; 71, 11; 72, 2; 74, 3; 77, 4; 80, 4; 81, 1; [85, 12]; 86, x+12);[142] and *ṯ nꜣ nṯr.w*, "taker of the gods" (graff. 19, 4 ; 34, 3 ; 62a, 3 ; 62a, 4–5 ; 62b, 4 ; 64b, 5 ; 69, 2 ; 74, 3 ; 74, 4 ; 77, 1) are most common in this corpus. The "great one of Thoth" was clearly responsible for the cult activity in the "place of rest." This official is certainly the most prominent figure in the graffiti. The "taker of the gods" was, as the name implies, in charge of carrying the sacred mummies.[143] The graffiti make it evident that there were numerous "takers of the gods" working in the "places of rest" at any one time. To judge from graff. 19 and 34, these positions may have been held for one year, although in graff. 64b the writer appears to declare that he has held them for three years. Several other titles associated with the ibis and falcon cult are worthy of note. "Pastophoroi of the place of rest" (graff. 49, 1) were presumably minor functionaries or guards assigned to the "places of rest."[144] The "lesonis of Thoth" (graff. 77, 6) was a more important official, of course, but this title only appears once in our corpus. The "men of (the) cage(?)" (graff. 77, 7) were probably in charge of the living ibises. The "men of the harbor" (graff. 19, 5 ; 74, 3) and the "great one of the men of the harbor" (graff. 34, 3) are rather puzzling. We suspect that these individuals may have been dockworkers connected with the ibis cult, possibly acting as stevedores responsible for the loading and unloading of the sacred birds.[145] A few other titles and professions reflect the Theban background of the graffiti. Of particular interest is the "great one of Thebes" (graff. 62a, 4 ; 62a, 5 ; 62b, 4), which occurs three times in one graffito. The title certainly sounds grand, and it is thus curious that we have found no other attestation in demotic. This man evidently held simultaneously three positions: "great one of Thoth, the taker of gods (and) great one of Thebes." The writer of graff. 62 was obviously impressed by his titles, repeating the fact that he acted as "the taker of gods (and) great one of Thebes at one time." Finally, the well-

142 See above, pp. 41–42.

143 See p. 63.

144 They perhaps had the keys to the "place of rest," see F. Hoffmann and J. Quack, "Pastophoros," in *A Good Scribe and an Exceedingly Wise Man: Studies in Honour of W. J. Tait*, ed. A. Dodson, J. Johnston, and W. Monkhouse, GHP Egyptology 21 (London: Golden House, 2014), 143. Very useful too is S. Thomas, "The *Pastophorion* Revisited: Owners and Users of 'Priests Houses' in Ptolemaic Pathyris and Elsewhere in Egypt," *JEA* 100 (2014): 111–32.

145 In graff. 19, 4–5, the taker of the gods may be either "of" *(n)* the "men of the harbor" or taking the gods "for" *(n)* the "men of the harbor." We wonder whether the "taker of the gods" is in this case "taking" the sacred animals from the "men of the harbor," and then transporting them to the "places of rest."

known Theban title of "overseer of the necropolis" (graff. 64d, 4 ; 67, 2 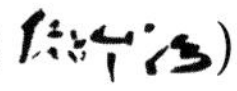) appears twice in the graffiti. We hardly need to emphasize that it is occasionally difficult to determine with certainty which individual holds which title. This is particularly the case with the list in graff. 77.[146]

The following titles are attested in the corpus; in a few cases we provide a fuller context in footnotes so that the possible relationships between the titles may become more apparent.

List of titles and professions mentioned in the corpus:

1. *ỉry.w-ꜥꜣ pꜣ ꜥ.wy ḥtp* "pastophoroi of the place of rest" [147]
   A list with the names of men holding this position given in graff. 49:
   49, 3: *Ḥr*, son of *Ns-Mn*
   49, 4: *ꜥnḫ-rn=f*, son of *Ns-Mn*
   49, 5: *Pa-tm*, son of *Ns-Mn*
   49, 6: *Pꜣ-nfr-ỉr-ḥr*, son of *Ḏ-ḥr*

2. *ỉt-ntr* "god's-father" 
   This otherwise common title only occurs in one text.
   64d, 1: ...
   64d, 2: ..., son of *Wsỉr-wr*
   64d, 4:[148] *Pꜣ-tỉ-Nfr-ḥtp*, son of ... — also *mr ḫꜣs.t*

3. *ꜥꜣ n nꜣ rmt.w n tꜣ mr.t* "great one of the men of the harbor" 
   34, 3:[149] unnamed

4. *ꜥꜣ Nw.t* "great one of Thebes" 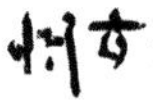[150]
   62a, 4:[151] *Pa-Wsr(?)*, son of *Pꜣ-šr-Mn* — also *wr Ḏḥwty* and *ṯ ntr.w*
   62b, 4: *Lwꜣ*, son of *Ḥr* — also *sẖ* and *ṯ ntr.w*
   62a, 5: refers(?) to *Pa-Wsr(?)*, son of *Pꜣ-šr-Mn* — also *ṯ ntr.w*

5. *ꜥntꜣy* "perfumer" 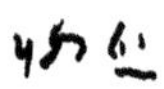
   77, 10: *Pa-nꜣ* — also *rmt wrṯ(?)* (in list), also(?) *ṯ ntr.w* (in list)

6. *wꜥb.w* "priests" 
   This otherwise common title only occurs once in connection with *rt*, "representative."
   64d, 3: only in *rt nꜣ wꜥb.w*

---

[146] Thus in the list of graff. 77, which begins with the heading: "The good name of the men who take the gods before Osiris..., their names," we have a subheading "the men of (the) cage(?)," followed by five names. Are these "men of (the) cage(?)" also "takers of the gods?"

[147] S. Grunert, *Thebanische Kaufverträge des 3. und 2. Jahrhunderts v. u. Z.*, Demotische Papyri aus den staatlichen Museen zu Berlin 2 (Berlin: Akademie, 1981), 9; *wn pꜣ ꜥ.wy ḥtp pꜣ hb n pꜣ bk*.

[148] 64d, 1–5 *ỉt-ntr PN ỉt-ntr PN nꜣ rt nꜣ wꜥb.w ỉt-ntr PN pꜣ mr ḫꜣs.t ỉrm nꜣ bꜣk.w sẖ PN tr=w* "God's-father PN, god's-father PN, the representatives of the priests, god's-father PN, the overseer of the necropolis and the servants of the scribe PN in their entirety."

[149] 34, 3: *nꜣy=w pꜣ ṯ nꜣ ntr.w ꜥꜣ n nꜣ rmt.w (n) tꜣ mr.t* "The ones of the taker of the gods, great one of the men (of) the harbor."

[150] We have not found a parallel for this title, but cf. *ꜥꜣ n* "Vorsteher von," *Glossar*, 54.

[151] 62, 2–5: *PN pꜣ wr Ḏḥwty pꜣ ṯ ntr.w ꜥꜣ Nw.t ỉw=f ỉ-ỉr pꜣ ṯ ntr.w ꜥꜣ Nw.t* "PN, great one of Thoth, the taker of gods (and) great one of Thebes, he acting as the taker of gods (and) great one of Thebes."

7. *wr Ḏḥwty* “great one of Thoth” 

4, 6; 54, 8; 55, 5; 57, 5; 60, 5; 71, 11; 85, 12; 86, x+12: *Pꜣ-šr-Mn,* son of *Ḏḥwty-sḏm*[152]
7, 2:[153] *Ḫnsw-Ḏḥwty,* son of *Pꜣ-ḥ.t-ntr* — also *ṯ ntr.w Pr-Mnṱ nb tꜣ*
8, 5; 9, 1: ...
18, 5: *Hr sꜣ ...*
19, 3–4:[154] *Mnḫ-pꜣ-Rꜥ(?),* son of *Pa-nꜣ-ḫṱ.w*
29, 3:[155] *Ỉmn-ḥtp(?),* son of *Pꜣ-...(?)* — also *ṯ ntr.w Pr-Mnṱ nb tꜣ*
30, 7: *Pa-ꜥnḫ(?),* son of *Pꜣ-tỉ-Ỉmn*
33a, 6; 53, 5: *Pꜣy=f-ṯꜣw-ꜥ.wy-Ḫnsw,* son of *Ns-Mn* — also *sẖ* (53, 5 only)
34, 1:[156] *Pꜣ-ỉšwr,* son of *Pꜣ-mrl*
45, 4: ...
62a, 3:[157] *Pa-Wsr(?),* son of *Pꜣ-šr-Mn* — also *ṯ ntr.w ꜥꜣ Nw.t*
67, 1:[158] [...]
69, 2:[159] *ꜣrꜥblws,* son of *Ỉy-m-ḥtp*
72, 2: *Pꜣ-šr-pꜣ-mwt,* son of *Ḏḥwty-ỉw*
74, 3:[160] *Ḥr-m-ḥb,* son of *Ḏ-ḥr(?)* — also *ṯ ntr.w*
77, 4: *Pꜣ-šr-Ḫnsw,* son of *Pꜣ-tỉ-Wsỉr* — also *ṯ ntr.w* (in list); his name placed first in list
80, 4; 81, 1: *Pꜣ-šr-Ḫnsw,* son of *Pꜣ-tỉ-Mn*

8. *bꜣk.w* “servants” 

All of the cult workers at Dra Abu el-Nagaꜥ were certainly implicitly or explicitly *bꜣk.w*, “servants” of Thoth.[161]
50, 4: unnamed
64d, 5:[162] unnamed

---

[152] He is the one who wrote all of these texts.

[153] 7, 1–2: *PN pꜣ wr Ḏḥwty n pꜣ ṯ ntr.w Pr-Mnṱ nb tꜣ* “PN, the great one of Thoth, namely, the taker of the gods (in) the House-of-Montu, lord of the land.”

[154] 19, 2–6: *PN pꜣ wr Ḏḥwty n pꜣ nt ṯ nꜣ ntr.w n nꜣ rmt.w tꜣ mr.t n ḥ.t-sp x r ḥ.t-sp x* “PN, the great one of Thoth, namely, the one who takes the gods of the men of the harbor from regnal year x to regnal year x.”

[155] 29, 2–4: *PN pꜣ wr Ḏḥwty pꜣ ṯ ntr.w Pr-Mnṱ nb tꜣ* “PN, the great one of Thoth, the taker of (the) gods (in) the House-of-Montu, lord of the land.”

[156] 34, 1–3: *PN pꜣ wr Ḏḥwty n ḥ.t-sp x r ḥ.t-sp x mn ty m-bꜣḥ pꜣ hb pꜣ bỉk ỉrm nꜣy=w pꜣ ṯ nꜣ ntr.w ꜥꜣ n nꜣ rmt.w (n) tꜣ mr.t n wꜥ sp* “PN, the great one of Thoth from regnal year x to regnal year x remains here before the ibis (and) the falcon together with the ones of the taker of the gods, the great one of the men (of) the harbor.”

[157] 62, 2–5: *PN pꜣ wr Ḏḥwty pꜣ ṯ ntr.w ꜥꜣ Nw.t ỉw=f ỉ-ỉr pꜣ ṯ ntr.w ꜥꜣ Nw.t wꜥ sp(?)* “PN, the great one of Thoth, the taker of gods (and) great one of Thebes, he acting as the taker of gods (and) great one of Thebes all together(?).”

[158] 67, 1–2: *[PN] pꜣ wr Ḏḥwty mn ty m-bꜣḥ Ḏḥwty nꜣ ntr.w n pꜣ ꜥ.wy ḥtp n pꜣ hb pꜣ bỉk* “[PN], the great one of Thoth remains here before Thoth (and) the gods of the place of rest⌉ of the ibis (and) the falcon until eternity.”

[159] 69, 1–2: *PN pꜣ wr Ḏḥwty ỉrm nꜣy=w pꜣ ṯ ntr.w wꜥ sp* “PN, the great one of Thoth, together with the men of the taker of gods all together.”

[160] 74, 3–4: *PN pꜣ wr Ḏḥwty pꜣ ṯ ntr.w nꜣ rmt.w tꜣ ml ỉrm nꜣy=w pꜣ ṯ ntr.w* “PN, the great one of Thoth, the taker of the gods, (and to) the men of the harbor, together with the ones of the taker of gods.”

[161] For “servants of Thoth,” see Ray, *Texts from the Baboon and Falcon Galleries*, 125.

[162] 64d, 1–5: *ỉt-ntr PN ỉt-ntr PN nꜣ rt nꜣ wꜥb.w ỉt-ntr PN pꜣ mr ḫꜣs.t ỉrm nꜣ bꜣk.w sẖ PN tr=w* “God’s-father PN, god’s-father PN, the representatives of the priests, god’s-father PN, the overseer of the necropolis and the servants of the scribe PN in their entirety.”

9. *pr-ꜥꜣ* "pharaoh" 

In 68, 1 "pharaoh" may designate the ibis itself.

68, 1: unnamed

10. *mr ḫꜣs.t* "overseer of the necropolis" 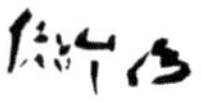

64d, 4:[163] *Pꜣ-tỉ-Nfr-ḥtp sꜣ ...*	also *ỉt-ntr*
67, 2: [...]	

11. *mr šn Ḏḥwty* "lesonis of Thoth" 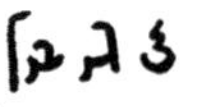

77, 6: *Ḥr-wn-nfr(?),* (son of) *Pꜣ-šr-...*	also *ṯ ntr.w* (in list)

12. *rmt.w ꜥy.w* "great people" 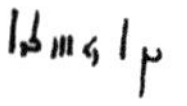

78, 2: *Pꜣ-šr-Ḫnsw,* son of *Hr*	(in list)
78, 3: *Pa-rt,* son of *Tny.t-Ḫnsw(?)*	(in list)
78, 4: ... *Pꜣ-šr-* ...	(in list),
78, 5: *[Pꜣy]-kꜣ(?),* son of *Pꜣ-šr-...*	(in list), also *sẖ*
78, 6: *Pa-Wsr,* son of *Twt*	(in list)
78, 7: *Hr,* son of *Ḥr-ỉw(?)*	(in list)
78, 8: *Ỉmn-* ... (son of) *Hr*	(in list), also *sẖ*
78, 9: *W...*	(in list), also *sẖ*
78, 10: *Ns-Ḫmn-ỉw,* son of *Hkl(?)*	(in list)

13. *rmt.w wrṯ(?)* "men of (the) cage(?)" 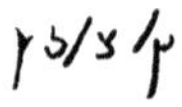

77, 8: *Plth,* son of *Pa-Ḏḥwty*	also(?) *ṯ ntr.w* (in list)
77, 9: *Ḫnsw-Ḏḥwty,* (son of) *Pꜣ-šr-ꜥ-pḥ.ty*	also(?) *ṯ ntr.w* (in list)
77, 10: *Pa-nꜣ*	also *ꜥnty*, also(?) *ṯ ntr.w* (in list)
77, 11: *Ḥr-Mw.t(?),* son of *Ḫnsw-Ḏḥwty*	also(?) *ṯ ntr.w* (in list)
77, 12: *Pꜣ-šr-n-Ḫnsw*	also(?) *ṯ ntr.w* (in list)

14. *rmt.w tꜣ mr.t* "men of the harbor" 

We do not have the personal names of any individuals holding this title. The "men of the harbor" seem to be associated with both the *wr Ḏḥwty* and the *ṯ nꜣ ntr.w.*

19, 5:[164] unnamed

74, 3:[165] unnamed

15. *rt nꜣ wꜥb.w* "representatives of the priests" 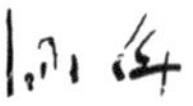

It is unclear in 64d which individuals hold this position.

64d, 3:[166] unnamed(?)

---

[163] 64d, 1–5: *ỉt-ntr PN ỉt-ntr PN nꜣ rt nꜣ wꜥb.w ỉt-ntr PN pꜣ mr ḫꜣs.t ỉrm nꜣ bꜣk.w sẖ PN tr=w* "God's-father PN, god's-father PN, the representatives of the priests, god's-father PN, the overseer of the necropolis and the servants of the scribe PN in their entirety."

[164] 19, 2–6: *PN pꜣ wr Ḏḥwty n pꜣ nt ṯ nꜣ ntr.w n nꜣ rmt.w tꜣ mr.t n ḥ.t-sp x r ḥ.t-sp x* "The great one of Thoth, namely, the one who takes the gods of the men of the harbor from regnal year x to regnal year x."

[165] 74, 2–5: *PN pꜣ wr Ḏḥwty pꜣ ṯ ntr.w nꜣ rmt.w tꜣ ml ỉrm nꜣy=w pꜣ ṯ ntr.w* "PN, the great one of Thoth, the taker of the gods, (and to) the men of the harbor, together with the ones of the taker of gods."

[166] 64d, 1–5: *ỉt-ntr PN ỉt-ntr PN nꜣ rt nꜣ wꜥb.w ỉt-ntr PN pꜣ mr ḫꜣs.t ỉrm nꜣ bꜣk.w sẖ PN tr=w* "God's-father PN, god's-father PN, the representatives of the priests, god's-father PN, the overseer of the necropolis and the servants of the scribe PN in their entirety."

16. *ḥry(?)* "chief" 
This otherwise common title is only attested once in a damaged context.
70, 2: unclear context

17. *sẖ* "scribe" 
33a, 4: *Pꜣy=f-ṯꜣw-[ꜥ.wy-Ḫnsw]*
34, 6: *Ns-Mn-...(?),* son of *Hr*
53, 4:[167] *Pꜣy=f-ṯꜣw-ꜥ.wy-Ḫnsw*, son of *Ns-Mn* — also *wr Ḏḥwty*
62b, 3:[168] *Lwꜣ*, son of *Ḥr* — also *ṯ ntr.w ꜥꜣ Nw.t*
64d, 5:[169] *Pꜣ-hb*
78, 5: *[Pꜣy]-kꜣ(?)*, son of *Pꜣ-šr-...* — *rmt ꜥꜣ* (in list)
78, 8: *ỉmn- ...*, (son of) *Hr* — *rmt ꜥꜣ* (in list)
78, 9: *W...* — *rmt ꜥꜣ* (in list)

17b. *sẖ.w(?)* "scribes" 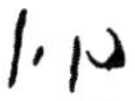
76, 8(?): unnamed

18. *sẖ pr-ḏ.t* "scribe of the House-of-Eternity" 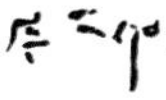 [170]
The reading and translation are not secure.
68, 3:[171] *Ḏḥwty-sḏm*, son of *Ns-nb-ꜥy*

19. *šms.w* "servants" 
The writer of graff. 50, 3 declares: "Numerous were his servants at the place." In this short three line text he mentions both *šms.w* and *bꜣk.w*, and one wonders if he made a distinction between the two terms.
50, 3:[172] unnamed

20. *skrṯ(?)* Greek title? 
The reading and translation are uncertain.
64d, 6:[173] *Hr*, son of *Pꜣ-hb*

21. *ṯ ntr.w/ṯ nꜣ ntr.w* "taker of the gods" 
The common title *ṯ ntr.w*, "bearer of the gods," occurs often in the corpus.[174] Evidently, the

---

[167] 53, 4–5: *sẖ.w sẖ PN pꜣ wr Ḏḥwty* "Has written the scribe, PN, the great one of Thoth."

[168] 62b, 3–4: *sẖ PN pꜣ sẖ pꜣ ṯ ntr.w ꜥꜣ Nw.t* "Has written PN, the scribe, the taker of gods, great one of Thebes."

[169] 64d, 1–5: *ỉt-ntr PN ỉt-ntr PN nꜣ rt nꜣ wꜥb.w ỉt-ntr PN pꜣ mr ḫꜣs.t ỉrm nꜣ bꜣk.w sẖ PN tr=w* "God's-father PN, god's-father PN, the representatives of the priests, god's-father PN, the overseer of the necropolis and the servants of the scribe PN in their entirety."

[170] While *pr-ḏ.t*, "House-of-Eternity," is attested in demotic (Vleeming, *Some Coins of Artaxerxes*, 312), the title "scribe of the House-of-Eternity," would seem to be very rare indeed. To our knowledge it is found in the Ramesside period, e.g., Bankes Stela 12; J. Černý, *Egyptian Stelae in the Bankes Collection* (Oxford: Oxford University Press, 1958), number 12.

[171] 68, 1–3: *pꜣ hb pr-ꜥꜣ rpy=k rpy ꜣḫ=k Wsỉr pꜣ hb Wsỉr pꜣ bỉk Wsỉr pꜣ ꜥḫm Wsỉr ⸢Twtw⸣(?) Wsỉr Ḥr nb Sḫm sẖ pr-ḏ.t PN* "O ibis of pharaoh, may you be rejuvenated! May your body be rejuvenated! O Osiris ibis, o Osiris falcon, o Osiris falcon, Osiris Tutu(?), Osiris Horus, Lord of Letopolis. Scribe of the House-of-Eternity PN."

[172] 50, 2–3: *pꜣ hb wn-nꜣ.w nꜣ-ꜥšꜣy nꜣy=f šms.w r pꜣ ꜥ.wy (ḥtp) sẖ bꜣk.w* "The ibis. Numerous were his servants at the place (of rest). Have written the servants."

[173] 64d, 1–6: *pꜣ(?) skrṯ(?) Pr-ỉmn Hr*, son of *Pꜣ-hb.*

[174] On the title *ṯ ntr.w*, Clarysse and Thompson, *Counting the People in Hellenistic Egypt* 1:90, remark that these were "probably bearers of the animal mummies in processions." See also Quaegebeur, "La Désignation 'porteur(s) des

same individual could be both a *wr Ḏḥwty* and a *ṯ ntr.w*. The *ṯ ntr.w* is generally understood to be the person responsible for transporting the deceased sacred animals "before Osiris ibis (and) Osiris falcon (and) the gods of the place of rest of the ibis" (graff. 77, 1). To judge from graff. 77 one could be a *ṯ ntr.w* while holding another occupation or title. The graffiti also mention men presumably under the supervision of the *ṯ ntr.w* (graff. 34, 3).

19, 4:[175] *Mnẖ-pꜣ-Rꜥ(?)*, son of *Pa-nꜣ-h̭ṱ.w*	also *wr Ḏḥwty*
34, 3:[176] unnamed	also(?) *ꜥꜣ n nꜣ rmt.w (n) tꜣ mr.t*
62a, 3:[177] *Pa-Wsr(?)*, son of *Pꜣ-šr-Mn*	also *wr Ḏḥwty, ꜥꜣ Nw.t*
62b, 4:[178] *Lwꜣ*, son of *Ḥr*	also *sẖ, ꜥꜣ Nw.t*
69, 2:[179] unnamed	
74, 3:[180] *Ḥr-m-ḥb*, son of *Ḏ-ḥr(?)*	also *wr Ḏḥwty*
77, 4:[181] *Pꜣ-šr-Ḫnsw*, son of *Pꜣ-ti-Wsỉr*	(in list); also *wr Ḏḥwty*
77, 5: *Grt(?)*, son of *Ḥr-wn-nfr(?)*	(in list)
77, 6(?): *Ḥr-wn-nfr(?)*, (son of) *Pꜣ-šr-* ...	(in list); also *mr šn Ḏḥwty*
77, 8(?): *Plth*, son of *Pa-Ḏḥwty*	(in list)(?); also *rmt wrṱ(?)* (in list)
77, 9(?): *Ḫnsw-Ḏḥwty*, (son of) *Pꜣ-šr-ꜥ-pḥ.ty*	(in list)(?); also *rmt wrṱ(?)* (in list)
77, 10(?): *Pa-nꜣ*	(in list)(?); also *ꜥntꜣy*, also *rmt wrṱ(?)* (in list)
77, 11(?): *Ḥr-Mw.t(?)*, son of *Ḫnsw-Ḏḥwty*	(in list)(?); also *rmt wrṱ(?)* (in list)
77, 12(?): *Pꜣ-šr-Ḫnsw*	(in list)(?); also *rmt wrṱ(?)* (in list)

22. *ṯ ntr.w Pr-Mnṯ nb tꜣ* "taker of the gods (in) the House-of-Montu, lord of the land" 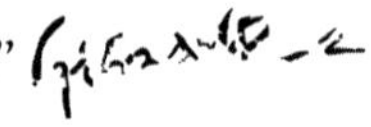

7, 1–2: *Ḫnsw-Ḏḥwty*, son of *Pꜣ-ḥ.t-ntr*	also *wr Ḏḥwty*,
29, 3–4: *Ỉmn-ḥtp(?)*, (son of) *Pꜣ-...(?)*	also *wr Ḏḥwty*

23. ... "taker(?) ..." 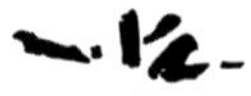

The reading and translation are uncertain.

31, 11(?): [...]

dieux,'" 161–76; T. Dousa, F. Gaudard, and J. Johnson, "P. Berlin 6848: A Roman Period Inventory," in *Res Severa Verum Gaudium: Festschrift für Karl-Theodor Zauzich zum 65. Geburtstag am 8. Juni 2004*, ed. F. Hoffmann and H.-J. Thissen, Studia Demotica 6 (Leuven: Peeters, 2004), 195, who comment that the title seems to refer to the porters "of the mummies of sacred animals."

175 19, 2–6: *PN pꜣ wr Ḏḥwty n pꜣ nt ṯ nꜣ ntr.w n nꜣ rmt.w tꜣ mr.t n ḥ.t-sp x r ḥ.t-sp x* "PN, the great one of Thoth, namely, the one who takes the gods of the men of the harbor from regnal year x to regnal year x."

176 34, 1–3: *PN pꜣ wr Ḏḥwty n ḥ.t-sp x r ḥ.t-sp x mn ty m-bꜣḥ pꜣ hb pꜣ bỉk ỉrm nꜣy=w pꜣ ṯ nꜣ ntr.w ꜥꜣ n nꜣ rmt.w (n) tꜣ mr.t n wꜥ sp* "PN, the great one of Thoth from regnal year x to regnal year x, remains here before the ibis (and) the falcon together with the ones of the taker of the gods, the great one of the men (of) the harbor."

177 62a, 2–5: *PN pꜣ wr Ḏḥwty pꜣ ṯ ntr.w ꜥꜣ Nw.t ỉw=f ỉ-ỉr pꜣ ṯ ntr.w ꜥꜣ Nw.t wꜥ sp(?)* "PN, the great one of Thoth, the taker of gods (and) great one of Thebes, he acting as the taker of gods (and) great one of Thebes at one time(?)."

178 62b, 4: *PN pꜣ sẖ pꜣ ṯ ntr.w ꜥꜣ Nw.t* "PN, the scribe, the taker of gods, great one of Thebes."

179 69, 1–2: *PN pꜣ wr Ḏḥwty ỉrm nꜣy=w pꜣ ṯ ntr.w wꜥ sp* "PN, the great one of Thoth, together with the men of the taker of gods all together."

180 74, 3–4: *PN pꜣ wr Ḏḥwty pꜣ ṯ ntr.w nꜣ rmt.w tꜣ ml ỉrm nꜣy=w pꜣ ṯ ntr.w* "PN, the great one of Thoth, the taker of the gods, (and to) the men of the harbor, together with the ones of the taker of gods."

181 77, 1–3: *pꜣ rn nfr nꜣ rmt.w ṯ ntr.w m-bꜣḥ Wsỉr pꜣ hb Wsỉr pꜣ bỉk nꜣ ntr.w pꜣ ꜥ.wy ḥtp pꜣ hb pꜣy=w rn PN* "The good name of the men who take the gods before Osiris the ibis (and) Osiris the falcon (and) the gods of the place of rest of the ibis. Their name(s): PNs."

REMARKS ON INDIVIDUALS ATTESTED ELSEWHERE AND PERSONAL NAMES IN THE GRAFFITI

Few of the individuals in these graffiti have been identified in other Theban Ptolemaic texts.[182] *Ḥr-pa-Is.t*, son of *Sylws* (graff. 68, 4) belongs to a well-documented family; his floruit would have been in the middle of the second century BCE.[183] *Ḥr*, son of *Ns-Mn* (graff. 49, 3), *ʿnḫ-rn=f*, son of *Ns-Mn* (graff. 49, 4), and *Pa-tm*, son of *Ns-Mn* (graff. 49, 5), are also members of this same family. Interestingly, a sale-document and a cession-document exist in which members of this family sell their share of a "place of rest of the ibis" in 198 BCE.[184] We suspect, moreover, that such a prominent individual as *Pꜣ-šr-Mn*, son of *Ḏḥwty-sḏm*, "great one of Thoth," will at some point be recognized in other contracts or ostraca from Ptolemaic Thebes, either as the party to a transaction or as a witness thereto.[185] As might be expected, the personal names in the graffiti reflect the local ibis cult (e.g., *Pꜣ-hb, Ḫnsw-Ḏḥwty, Ḏ-ḥr, Ḏḥwty-ỉw, Ḏḥwty-sḏm*). Also popular are such names as *ʾIy-m-ḥtp* and *ʾImn-ḥtp*, associated with nearby Deir el-Bahari. Distinctly Greek names are rare (*Sylws* [Zoïlos] in graff. 68, 4; *Hrgls* in graff. 14, 5).[186] The relatively sparse prosopographical information in these graffiti does not enable one to reconstruct detailed family trees; only graff. 48, 80, and 81 provide material for a genealogy. We present below the genealogies and a list of individuals with titles. For a complete list of personal names, see the glossary.

GENEALOGIES OF INDIVIDUALS MENTIONED IN GRAFFITI 48, 80, AND 81

Graffito 48, 2–3: *Wsỉr-wr sꜣ Ḥr sꜣ Gl-šr sꜣ Ḥr*

The proposed genealogy is tentative, and assumes that nothing is lost to the left of the preserved text.

Ḥr
|
Gl-šr
|
Ḥr
|
Wsỉr-wr

[182] We should mention here that in ostracon 1, 1 (= O. DAN 2066), found in the southwest of TT 11, a certain *Ḏ-ḥr* "(of) the place of rest" is named on a receipt for price of oil. This ostracon is probably to be dated to 252/251 BCE. Muhs has proposed that this individual may well be identical to the ibis-keeper Teos, son of Patemis, who is known from three bilingual receipts published in *UPZ* 2, nos. 153–155, which date to year 30 of Ptolemy II. The demotic material from the forecourt seems to be considerably earlier than the graffiti published in this volume.

[183] Vleeming, *Graffiti*, 122, cites the genealogy presented in Pestman, *Recueil de textes démotiques*, vol. 2, pl. opposite p. 73.

[184] Pestman, *Recueil de textes démotiques* 2:82–83. Pestman, p. 77, suggests that the "place of rest" being sold in this document may have been located in Dra Abu el-Nagaʿ, near TT 11 and TT 12. He also provides, at graff. 77–78, a valuable discussion of the phrase *ʿ.wy ḥtp*.

[185] See p. 43. Similarly, it is probable that the "overseer of the necropolis" *Pꜣ-tỉ-Nfr-ḥtp* (graff. 64d, 4) will be found in other Theban texts. One wonders, e.g., whether this "great one of Thoth," *Pꜣ-šr-ʾImn*, son of *Ḏḥwty-sḏm*, is related to the *Ḏḥwty-sḏm*, son of *Pꜣ-šr-ʾImn*, attested in line 3 of the witness list for P. BM 10387 (227 BCE); Andrews, *Legal Texts*, 84. On the significance the name *Ḏḥwty-sḏm*, "the hearing ear," and the related name *Msḏr-sḏm*, "the hearing ear," in this Thothian context, see Ray, *Texts from the Baboon and Falcon Galleries*, 62.

[186] See also the note (a) on graff. 69, 1 (*ꜣrʿblws*); note (a) on graff. 77, 8 (*Plth*).

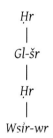

Graffiti 80 and 81: *Pꜣ-tỉ-Mn, Pꜣ-šr-Ḫnsw* and *Ḫnsw-Ḏḥwty*

Genealogies based on graff. 80 and 81 incorporating Chauveau, "Un été 145," 130–31 reading *Pꜣ-šr-Ḫnsw* in place of Spiegelberg's *Pꜣ-šr-n-tꜣ-ỉḥ.t*.

Pꜣ-tỉ-Mn		*Pꜣ-tỉ-Mn*	*Pꜣ-tỉ-Mn*	
|80, 4[187]		|80, 3[190]	|81, 1[191]	*Pꜣ-šr-Ḫnsw*
Pꜣ-šr-Ḫnsw pꜣ wr Ḏḥwty	*Pꜣ-šr-Ḫnsw*	*Pꜣ-šr-Ḫnsw*	*Pꜣ-šr-Ḫnsw pꜣ wr Ḏḥwty*	|81, 4[192]
(pꜣy=y ỉṱ)[188]	|80, 1[189]	|80, 3		*Ḫnsw-Ḏḥwty*
	Ḫnsw-Ḏḥwty	*Ḫnsw-Ḏḥwty*		*(pꜣy=f šr)*[193]

Combining these "partial" genealogies of graff. 80 and 81 produces the following result:

Pꜣ-tỉ-Mn

80, 1, |80, 4; 81, 1

Pꜣ-šr-Ḫnsw pꜣ wr Ḏḥwty

80, 1; |80, 3; 81, 4

Ḫnsw-Ḏḥwty

PERSONAL NAMES WITH TITLES

ꜣrꜥblws, son of *ʾIy-m-ḥtp*	69, 1	*wr Ḏḥwty*
ʾImn-ḥtp(?), son of *Pꜣ...(?)*	29, 2–3	*wr Ḏḥwty*, *ṯ nṯr.w Pr-Mnṱ nb tꜣ*
ʾImn-..., son of *Hr*	78, 8	*sḫ, rmt ꜥꜣ* (in list)
ꜥnḫ-rn=f, son of *Ns-Mn*	49, 4	*ỉry-ꜥꜣ pꜣ ꜥ.wy ḥtp* (in list)
W...	78, 9	*sḫ, rmt ꜥꜣ* (in list)
Pꜣ-ỉšwr, son of *Pꜣ-mrl*	34, 1	*wr Ḏḥwty*
Pꜣ-nfr-ỉr-ḥr, son of *Ḏ-ḥr*	49, 6	*ỉry-ꜥꜣ pꜣ ꜥ.wy ḥtp* (in list)
Pꜣ-hb	64d, 5	*sḫ*
Pꜣ-šr-pꜣ-Mwt, son of *Ḏḥwty-ỉw*(?)	72, 1–2	*wr Ḏḥwty*
Pꜣ-šr-Mn, son of *Ḏḥwty-sḏm*	4, 4; 54, 7; 55, 4; 56, 3; 57, 4; 58, 6; 60, 4; 71, 10; [85, 12]; 86, x+12; *wr Ḏḥwty*;	

In graff. 70, 4; 75, 5; 85, 4–5; 87, 5, the name *Pꜣ-šr-Mn*, son of *Ḏḥwty-sḏm* appears; it is most probably the same person, but either the title *wr Ḏḥwty* is destroyed or, as in graff. 85, is omitted.

Pꜣ-šr-Ḫnsw	77, 12	*rmt wrṱ(?)* (in list), *ṯ nṯr.w* (in list)(?)
Pꜣ-šr-Ḫnsw, son of *Pꜣ-tỉ-Wsỉr*	77, 4	*wr Ḏḥwty; ṯ nṯr.w* (in list)

187 80, 4: *Pꜣ-šr-Ḫnsw sꜣ Pꜣ-tỉ-Mn pꜣy=y ỉṱ pꜣ wr Ḏḥwty*

188 In 80, 4 *Pꜣ-šr-Ḫnsw* explicitly refers to *Pꜣ-tỉ-Mn* as "my father."

189 80, 1: *Ḫnsw-Ḏḥwty sꜣ Pꜣ-šr-Ḫnsw*

190 80, 3: *Ḫnsw-Ḏḥwty sꜣ Pꜣ-šr-Ḫnsw sꜣ Pꜣ-tỉ-Mn*

191 81, 1: *Pꜣ-šr-Ḫnsw sꜣ Pꜣ-tỉ-Mn pꜣ wr Ḏḥwty*

192 81, 4: *Ḫnsw-Ḏḥwty sꜣ Pꜣ-šr-Ḫnsw pꜣy=f šr*

193 In 81, 4 *Ḫnsw-Ḏḥwty* explicitly refers to himself as "his (i.e., *Pꜣ-šr-Ḫnsw*'s) son."

Pꜣ-šr-Ḫnsw, son of *Pꜣ-ti-Mn*	80, 4; 81, 1	*wr Ḏḥwty*
Pꜣ-šr-Ḫnsw, son of *Hr*	78, 2	*rmt ꜥꜣ* (in list)
Pꜣ-šr-..., father of ...(?)	78, 4	*rmt ꜥꜣ* (in list)
Pꜣ-ti-Nfr-ḥtp, son of ...	64d, 4	*it-ntr, mr ḫꜣs.t*
Pa-ꜥnḫ(?), son of *Pꜣ-ti-ꜣImn*	30, 6–7	*wr Ḏḥwty*
Pa-Wsr(?), son of *Pꜣ-šr-Mn*	62a, 2	*wr Ḏḥwty, ṯ ntr.w* (2x), *ꜥꜣ Nw.t* (2x)
Pa-Wsr, son of *Twt*	78, 6	*rmt ꜥꜣ* (in list)
Pa-nꜣ	77, 10	*rmt wrṯ(?)* (in list), *ꜥntꜣy, ṯ ntr.w* (in list)(?)
Pa-rt, son of *Tny.t-Ḫnsw*(?)	78, 3	*rmt ꜥꜣ* (in list)
Pa-tm, son of *Ns-Mn*	49, 5	*iry-ꜥꜣ pꜣ ꜥ.wy ḥtp* (in list)
Pꜣy=f-ṯꜣw-[ꜥ.wy-Ḫnsw]	33a, 4	*sḫ* same(?) individual as in graff. 33a, 5
Pꜣy=f-ṯꜣw-ꜥ.wy-Ḫnsw, son of *Ns-Mn*	33a, 5; 53, 4	*wr Ḏḥwty, sḫ* (only in 33a, 5)
[Pꜣy]-kꜣ(?), son of *Pꜣ-šr-...*	78, 5	*sḫ, rmt ꜥꜣ* (in list)
Plth, son of *Pa-Ḏḥwty*	77, 8	*rmt wrṯ(?)* (in list), *ṯ ntr.w* (in list)(?)
Mnḫ-pꜣ-Rꜥ(?), son of *Pa-nꜣ-ḫṯ.w*	19, 2–3	*wr Ḏḥwty, ṯ ntr.w*
Ns-Mn-...(?), son of *Hr*	34, 6	*sḫ*
Ns-Ḫmn-iw, son of *Hkl(?)*	78, 10	*rmt ꜥꜣ* (in list)
Lwꜣ, son of *Ḥr*	62b, 3	*sḫ, ṯ ntr.w, ꜥꜣ Nw.t*
Hr, son of *Pꜣ-hb*	64d, 7	*skrṯ(?) Pr-ꜣImn*
Hr, son of *Ḥr-iw(?)*	78, 7	*rmt ꜥꜣ* (in list)
Hr, son of ...(?)	18, 5	*wr Ḏḥwty*
Ḥr, son of *Ns-Mn*	49, 3	*iry-ꜥꜣ pꜣ ꜥ.wy ḥtp*
Ḥr-wn-nfr(?), (son of) *Pꜣ-šr-...*	77, 6	*mr šn Ḏḥwty, ṯ ntr.w* (in list)
Ḥr-m-ḥb, son of *Ḏ-ḥr(?)*	74, 2	*wr Ḏḥwty, ṯ ntr.w*
Ḥr-Mw.t(?), son of *Ḫnsw-Ḏḥwty*	77, 11	*rmt wrṯ(?)* (in list), *ṯ ntr.w* (in list)(?)
Ḫnsw-Ḏḥwty, son of *Pꜣ-ḥ.t-ntr*	7, 1	*wr Ḏḥwty*
Ḫnsw-Ḏḥwty, son of *Pꜣ-šr-ꜥ-pḥ.ty*	77, 9	*rmt wrṯ(?)* (in list), *ṯ ntr.w* (in list)(?)
Grt(?), son of *Ḥr-wn-nfr*(?)	77, 5	*ṯ ntr.w* (in list)
Ḏḥwty-sḏm, son of *Ns-nb-ꜥy*	68, 3	*sḫ pr-ḏ.t*
..., son of *Wsir-wr*	64d, 2	*it-ntr*
... *Pꜣ-šr-* ...	78, 4	*rmt ꜥy* (in list)
...	45, 4	*wr Ḏḥwty*
...	64d, 1	*it-ntr*
...	9, 1	*wr Ḏḥwty*
...	67, 1	*wr Ḏḥwty*

TEXT EDITIONS OF GRAFFITI

TOMB OF DJEHUTY (TT 11)

SOUTH WALL

1. **Graffito TT 11/1** (Plate 11)

Location: Main corridor, S-wall

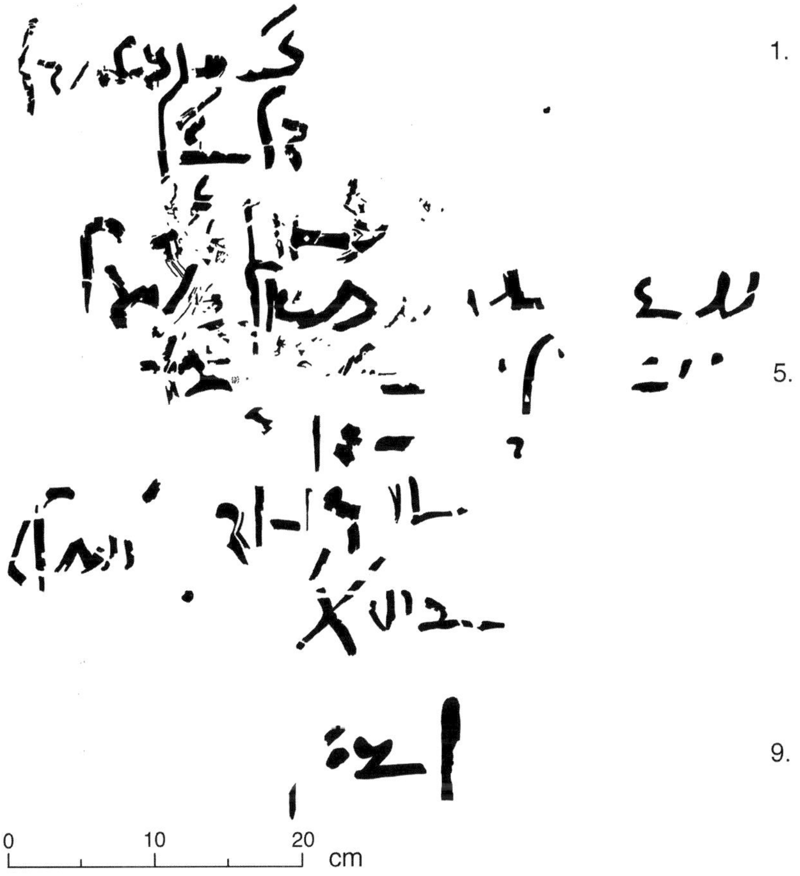

TRANSLITERATION

1. *Ḏ-ḥr-m-ḥb*
2. *ʾImn-ḥtp*
3. ... *Ḏw-*⌜*ʿḫy*⌝
4. *pꜣ rn nfr Pꜣ-hb* ...
5. ...
6. ...
7. *[pꜣ rn] nfr* ...
8. ... *mn ty* ...
9. *[... Pꜣ]-tỉ-Wsỉr* ...

TRANSLATION

1. *Ḏ-ḥr-m-ḥb*
2. *ʾImn-ḥtp*
3. ... *Ḏw-*⌜*ʿḫy*⌝
4. The good name of *Pꜣ-hb* ...
5. ...
6. ...
7. [The] good [name] ...
8. ... remains here ...
9. [... *Pꜣ*]*-tỉ-Wsỉr* ...

Commentary
(Spiegelberg #23, pl. 29; Vleeming, *Graffiti*, 115 [#1470; first three lines])

Line 1
(a) *Ḏ-ḥr-m-ḥb* appears to be the best reading. However, we can offer no other example of the name.

Line 3
(a) We had first read *sꜣ*, "son," before *Ḏw-ꜥẖy*, but this is questionable.
(b) *Ḏw-ꜥẖy* fits the traces, comparing *Ṯꜣw-ꜥẖy*, *Demot. Nb.*, 1355, but it is a mere guess.

Line 4
(a) Perhaps *Hb*, *Demot. Nb.*, 740. It may be that the text of lines 4–9 belong to a different graffito from the text preserved in lines 1–3.
(b) Is *hr* to be transliterated at the end of the line?

2. Graffito TT 11/2 (Plate 12)

Location: Main corridor, S-wall

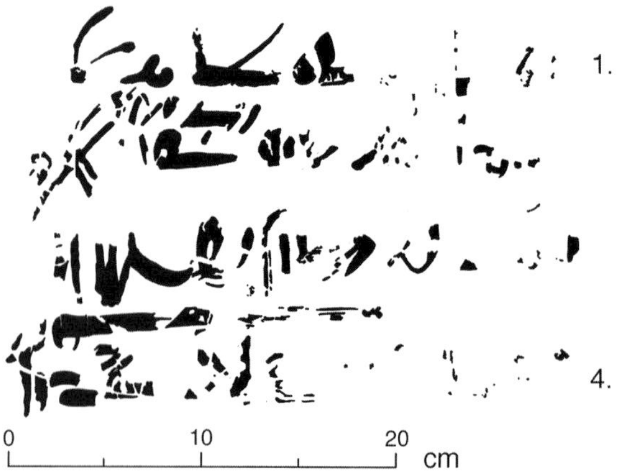

TRANSLITERATION
1. ⸢*pꜣ rn*⸣ *nfr(?) Ns-*⸢*pꜣ-Rꜥ(?)*⸣
2a. ... *pꜣ* ...
2b. ... *mn ty*
3. ... ⸢*m-bꜣh*⸣ *pꜣ hb pꜣ bik*
4. ... *ꜥ.wy ḥtp*

TRANSLATION
1. ⸢The⸣ good(?) ⸢name⸣ *Ns-*⸢*pꜣ-Rꜥ(?)*⸣
2a. ... the ...
2b. ... remains here
3. ... ⸢before⸣ the ibis (and) the falcon
4. ... place of rest

Commentary

Line 1
(a) The name clearly concludes with the divine determinative. *Ns-pꜣ-Rꜥ*, *Demot. Nb.*, 669, is one possibility, but this is an uncommon name.

3. Graffito TT 11/3 (Plate 13)

Location: Main corridor, S-wall

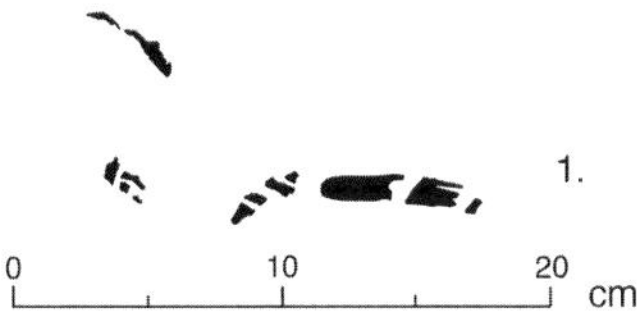

TRANSLITERATION	TRANSLATION
1. ...	1. ...

Commentary

(a) These are the only traces that are visible beneath the burnt layer.

4. Graffito TT 11/4 (Plate 12)

Location: Main corridor, S-wall

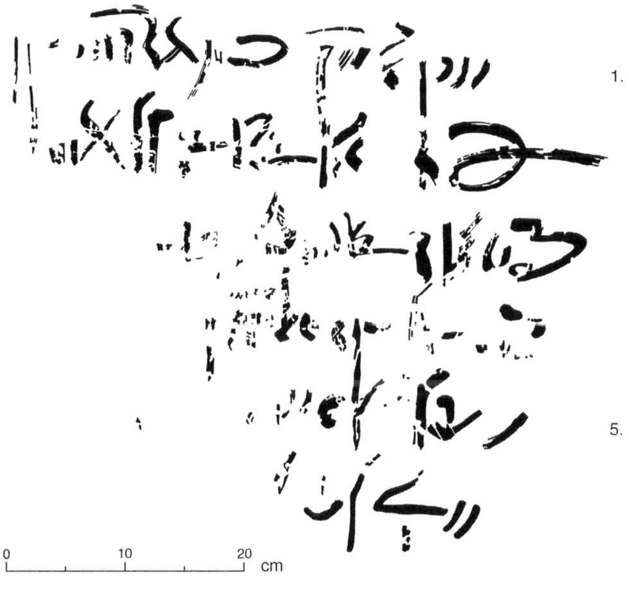

TRANSLITERATION	TRANSLATION
1. *pꜣ rmt nb (n) pꜣ tꜣ nt ỉw=f (r) ꜥš nꜣy sẖ.w*	1. As for every man (in) the world who will read these writings,
2. *m-ỉr tỉ.t tỉ ḥtp ntr ty*	2. do not let a god be at rest here
3. *šꜥ-tw nꜣ ꜥ.wy.w ẖry.w ...*	3. until the lower chambers ...
4. *⌈wn⌉(?) sẖ Pꜣ-šr-Mn*	4. ⌈open⌉(?). Has written *Pꜣ-šr-Mn*,
5. *sꜣ Ḏḥwty-sḏm*	5. son of *Ḏḥwty-sḏm*,
6. *pꜣ wr Ḏḥwty*	6. the great one of Thoth

Commentary

Line 1

(a) This graffito addresses the evidently literate animal cult workers.

Line 2

(a) The sacred animal mummies should apparently not be buried or interred in this area. Presumably, they should be placed in the "lower chambers." One assumes that the writer wishes that the mummies should be moved through the tombs to their final resting place as quickly as possible.

Line 3

(a) *ẖry.w* is a reasonable transliteration, but not secure.

Line 4

(a) *wn*, "öffnen," *Glossar*, 89, fits the traces.

Line 5

(a) The ends of the lines are damaged, but the writer is almost certainly *Pꜣ-šr-Mn sꜣ Ḏḥwty-sḏm*.

5. Graffito TT 11/5 (Plate 13)

Location: Main corridor, S-wall

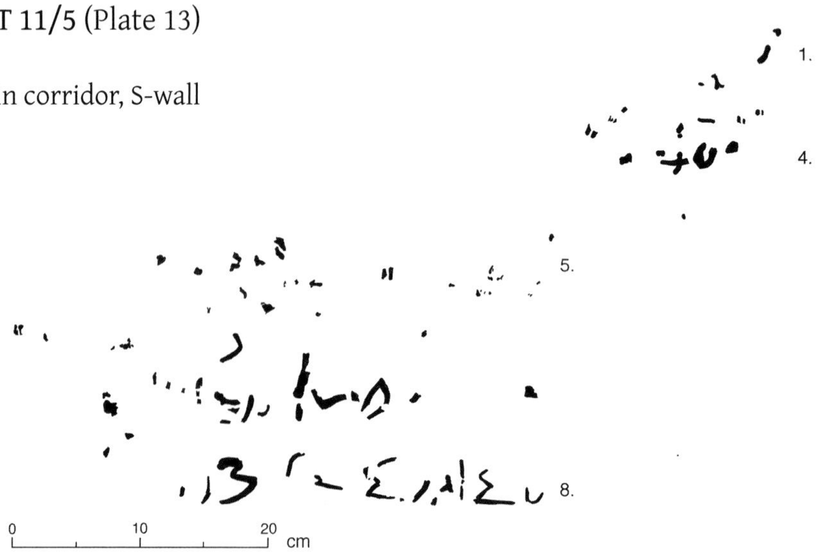

Transliteration

1–3. illegible traces

4. *Pꜣ-⌜mꜣy⌝(?) ...*

5. *[...] ⌜...⌝ [...]*

6. ...

7. *[...] ⌜pꜣ hb pꜣ bi͗k(?)⌝ [...]*

8. *pꜣ ꜥ.wy ḥtp šꜥ [...]*

Translation

1–3. illegible traces

4. *Pꜣ-⌜mꜣy⌝(?)* ...

5. [...] ⌜...⌝ [...]

6. ...

7. [...] ⌜the ibis (and) the falcon(?)⌝ [...]

8. the place of rest until [...]

Commentary

Line 4

(a) Compare *Pꜣ-mꜣy*, *Demot. Nb.*, 186.

6. **Graffito TT 11/6** (Plate 14)

Location: Main corridor, S-wall

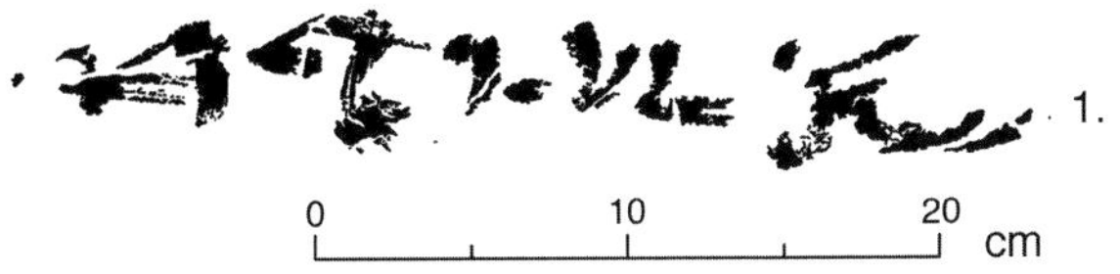

Transliteration

1. *pꜣ rn nfr n Pa-Wsr*

Translation

1. The good name of *Pa-Wsr*

Commentary

(Spiegelberg #22, pl. 29; see also Vleeming, *Graffiti*, 115 [#1469])

Line 1

(a) For *Pa-Wsr*, see *Demot. Nb.*, 361. A *Pa-Wsr*, son of *Twt*, appears in graff. 78, 6.

7. **Graffito TT 11/7** (Plate 14)

Location: Main corridor, S-wall

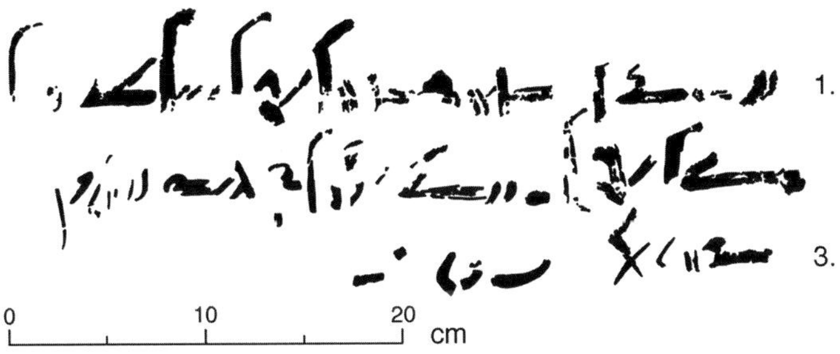

Transliteration

1. *pꜣ rn nfr Ḫnsw-Ḏḥwty sꜣ Pꜣ-ḥ.t-ntr*
2. *pꜣ wr Ḏḥwty n pꜣ ṯ* ⸢*ntr.w Pr-Mnṱ nb tꜣ*⸣
3. *mn ty* ⸢*šꜥ ḏ*⸣*[.t]*

Translation

1. The good name of *Ḫnsw-Ḏḥwty*, son of *Pꜣ-ḥ.t-ntr*,
2. the great one of Thoth, namely, the taker of the ⸢gods (in) the House-of-Montu, lord of the land,⸣
3. remains here ⸢fore⸣[ver.]

Commentary

(Spiegelberg #21, pl. 29; see also Vleeming, *Graffiti*, 115 [#1468])

Line 1

(a) We had first read *Hb-Ḏḥwty*, but the name actually looks more like *Ḫnsw-Ḏḥwty*, *Demot. Nb.*, 881–82.

(b) We take *Pꜣ-ḥ.t-ntr* to be a variant of *Pa-ḥ.t-ntr*, *Demot. Nb.*, 396.

Line 2

(a) This line is problematic. We have taken *n* as old *m*, in the sense of "namely." Still, the construction seems awkward. It is not likely that the *n* after the *Ḏḥwty* is genitival. Vleeming, *Graffiti*, 115, reads ⸢*ỉrm*⸣ for *n pꜣ*, but this also does not yield very attractive sense. The reading *ṯ ntr.w* is secure.

(b) *Pr-Mnṱ*, "domain of Mont," *CDD M*, 123, s.v. *Mnṱ*. The same place name, presumably Armant, occurs also in graff. 29, 4.

(c) For *nb tꜣ*, "Der Herr der Erde," see Leitz, *LGG* 3:768–69. We have not found this epithet elsewhere in demotic texts.

8. **Graffito TT 11/8** (Plate 15)

Location: Main corridor, S-wall

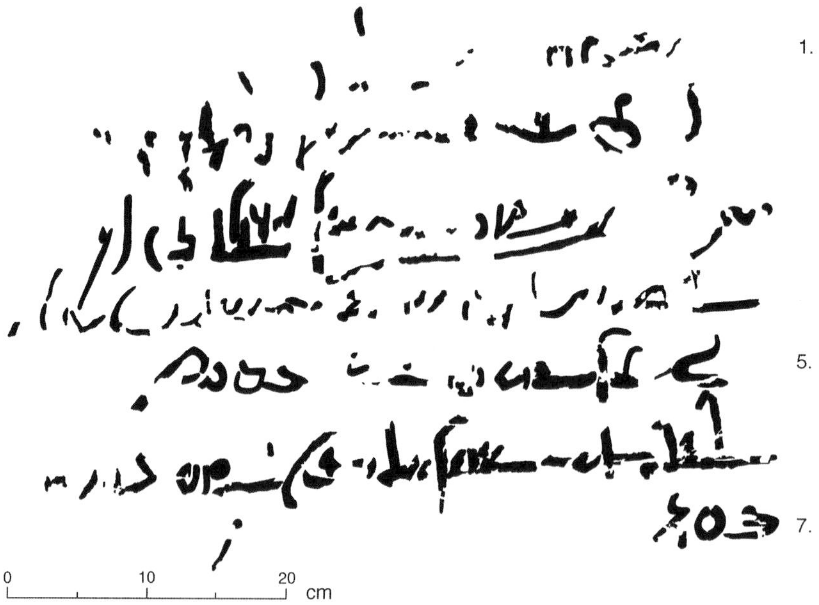

Transliteration	Translation
1. *[pꜣ rn]* ⸢*nfr ...*⸣	1. [The] ⸢good⸣ [name] ...
2. ...	2. ...
3. ... *pꜣ hb pꜣ bik ... tỉ=f*	3. ... the ibis (and) the falcon ... he cause
4. *ḥtp ....*	4. to rest ...
5. *[pꜣ] wr Ḏḥwty mn ...*	5. [the] great one of Thoth remains ...
6. *pꜣ rn nfr n ʾIy-m-ḥtp (sꜣ) Pꜣ-šr-pꜣ-mwt mn ty ...*	6. The good name of *ʾIy-m-ḥtp*, (son of) *Pꜣ-šr-pꜣ-mwt*, remains here ...
7. *šꜥ ḏ.t*	7. forever.

Commentary

Line 3

(a) *tỉ=f* is plausible, but perhaps read simply *ỉw=f*.

Line 4
(a) Perhaps read rather *ꜥq*, “to enter,” at the beginning of the line.
(b) There are presumably personal names in this line. One might suggest *sꜣ Pꜣ-šr-...* toward the end.

Line 5
(a) Admittedly the traces strongly suggest *wr-tỉw*, but this is difficult to interpret in view of the following probable *Ḏḥwty*.
(b) Perhaps *nt ḥry* may be read at the end of the line.

9. **Graffito TT 11/9** (Plate 16)

Location: Main corridor, S-wall

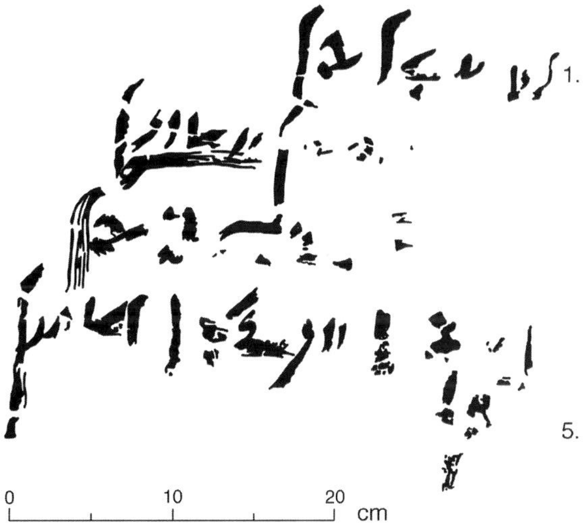

TRANSLITERATION	TRANSLATION
1. ... *pꜣ wr Ḏḥwty*	1. ... the great one of Thoth
2. ...⸢*pꜣ hb*⸣ *pꜣ bỉk*	2. ... ⸢the ibis⸣ (and) the falcon,
3. ...*ꜥq(?)* ... *Ḏḥwty*	3. ... cause to enter(?) ... Thoth
4. ... *ỉw=f ḥtp (n) ḥ.t-ntr*	4. ... he resting (in) the temple.
5. ...	5. ...

Commentary
(Spiegelberg, #20, pl. 29; Vleeming, *Graffiti*, 114–15 [#1467])

Line 1
(a) The personal name is unfortunately lost.

Line 3
(a) *ꜥq*, “eintreten,” *Glossar*, 72, would have in these texts a causative force, see, for example, M. Smith, *The Mortuary Texts of Papyrus British Museum 10507*, Catalogue of Demotic Papyri in the British Museum 3 (London: British Museum Publications), 64–65.[194]

[194] We owe this interpretation of *ꜥq* to Joachim Quack, who suggested this possibility in the discussion following our presentation of these graffiti at the Twelfth International Congress of Demotic Studies in Würzburg (August 30, 2014).

(b) Vleeming, *Graffiti*, 114, reads *Pa-Ḏḥwty*.

Line 4
(a) This statement presumably refers to Thoth, as embodied in the ibis mummies.

10. Graffito TT 11/10 (Plate 16)

Location: Main corridor, S-wall

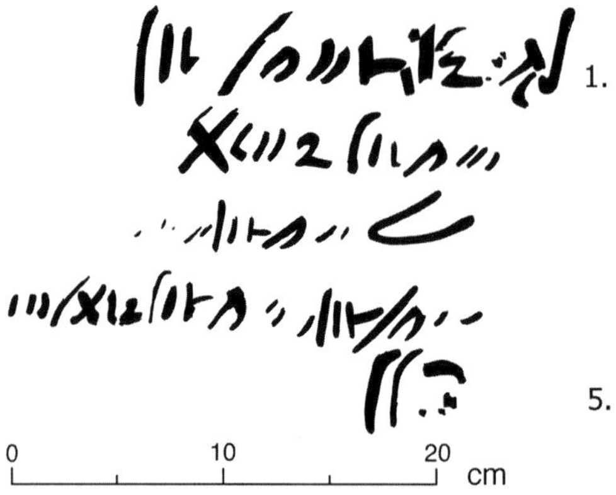

Transliteration	Translation
1. Ḥ.t-sp 11.t <pꜣ> rn nfr Hr	1. Regnal year 11. <The> good name of *Hr*,
2. sꜣ Pꜣ-hb mn ty	2. son of *Pꜣ-hb*, remains here
3. [m]-bꜣḥ pꜣ hb	3. [be]fore the ibis.
4. ... Hr sꜣ Pꜣ-hb mn ty	4. ... *Hr*, son of *Pꜣ-hb*, remains here
5. ... ntr(?) ...	5. ... god(?) ...

Commentary

Line 1
(a) The *pꜣ* is difficult to see, and may have been omitted by the scribe.

Line 5
(a) *ntr* is possible, but hardly certain.

11. Graffito TT 11/11 (Plate 17)

Location: Main corridor, S-wall

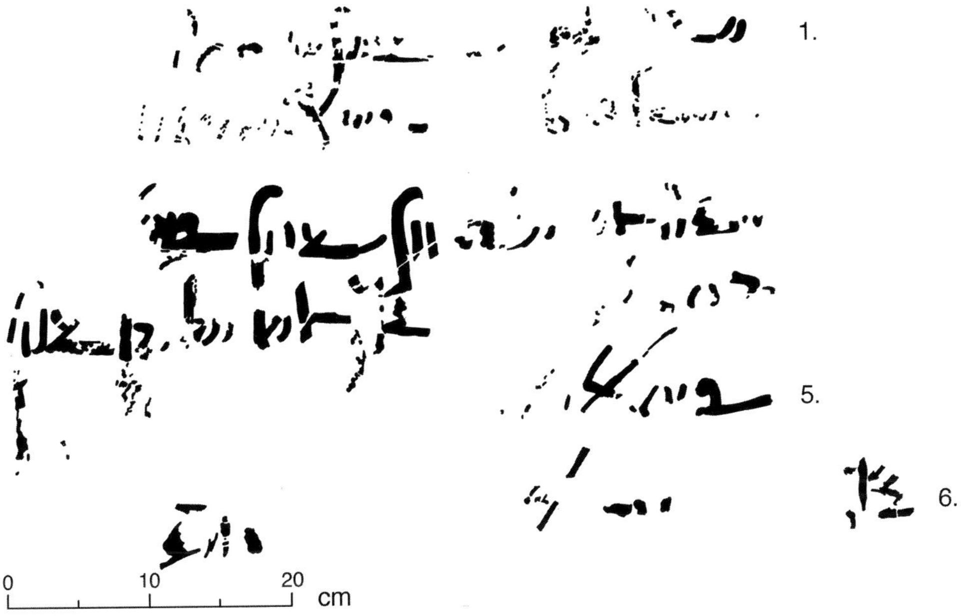

TRANSLITERATION

1. *pꜣ rn nfr ... ʾIy-m-ḥtp* ⸢*sꜣ*⸣ *Pꜣ-šr-...*
2. *... mn ty ...*
3. *pꜣ rn nfr Pꜣ-hb sꜣ ʾIy-m-ḥtp mn* ⸢*ty*⸣
4. ⸢*šʿ ḏ.t*⸣ *... [pꜣ] rn nfr Pꜣ-šr-ʾImn(?) (sꜣ) ʾIy-m-ḥtp(?)*
5. *mn ty ...*
6. *rn [nfr] ...* ⸢*mn ty*⸣*...*

TRANSLATION

1. The good name ... *ʾIy-m-ḥtp*, ⸢son of⸣ *Pꜣ-šr-...*
2. ... remains here ...
3. The good name of *Pꜣ-hb*, son of *ʾIy-m-ḥtp*, remains ⸢here⸣
4. ⸢forever⸣ ... [the] good name of *Pꜣ-šr-ʾImn(?)*, (son of) *ʾIy-m-ḥtp(?)*,
5. remains here ...
6. [good] name ... ⸢remains here⸣ ...

Commentary

Line 2

(a) The initial preserved group seems to end with the divine determinative.

12. Graffito TT 11/12 (Plate 17)

Location: Main corridor, S-wall

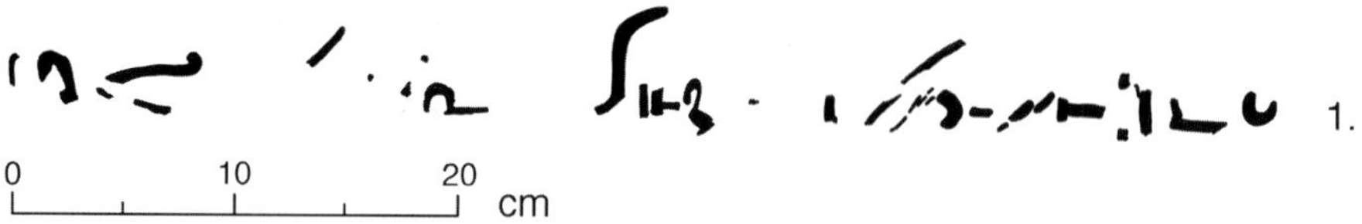

Transliteration

1. *pꜣ rn nfr n Hr* ... *Ḫnsw-*... ⸢*mn ty m-bꜣḥ Ḏḥwty*⸣ ...

Translation

1. The good name of *Hr* ... *Ḫnsw-*... ⸢remains here before Thoth⸣ ...

Commentary

Line 1

(a) The genitive *n* is not generally found after *rn nfr*. The reading is not secure.

13. Graffito TT 11/13 (Plate 18)

Location: Main corridor, S-wall

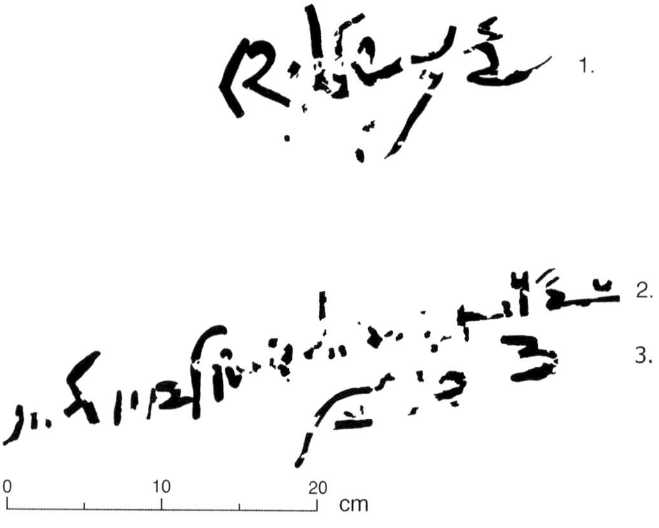

Transliteration

1. *ʿq=f Ḏḥwty ḥ.t-sp 9.t*
2. *pꜣ rn nfr* ⸢...⸣ (*sꜣ*) *Pꜣ-šr-Ḫnsw mn ty*
3. *šʿ ḏ.t*

Translation

1. He caused to enter Thoth (in) regnal year 9.
2. The good name of ⸢...⸣ (son of) *Pꜣ-šr-Ḫnsw* remains here
3. forever.

Commentary

Line 1

(a) Once more *ʿq*, "to cause to enter," is employed in a technical sense, denoting presumably the interment of an ibis or falcon mummy; see note (a) on 9, 3.

14. Graffito TT 11/14 (Plate19)

Location: Main corridor, S-wall

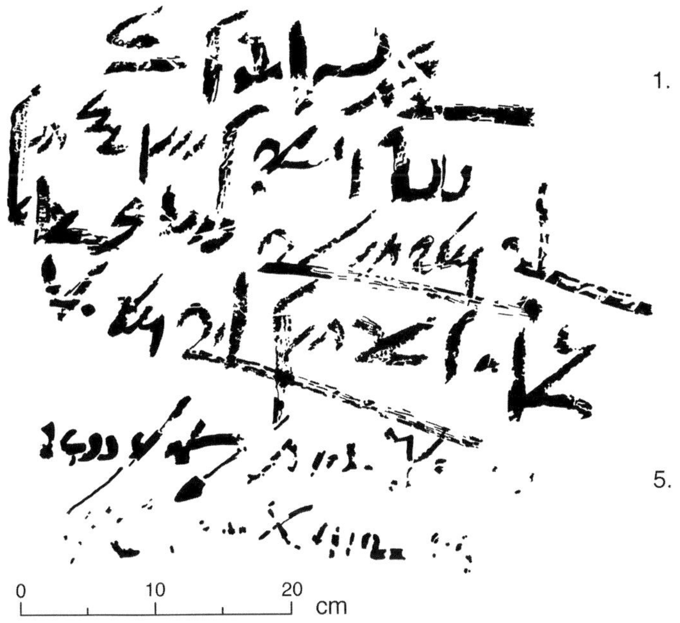

TRANSLITERATION	TRANSLATION
1. *ʿq=w Ḏḥwty ḫn*	1. They caused to enter Thoth, foremost
2. *ṱ Wsr r pꜣ ỉrpy*	2. of Thebes, to the divine chapel
3. *(n) ḥ.t-sp 9 ỉbt 4 pr.t sw 19 m-sꜣ ỉr rnp.t*	3. (in) regnal year 9, fourth month of winter, day 19, after spending
4. *ʿšꜣy n ḥ.t-ntr ḥ.t-sp 9 ỉbt 3 sw 11*	4. many years in the temple. Regnal year 9, third month, day 11.
5. ⸢*pꜣ rn*⸣ *nfr Hrgls*	5. ⸢The⸣ good ⸢name⸣ of *Hrgls*
6. *mn ty m-bꜣḥ [Ḏḥwty ...]*	6. remains here before [Thoth ...]

Commentary

(Spiegelberg #27, pl. 28; Vleeming, *Graffiti*, 116 [#1471])

This graffito is virtually identical to graff. 63. This text formula deserves close study. Is Thoth, “foremost one of Thebes” the name or epithet of a particular ibis? We suggest that the *ỉrpy* is the tomb-chapel, while the *ḥ.t-ntr* is the place where the living birds were kept; see pp. 53–54 One naturally thinks of Medinet Habu, Qasr el-Aguz, or the Seti I Temple at Qurna. However, there is no archaeological evidence for such breeding installations at these sites, to our knowledge.

Line 1

(a) Again, *ʿq* is employed in a technical sense; see note (a) on 9, 3.

Line 2

(a) *Ḏḥwty ḫnṱ Wsr* seems to stand for “Thoth, the foremost one of Thebes.” On *Wsr* for *Ws.t*, “Thebes,” see *Glossar*, 99. Could this be an individual ibis, who received the special epithet? See perhaps Kessler and Nur el-Din, “Tuna al-Gebel,” 128. Especially interesting in this regard is the on-go-ing scientific work of Sally Wasef and her collaborators, who write, "A small number of sacred Ibis were chosen as 'sacred animals', based on physical markings, and were reared for the temples," S. Wasef et al. "Radiocarbon Dating of Sacred Ibis Mummies from Ancient Egypt," *Journal of Archaeological Science: Reports* 4 (2015), 355.

(b) *ỉrpy*, "divine chapel," may here denote the tomb.

Line 3

(a) The interment thus occurred in the ninth year of an unnamed Ptolemy. Vleeming, *Graffiti*, 116, reads *šmw*.

Line 4

(a) It is difficult to determine the force of these statements. The writer seems to distinguish between the *ỉrpy* in line 2 and the *ḥ.t-ntr* in line 4. One wonders whether the *ỉrpy* designates the tomb, while the *ḥ.t-ntr* would be the sphere of the living animal. Or is *ḥ.t-ntr* a term for another section of the tomb? See Kessler and Nur el-Din, "Tuna al-Gebel," 128, 156 "all remains of sacred animals kept around the local ibis breeding area that was connected to a temple institution were collected and sent to Tuna regardless of their species."

(b) "Day 11" is the most common day named in these graffiti. Did the cult workers carry out their activities on this particular day? Vleeming, *Graffiti*, 116, reads *ibt 4 šmw (sw) xy*.

Line 5

(a) *Hrgls* is *Hrꜣqlꜣs, Demot. Nb.*, 744.

15. Graffito TT 11/15 (Plate 20)

Location: Main corridor, S-wall

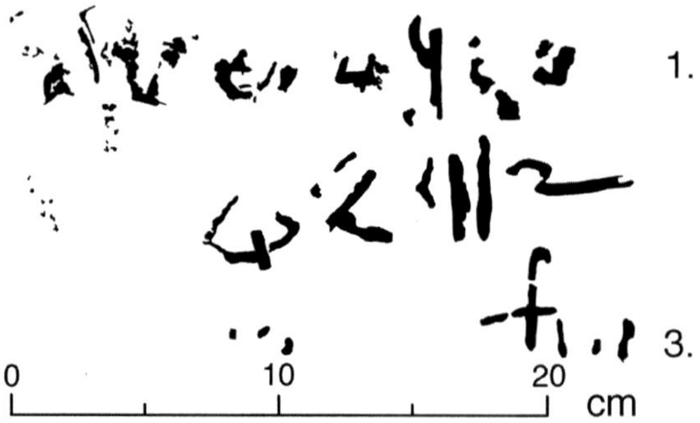

TRANSLITERATION	TRANSLATION
1. *pꜣ rn nfr* ...	1. The good name ...
2. *mn ty m-bꜣḥ* ...	2. remains here before ...
3. ...	3. ...

Commentary

Line 1

(a) Does the name begin with *Ḏḥwty*?

16. **Graffito TT 11/16** (Plate 20)

Location: Main corridor, S-wall

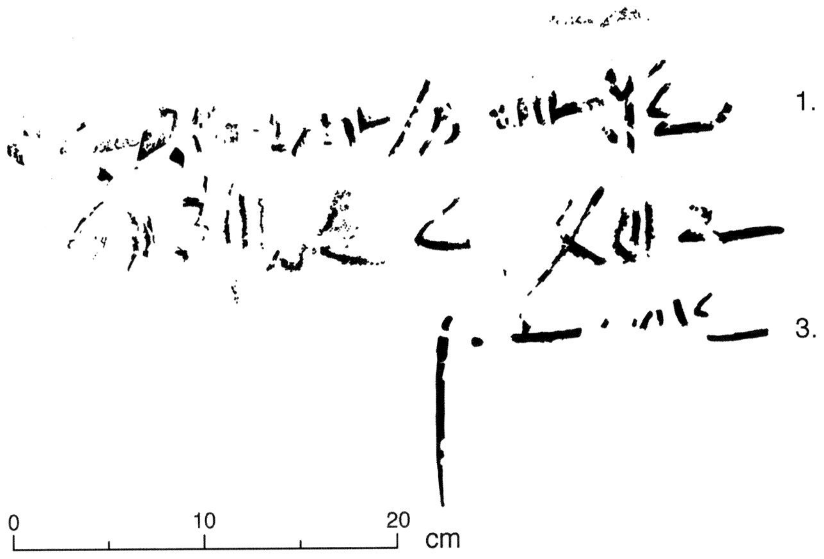

Transliteration

1. ⌜*pꜣ*⌝ *rn nfr Hr sꜣ* ...
2. *mn ty m-bꜣḥ* ...
3. ⌜*ꜥ.wy ḥtp*⌝ *sẖ*

Translation

1. ⌜The⌝ good name of *Hr*, son of ...,
2. remains here before ...
3. ⌜place of rest⌝. Written.

Commentary

Line 2

(a) It is difficult to see the expected *pꜣ hb pꜣ bꞽk* in the preserved traces.

17. **Graffito TT 11/17** (Plate 20)

Location: Main corridor, S-wall

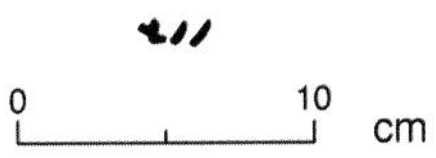

Transliteration

1. ...

Translation

1. ...

Commentary

There do not seem to be traces of any other signs.

18. Graffito TT 11/18 (Plate 21)

Location: Main corridor, S-wall

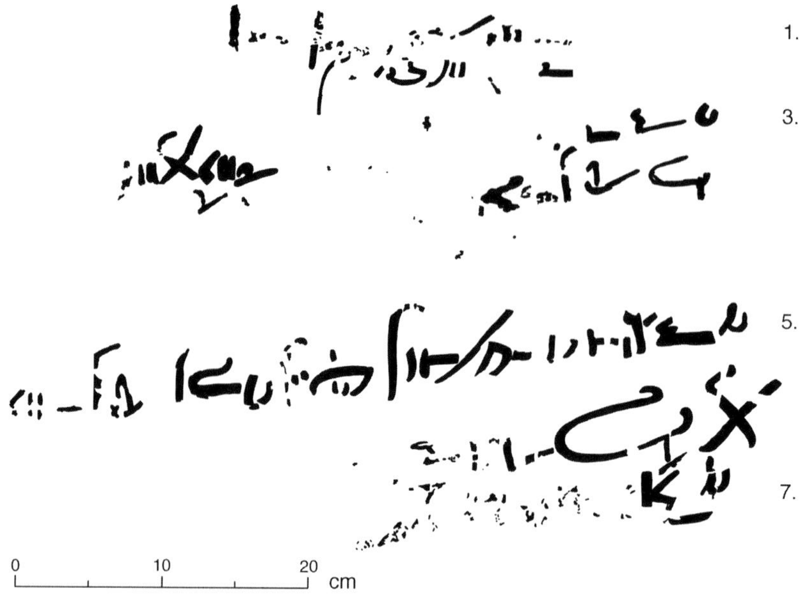

Transliteration	Translation
1. ⸢*pꜣ rn nfr*⸣ ...	1. ⸢The good name⸣ ...
2. *mn ty šʿ ḏ.t*	2. remains here forever.
3. *pꜣ rn nfr ... mn ty*	3. The good name ... remains here
4. *m-bꜣḥ Ḏḥwty* ⸢*šʿ*⸣ *[ḏ.t]*	4. before Thoth ⸢for⸣[ever.]
5. *pꜣ rn nfr n Hr sꜣ ... pꜣ wr Ḏḥwty mn*	5. The good name of *Hr*, son of ..., the great one of Thoth, remains
6. *ty m-bꜣḥ Ḏḥwty šʿ [ḏ.t]*	6. here before Thoth for[ever.]
7. *pꜣ rn nfr ...*	7. The good name ...

Commentary

Line 5

(a) The traces of the father's name resemble ʿꜣ, but this is very uncertain.

19. Graffito TT 11/19 (Plate 22)

Location: Main corridor, S-wall

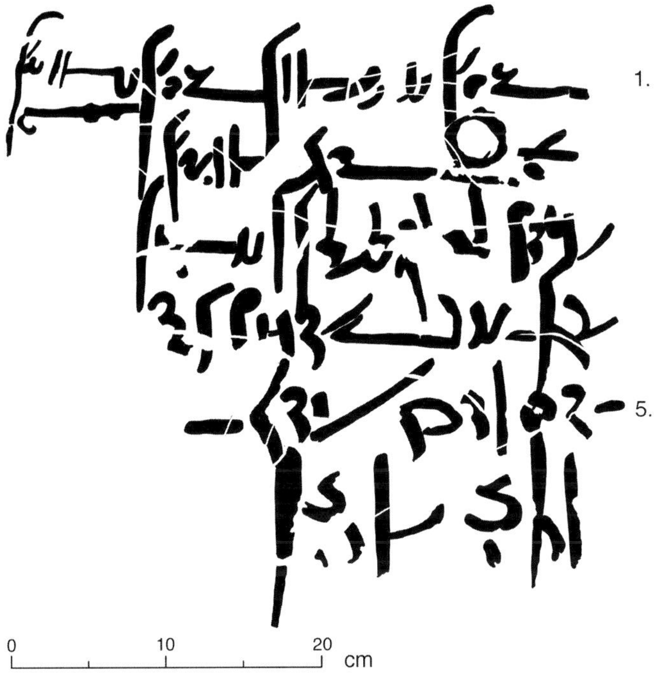

Transliteration

1. *Wsi͗r pꜣ hb Wsi͗r pꜣ bi͗k*
2. *ti͗.t ꜥnḫ (n) Mnḫ-pꜣ-Rꜥ(?)*
3. *sꜣ Pa-nꜣ-ḫṱ.w pꜣ wr*
4. *Ḏḥwty n pꜣ nt ṯ nꜣ nṯr.w*
5. *n nꜣ rmt.w tꜣ mr.t n*
6. *ḥ.t-sp 20.t r ḥ.t-sp 21.t*

Translation

1. Osiris the ibis (and) Osiris the falcon,
2. give life (to) *Mnḫ-pꜣ-Rꜥ(?)*,
3. son of *Pa-nꜣ-ḫṱ.w*, the great one of
4. Thoth, namely, the one who takes the gods
5. of the men of the harbor from
6. regnal year 20 to regnal year 21.

Commentary

Line 1

(a) This typical formula is not common in these graffiti (see pp. 45–46). The phraseology of the entire text is unusual.

Line 2

(a) The hieroglyphic writing of *ꜥnḫ* is striking.

(b) *Mnḫ* and *Rꜥ* are clear, but the *pꜣ* is difficult to see; for *Mnḫ-pꜣ-Rꜥ*, *Demot. Nb.*, 595.

Line 3

(a) For *Pa-nꜣ-ḫṱ.w*, *Demot. Nb.*, 382–83.

Line 4

(a) We had first understood this *n* as "to," rendering "(and) to," and assumed there were two different individuals. However, since this second individual would not have a name, we now think it preferable to translate *n* as "namely," and propose that the writer has the functions of both "great one of Thoth" and "taker of the gods." This combination of titles is found in graff. 62a, 74, and 77.

(b) For the *ṯ n3 ntr.w* , see pp. 63–64.

Line 5

(a) "The men of the harbor" occur three times in this corpus. *Rmt t3 mr.t*, "man of the harbor," is cited in *Glossar*, 168; *CDD M*, 151 ("man of the harbor," "dockworker"). In graff. 34, 3 a "great one of the men of the harbor" is mentioned. The identification of the "harbor" is somewhat mysterious. Does this refer to the river-edge at the time of inundation? We are probably to understand *mr.t* as a simple canal "docking-place."[195] The "men of the harbor" probably were stevedores charged with the loading and unloading of the sacred birds. On such harbor activities, see S. Vinson, *The Nile Boatman at Work*, MÄS 48 (Munich: von Zabern, 1998), 156–59. One might expect "from the men of the harbor," but *n* does not generally have that meaning.

Line 6

(a) Were these offices held for a year?

20. **Graffito TT 11/20** (Plate 23)

Location: Main corridor, S-wall

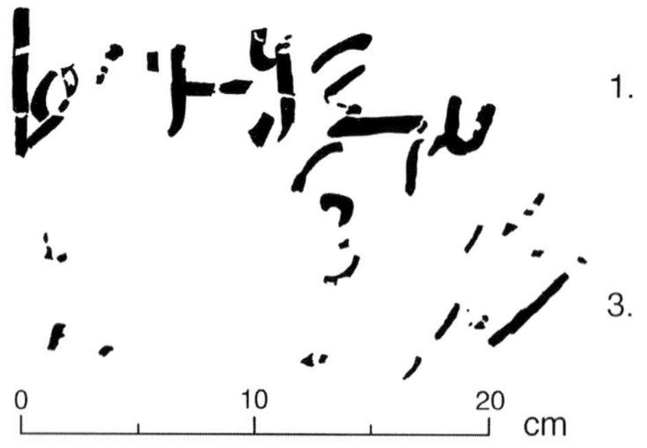

TRANSLITERATION	TRANSLATION
1. *p3 rn nfr* ...	1. The good name ...
2. ...	2. ...
3. ...	3. ...

[195] We have also considered whether *mr.t* is not *mr.t*, "harbor," but rather to be identified with the much-discussed *ml*, "chapel," *CDD M*, 162–63, for which see Pestman, *Recueil de textes démotiques*, vol. 2:79. To be sure, *ml*, "chapel," is masculine, whereas the word in these graffiti seems to be feminine.

21. Graffito TT 11/21 (Plate 23)

Location: Main corridor, S-wall

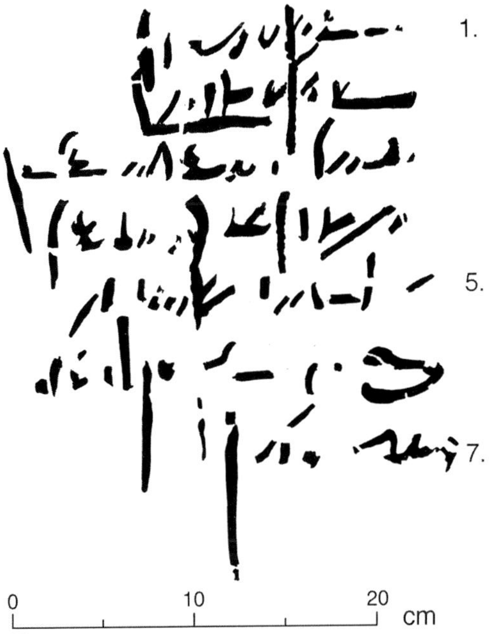

Transliteration

1. *Wsỉr pꜣ hb*
2. *Wsỉr pꜣ bỉk*
3. ⸢*ꜥq*⸣*=w n pꜣ ꜥ.wy ḥtp*
4. *Hr ... Pꜣ-šr-Mn(?)*
5. *r ḥ.t-ntr(?) ...*
6. *šꜥ ḏ.t sẖ ḥ.t-sp 21.t(?)*
7. *ỉbt 3 [p]*⸢*r.t*⸣*(?) sw 11*

Translation

1. Osiris the ibis (and)
2. Osiris the falcon,
3. ⸢causing⸣ them to enter in the place of rest
4. *Hr ... Pꜣ-šr-Mn(?)*
5. to the temple(?) ...
6. forever. Written (in) regnal year 21(?)
7. third month of [win]⸢ter⸣(?), day 11

Commentary

Line 3

(a) The transliteration *ꜥq* is tentative. Could this be a stative form, with a *w* ending, translating "Osiris, the ibis (and) Osiris, the falcon, are caused to enter?" Alternatively, one could take the vertical stroke as the divine determinative.

Line 4

(a) More than simply *Hr* seems to be written. The syntax of the text is obscure. Presumably *Hr* was responsible for the interment of the birds.

Line 5

(a) The traces may be misleading and therefore the reading is questionable. Elsewhere *ḥ.t-ntr* seems to denote the place where the living birds were kept, while *ỉrpy* would designate the tomb; see note (a) on line 4 in graff. 14.

22. Graffito TT 11/22 (Plate 24)

Location: Main corridor, S-wall

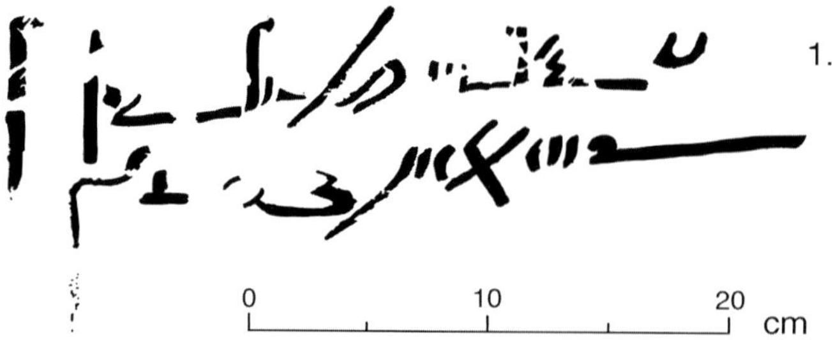

TRANSLITERATION
1. *pꜣ rn nfr Hr (sꜣ) ꞽIy-m-ḥtp(?)*
2. *mn ty šꜥ ḏ.t*

TRANSLATION
1. The good name of *Hr*, (son of) *ꞽIy-m-ḥtp(?)*,
2. remains here for ever.

23. Graffito TT 11/23 (Plate 24)

Location: Main corridor, S-wall

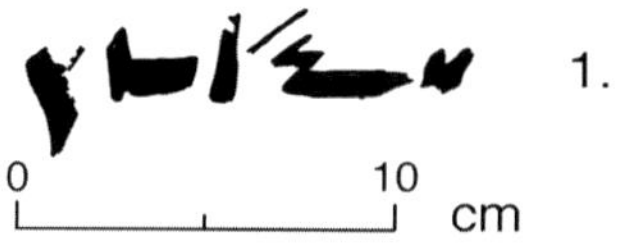

TRANSLITERATION
1. *pꜣ rn nfr*

TRANSLATION
1. The good name

Commentary
Nothing seems to be lost after *pꜣ rn nfr*.

24. **Graffito TT 11/24** (Plate 25)

Location: Main corridor, S-wall

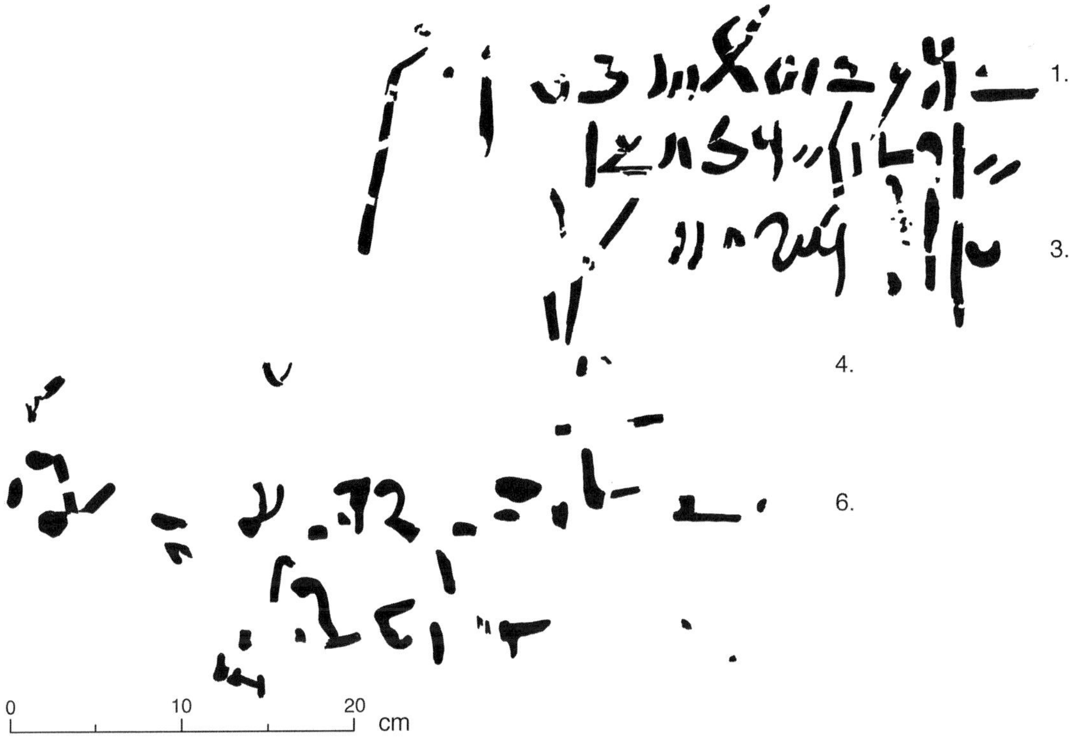

TRANSLITERATION

1. *rn=f mn ty šʿ ⸢ḏ.t⸣*
2. *Pꜣ-ti͗-Ḫnsw-pꜣ-sẖy*
3. *sẖ (n) ḥ.t-sp ⸢10.t⸣(?) i͗bt 4 pr.t sw 11*
4. ...
5. ...
6. *⸢pꜣ rn nfr⸣ ... Ḏḥwty*
7. *... ⸢ ty(?) m-bꜣḥ Ḏḥwty⸣ ...*

TRANSLATION

1. His name remains here for⸢ever⸣
2. *Pꜣ-ti͗-Ḫnsw-pꜣ-sẖy.*
3. Written (in) regnal year ⸢10.t⸣(?) fourth month of winter, day 11
4. ...
5. ...
6. ⸢The good name⸣ ... Thoth
7. ... ⸢here(?) before Thoth⸣ ...

Commentary

Line 1
(a) *rn=f mn* is not a very typical initial phrase in these graffiti.

Line 2
(a) *Pꜣ-ti͗-Ḫnsw-pꜣ-sẖy* is perhaps a variant of *Pꜣ-ti͗-Ḫnsw-pꜣ-i͗-i͗r-sẖy*, *Demot. Nb.*, 338. However, the reading is not secure.

Line 3
(a) *sw 11* is the most common day named in the corpus.

25. Graffito TT 11/25 (Plate 26)

Location: Main corridor, S-wall

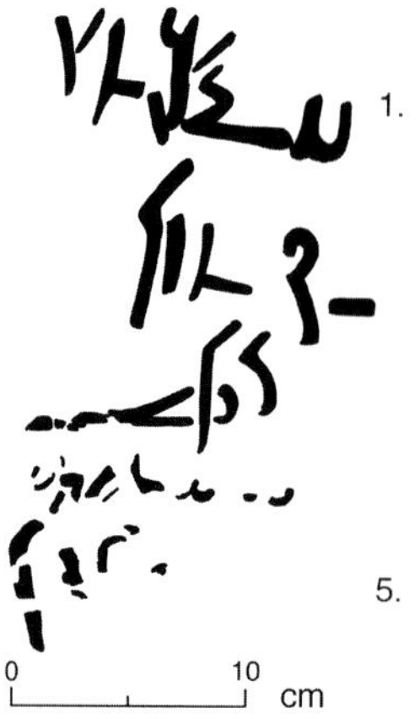

TRANSLITERATION
1. *pꜣ rn nfr* ...
2. *n Ḫnsw-*
3. ...
4. ...
5. ...

TRANSLATION
1. The good name ...
2. of(?) *Ḫnsw-*
3. ...
4. ...
5. ...

Commentary

Line 3
(a) Perhaps read *ḥꜣ.ṯ=w* or *ḥꜣ.ṯ* followed by the divine determinative at the beginning of the preserved line.

Line 4
(a) Possibly read *pꜣ rn nfr* toward the end of the preserved traces.

26. Graffito TT 11/26 (Plate 26)

Location: Main corridor, S-wall

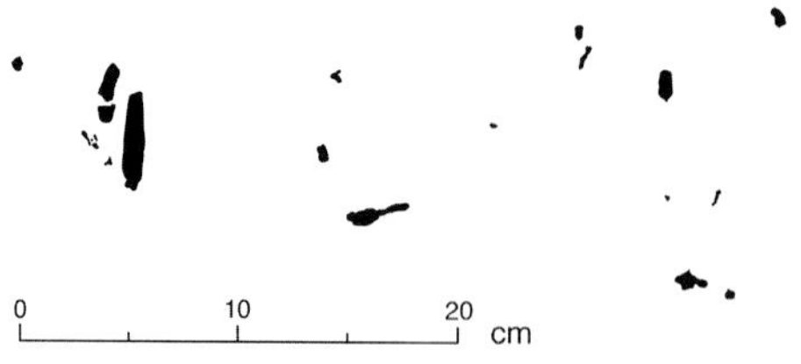

TRANSLITERATION
1. ...

TRANSLATION
1. ...

27. Graffito TT 11/27 (Plate 26)

Location: Main corridor, S-wall

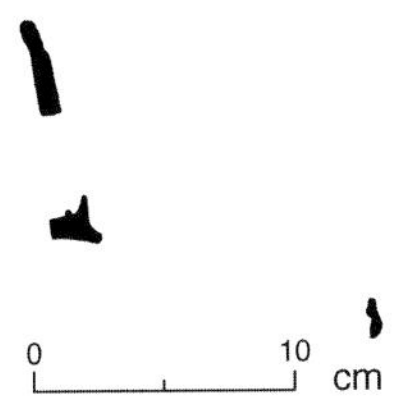

TRANSLITERATION	TRANSLATION
1. ...	1. ...

NORTH WALL

28. Graffito TT 11/28 (Plate 27)

Location: Main corridor, N-wall

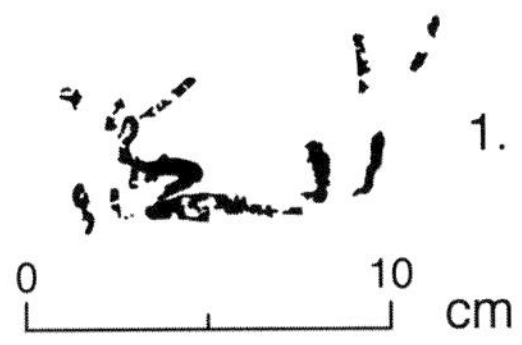

TRANSLITERATION	TRANSLATION
1. *pꜣ rn*	1. The name

Commentary

The red traces around *pꜣ rn* indicate that there was originally more of this inscription although the wall surface does not appear damaged.

29. Graffito TT 11/29 (Plate 27)

Location: Main corridor, N-wall

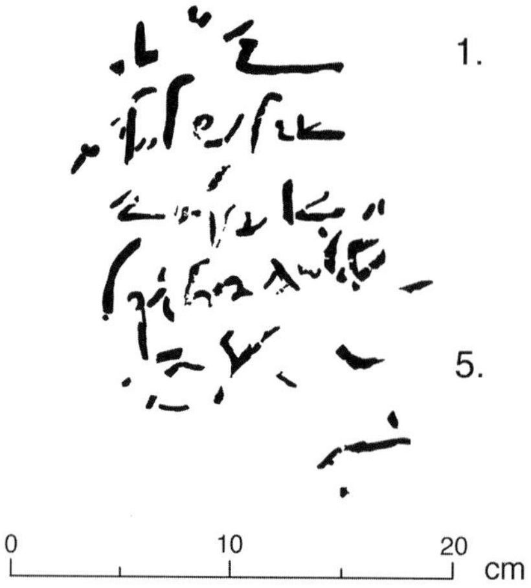

Transliteration	Translation
1. *[pꜣ] rn nfr*	1. [The] good name
2. *ʾImn-ḥtp(?) (sꜣ) Pꜣ-...(?)*	2. of *ʾImn-ḥtp(?)*, (son of) *Pꜣ-...(?)*,
3. *pꜣ wr Ḏḥwty pꜣ ṯ*	3. the great one of Thoth, the taker of
4. *ntr.w Pr-Mnṯ nb tꜣ*	4. (the) gods (in) the House-of-Montu, lord of the land,
5. ⸢*mn ty šꜥ*	5. ⸢remains here for-
6. *ḏ.t*⸣	6. ever.⸣

Commentary

Line 2

(a) *ʾImn-ḥtp* is very uncertain. The second element of the name rather resembles *m-ḥb*.

Line 4

(a) The same place name, presumably Armant, occurs also in graff. 7, 2.

30. Graffito TT 11/30 (Plate 28)

Location: Main corridor, N-wall

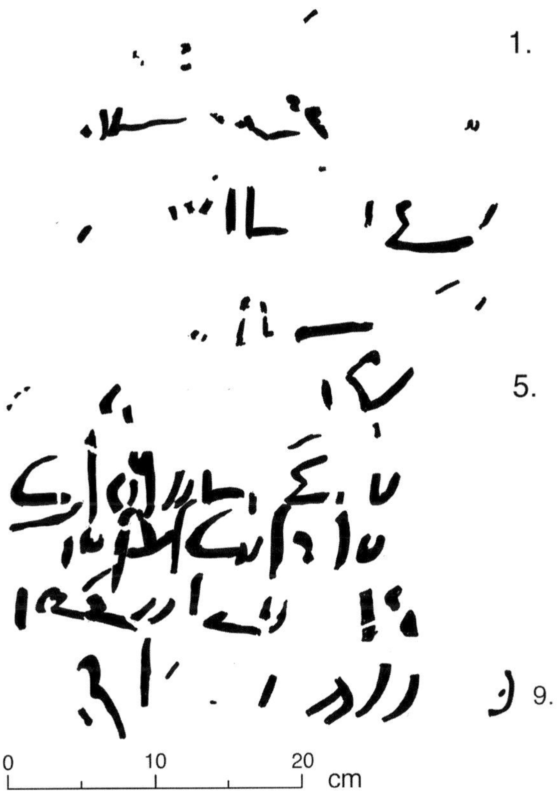

TRANSLITERATION

1. ...
2. ...
3. ⸢*pꜣ rn nfr*⸣ ...
4. ...
5. *ty* ...
6. *pꜣ rn nfr Pa-ꜥnḫ(?) (sꜣ?)*
7. *Pꜣ-ti͗-Ꞽmn pꜣ wr Ḏḥwty* ...
8. ... *pꜣ ꜥ.wy ḥtp* ...
9. ... *ḥ.t-sp 9.t(?)* [...]

TRANSLATION

1. ...
2. ...
3. ⸢The good name⸣ ...
4. ...
5. here(?) ...
6. The good name of *Pa-ꜥnḫ(?)*, (son of?)
7. *Pꜣ-ti͗-Ꞽmn*, the great one of Thoth, ...
8. ... the place of rest ...
9. ... regnal year 9(?) [...]

Commentary

Line 6

(a) *Pa-ꜥnḫ* is possible, but not certain; compare *Pꜣ-ꜥnḫ/ Pa-ꜥnḫ, Demot. Nb.*, 162. *Sꜥnḫ* is a less attractive reading.

31. Graffito TT 11/13 (Plate 29)

Location: Main corridor, N-wall

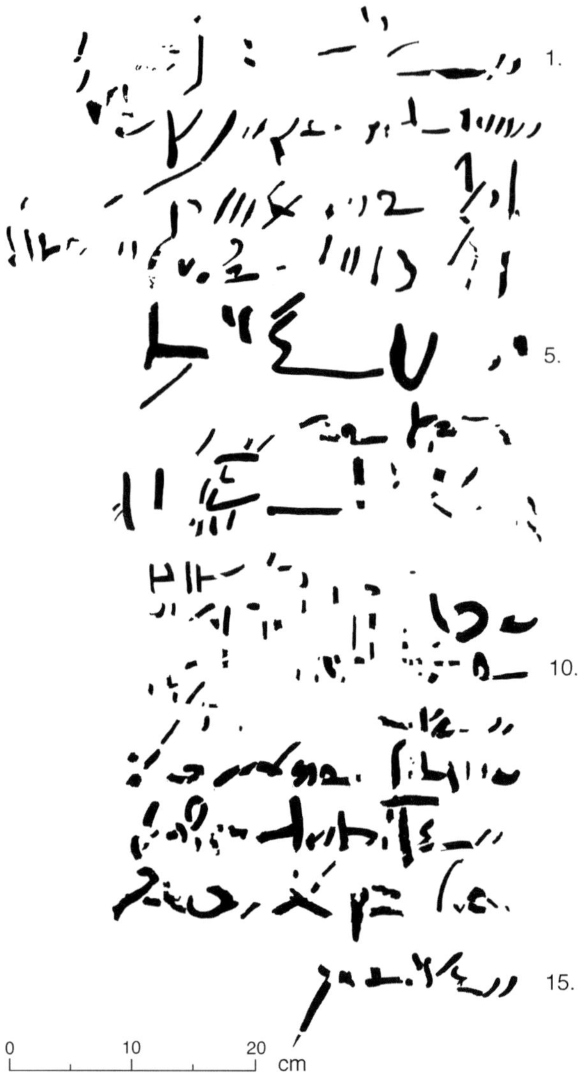

Transliteration

1. ⸢*pꜣ rn nfr*⸣ ...
2. *sꜣ Pꜣy=s-nfr(?)* ...
3. *ḥ.t-sp 5.t mn ty* ⸢*m-bꜣḥ*⸣ *[pꜣ] hb*
4. ... ⸢*ꜥ.wy.w*⸣*(?) n ḥtp*
5. ... *pꜣ rn nfr* ...
6. ... *mn ty(?)* ...
7. ...
8. ...
9. *pꜣ* ...
10. ...

Translation

1. ⸢The good name⸣ ...
2. son of *Pꜣy=s-nfr(?)* ...
3. regnal year 5 remains here ⸢before⸣ [the] ibis
4. ... ⸢places⸣(?) of rest
5. ... The good name ...
6. ... remains here(?) ...
7. ...
8. ...
9. the ...
10. ...

11. *pꜣ ṯ(?)* ...	11. the taker(?) ...
12. *Pꜣ-ti-Ḫnsw mn ty* ⸢*šꜥ ḏ.t*⸣	12. *Pꜣ-ti-Ḫnsw* remains here ⸢for ever⸣.
13. *pꜣ rn nfr* ...	13. The good name ...
14. ... *mn ty šꜥ ḏ.t*	14. ... remains here forever.
15. *pꜣ rn nfr* ...	15. The good name ...

Commentary

Line 2

(a) *Pꜣy=s(?)* would presumably be part of a personal name, perhaps *Pꜣy=s-nfr, Demot. Nb.*, 448.

Line 4

(a) One might expect *pꜣ bik* at the beginning of the line, but the traces are too vague to interpret.

(b) We had first read *[nꜣ] ꜥ.wy.w ẖry.w*, "[the] lower places," already mentioned in graff. 4, 3, which would designate back chambers of the tomb. We are now doubtful of this transliteration here.

Line 11

(a) *Ṯ* is plausible, but it does not seem possible to read *ntr.w* after it.

32. Graffito TT 11/32 (Plate 27)

Location: Main corridor, N-wall

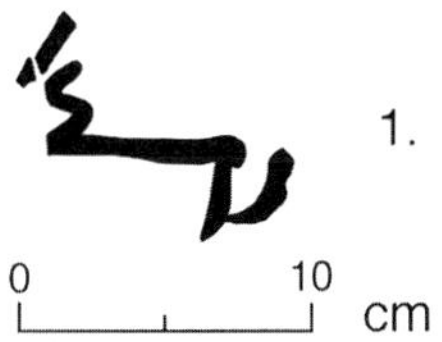

Transliteration	Translation
1. *pꜣ rn*	1. the name

Commentary

The graffito seems never to have been finished.

33a and 33b. Graffito TT 11/33 (Plate 30)

Location: Main corridor, N-wall

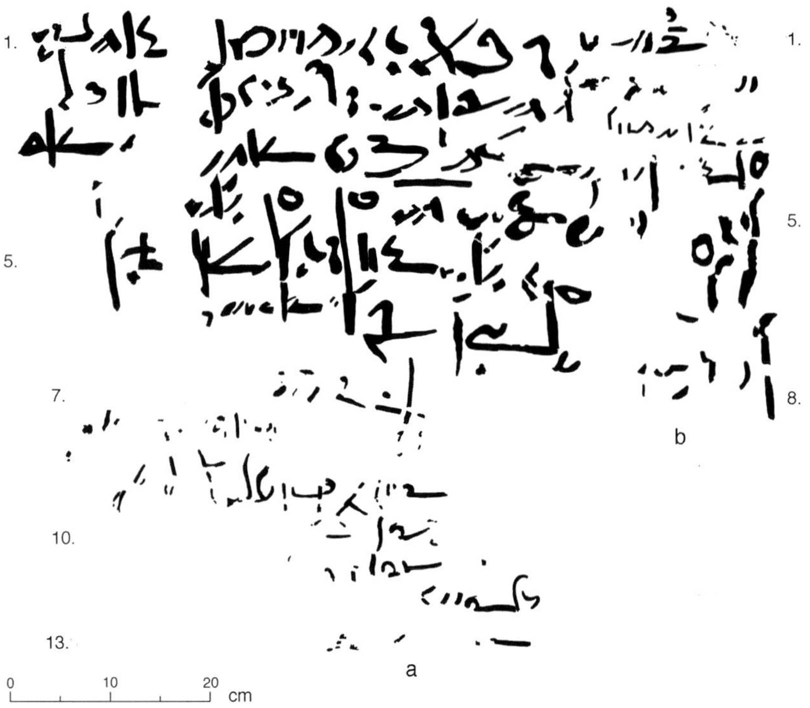

TRANSLITERATION A

1. *tꜣ mỉ.t r ⸢hyn.w⸣ ꜥ.wy.w ḥtp*
2. *r(?) pr ỉmnṱ n tꜣ ẖ.t mḥ-3.t ḏm*
3. *⸢r pḥ⸣ šꜥ rꜣ [r] ⸢tꜣ⸣ rnp.t*
4. *pꜣ bnr nꜣy sẖ sẖ Pꜣy=f-ṯꜣw-[ꜥ.wy-Ḫnsw]*
5. *sẖ Pꜣy=f-ṯꜣw-ꜥ.wy- Ḫnsw sꜣ Ns-Mn*
6. *pꜣ wr Ḏḥwty ...*
7. *ḥ.t-sp 9 ⸢ỉbt 3⸣(?) ...*
8. ...
9. *mn ty m-bꜣḥ Ḏḥwty ...*
10. ...
11. ...
12. ... *mn* ...
13. ...

TRANSLATION A

1. The path to ⸢some⸣ places of rest
2. for/to(?) the west of the third group of offspring
3. ⸢to arrive⸣ up to the entrance [for] ⸢the⸣ year
4. outside of these (areas?). Has written the scribe *Pꜣy=f-ṯꜣw-[ꜥ.wy-Ḫnsw].*
5. Has written *Pꜣy=f-ṯꜣw-ꜥ.wy-Ḫnsw*, son of *Ns-Mn*,
6. the great one of Thoth, ...
7. regnal year 9, ⸢third month⸣(?) ...
8. ...
9. remains here before Thoth ...
10. ...
11. ...
12. ... remains ...
13. ...

Commentary

The graffiti here seem in part to be superimposed upon one another. It is consequently difficult to distinguish the texts. The line numbers for graff. 33a are shown on the left side of the text and the ones for graff. 33b on the right side. We took the faint inscription on the bottom as part of graff. 33a, but it could very well belong to graff. 33b or even be a different graffito altogether. A closely related graffito written by the same scribe is graff. 53.

Line 1

(a) *Mỉ.t*, "der Weg," *Glossar*, 152, is a plausible reading. This is obviously a directional text.

(b) *ꜥ.wy* is clear, but there is much damage to the end of the line. The vertical stroke after the place determinative is probably the plural *w* ending. The following traces fit *ḥtp* fairly well.

Line 2

(a) Since *ḏm*, "Nachkomme," *Glossar*, 678, clearly designates the sacred birds, the interesting expression "the third group/body of the offspring," may perhaps refer to the third collective burial of the ibis and falcon mummies. There are indeed such clusterings in the Upper Gallery, tomb -399-/ TT 12 Hery. Thus this graffito may refer to the "third" collective burial.

Line 3

(a) This passage evidently describes the location of the burials of the sacred birds. Graffito 53, which has a very similar content, is written by the same person.

(b) There is little lost here and we thus restore a preposition, for example, *r* or *n*.

(c) The trace before *rnp.t* may be the upper part of the definite article *tꜣ*.

(d) The force of "for the year" is uncertain. Does this refer to the burial or delivery of sacred mummies for the year?

Line 4

(a) *Pꜣ bnr*, "ausserhalb," *Glossar*, 118.

(b) We understand *nꜣy* as the demonstrative pronoun, "diese," *Glossar*, 203. Does it refer to the burial areas (i.e., "these places of rest") or perhaps even to the sacred mummies themselves?

(c) The writer seems to have become confused. He wrote his name again in line 5, adding the title *wr Ḏḥwty* after his name to the title of *sẖ*, "scribe," written before his name here in line 4. In graff. 53 the same man appears with the two titles (*sẖ* and *wr Ḏḥwty*).[196]

Line 5

(a) The same scribe wrote graff. 53. For the name *Pꜣy=f-ṯꜣw=ꜥ.wy-Ḫnsw*, see *Demot. Nb.*, 447.

Transliteration B	Translation B
1. ... *ꜥq(?) ...*	1. ... to cause to enter(?) ...
2. ...	2. ...
3. ... *pꜣ hb ...*	3. ... the ibis ...
4. *sẖ(?) ...*	4. Has written(?) ...
5. ...	5. ...
6. ...	6. ...
7. ...	7. ...
8. ...	8. ...

Commentary

Line 1

(a) *ꜥq*,"to cause to enter," is the technical term for the process of interment of the sacred birds; see note (a) on graff. 9, 3.

[196] Graffito 53, 4–5: *sẖ.w sẖ Pꜣy=f-ṯꜣw-ꜥ.wy-Ḫnsw sꜣ Ns-Mn pꜣ wr Ḏḥwty*.

34. Graffito TT 11/34 (Plate 31)

Location: Main corridor, N-wall[197]

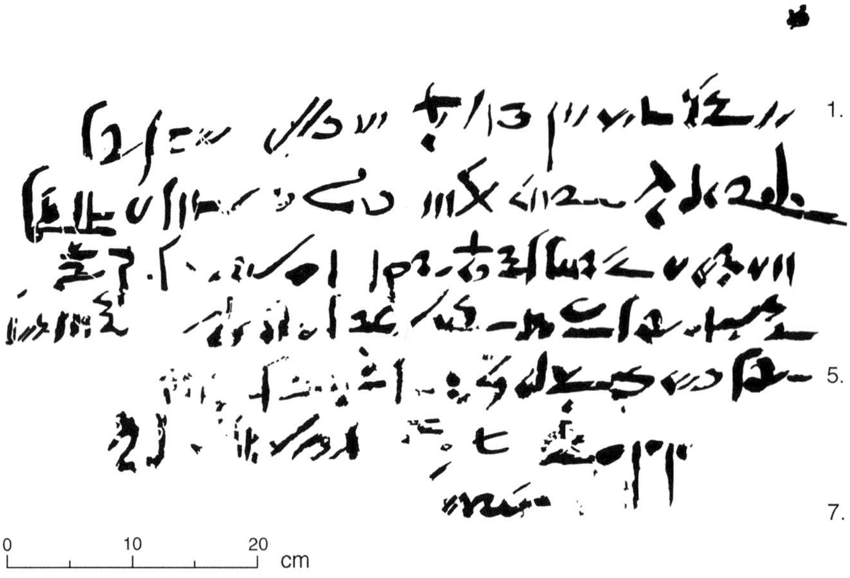

TRANSLITERATION	TRANSLATION
1. *pꜣ rn nfr Pꜣ-ỉšwr sꜣ Pꜣ-mrl pꜣ wr Ḏḥwty*	1. The good name of *Pꜣ-ỉšwr*, son of *Pꜣ-mrl*, the great one of Thoth
2. *n ḥ.t-sp 9.t r ḥ.t-sp 10.t mn ty m-bꜣḥ pꜣ hb pꜣ bỉk*	2. from regnal year 9 to regnal year 10 remains here before the ibis (and) the falcon
3. *ỉrm nꜣy=w pꜣ ṯ nꜣ ntr.w ꜥꜣ n nꜣ rmt.w (n) tꜣ mr.t n wꜥ sp*	3. together with the ones of the taker of the gods, the great one of the men (of) the harbor at one time.
4. *ꜥq=w Ḏḥwty ḫnṱ Wsr ... r [pꜣ] ỉrpy*	4. They caused to enter Thoth, foremost of Thebes ... to [the] divine chapel
5. *n Ḏḥwty m-sꜣ ỉr rnp.t ꜥšꜣ.w n ḥ.t-ntr ...*	5. of Thoth after spending many years in the temple ....
6. *[...] sẖ sẖ Ns-Mn-...(?) sꜣ Hr ... ḥ.t-sp 10.t(?)*	6. [...] Has written the scribe *Ns-Mn-...(?)*, son of *Hr* ... regnal year 10(?)
7. *... ỉbt 3(?) pr.t ...*	7. ... third(?) month of winter ...

Commentary

Line 1

(a) For *Pꜣ-ỉšwr*, see *Demot. Nb.*, 158.

(b) For *Pꜣ-mrl*, see *Demot. Nb.*, 190. An alternative reading is *Pꜣ-šrr*, compare *Pꜣ-šll* in graff. 83, 2 and 84, 1, but *Pꜣ-mrl* occurs also in graff. 34, 1 and 45, 5.

---

[197] For an image of the conservator Nieves López Meijueiro during cleaning graff. 34, see https://proyectodjehuty.com/30-enero-2013/.

Line 2

(a) Was the position of "great one of Thoth" held for one year?

Line 3

(a) "The ones of the taker of the gods" seems to designate the staff of that office or, alternatively, his family; for the *ṯ nꜣ ntr.w* , see pp. 63-64.

(b) "The great one of the men of the harbor" is an otherwise unattested title. The "men of the harbor" appear also in graff. 19, 5 and 74, 3.

Line 4

(a) Once more the verb *ꜥq* denotes the interment of the sacred bird; see note (a) on graff. 9, 3. This bird receives the epithet "foremost of Thebes." This epithet occurs also in graff. 14, 1–2.

(b) We understand the short horizontal stroke to belong to *ḫnṱ*, and not as the genitive *n*.

(c) In graff. 14, 1–2, *ḫnty Wsr* concludes with the divine determinative. We had first thought that a place determinative came here after *ḫnty Wsr*. However, we now suspect that what follows should be the date of the burial of the sacred ibis. Thus, one would like to read at least *ḥ.t-sp 10.t ỉbt x*. The available space seems insufficient for a season and day. Unfortunately, even with digital enhancement, the visible traces do not permit certainty.

(d) *ỉrpy* would appear to refer to the tomb, while the *ḥ.t-ntr* in line 5 would denote the space of the living birds.

Line 6

(a) *Ns-Mn-...(?)* is a mere suggestion, although it does seem that *Mn* may be read. There is clearly too much written here for only *Ns-Mn*.

Line 7

(a) Perhaps read *ỉbt 4* .

35. Graffito TT 11/35 (Plate 32)

Location: Main corridor, N-wall

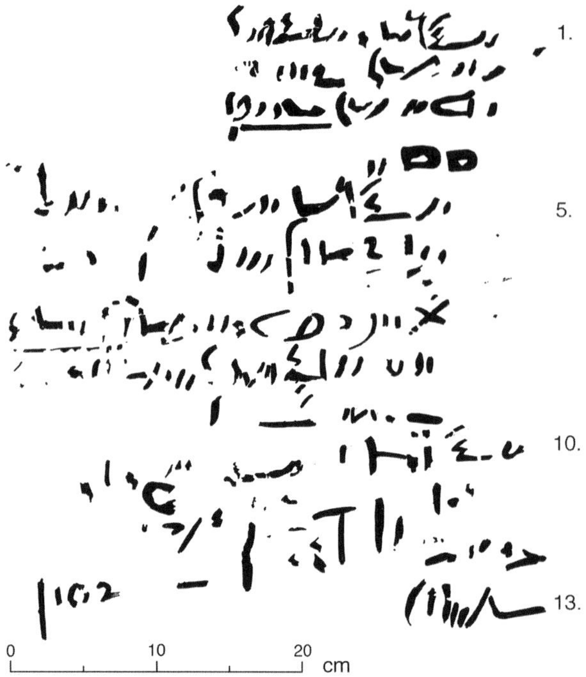

Transliteration

1. *pꜣ rn nfr Pꜣ-...*
2. *sꜣ Pꜣ-hb mn* ⸢*ty*⸣
3. *m-bꜣḥ pꜣ hb pꜣ bỉk*
4. ⸢*šꜥ ḏ.t(?)*⸣ ...
5. *pꜣ rn nfr Ḏḥwty-*⸢*sḏm*⸣ *sꜣ Pꜣ-šr-[Mn]*
6. *Pꜣ-šr-Ḫnsw sꜣ Pꜣ-šr-... [mn]*
7. *ty m-bꜣḥ pꜣ hb pꜣ bỉk*
8. *ỉrm Pꜣ-...* ⸢*sꜣ Pꜣ-hb*⸣
9. ...
10. *pꜣ rn nfr* ⸢*Pꜣ-hb*⸣*(?) ...*
11. ...
12. ...
13. ...

Translation

1. The good name *Pꜣ-...*,
2. son of *Pꜣ-hb*, remains ⸢here⸣
3. before the ibis (and) the falcon
4. ⸢forever(?)⸣ ...
5. The good name *Ḏḥwty-*⸢*sḏm*⸣, son of *Pꜣ-šr-[Mn]*,
6. *Pꜣ-šr-Ḫnsw*, son of *Pꜣ-šr-...* [remains]
7. here before the ibis (and) the falcon
8. together with *Pꜣ-...*, ⸢son of *Pꜣ-hb*⸣
9. ...
10. The good name of ⸢*Pꜣ-hb*⸣*(?)* ...,
11. ...
12. ...
13. ...

Commentary

Line 1

(a) We are unable to read the name. It seems to begin with *Pꜣ*, but the remaining group puzzles us. The last sign may be the divine determinative. The same name almost certainly occurs in line 8.

Line 8

(a) *Pꜣ-...* may be the same name as in line 1.

36. Graffito TT 11/36 (Plate 33)

Location: Main corridor, N-wall

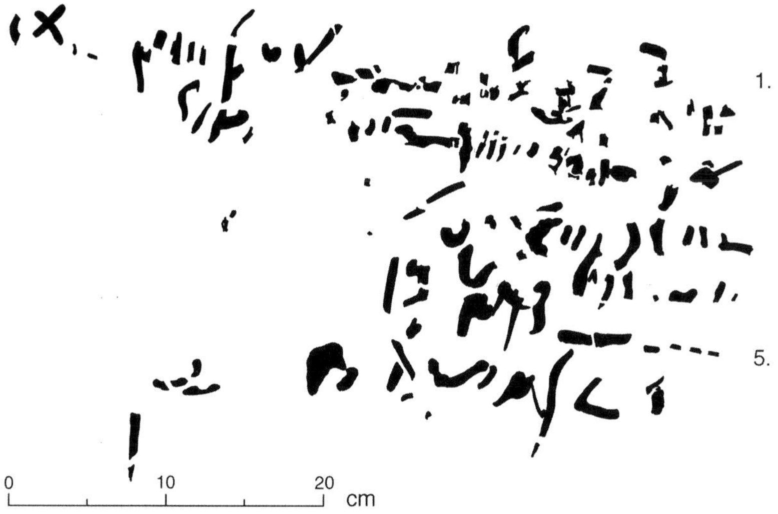

This graffito is illegible apart from a few isolated signs. One might perhaps suggest *ty*, "here," in line 1 and *ỉnp* in line 2 .

37. Graffito TT 11/37 (Plate 34)

Location: Main corridor, N-wall

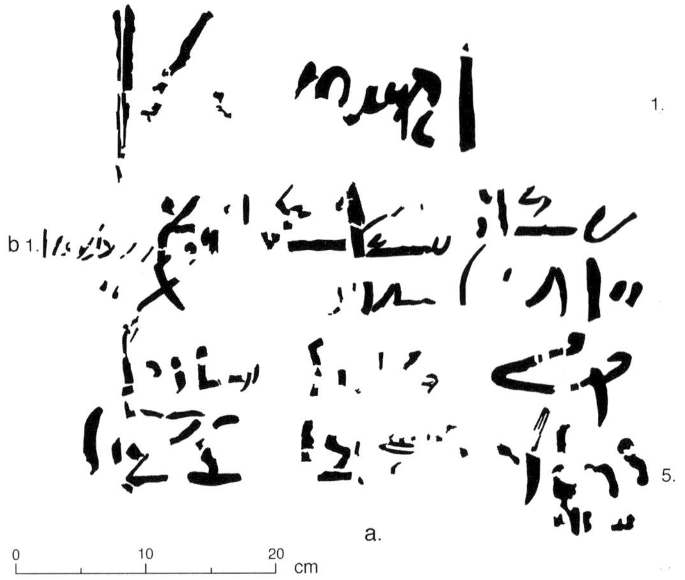

Transliteration A	Translation A
1. *Ḥ.t-sp 10.t ỉbt 4 … sw 11*	1. Regnal year 10, fourth month of …, day 11.
2. *pꜣ rn nfr …-ꜣIs.t (sꜣ)*	2. The good name of …-*ꜣIs.t*, (son of)
3. *Pꜣ-tỉ-… […mn] ty*	3. *Pꜣ-tỉ-…* […remains] here
4. *m-bꜣḥ ⌜pꜣ hb⌝ pꜣ bỉk*	4. before ⌜the ibis⌝ (and) the falcon
5. *…ꜥ.wy ḥtp*	5. … place of rest
6. …	6. …

Commentary

Line 1

(a) "Day 11" is strikingly common in this corpus of graffiti.

Line 3

(a) Perhaps read rather *Pꜣ-ỉhy* at the beginning of the line, compare *Demot. Nb.*, 157.

Transliteration B	Translation B
1. *pꜣ rn nfr …*	1. The good name of …

Commentary

Line 1

(a) Graffito 37a almost completely covers graff. 37b; only this one line seems to be preserved.

38. Graffito TT 11/38 (Plate 35)

Location: Main corridor, N-wall

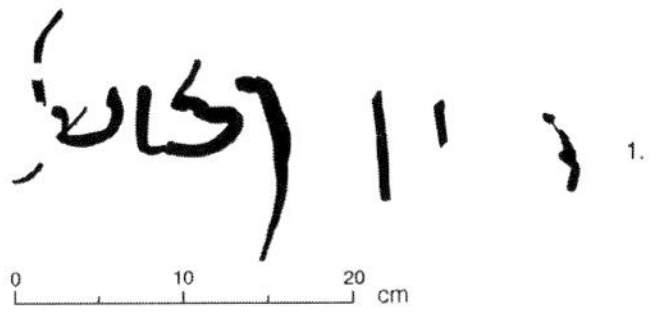

Transliteration	Translation
1. ...	1. ...

39. Graffito TT 11/39 (Plate 35)

Location: Main corridor, N-wall

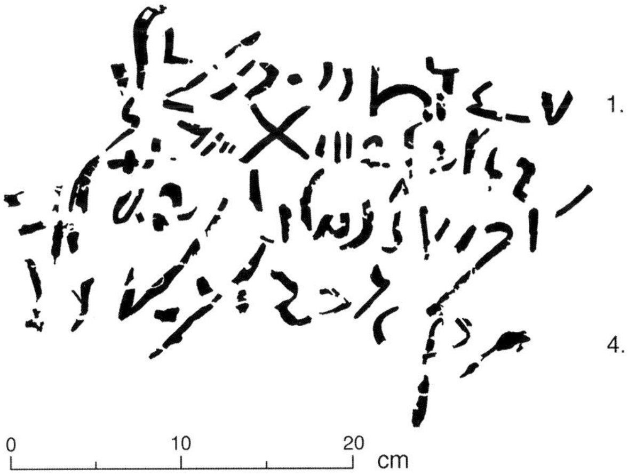

Transliteration	Translation
1. *pꜣ rn nfr Hr*	1. The good name of *Hr,*
2. *sꜣ Ḫnsw-Ḏḥwty mn ty šꜥ ḏ.t*	2. son of *Ḫnsw-Ḏḥwty*, remains here forever
3. *ḥnꜥ Pꜣ-ti-Ḥr-pꜣ-ẖrṱ(?) sꜣ Ḏḥwty-⌜...⌝(?)*	3. together with *Pꜣ-ti-Ḥr-pꜣ-ẖrṱ*(?), son of *Ḏḥwty-⌜...⌝*(?)
4. ... *rmt nb nt ꜣlr*	4. ... every man who is (in) mourning.

Commentary

Line 1

(a) Perhaps *n Hr.*

Line 4

(a) Restore possibly *ḥnꜥ*, "together with," at the beginning of the line.

(b) For *ꜣlr*, compare *ꜣrl*, "Klage," *Glossar*, 6; *ꜣll*, "to cry out," *CDD* ꜣ, 55. The traces at the end of the word are damaged. This seems to designate the cult workers, who are described as mourning for the deceased sacred animals.

40. Graffito TT 11/40 (Plate 36)

Location: Main corridor, N-wall

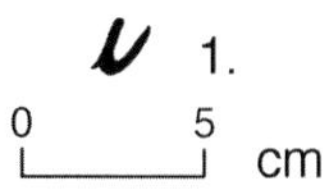

Transliteration	Translation
1. *pꜣ*	1. The

Commentary
This graffito seems never to have been finished.

41. Graffito TT 11/41 (Plate 36)

Location: Doorway between main corridor and chapel, N-jamb, E-face

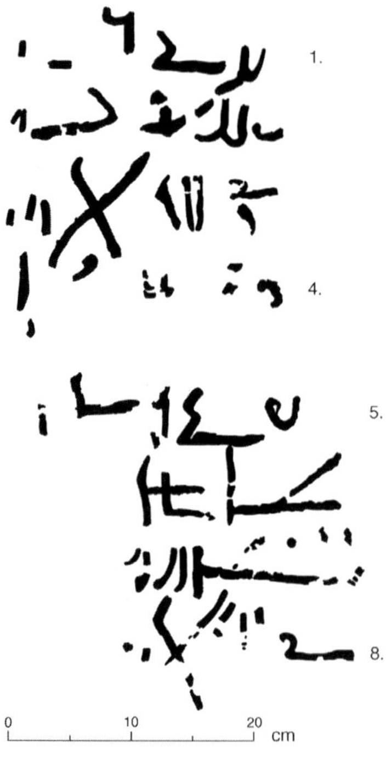

Transliteration	Translation
1. *pꜣ rn* ⸢*nfr*⸣	1. The ⸢good⸣ name of
2. ... *Ḥr-Ḏḥwty(?)* ...	2. ... *Ḥr-Ḏḥwty(?)* ...
3. *mn ty*	3. remains here
4. ⸢*m-bꜣḥ*⸣ ...	4. ⸢before⸣ ...
5. *pꜣ rn nfr*	5. The good name of
6. *Ns-Mn*	6. *Ns-Mn*,
7. *sꜣ Ns(?)-...*	7. son of *Ns(?)-...*
8. *mn ty*	8. remains here.

Commentary

Line 2

(a) Perhaps *sꜣ*, "son," at the beginning of the line.

Line 7

(a) Possibly *Ns* may be recognized in this line.

42. Graffito TT 11/42 (Plate 37)

Location: Doorway between main corridor and chapel, N-jamb, S-face

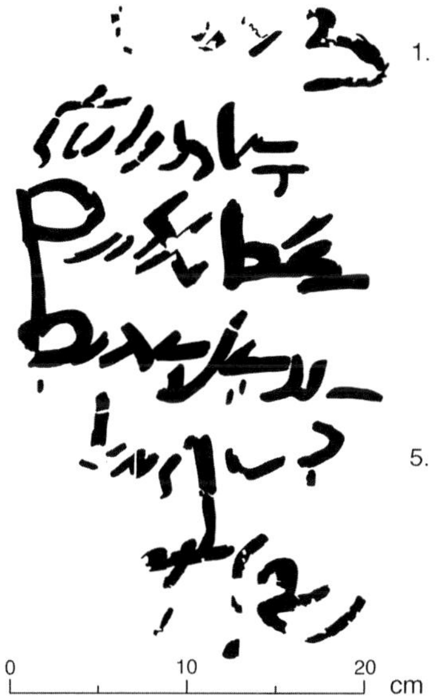

Transliteration	Translation
1. *wn ...*	1. There are/is ...
2. *qs(.t)(?) ꜥꜣ.t*	2. a great burial(?)
3. *ḥtp ty ḥry*	3. (at) rest here above
4. *n pꜣ trt ḥry(?)*	4. the stairs above(?).
5. *... sẖ Pꜣ-šr-[Ỉmn]*	5. ... Has written *Pꜣ-šr-[Ỉmn]*,
6. *sꜣ Ḏḥwty-⸢sḏm⸣*	6. son of *Ḏḥwty-⸢sḏm⸣*

Commentary

Line 1

(a) This graffito is evidently a directional text. Perhaps restore *hyn.w*, "some," after *wn*?

Line 2

(a) We tentatively propose *qs.t*, "Begräbnis," *Glossar*, 549. The reading is quite uncertain, but the point of the graffito seems to inform cult workers that certain burials are above the stairs, which is located nearby. *ꜥꜣ.t* is secure.

Line 3

(a) The syntax is obscure here. It is difficult to determine how *ḥtp* relates to the previous lines.

Line 4
(a) It is odd that *ḥry* is repeated in both lines 3 and 4.

Line 5
(a) Perhaps read *ꜥn* "also," at the beginning of line.

43. Graffito TT 11/43 (Plate 37)

Location: Doorway between main corridor and chapel, N-jamb, E-face

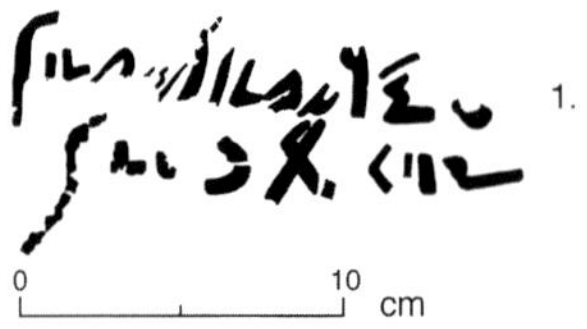

Transliteration	Translation
1. *pꜣ rn Pꜣ-hb sꜣ Pꜣ-hb*	1. The name of *Pꜣ-hb*, son of *Pꜣ-hb*,
2. *mn ty šꜥ ḏ.t*	2. remains here forever.

Commentary

Line 1
(a) Curiously *nfr* is absent in this line.

44. Graffito TT 11/44 (Plate 38)

Location: Chapel, E-wall

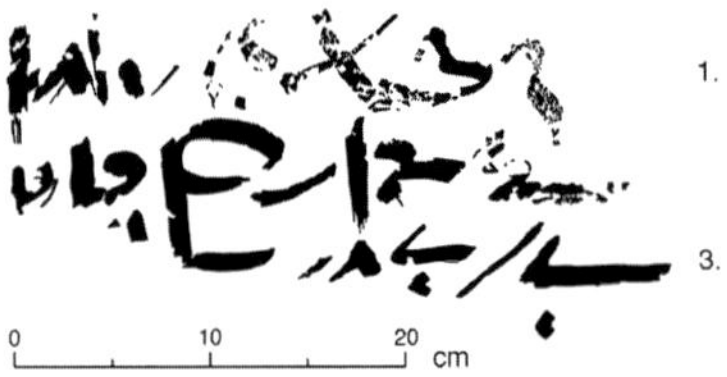

Transliteration	Translation
1. *tꜣ mi̓.t r nꜣ ꜥ.wy.w*	1. The path to the places of
2. *ḥtp r-ḥry ḥr pꜣ*	2. rest above upon the
3. *trt …*	3. stairs …

Commentary

Line 1
(a) This is another directional text, obviously related to the stairway close by.

TOMB –399–

45. Graffito Tomb –399–/1 (Plate 39)

Location: Tomb –399-, underground chamber UE 245, N-wall

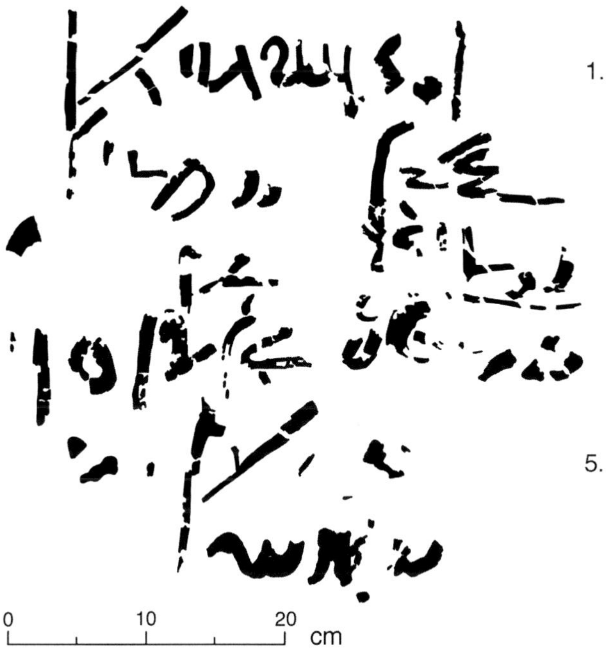

Transliteration	Translation
1. *ḥ.t-sp 20 ỉbt 4 pr.t sw 11*	1. Regnal year 20, fourth month of winter, day 11
2. *ḥtp pꜣ hb*	2. resting-(place?) (of) the ibis (and)
3. *pꜣ bỉk ...*	3. the falcon ...
4. ... *pꜣ wr Ḏḥwty sẖ*	4. ... the great one of Thoth. Has written
5. ... *[Pꜣ-]⸢mrl⸣ ...*	5. ... *[Pꜣ-]⸢mrl⸣ ...*
6. ... *ỉbt 3(?) ...*	6. ... third month(?) ...

Commentary

Line 1

(a) Again, we have the striking appearance of day 11.

Line 2

(a) The force of *ḥtp* is difficult. Is this an infinitive, "the resting in peace (of)"? One suspects that the graffito records the interment of the sacred animal mummies.

Lines 3–4

(a) The name of the "great one of Thoth," and perhaps his father, are lost.

Line 5

(a) Compare *Pꜣ-mrl*, *Demot. Nb.*, 190–91. The same name seems to appear in graff. 34, 1.

46. Graffito Tomb –399–/2 (Plate 42)

Location: Tomb –399–, underground chamber UE 245, E-wall

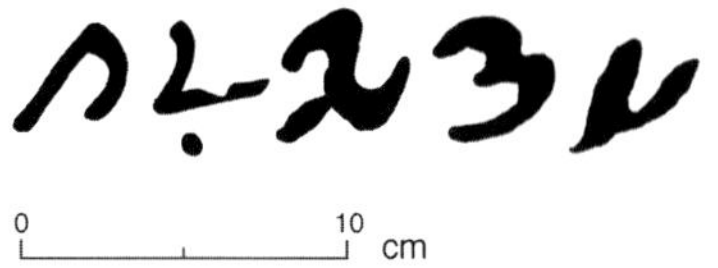

1.

TRANSLITERATION

1. *p3 m3t (r-)ḥry(?)*

TRANSLATION

1. The path up(?)

Commentary

Line 1

(a) *m3t* appears to be a variant of *myt*, "der Weg," *Glossar*, 153. Perhaps read *r-ḥry*, "up, upwards, above," or *ḥry* after *m3t*, that is, "upper path," or "the path above," but then the determinative is absent. In any case the determinative (the house determinative) would be strangely formed. We have considered *m3q*, comparing *mky*, "Leiter," *Glossar*, 183, but this is also problematic. It may be simplest to observe that this graffito with the directional sign, "the path up(?)," was visible to those workers returning up the staircase after depositing the mummies (see fig. 7).

TOMB OF HERY (TT 12)

For a keyplan of the S-wall of the tomb of Hery (TT 12) showing the locations of the graffiti, see plates 40 and 41.[198]

47. **Graffito TT 12/1** (Plate 43)

Location: Thickness of the passage/break connecting tomb -399- with TT 12, E-wall

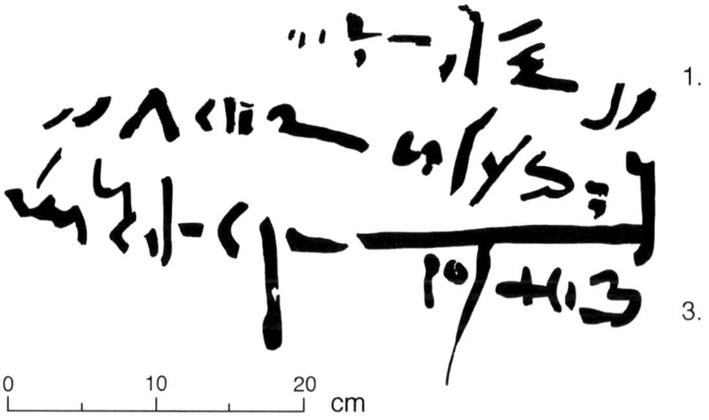

TRANSLITERATION

1. *pꜣ rn nfr [...]*
2. *mw.t=f Tꜣy-lwꜣ(?) mn* ⸢*ty*⸣
3. *šꜥ ḏ.t sẖ(?) sẖ n ḥ.t-sp 2.t ỉbt 3 [...]*

TRANSLATION

1. The good name of [...]
2. whose mother is *Tꜣy-lwꜣ(?)*, remains ⸢here⸣
3. forever. Written(?). Written in regnal year 2, third month [...]

Commentary

This graffito was added after a passageway was broken through the wall between tomb -399- and TT 12 (Hery). For a description of the damage suffered by the walls of the tomb of Hery and the valuable information conveyed in Spiegelberg's squeezes kept at the Griffith Institute in Oxford, see Galán and Menéndez, "Funerary Banquet of Hery," 143–66.

Line 2

(a) *Tꜣy-lwꜣ* is very insecure, compare *Demot. Nb.*, 1199.

Line 3

(a) The suggested *sẖ* after *ḏ.t* is not certain.

198 See appendix B for additional recently discovered graffiti from this tomb. The wall drawings of TT 12 are by G. Menéndez.

48. Graffito TT 12/2 (Plate 42)

Location: Main corridor, S-wall

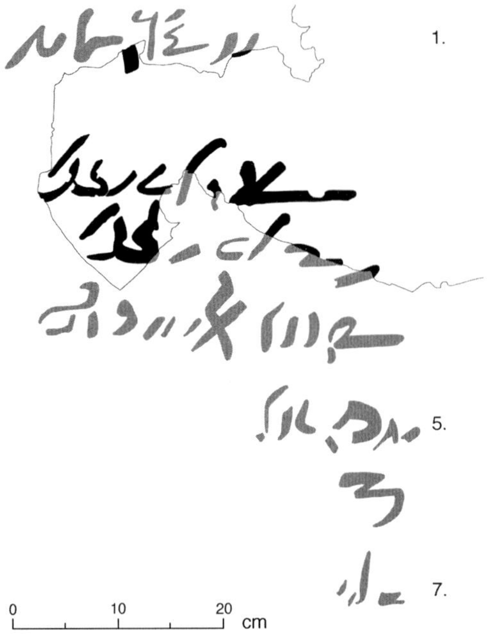

Transliteration

1. *pꜣ rn nfr*
2. *Wsỉr-wr sꜣ Ḥr*
3. *sꜣ Gl-šr sꜣ Ḥr*
4. *mn ty m-bꜣḥ*
5. *pꜣ hb ...*
6. *š[ꜥ ḏ.t(?) ...]*
7. *n ḥ.t-sp ...*

Translation

1. The good name
2. of *Wsỉr-wr*, son of *Ḥr*,
3. son of *Gl-šr*, son of *Ḥr*,
4. remains here before
5. the ibis ...
6. for[ever (?) ...]
7. in regnal year ...

Commentary

(Spiegelberg #29, pl. 30; Vleeming, *Graffiti*, 117–18 [#1473])

The graffito has suffered serious damage since Spiegelberg copied it. The lost text is represented in the hand-copy by gray.

Line 3

(a) The initial stroke looks like *sꜣ*, but the sequence is certainly awkward. The extended genealogy would be unusual; see the comments of Vleeming, *Graffiti*, 118.

Line 7

(a) Vleeming, *Graffiti*, 118 reads ⸢*nḥḥ.*⸣

49. Graffito TT 12/3 (Plate 44)

Location: Main corridor, S-wall

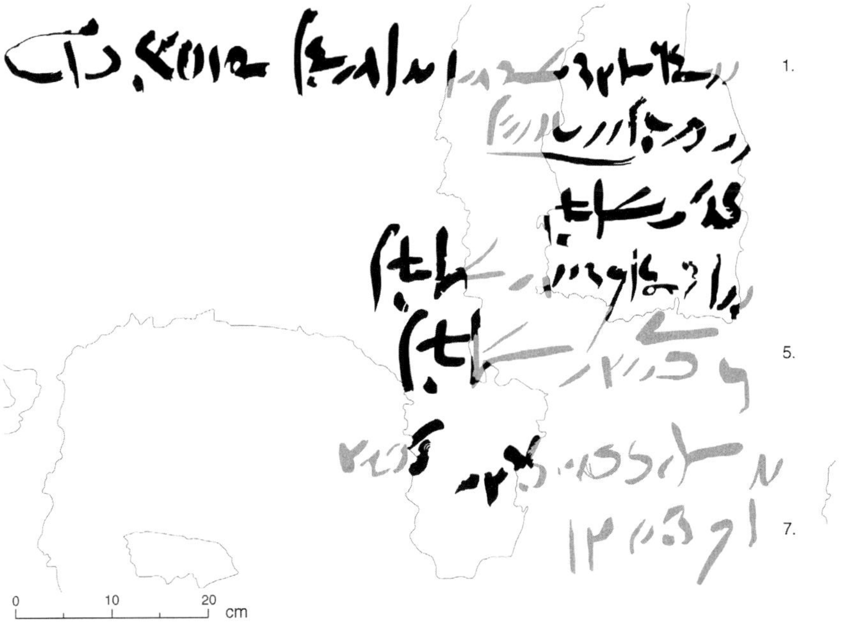

Transliteration	Translation
1. *pꜣ rn nfr nꜣ ỉry.w-ꜥꜣ pꜣ ꜥ.wy ḥtp mn ty m-bꜣḥ*	1. The good name of the pastophoroi of the place of rest remains here before
2. *pꜣ hb pꜣ bỉk*	2. the ibis (and) the falcon:
3. *Ḥr sꜣ Ns-Mn*	3. *Ḥr*, son of *Ns-Mn*
4. *ꜥnḫ-rn=f sꜣ Ns-Mn*	4. *ꜥnḫ-rn=f*, son of *Ns-Mn*
5. *Pa-tm sꜣ Ns-Mn*	5. *Pa-tm*, son of *Ns-Mn*
6. *Pꜣ-nfr-ỉr-ḥr sꜣ Ḏ-ḥr*	6. *Pꜣ-nfr-ỉr-ḥr*, son of *Ḏ-ḥr*
7. *ḥnꜥ nꜣy=w rmt.w*	7. together with their people.

Commentary

(Spiegelberg #28, pl. 30; Vleeming, *Graffiti*, 117 [#1472])

The graffito has suffered serious damage since Spiegelberg copied it. The lost text is represented in the hand-copy by gray.

Line 1

(a) The "pastophoroi of the place of rest" are only mentioned in this graffito. The title of *ỉry-ꜥꜣ* is otherwise not associated with the sacred animal cult in this corpus. See, however, Scalf, "Resurrecting an Ibis Cult," 368. For the reading *ỉry-ꜥꜣ*, see Hoffmann and Quack, "Pastophoros," 127–55.

Line 3

(a) Vleeming, *Graffiti*, 117, observes: "Three sons of Esmin are here commemorated together with Pneferho. They belong to a priestly family known from several papyri," citing Pestman, *Recueil de textes démotiques*, vol. 2, table opposite p. 73. Pestman (table) remarks that Horus seems to have died about 176 BC.

Line 4

(a) The damaged first preserved sign might be *pꜣ*, but this is not secure. The traces suggest *m/ nt ꜥ.wy=f*, but we cannot read this name with confidence. Perhaps *Pꜣ-tỉ-nꜣ-bꜣk.w*, *Demot. Nb.*, 315? Vleeming, *Graffiti*, 117, reads *ꜥnḫ-rn=f.*

Line 5

(a) For *Pꜣ-nfr-ḥr*, see *Demot. Nb.*, 192–93.

50. Graffito TT 12/4 (Plate 45)

Location: Main corridor, S-wall[199]

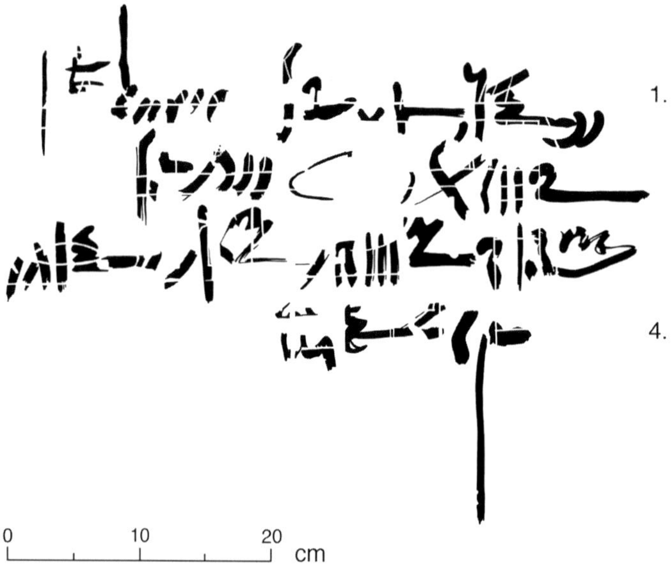

Transliteration

1. *pꜣ rn nfr Ḏḥwty-⸢sḏm⸣ (sꜣ) Pꜣ-šr-Mn*
2. *mn ty m-bꜣḥ pꜣ hb*
3. *wn-nꜣ.w nꜣ-ꜥšꜣy nꜣy=f šms.w r pꜣ ꜥ.wy (ḥtp)*
4. *sḫ bꜣk.w*

Translation

1. The good name of *Ḏḥwty-⸢sḏm⸣*, (son of) *Pꜣ-šr-Mn*,
2. remains here before the ibis.
3. Numerous were his servants at the place (of rest).
4. Have written the servants.

Commentary

(Spiegelberg #30, pl. 30; Vleeming, *Graffiti*, 118 [#1474])

Line 1

(a) The transliteration *Ḏḥwty-sḏm* is reasonable, although the *sḏm* is much damaged.

Line 3

(a) The imperfect converter is followed by the adjective verb *nꜣ-ꜥšꜣ*, a rather elaborate construction for a graffito.

(b) *šms*, "Diener," *Glossar*, 511, is a plausible reading. The writer proudly asserts that there were many individuals participating in the ibis cult in this section of the tomb. Vleeming, *Graffiti*, 118, has

[199] https://proyectodjehuty.com/09-febrero-2019/.

with hesitation followed Spiegelberg's translation: "The favoured ones had been brought(?) into the place."

Line 4

(a) One expects, of course, just a personal name after *sẖ*, but this seems to be the title or phrase *sẖ b3k.w*, "written by the servants," *CDD B*, 15, s.v. *b3k*; H. Thissen, "Zu den demotischen Graffiti von Medinet Habu," *Enchoria* 2 (1972): 49.

51. Graffito TT 12/5 (Plate 46)

Location: Main corridor, N-wall

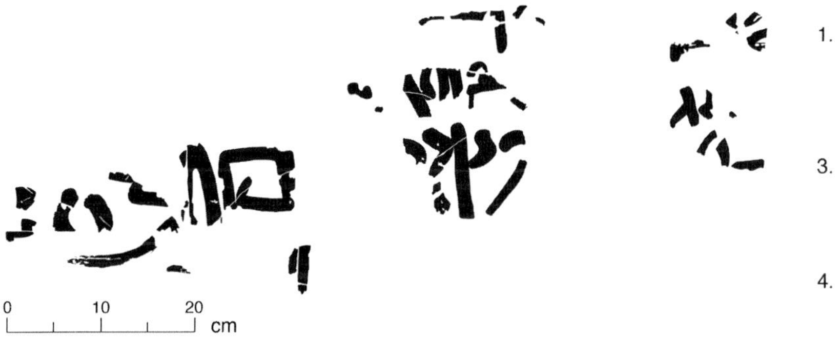

Transliteration	Translation
1. *[p3]* ⸢*rn nfr*⸣ ...	1. [The] ⸢good name of⸣ ...
2. ... *mn* ⸢*ty*⸣ ...	2. ... remains ⸢here⸣ ...
3. ... *rmt nb* ⸢*nt*⸣*[...]* ... ⸢*šʿ ḏ.t*⸣	3. ... every man ⸢who⸣ [...] ... ⸢forever.⸣
4. *[...]* ... *[...]*	4. [...] ... [...]

Commentary

Initially only one small section of the graffito was in situ. The conservator Miguel Ángel Navarro joined several loose fragments of this inscription found in the debris and returned them to their proper position on the wall.[200] There is still, however, considerable damage to the text, and there may be more than one graffito here.

Line 3

(a) *Nt* seems to be a plausible restoration; compare, for example, graff. 4, 1 and 39, 4.

(b) *šʿ ḏ.t* is a reasonable reading of the traces, but hardly certain, given the lack of context.

[200] https://proyectodjehuty.com/19-febrero-2017/.

52. Graffito TT 12/6 (Plate 50)

Location: Chapel, E-wall

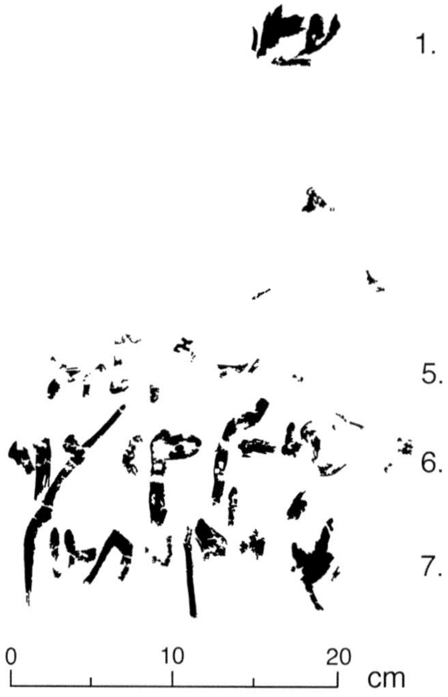

TRANSLITERATION	TRANSLATION
1. *[...] pꜣ b[ỉ]k(?) [...]*	1. [...] the fa[l]con(?) [...]
Presumably numerous lines lost	Presumably numerous lines lost
6. *[š]ꜥ ḏ.t sẖ Lwꜣ*	6. [for]ever. Has written *Lwꜣ*,
7. *sꜣ Ḥr sẖ Pꜣ-hb*	7. son of *Ḥr*. Has written *Pꜣ-hb*

Commentary

Line 6

(a) *Lwꜣ*, son of *Ḥr*, appears also in graff. 62b, 3 and in the unplaced fragment graff. 59c.

Line 7

(a) Alternatively translate "the scribe *Pꜣ-hb*."

EASTERN GALLERIES

53. Graffito UE 212/1 (Plate 51)

Location: UE 212, W-wall[201]

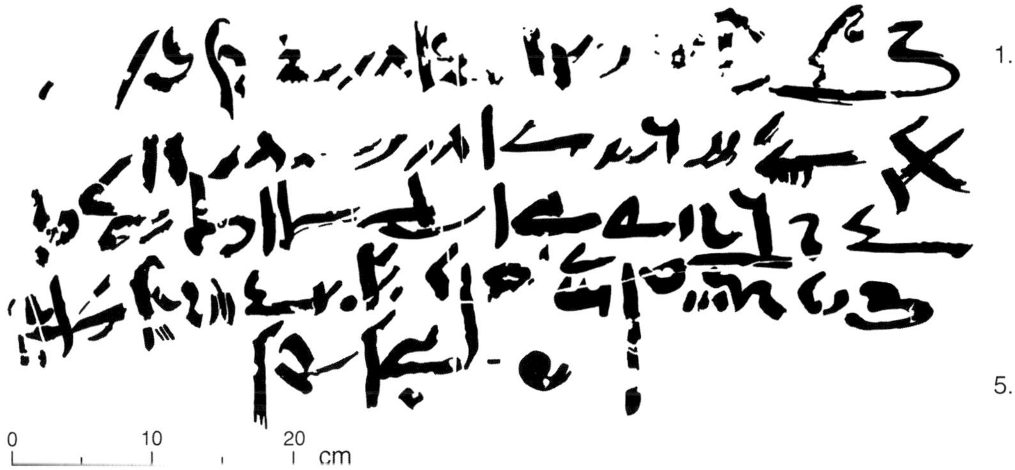

Transliteration

1. *wn* ⸢*hyn.w*⸣ *ꜥ.wy ḥtp ẖry*
2. *ty ṯ(?) pꜣy rꜣ r-[ẖ]n ỉw*
3. *bn nꜣ-sbk=w ỉn ḏm r pḥ*
4. *šꜥ nꜣy sẖ.w sẖ Pꜣy=f-ṯꜣw-ꜥ.wy-Ḫnsw sꜣ Ns-Mn*
5. *pꜣ wr Ḏḥwty*

Translation

1. There are ⸢some⸣ (more) places of rest below
2. here from(?) this entrance [in]side, since
3. they are not few, namely, the offspring, to reach
4. until these (areas). Has written the scribe, *Pꜣy=f-ṯꜣw-ꜥ.wy-Ḫnsw*, son of *Ns-Mn*,
5. the great one of Thoth.

Commentary

Line 1

(a) *wn* is slightly damaged, but certain.
(b) *hyn.w* fits the traces well. This graffito is clearly a directional text.

Line 2

(a) We had first understood the group after *ty* as *ṯsy*, "aufsteigen," *Glossar*, 670–71, but now think that *ṯ*, "from, since," *Glossar*, 667, is preferable. The writing is admittedly rather strange; there are unusual short strokes beneath the long horizontal line of *ṯ*. Moreover, we include the sign following the *ṯ*-group as part of the preposition, although it is hard to explain. Nevertheless, the preposition *ṯ* "from" yields the best sense in the context.
(b) *rꜣ*, "Eingang," *Glossar*, 240, seems most likely.
(c) Again, we had initially considered the two strokes as *sw* 6, "day 6," *Glossar*, 708, or *mỉ-nn*, "ebenso," *Glossar*, 152. We now think that the circumstantial converter *ỉw* is the simplest solution.

---

[201] For an illustration of graff. 53 being revealed during excavation, see https://proyectodjehuty.com/19-enero-2012/.

Line 3

(a) *ỉw bn ... ỉn* is the circumstantial negative first present construction.

(b) *nꜣ-sbk*, "klein ist," *Glossar*, 422.

(c) *ḏm*, "Geschlecht, Nachkomme, Generation," *Glossar*, 678, refers, we suggest, in these graffiti to the sacred birds. Apparently, the writer is emphasizing that there are additional (new) places of rest beyond this point. He then, in rather elaborate terms, declares that many birds have been laid to rest already in the shafts up to this area in the tomb.

(d) Is *r pḥ* an infinitive construction, or rather a perfect participle, the "generations who have reached?" A similar phrase occurs in graff. 33, 3.

Line 4

(a) *šꜥ* is clear, but what is the small stroke between *šꜥ* and *nꜣ*? Is this the walking legs determinative or the book-roll determinative of *šꜥ*, "bis," *Glossar*, 487–88?

(b) *nꜣy* is possible after *šꜥ*. We understand this to be the demonstrative pronoun "diese," *Glossar,* 203. The sense would be "these (areas/places)," that is, "up to here."

(c) The noun *sẖ.w*, *Glossar*, 459, seems here to be written for the verb *sẖ*. We had also considered the reading *nꜣy sẖ.w*, "these scribes," but that translation does not appear to yield sense here.

(d) For *Pꜣy=f-ṯꜣw-ꜥ.wy-Ḫnsw*, see *Demot. Nb.*, 447.

54. Graffito UE 212/2 (Plate 52)

Location: UE 212, N-wall

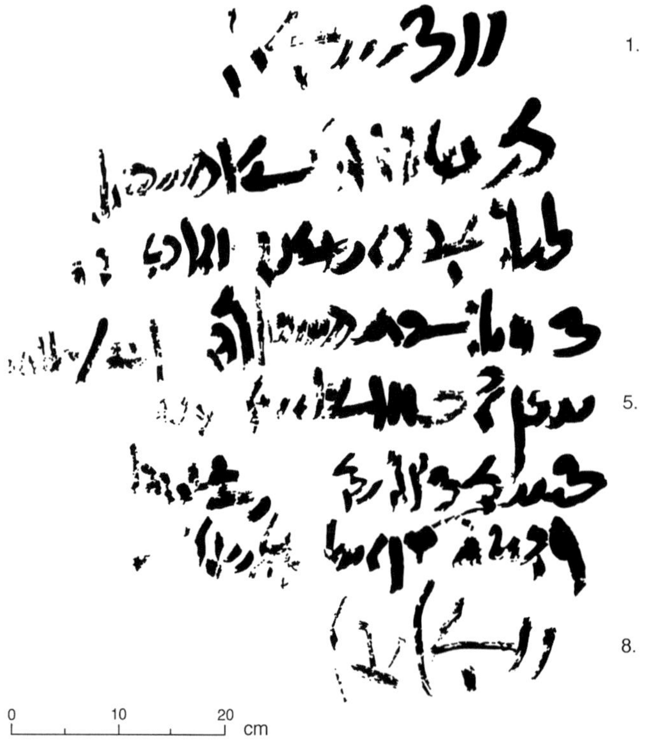

Transliteration	Translation
1. *pꜣ myt*	1. The path.
2. *tꜣy kꜣ.t ṯ=w hyn.w*	2. As for this chapel, they took some
3. *mt nḫṱ.t r-r=s ỉw=w ...*	3. thing(s) of protection(?) to it, they being ...
4. ... *ẖn hyn.w ḥnw bry*	4. ... in some new jars.
5. *pꜣ rmt nb nt ỉw=w (r) ỉy n-ỉm=s ...*	5. As for every man who will come therein (the chapel?) ...
6. *my ỉr=f šw(?) r-r=w r qs=w*	6. Let him do right(?) to them (the ibises) so as to bury them
7. *sf ... sẖ Pꜣ-[šr-M]n sꜣ Ḏḥwty-⌜sḏm⌝*	7. (with) resin. Has written *Pꜣ-[šr-M]n*, son of *Ḏḥwty-⌜sḏm⌝*,
8. *pꜣ wr Ḏḥwty*	8. the great one of Thoth.

Commentary

Line 1

(a) *myt*, "der Weg," *Glossar*, 153, is a plausible transliteration. There does not seem to be anything missing after *myt*. Is it a sort of heading? This text appears to contain both statements about the chapel and directives to the cult workers regarding the proper treatment of the animal mummies.

Line 2

(a) We think the word following *tꜣy* is a damaged writing of *gꜣ.t* "Kapelle," *Glossar*, 70, or *ꜥꜣb.t?*

(b) *ṯ=w* is reasonable, but the traces following are obscure. We propose *hyn.w*. Nothing is lost at the end of the line.

Line 3

(a) *mt nḫṱ.t* is the most obvious transliteration, but it is difficult to determine the force of the phrase, which we have not found elsewhere. *Mt nḫṱ.t* should probably be modified by *hyn.w* and function as the object of *ṯ=w*. We believe that *nḫṱ.t* is most likely to be identified with *nḫṱ.t*, "strength, protection," *CDD N*, 117–18, s.v. *nḫṱ.t*. Given that the intelligible later lines of the graffito deal with specific mummification materials, such as *sf*, "resin," we wonder whether *mt nḫṱ.t* is literally to be translated "a thing of protection," and signifies such embalming materials or similar. Compare perhaps *hn.w r nḫṱ*, "vessels for protection," in graff. 58, 2–3.

(b) The suffix pronoun of *r-r=s* would refer back to *kꜣ.t*.

(c) Our first reading *mtre* after *ỉw=w* does not yield satisfactory sense and is hardly palaeographically convincing. One also thinks of *mḫj*, "ehren," *Glossar*, 176. The subject of *ỉw=w* is presumably *hyn.w mt nḫṱ.t*. One expects a verb or series of nouns that explicates the antecedent. The crack visible in the image was probably already there when the graffito was written. Little was therefore probably lost of the word or words at the end of the line. Still, the final traces are damaged and we cannot decipher them.

Line 4

(a) We were initially inclined to read the first word as *my* or *šy*, with the man with hand to mouth determinative. The supposed *y* is dubious, however, and we could offer no good translation of *my* or *šy*. We then thought that *m-šs*, "gewiss," *Glossar*, 521–22, was a better alternative but are now also skeptical of this as well. We thus leave the word unread.

(b) *ḥn.w* fits the traces well, "Topf," *Glossar*, 313; *CDD Ḥ*, 158.

(c) *bry*, "neu," *Glossar*, 119, is reasonable. One might suggest that these new jars might have been used for the ibis mummies were it not the case that these sacred birds were not placed in such jars in Dra Abu el-Nagaʿ, unlike their counterparts in Saqqara or Tuna el-Gebel; see Scalf, "Resurrecting an Ibis Cult," 364–65.

Line 5

(a) This is clearly a formulaic phrase toward the end of such an inscription, encouraging the cult workers to do their utmost for the sacred birds.

Line 6

(a) We consider *šw*, "geeignet, nützlich, würdig," *Glossar*, 493, most likely. Less attractive is *mꜣꜥ.t*, "das Rechte," *Glossar*, 149–50. This line particularly benefited very much from DStretch.

(b) For *qs*, "begraben," *Glossar,* 548–59.

Line 7

(a) We think most probable is *sf*, "Harz," *Glossar*, 429, with the jar determinative. There seem to be traces after this jar determinative.

(b) The great one of Thoth *Pꜣ-šr-Mn* is the most prominent individual in these graffiti; see p. 65.

55. Graffito UE 270/1 (Plate 53)

Location: UE 270, W-wall

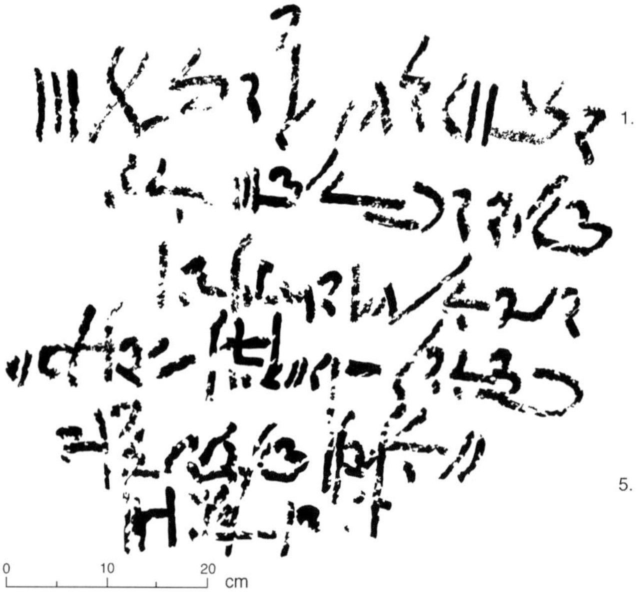

Transliteration	Translation
1. *tꜣ wsḫ mḥ-1.t tꜣ(?) tꜣy ty*	1. This is here the First Hall.
2. *mtw=s tꜣ nt ṯ-myt*	2. It is the one that leads
3. *(r) nꜣ ꜣtr.w nꜣ nṯr.w*	3. (to) the chapels of the gods
4. *nt mqḥ sẖ Pꜣ-šr-Mn sꜣ Ḏḥwty-sḏm*	4. who are mourned. Has written *Pꜣ-šr-Mn*, son of *Ḏḥwty-sḏm*,
5. *pꜣ wr Ḏḥwty mtw⸢=f⸣ nt ti͗.t ḥtp*	5. the great one of Thoth. ⸢He⸣ is the one who causes that
6. *[nꜣ nṯr]⸢.w⸣ rn.w nfr(?)*	6. [the] aforesaid [god]⸢s⸣ rest well(?).

Commentary

When this area first became accessible during excavation, it was striking to observe how the vivid red ink of the graffito stood out in that dark space when even minimal light shone upon it.

Line 1

(a) This is again a directional text. Apparently the individual chambers of the tomb were numbered by those involved in the ibis and falcon cult.

(b) *wsḫ.t*, "broad court, hall," *CDD W*, 164–67, is a deeply significant word in demotic. While it can often be used with regard to actual buildings (e.g., as the "broad hall of Pharaoh," *CDD W*, 165), *wsḫ.t* is also employed to designate sections of the underworld, most notably in Setne II. In 2/2, for example, Siosiris and his father Setne go to the *wsḫ.t mḥ-5.t*, "the Fifth Hall" of the underworld, F. Ll. Griffith, *Stories of the High Priests of Memphis: The Sethon of Herodotus and the Demotic Tales of Khamuas* (Oxford: Clarendon, 1900), 150–51.

(c) There seems to be a sign between *mḥ-1.t* and *tȝy*. But what can this be? We think that *tȝ* is most probable, perhaps functioning as a demonstrative pronoun(?).

Line 2

(a) *mtw=s* is the independent pronoun. The cleft sentence is more elaborate than is generally found in such graffiti. The writer employs the same construction in line 5.

(b) For *ṯ-myt*, "den Weg weisen," *Glossar*, 666.

Line 3

(a) *ȝtr*, "chapel," *CDD, ȝ*, 108, is virtually a technical term in the ibis or animal cult. This is *ȝtr.t*, "shrine containing images of gods," Wilson, *Lexikon*, 123–24.

Line 4

(a) *mqḥ*,"betrübt sein, Trauer," *Glossar*, 183. It is presumably a stative form. This would seem to refer to the dead ibises; on the word, see p. 47.

Line 5

(a) *Pȝ-šr-Mn* is the most prominent individual involved in the ibis and falcon cult.

(b) *nt* is not absolutely secure, but seems reasonable.

Line 6

(a) *nfr* is a suggestion, but hardly certain. It would appear to function here as an adverb.

56. **Graffito UE 276/1** (Plate 54)

Location: UE 276, E-wall of the passage/break connecting the tomb parallel to that of Hery to the north, with the next rock-cut tomb to the north, still unexcavated, located below the New Kingdom tomb of the overseer of the weavers Ay.[202]

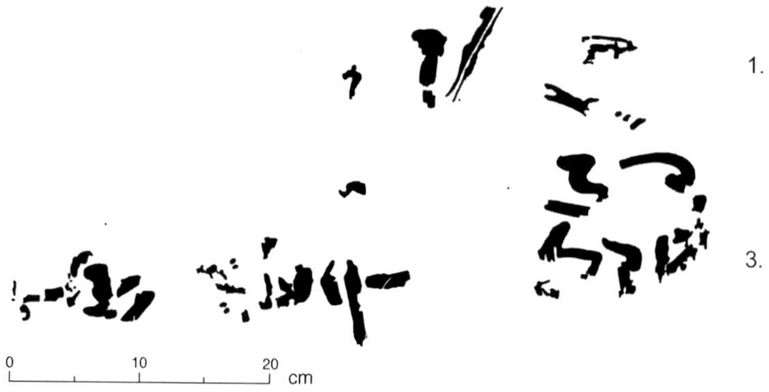

TRANSLITERATION
1. ...
2. ...
3. ... *tꜣ(?) tꜣy [...] sẖ Pꜣ-šr-Mn sꜣ Ḏḥwty-sḏm*

TRANSLATION
1. ...
2. ...
3. ... Has written *Pꜣ-šr-Mn*, son of *Ḏḥwty-sḏm*.

Commentary

Line 3

(a) Compare graff. 55, 1 *tꜣ wsḫ mḥ-1.t tꜣ(?) tꜣy ty* "This is here the First Hall." This is probably also a directional text.

(b) There is not much space available after the name, but *pꜣ wr Ḏḥwty*, "the great one of Thoth" is almost certainly to be restored here.

[202] On the tomb of Ay, see the description of the 2012 excavation season by Galán at: https://proyectodjehuty.com/report-campaign-2012/. The Middle Kingdom tomb below Ay, which was incorporated in the Ptolemaic period to the animal galleries, was discovered in the 2018 excavation season: see Bosch-Puche and Ikram in this volume.

57. Graffito UE 276/2 (Plate 55)

Location: UE 276, N-wall

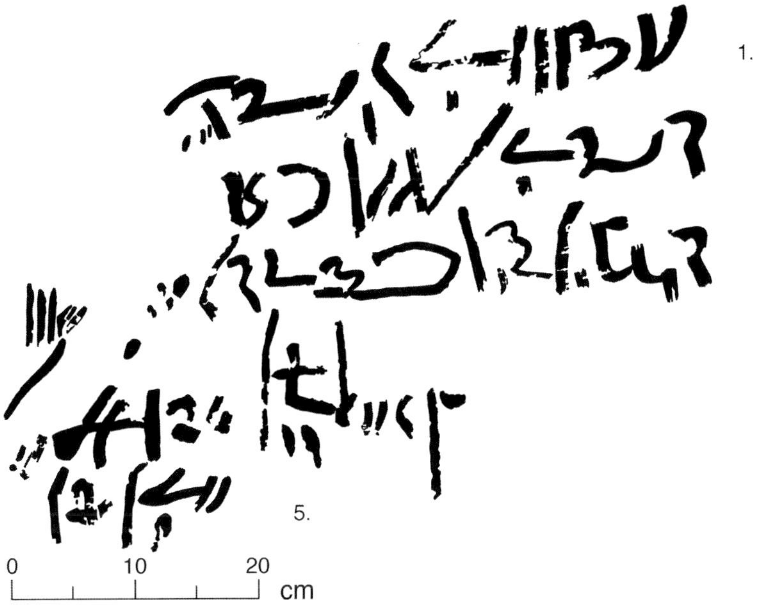

Transliteration

1. *pꜣ myt r-ẖn*
2. *nꜣ ꜣtr.w nt ẖr*
3. *nꜣ ntr.w nt mqḥ pꜣy pꜣy*
4. *sẖ Pꜣ-šr-Mn sꜣ Ḏḥwty-sḏm*
5. *pꜣ wr Ḏḥwty*

Translation

1. This is the path into
2. the chapels that contain
3. the gods who are mourned.
4. Has written *Pꜣ-šr-Mn*, son of *Ḏḥwty-sḏm*,
5. the great one of Thoth.

Commentary

Line 1

(a) Compare graff. 55, which is by the same scribe, *Pꜣ-šr-Mn*. Once more, this is obviously a directional text.

Line 3

(a) The line interestingly concludes with both the copula and demonstrative pronoun. The scribe has differentiated the writings of the like-sounding words, see K.-Th. Zauzich, "Differenzierende Schreibungen bei differierender Wortbedeutung," in *Aspects of Demotic Lexicography: Acts of the Second International Conference for Demotic Studies, Leiden, 19–21 September 1984*, ed. S. Vleeming, Studia Demotica 1 (Leuven: Peeters, 1987), 109–13.

58. **Graffito UE 277/1** (Plate 56)

Location: UE 277, NE-corner, connecting to UE 325

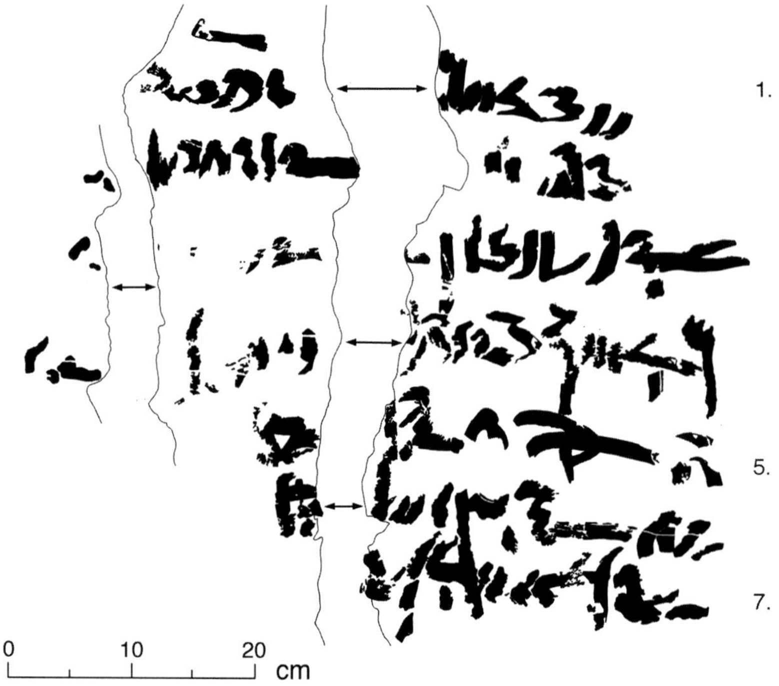

Transliteration
1. *pꜣ mtre nꜣ thm nb*
2. *mꜣꜥ ỉw(?) ỉn=w nꜣ hn.w r*
3. *nḫṯ bw-ỉr=w ⸢ỉp⸣ r*
4. *sty šꜥ nꜣ(?) ...*
5. *... m-ỉr tỉ.t ḥtp*
6. *r pꜣy=w bnr sẖ Pꜣ-šr-Mn*
7. *sꜣ(?) Ḏḥwty-sḏm pꜣ wr Ḏḥwty*

Translation
1. The proper mode of conduct(?) for anyone who enters
2. a place (in which) they have brought the vessels for
3. protection. They do not ⸢reckon⸣ on
4. a flame up to the(?) ...
5. ... Do not let rest here
6. outside of them. Has written *Pꜣ-šr-Mn,*
7. son of(?) *Ḏḥwty-sḏm*, the great one of Thoth.

Commentary

This graffito wraps around the rough and unfinished corner where the path turns north. There is nothing lost in these lines; the arrows merely indicate that the text continues around the corner or bend in the wall.

Line 1

(a) This graffito seems to be an instructional text. It may perhaps deal with the proper handling of torches or lamps in the highly flammable environment. For *mtre* at the beginning of a graffito, compare graff. 70, 1. The translation "proper mode of conduct," is a proposal based on the general tenor of the text. Other renderings are naturally possible, for example, assuming that *mtre* is a variant of *myt*, "path."

(b) *thm*, "pierce, enter, tread." *Glossar*, 650; *CDD T*, 269–70 ("to summon, invite, load"). The word here has the expected walking-legs determinative. While the reading *thm* appears secure, the grammar is less so. We assume that *thm* is a participle, but that is clearly an archaic form. We therefore offer this translation with reserve.

Line 2

(a) *mꜣꜥ* does not seem to be defined, which suggests then the circumstantial *iw* is to be read following it.

(b) *hn.w* is probably here *ḥnw*, "Topf," *Glossar*, 313, *ḥnw*, "Särge," *Glossar*, 313, *hn*, "Art Krug," *Glossar*, 277. Since the ibises in Dra Abu el-Nagaꜥ were not buried in jars, as in Saqqara, it seems more likely that *hn.w* here refers to the jars containing embalming materials (e.g., resins) or oil for lighting and consecration. *Ḥn.w*, "jars," occurs also in graff. 54, 4. Since *ḥn* is such a general term, it is difficult to determine the force of the phrase here. It is, of course, also possible that *hn.w* is in fact *hn*, *Glossar*, 277, "Art Krug," "Kasten," and that "boxes" or "containers," is to be understood. But what would "containers of protection" mean in this context? This would be a reasonable designation of a coffin, but, again, the sacred birds were only wrapped in linen in Dra Abu el-Nagaꜥ.

(c) The reading of *r* is plausible, given the following *nẖt*.

Line 3

(a) We understand *nẖt* to mean here, "protection," *Glossar*, 226.

(b) *bw-ir=w* is secure, but it is harder to propose a convincing reading of the damaged verb. We suggest *ip*, "prüfen, denken," *Glossar*, 28; perhaps understand *bw-ir=w ip r sty.t*, "They do not reckon/think about fire."

(c) Again, *r* is reasonable at the end of the line, but hardly certain.

Line 4

(a) *sty.t*, "Feuer, Flamme," *Glossar*, 475–76. Does this refer to a fire or to a lamp/torch?

(b) We have devoted considerable thought to the traces following *sty*. Unfortunately, we can offer no secure reading. Most likely is *šꜥ*, but, since we are unable to read confidently the traces after this, the transliteration remains a mere suggestion. We have the impression that the writer is concerned with the handling of torches or lamps, being understandably afraid of fire. It may be therefore that the reader is warned about where in the tomb fire is allowed for illumination or where fire could by accident come into being.

(c) *nꜣ* is simply one possibility. Perhaps rather *šꜥ-tw=f*?

(d) We can make nothing of the faint and damaged traces at the end of this line.

Line 5

(a) Presumably the initial word concludes the previous statement (*nꜣy*?).

(b) Perhaps restore or understand *wꜥ ntr*, "a god," following *ḥtp* based on the similar vetitive in graff. 88, 3. It would seem that the head of the cult workers did not want the ibis and falcon mummies to accumulate in this chamber. They should rather be brought to the *ꜥ.wy.w ḥtp* deeper in the tomb. One wonders whether such mummies would in themselves have also posed a fire hazard.

Line 6

(a) *r pꜣy=w* seems plausible, but is not secure; compare, for example, *n pꜣy=k bnr*, "except for you," *CDD B*, 54, s.v. *bnr*.

Line 7

(a) We assume the horizontal stroke before *Ḏḥwty-sḏm* is *sꜣ*, although it resembles more closely *n*.

59. Graffito UE 277/2 (Plate 57)

Location: a. UE 277, NW-corner, connecting to UE 325 (b.–c. unplaced fragments)

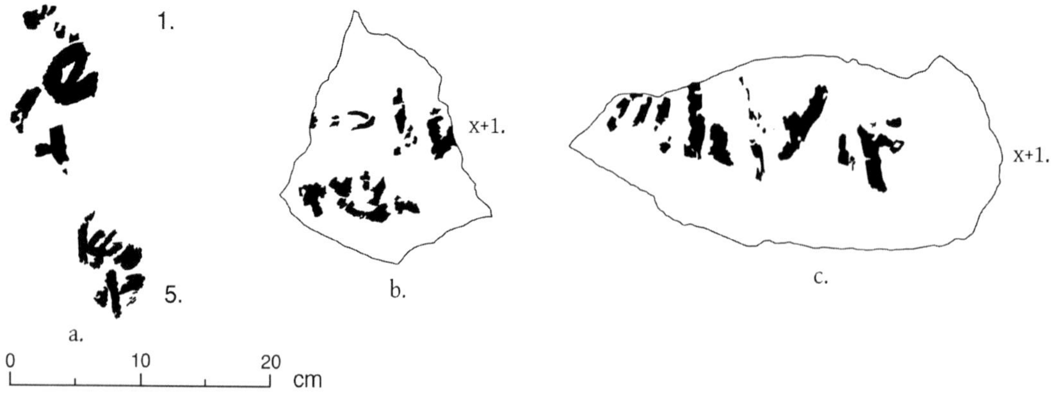

TRANSLITERATION A
1. *[...]* ⸢...⸣ *[...]*
2. *[...] pꜣ [...]*
3. *[...]* ⸢...⸣ *[...]*
4. *[...] Pꜣ-ti͗-[...]*
5. *[...] sẖ(?) [...]*

TRANSLATION A
1. [...] ⸢...⸣ [...]
2. [...] the [...]
3. [...] ⸢...⸣ [...]
4. [...] *Pꜣ-ti͗-[...]*
5. [...] written(?) [...]

Commentary
This graffito is located directly opposite of graff. 58. Both of these are written on the corners of their respective paths. They are clearly intended to inform the cult workers of the proper routes to the chambers in use. This is no small matter, given the multiplicity of shafts branching off in different directions. In the course of the 2018 excavation season two small fragments were found near graff. 59a, to which they probably belong.[203] The two unplaced fragments are labeled here b and c.

Line 4
(a) Perhaps *Pꜣ-ti͗=w, Demot. Nb.*, 296.

TRANSLITERATION B
x+1. *[...]* ⸢...⸣ *[...]*
x+2. *[...] ... [...]*

TRANSLATION B
x+1. [...] ⸢...⸣ [...]
x+2. [...] ... [...]

Commentary

Line x+1
(a) Perhaps read *Pꜣ-šr-....*

[203] They have received the excavation number 6898 (email of F. Bosch-Puche, February 15, 2019).

Transliteration C	Translation C
x+1. *sẖ Lwꜣ* ⸢*sꜣ Ḥr*⸣ [...]	x+1. Has written *Lwꜣ*, ⸢son of *Ḥr*⸣ [...]

Commentary

(a) The same man occurs also in graff. 52, 6 and 62b, 3, where he has the titles *sẖ*, *ṯ ntr.w*, and *ꜥꜣ Nw.t*, "scribe," "taker of gods," and "great one of Thebes."

60. Graffito UE 277/3 (Plate 58)

Location: UE 277, S-wall

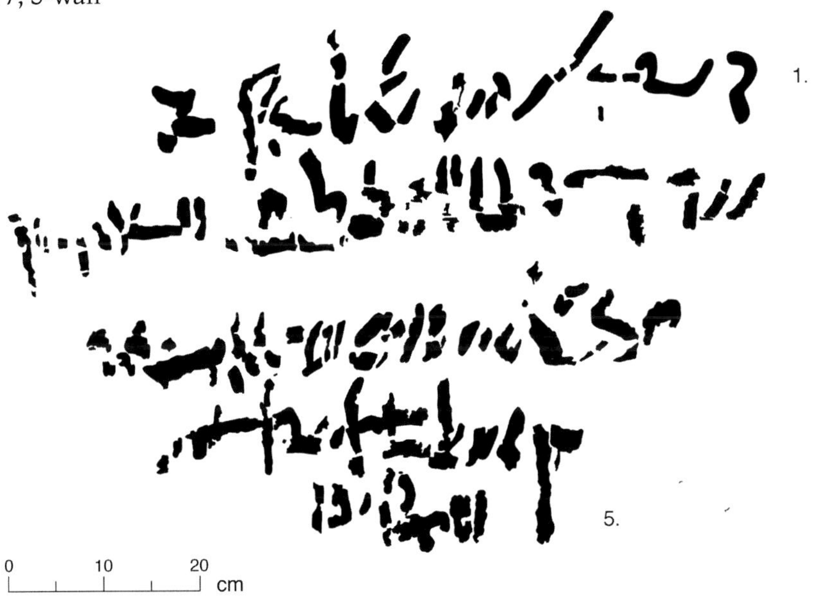

Transliteration	Translation
1. *tꜣ ꜣtr.t r ti͗.t ḥtp*	1. The chapel to cause to rest (the gods)
2. ⸢*r-tbꜣ*⸣ *nꜣ mt.w i͗-i͗r ḫpr my ṯꜣy=w nꜣ ntr.w*	2. ⸢on account of⸣ the things which happened. Let the gods be taken (there).
3. *tꜣ tꜣy ty pꜣ(?) myt r-r=s*	3. This is here the(?) path to it.
4. *sẖ Pꜣ-šr-Mn sꜣ Ḏḥwty-sḏm*	4. Has written *Pꜣ-šr-Mn*, son of *Ḏḥwty-sḏm*,
5. *pꜣ wr Ḏḥwty*	5. the great one of Thoth.

Commentary

Line 1

(a) The transliteration *r ti͗.t* is not certain; we understand this to be *r* followed by the infinitive of *ti͗*, *Glossar*, 605. *r ti͗.t ḥtp* has here the sense of *ti͗ ḥtp*, "to bury," *CDD Ḥ*, 299, s.v. *ḥtp*. Perhaps render "the chapel for burying." This is evidently a directional text.

Line 2

(a) We tentatively interpret the damaged traces of the first word to be *r-tbꜣ*, *Glossar*, 620–21. The idea may be that the ibis and falcon mummies should be placed in a different chapel or tomb chamber from the one employed earlier because of some mishap or problem (a fire?).

Line 3

(a) Compare graff. 55.1. The definite article *pꜣ* is problematic, noting especially the gender discrepancy between *tꜣ tꜣy* and *pꜣ(?) myt.* One can just recognize the radical *t* and the walking legs determinative of *myt.*

61. Graffito in Unexcavated Chamber of Middle Kingdom Tomb below Tomb of Ay (Plate 57)

Location: E-wall of an unexcavated chamber of Middle Kingdom tomb below the New Kingdom tomb of the overseer of the weavers, Ay.

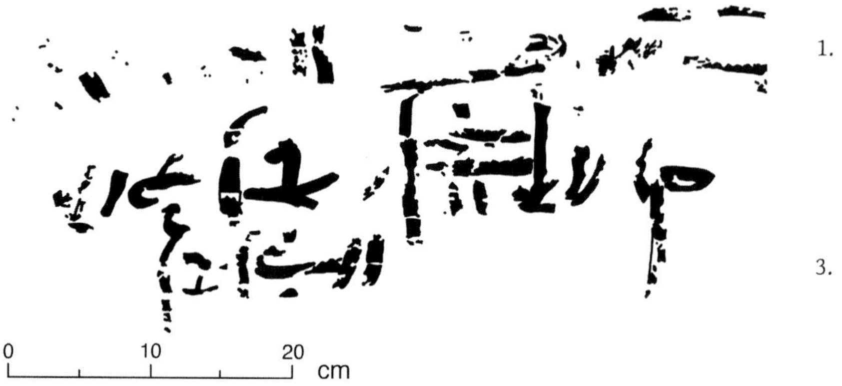

Transliteration	Translation
1. ...	1. ...
2. *sẖ Pꜣ-šr-Mn sꜣ Ḏḥwty-sḏm*	2. Has written *Pꜣ-šr-Mn*, son of *Ḏḥwty-sḏm*,
3. *pꜣ wr Ḏḥwty*	3. the great one of Thoth.

Commentary

Line 1

(a) Unfortunately we can read nothing of this line.

UPPER GALLERY (PLATES 59 AND 60)

62. **Graffito Upper Gallery 1** (Plates 60a and 61)

Location: Upper Gallery, chamber F (above entrance to chamber H), W-wall

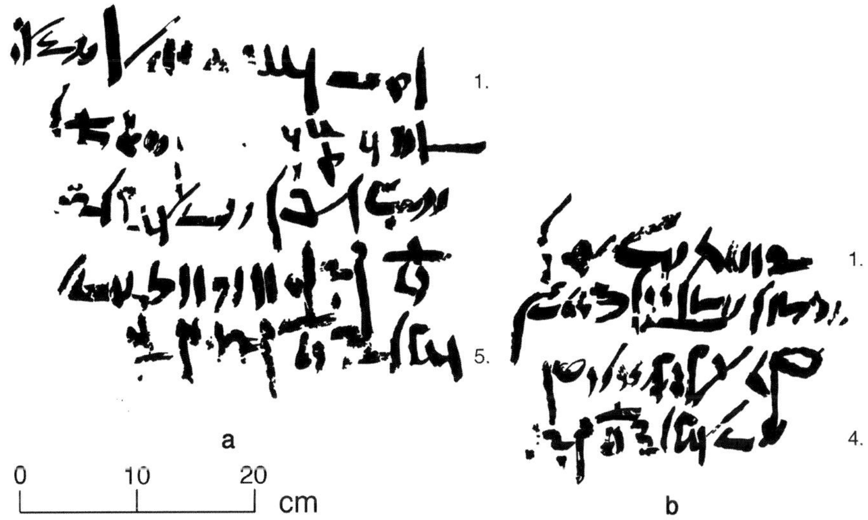

TRANSLITERATION A

1. *ḥ.t-sp 7 ỉbt 4 ⸢pr.t⸣ sw* 11 *pꜣ rn*
2. *nfr Pa-⸢Wsr⸣(?) ⸢sꜣ⸣ Pꜣ-šr-Mn*
3. *pꜣ wr Ḏḥwty pꜣ ṯ ntr.w*
4. *ꜥꜣ Nw.t ỉw=f ỉ-ỉr pꜣ ṯ*
5. *ntr.w ꜥꜣ Nw.t wꜥ ⸢sp⸣(?)*

TRANSLATION A

1. Regnal year 7, fourth month ⸢winter⸣, day 11. The good
2. name of *Pa-⸢Wsr⸣(?)* ⸢son of⸣ *Pꜣ-šr-Mn*,
3. the great one of Thoth, the taker of gods (and)
4. great one of Thebes, he acting as the taker
5. of gods (and) great one of Thebes all ⸢together⸣(?).

TRANSLITERATION B

1. *mn ty m-bꜣḥ Ḏḥwty*
2. *pꜣ hb pꜣ bỉk šꜥ ḏ.t*
3. *sẖ Lwꜣ sꜣ Ḥr pꜣ sẖ*
4. *pꜣ ṯ ntr.w ꜥꜣ Nw.t*

TRANSLATION B

1. remains here before Thoth,
2. the ibis, (and) the falcon forever.
3. Has written *Lwꜣ*, son of *Ḥr*, the scribe,
4. the taker of gods, great one of Thebes.

Commentary a

Line 1

(a) We take this to be "7," *Glossar*, 698; "40" is less likely, compare *Glossar*, 700.

(b) For *sw 11*, *Glossar*, 709. This is the most common day named in the graffiti.

Line 3

(a) For *Pa-Wsr*, see graff. 6, 1.

Line 4

(a) We have not found a parallel for this title, but compare *ꜥꜣ n*, "Vorsteher von," *Glossar*, 54.

(b) After some deliberation, we tentatively propose that the circular sign and the short vertical stroke are an elaborate place determinative following *Nw.t*. If correct, we can then read *ỉw=f* after *Nw.t*.

(c) *ỉ-ỉr* is possible, but not secure. It would seem to be here a mere variant of *ỉr*.

Line 5

(a) The writer apparently claims that he held the distinction of occupying these two positions at the same time.

Commentary b

Line 1

(a) We do not believe that there is anything lost here. A and b actually comprise one text. The writer of the graffito started in the center of the doorway, but then ran out of space and had to continue to the right in a second column.

Line 3

(a) For *Lwꜣ*, see *Lw/ Lwꜣ*, *Demot. Nb.*, 722. *Lwꜣ*, son of *Ḥr*, appears also in graff. 52, 6 and in the unplaced fragment graff. 59c.

(b) The *pꜣ* before *sẖ* is unclear.

63. Graffito Upper Gallery 2 (Plates 60b and 62)

Location: Upper Gallery, chamber G, S-wall

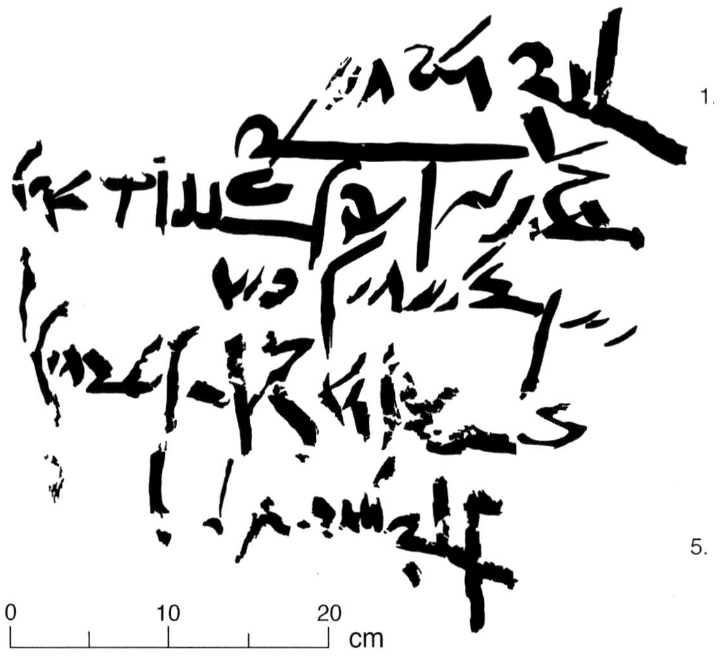

Transliteration	Translation
1. *ḥ.t-sp 9.t ỉbt 3 pr.t*	1. Regnal year 9, third month of winter,
2. *(sw) 19*	2. (day) 19.
3. *ʿq=w Ḏḥwty ḫnṯ Wsr*	3. They caused to enter (i.e., buried) Thoth, foremost one of Thebes,
4. *r pꜣ ỉrpy m-sꜣ*	4. into the divine chapel after
5. *ỉr rnp.(w)t ʿšꜣ n ḥ.t-ntr*	5. spending many years in the temple.
6. *sẖ (n) ḥ.t-sp 9.t ỉbt 4 pr.t sw 11*	6. Written (in) regnal year 9, fourth month of winter, day 11.

Commentary

This graffito is virtually identical to graff. 14; see the commentary on that text.

Line 3

(a) We understand "Thoth, foremost one of Thebes," to be the name or epithet of a particular individual sacred ibis.

Line 4

(a) Again, the use of both *ỉrpy* and *ḥ.t-ntr* is intriguing.

(b) The irregular long vertical stroke at the very end of the line is probably just a drip down from the divine determinative of *Wsr.*

64. Graffito Upper Gallery 3a–d (Plates 60b, 63, and 64)

These four graffiti are distinct texts that have been discovered over an extended period of time in this mostly unexcavated chamber. They have been assigned the designations 64a–d.

64a. Graffito Upper Gallery 3a (Plate 64)

Location: Upper Gallery, chamber G, N-wall

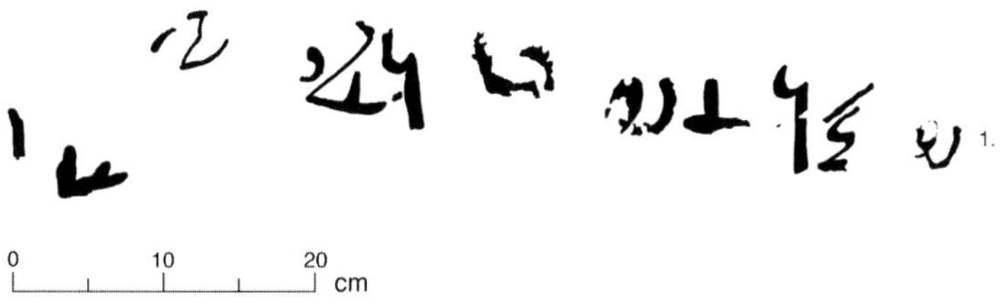

Transliteration	Translation
1. *pꜣ rn nfr ...*	1. The good name ...
2. ...	2. ...

Commentary

Line 1

(a) On the basis of graff. 64b, 2, we had first considered reading *Pa-Wsr* here, but now consider this too insecure.

64b. Graffito Upper Gallery 3b (Plate 65)

Location: Upper Gallery, chamber G, N-wall

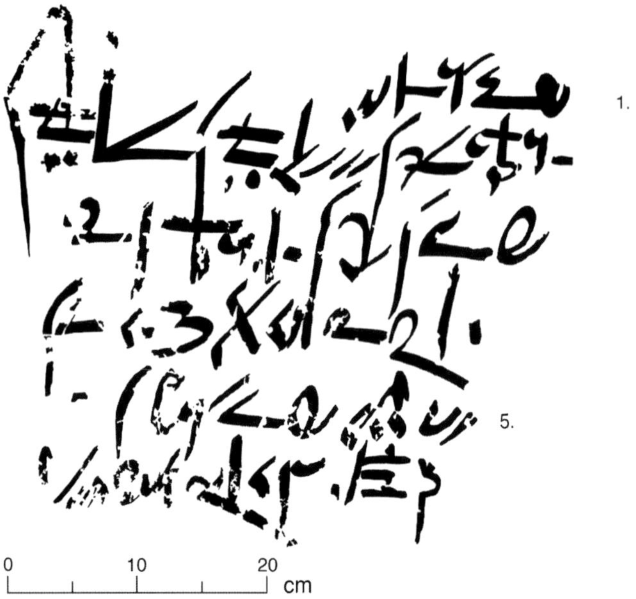

Transliteration	Translation
1. *pꜣ rn nfr*	1. The good name
2. *n Pa-Wsr sꜣ Pꜣ-šr-Mn (sꜣ) Ns-Mn*	2. of *Pa-Wsr*, son of *Pꜣ-šr-Mn*, son of *Ns-Mn*,
3. *pꜣ wr Ḏḥwty n ḥ.t-sp 7.t ḥ.t-sp 8.t*	3. the great one of Thoth, in regnal year 7, regnal year 8,
4. *n ḥ.t-sp 9.t mn ty šꜥ ḏ.t*	4. in regnal year 9, remains here forever
5. *ỉrm nꜣy=w pꜣ ṯ ntr.w*	5. with the men of the taker of gods,
6. *wꜥ sp sẖ (n) ḥ.t-sp 9 ỉbt 4 pr.t sw 11*	6. all together. Written (in) regnal year 9, fourth month of winter, day 11.

Commentary

Line 2

(a) *Pa-Wsr*, son of *Pꜣ-šr-Mn*, appears also in graff. 62a, 2.

Line 3

(a) *Pa-Wsr* seems to have held the office of "great one of Thoth" for three years.

64c. Graffito Upper Gallery 3c (Plate 66)

Location: Upper Gallery, chamber G, N-wall

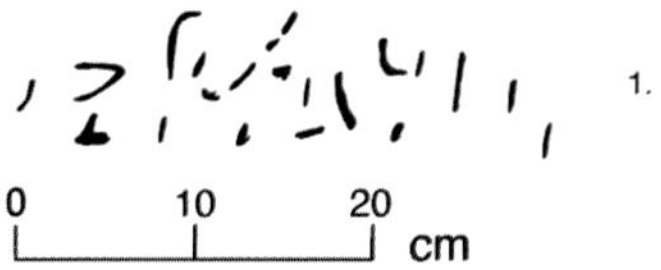

TRANSLITERATION	TRANSLATION
1. ...	1. ...

Commentary

We can only recognize a possible divine determinative in these vague traces.

64d. Graffito Upper Gallery 3d (Plate 66)

Location: Upper Gallery, chamber G, N-wall

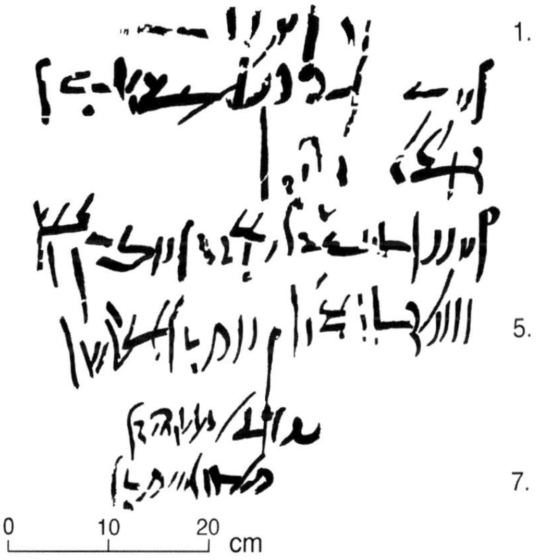

TRANSLITERATION	TRANSLATION
1. ⸢*ỉt-nṯr* ...⸣	1. ⸢God's-father ...⸣,
2. *ỉt-nṯr ... sꜣ Wsỉr-wr*	2. god's-father ..., son of *Wsỉr-wr*,
3. *nꜣ rt nꜣ wꜥb.w*	3. the representatives of the priests,
4. *ỉt-nṯr Pꜣ-tỉ-Nfr-ḥtp sꜣ ... pꜣ mr ḫꜣs.t*	4. god's-father *Pꜣ-tỉ-Nfr-ḥtp*, son of ..., the overseer of the necropolis
5. *ỉrm nꜣ bꜣk.w sẖ Pꜣ-hb tr=w*	5. and the servants of the scribe *Pꜣ-hb* in their entirety.
6. *pꜣ(?) sk̭rṯ(?) Pr-Ỉmn*	6. The(?) *sk̭rṯ(?)* of the House-of-Amun
7. *Hr sꜣ Pꜣ-hb*	7. *Hr*, son of *Pꜣ-hb*.

Commentary

The surface upon which this graffito is written is exceptionally uneven, and thus the photographic images are distorted. The above hand-copy represents an attempt to regularize the appearance. The hand-copy on plate 62 shows the graffito as seen on the photograph.

Line 1

(a) The standard title "god's-father" is otherwise not attested in this corpus of graffiti.

Line 2

(a) We are unable to read this name, which seems to end with a divine determinative.

Line 3

(a) This title is also not found elsewhere in the corpus. For *pꜣ rt nꜣ wꜥb.w*, see *CDD R*, 77, "the agent of the priests."

Line 4

(a) We have not been able to read the name of the father of *Pꜣ-ti-Nfr-ḥtp* (perhaps *Pa-Ḫnsw*?).

(b) The title *mr ḫꜣs.t*, "overseer of the necropolis," is also found in graff. 67, 2. "Vorsteher der Nekropole," *Glossar,* 166, 348; *CDD Ḫ* 13-14, s.v. *ḫꜣs.t*, "necropolis," is, of course, a well-known official in Thebes. The overseer of the necropolis is indeed associated with the ibis cult, Kessler, *Die Heiligen Tiere und der König*, 162, but the title otherwise appears in this corpus only in graff. 67, 2. The office is perhaps best known from the tax or payment made to the holder, see, for example, S. M. Wahid El-Din, "The Chief of the Necropolis Tax," in Hoffmann and Thissen, *Res Severa Verum Gaudium*, 639–49; M. Depauw, *The Archive of Teos and Thabis from Early Ptolemaic Thebes: P. Brux. Dem. Inv. E. 8252–8256*, MRE 8 (Brepols: Fondation Égyptologique Reine Élisabeth, 2000), 189–93.

Line 5

(a) The scribe *Pꜣ-hb* appears also in graff. 10, 2. His son *Hr* is named in line 7.

(b) For *tr,* "ganz," *Glossar*, 641–42.

Line 6

(a) We have tentatively transliterated *pꜣ skrṱ*, but this is very uncertain. In view of the clear *Pr-ỉmn* at the end, we propose that this is a (Greek?) title. However, we have no parallel.

APPENDIX A

GRAFFITI COPIED BY SPIEGELBERG IN A "TOMB ABOVE HERY" (TT 12) AND "THE GREAT TOMB OF THE IBIS AND HAWKS," PRESENT LOCATION UNKNOWN.

A. TOMB ABOVE HERY (TT 12)

65. Graffito Spiegelberg #31 (Plate 67a)

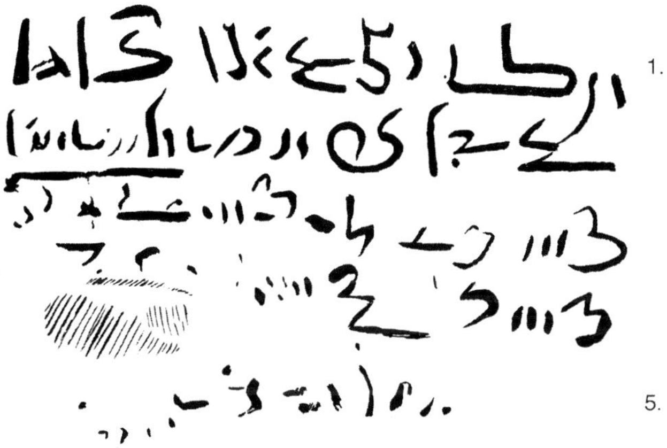

no scale

TRANSLITERATION

1. *ỉw=f ḫ̮pr ỉw wḫ̮ꜣ=w n ỉr(?) ꜥ.wy.w*
2. *ḥtp ẖr pꜣ hb pꜣ bỉk*
3. *my wn[=w]* ⌜*w*ꜥ⌝ *myt*
4. *my ỉr=*⌜*w wpy.t nb*⌝
5. ...

TRANSLATION

1. If it happens that they have desired to make(?) places
2. of rest for the ibis (and) the falcon,
3. let [one] open ⌜a⌝ path,
4. let ⌜one⌝ make ⌜all work.⌝
5. ...

Commentary

(Spiegelberg #31, pl. 30; Vleeming, *Graffiti*, 119 [#1475])

Line 1

(a) Spiegelberg also read *n ỉr*, but the syntax is unusual. One would expect a simple infinitive after *wḫ̮ꜣ*. It is unclear to us if there is any association between this *n ỉr* and the grammatical point (*n dỉ.t* versus *r dỉ.t)* discussed by L. Depuydt, "Demotic Script and Demotic Grammar (II): Dummy Prepositions Preceding Infinitives," *Enchoria* 27 (2001): 3–35. This would also seem to be a directional text.

Line 3

(a) The *w* suffix pronoun is lost.

(b) *w*ꜥ, *Glossar*, 81, is a reasonable transliteration. This text may refer to the construction work involved in preparing these New Kingdom tombs for the burial of the sacred animals. They may have had to clear a considerable amount of accumulated debris and also build the stairs that connect the various tombs.

Line 4
(a) We adopt the attractive reading of this line in Vleeming, *Graffiti*, 119.

Line 5
(a) The first series of traces fits *n-ỉm=w*, *Glossar*, 200. Of course, other readings are also possible.

66. Graffito Spiegelberg #32 (Plate 67b)

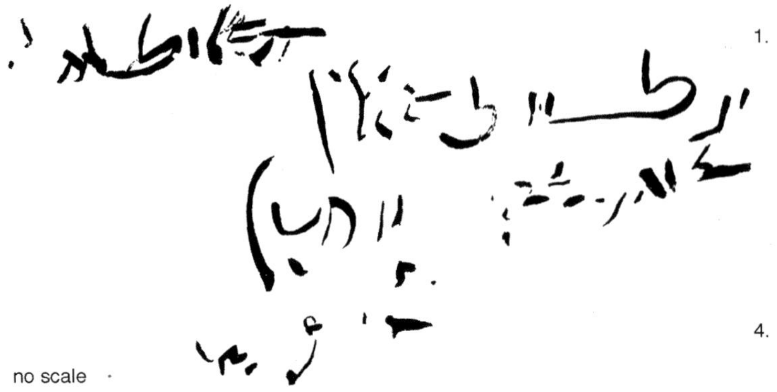

TRANSLITERATION	TRANSLATION
1. ... *Ns-Mn(?)* ...	1. ... *Ns-Mn(?)* ...
2. *ỉw=f ḫpr ỉw wḫꜣ=w [n ỉr]*	2. If it happens that they have desired [to make]
3. *ʿ.wy ḥtp [ẖr] pꜣ hb*	3. a place of rest [for] the ibis (and)
4. *[pꜣ bỉk]* ...	4. [the falcon] ...

Commentary
(Spiegelberg #32, pl. 30; Vleeming, *Graffiti*, 119 [#1476])

Line 1
(a) *Mn* is an insecure reading.

Line 2
(a) This graffito is obviously associated with graff. 65. Vleeming, *Graffiti*, 119, suggests *[n ỉr]*.

B. *"THE GREAT TOMB OF THE IBIS AND HAWKS"*

67. Graffito Spiegelberg #1 (Plate 67c)

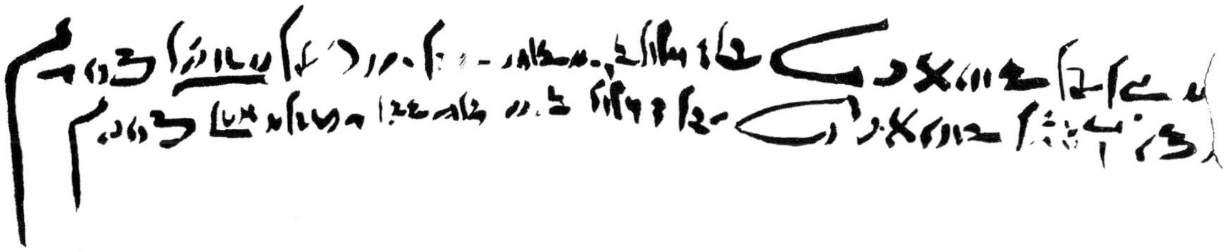

1.

no scale

TRANSLITERATION

1. *[pꜣ rn nfr ...] pꜣ wr Ḏḥwty mn ty m-bꜣḥ Ḏḥwty nꜣ nṯr.w n pꜣ ꜥ.wy ⸢ḥtp⸣ n pꜣ hb pꜣ bik šꜥ ḏ.t*

2. *[pꜣ rn nfr ... p]ꜣ mr ḫꜣs.t mn ty m-bꜣḥ Ḏḥwty nꜣ nṯr.w n ⸢pꜣ⸣ ꜥ.wy ḥtp (n) pꜣ hb pꜣ bik šꜥ ḏ.t*

TRANSLATION

1. [The good name of ...] the great one of Thoth remains here before Thoth (and) the gods of the place of ⸢rest⸣ of the ibis (and) the falcon forever.
2. [The good name of ... t]he overseer of the necropolis remains here before Thoth (and) the gods of ⸢the⸣ place of rest (of) the ibis (and) the falcon forever.

Commentary

(Spiegelberg #1, pl. 26; Vleeming, *Graffiti*, 121 [#1480])

Line 1

(a) For the correction of Spiegelberg's *Pꜣ-iꜥḥ-Ḏḥwty* to *pꜣ wr Ḏḥwty*, see den Brinker, Muhs, and Vleeming, *Berichtigungsliste*, 518; Vleeming, *Graffiti*, 121.

Line 2

(a) For the overseer of the necropolis, see note (a) 64d, 4.

68. Graffito Spiegelberg #2 (Plate 68a)

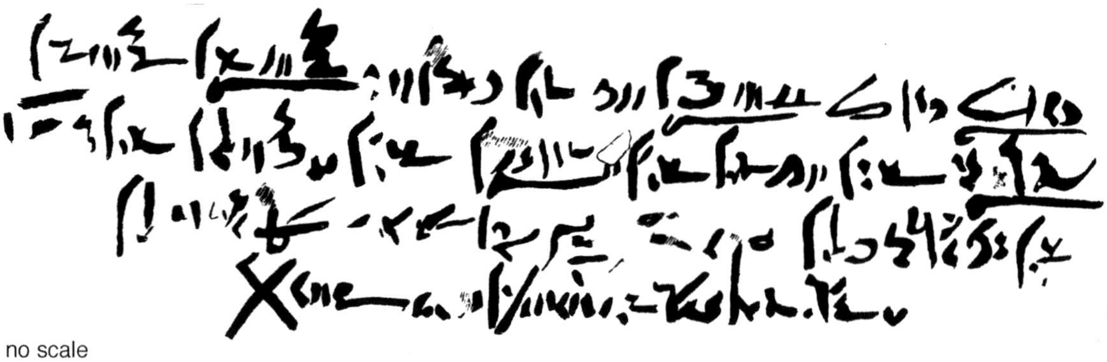

1.

4.

no scale

TRANSLITERATION	TRANSLATION
1. *ʿnḫ=k ʿnḫ by=k pꜣ hb pr-ʿꜣ rpy=k rpy*	1. May you live! May your ba live! O ibis of pharaoh, may you be rejuvenated!
2. *ꜣḫ=k Wsỉr pꜣ hb Wsỉr pꜣ bỉk Wsỉr pꜣ ʿḫm Wsỉr ⌜Twtw⌝(?)*	2. May your body be rejuvenated! O Osiris ibis, o Osiris falcon, o Osiris *ʿḫm*-falcon, Osiris ⌜Tutu⌝(?),
3. *Wsỉr Ḥr nb Sḫ̭m sẖ pr-ḏ.t Ḏḥwty-sḏm sꜣ Ns-nb-ʿy*	3. Osiris Horus, Lord of Letopolis. Scribe of the House-of-Eternity, *Ḏḥwty-sḏm*, son of *Ns-nb-ʿy*.
4. *pꜣ rn nfr Ḥr-pa-ꜣIs.t sꜣ Sylws mn ty*	4. The good name of *Ḥr-pa-ꜣIs.t*, son of *Sylws*, remains here.

Commentary

(Spiegelberg #2, pl. 26; Vleeming, *Graffiti*, 121–22 [##1481–1482]; Colin, "Un jeu de déterminatifs," 179–84)

Line 1

(a) We understand this text as a votive prayer offered by *Ḥr-pa-ꜣIs.t* on behalf of *Ḏḥwty-sḏm*, son of *Ns-nb-ʿy*. On this interpretation *Ḏḥwty-sḏm* is both identified with these various ibis and falcon deities and called an "ibis of pharaoh." Vleeming offers an alternative rendering, certainly worthy of consideration, "o Ibis, King$^{l.p.h.}$." Graffiti containing such good wishes as *ʿnḫ=k* and *ʿnḫ by=k* are well-attested at Medinet Habu, for example, number 49, Thissen, *Die demotischen Graffiti von Medinet Habu*, 47–48, and 218.

Line 2

(a) *ꜣḫ* is presumably *ḫʿ*, "Körper," *Glossar*, 292.

(b) Colin, "Un jeu de déterminatifs," 180, renders *pꜣ ʿḫm Wsỉr*, as "Osiris-l'image de faucon."

(c) Colin, "Un jeu de déterminatifs," 180, suggests *Twtw* at the end of the line, rendering "Osiris-Toutou." This would be the Horus-type god of Dakhla Oasis.

Line 3

(a) For "Horus, Lord of Letopolis," see *CDD S*, 376; Jasnow et al., *Demotic and Hieratic Papyri in the Suzuki Collection*, 51.

(b) The title "scribe of the House-of-Eternity," is uncertain. See Colin, "Un jeu de déterminatifs," 183, on the House of Eternity. Vleeming, *Graffiti*, 121, transliterates: *Sẖ-(bꜣk)* ⌜*pr*⌝ *ḏ.t*, "In writing of the servant of the House-of-Eternity." Less likely is an alternative reading *sẖ* ⌜*šʿ*⌝ *ḏ.t*, "written ⌜for⌝ever."

(c) For *Ns-nb-ʿy*, see *Demot. Nb.*, 682–83.

Line 4

(a) For *Sylws*, see *Demot. Nb.*, 907. Vleeming, *Graffiti*, 122, suggests that this is a separate graffito. He notes further that the mention of *Ḥr-pa-ʾIs.t*, son of *Sylws* (Greek Zoïlos), a known individual, "places the date of our text in the middle of the 2nd century BC."

69. Graffito Spiegelberg #3 (Plate 68b)

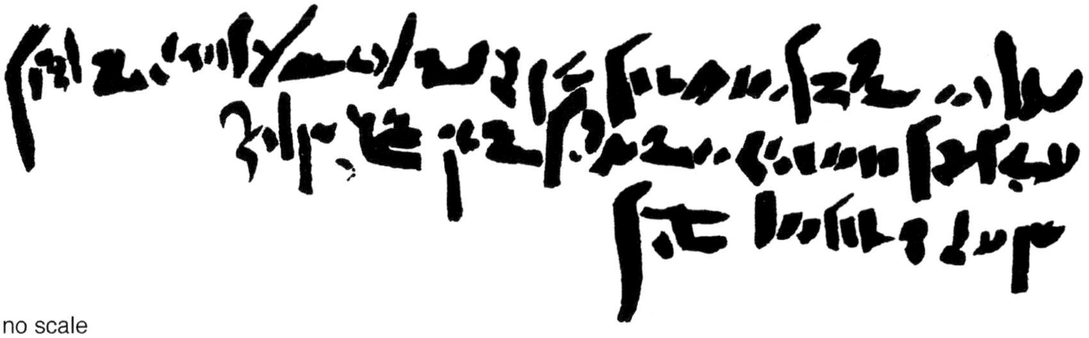

1.

no scale

Transliteration	Translation
1. *pꜣ ꜥ.wy ḥtp n pꜣ hb tr.t ꜣrꜥblws (sꜣ) ʾIy-m-ḥtp*	1. The place of rest of the ibis is in the hand of *ꜣrꜥblws*, (son of) *ʾIy-m-ḥtp*,
2. *pꜣ wr Ḏḥwty ỉrm nꜣy=w* ⸢*pꜣ ṯ ntr.w wꜥ sp*⸣ *sẖ ḥ.t-sp 5.t*	2. the great one of Thoth, together with ⸢the men of the taker of gods all together⸣. Written in regnal year 5.
3. *sẖ Pꜣ-šr-Ḫnsw (sꜣ) Pꜣ-tỉ-Mn*	3. Has written *Pꜣ-šr-Ḫnsw*, (son of) *Pꜣ-tỉ-Mn.*

Commentary

(Spiegelberg #3 pl. 26; Vleeming, *Graffiti*, 122–23 [#1483])

Line 1

(a) Spiegelberg tentatively reads *ꜣlbws*. *Demot. Nb.*, 27, reads *ꜣrꜥblws*. Vleeming, *Graffiti*, 123, quotes a suggestion of Clarysse that one might perhaps transliterate *ꜣrꜥglws* or *ꜣrqylws* for Archelaos.

(b) The phrase "in the hand of" is intriguing. Presumably *ꜣrꜥblws* was responsible, as "great one of Thoth," for the burial chambers of these particular sacred birds.

Line 2

(a) Vleeming, *Graffiti*, 123, renders *ṯ* as "(crew of) bearers." See also Kessler, *Die Heiligen Tiere und der König*, 162.

70. Graffito Spiegelberg #4 (Plate 68c)

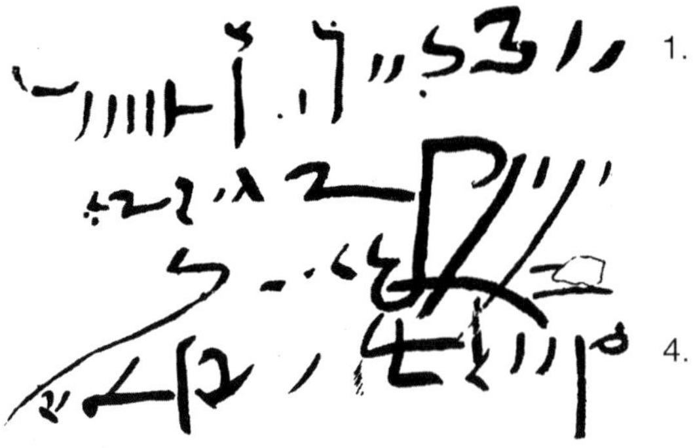

Transliteration	Translation
1. *pꜣ mtre n ḥꜣṯ(?)*	1. The correct of heart(?)
2. ... *ḥry ẖn tꜣ* ...	2. ... above/chief(?) in the ...
3. ⸢*m-ỉr*⸣*(?) šm r-r=f*	3. ⸢Do not⸣(?) go to it/him.
4. *sẖ Pꜣ-šr-Mn sꜣ Ḏḥwty-sḏm*	4. Has written *Pꜣ-šr-Mn*, son of *Ḏḥwty-sḏm.*

Commentary

(Spiegelberg #4, pl. 26; Vleeming, *Graffiti*, 126 [#1487])

Line 1

(a) The reading *mtre* is secure, but the translation less so. We have interpreted this as similar to the *mtre,* "proper mode of conduct," found in graff. 58, 1. However, the rendering is quite tentative. Possible is also a vocative, "o, one correct of heart." Is *pꜣ mtre* part of a personal name *Ns-pꜣ-mtr*? Another alternative is understanding *mtre* as an unorthographic writing of *myt*, "path."

(b) Instead of *ḥꜣt* (as Spiegelberg), read perhaps *wꜥ ḏy*, "a boat?" Vleeming, *Graffiti*, 126, prefers .... Another possibility is *by*, "stone mason," *CDD B*, 26–28, s.v. *by*, "stonemason."

Line 2

(a) Perhaps read *pꜣy pꜣy*, "This is." If so, possibly there is a statement following the pattern: "This is the *mtre* ... above in the ...."

Line 3

(a) *M-ỉr* is a plausible reading. Is the force of this text that *Pꜣ-šr-Mn*, son of *Ḏḥwty-sḏm*, a "great one of Thoth," was in charge of this area, and one should not trespass on his sphere of authority?

Line 4

(a) This individual is certainly the *Pꜣ-šr-Mn*, son of *Ḏḥwty-sḏm*, the "great one of Thoth" frequently appearing in these graffiti.

71. Graffito Spiegelberg #5 (Plate 69a)

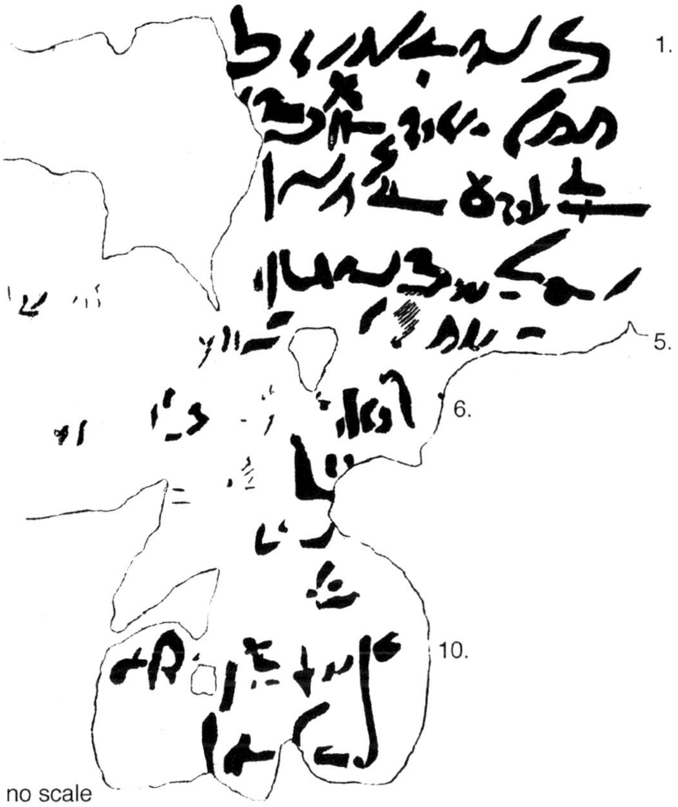

no scale

TRANSLITERATION	TRANSLATION
1. *tꜣy ꜣtr.t ẖpr*	1. As for this chapel, it happened that
2. *hh n-ỉm=s wḥm⌜=w⌝*	2. fire was in it. ⌜They⌝ repeated
3. *qs(.t) ꜥq=w*	3. burial. They entered
4. *r pḥ r pꜣ mꜣ(?)*	4. so as to reach the place(?)
5. *n pꜣ hh ... ỉw=f ... [...]*	5. of the fire..., it being ... [...]
6. *[...] ẖ.wt(?) ... [...]*	6. [...] bodies(?) ... [...]
7. *[...] ... [...]*	7. [...] ... [...]
8. *[...] ... [...]*	8. [...] ... [...]
9. *[...] ... [...]*	9. [...] ... [...]
10. *[...] sẖ Pꜣ-šr-Mn (sꜣ) Ḏḥwty-sḏm*	10. [...] Has written *Pꜣ-šr-Mn*, (son of) *Ḏḥwty-sḏm*,
11. *pꜣ wr Ḏḥwty [...]*	11. the great one of Thoth [...]

Commentary

(Spiegelberg #5, pl. 26; Vleeming, *Graffiti*, 123–24 [#1484])

Line 1

(a) This text clearly describes events associated with this chapel or chamber. We have benefited from the edition of Vleeming, *Graffiti*, 123–24.

Line 2

(a) *hh*, “Flamme, Feuer,” *Glossar*, 281. For *hh*, “fire,” with the evil determinative, see the examples from the *CDD H*, 96 (O. Hor 18, 1).

(b) Or, as in Kessler, *Die Heiligen Tiere und der König*, 162, simply *wḥm qrs.t*, “die Wiederholung der Bestattung.”

Line 3

(a) *ʿq* may have the transitive force found elsewhere in these texts, that is, “to cause to enter” a sacred mummy into the tomb.

Line 4

(a) Understanding this group as an unusual writing of *mꜣ*, “Ort,” *Glossar*, 147, is just possible, but one might also consider *mꜣt*, as a variation of the masculine *myt*, “Weg,” *Glossar*, 153–54, as in graff. 46, 1. Vleeming, *Graffiti*, 123, reads *mꜣq*, “ladder,” but that sense seems difficult as well.

Line 6

(a) The reading *ẖ.t*, “Leib,” *Glossar*, 373–74, is reasonable, but lack of context prevents a secure translation.

72. Graffito Spiegelberg #6 (Plate 69b)

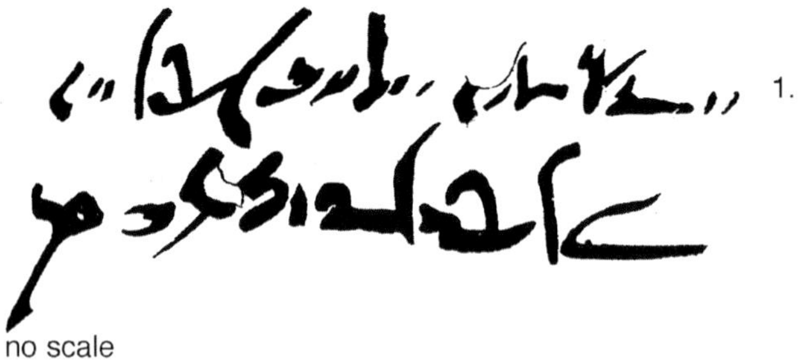

TRANSLITERATION	TRANSLATION
1. *pꜣ rn nfr Pꜣ-šr-pꜣ-mwt (sꜣ) Ḏḥwty-ỉw*	1. The good name of *Pꜣ-šr-pꜣ-mwt*, (son of) *Ḏḥwty-ỉw*,
2. *wr Ḏḥwty mn ty šʿ ḏ.t*	2. great one of Thoth, remains here forever.

Commentary

(Spiegelberg #6, pl. 26; Vleeming, *Graffiti*, 129 [#1490])

Line 1

(a) For *Pꜣ-šr-pꜣ-Mwt*, see *Demot. Nb.*, 236.

(b) For *Ḏḥwty-ỉw*, see *Demot. Nb.*, 1298–99. The reading is not certain.

Line 2

(a) One would expect *pꜣ* before *wr Ḏḥwty*.

73. Graffito Spiegelberg #7 (Plate 69c)

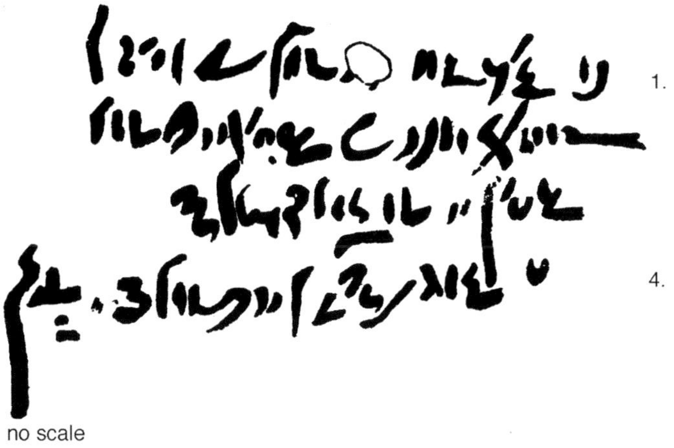

TRANSLITERATION

1. *pꜣ rn nfr <Pꜣ->hb (sꜣ) ʾỈy-m-ḥtp*
2. *mn ty m-bꜣḥ Wsỉr pꜣ hb*
3. *Wsỉr pꜣ bỉk nꜣ ntr.w*
4. *pꜣ ꜥ.wy ḥtp pꜣ hb šꜥ ḏ.t*

TRANSLATION

1. The good name of *<Pꜣ->hb*, (son of) *ʾỈy-m-ḥtp*,
2. remains here before Osiris the ibis
3. (and) Osiris the falcon, the gods
4. of the place of rest of the ibis, forever.

Commentary

(Spiegelberg #7, pl. 26; Vleeming, *Graffiti*, 129–30 [#1491])

Line 1

(a) The writing of *pꜣ* is odd, but the reading is obviously required.

74. Graffito Spiegelberg #8 (Plate 70a)

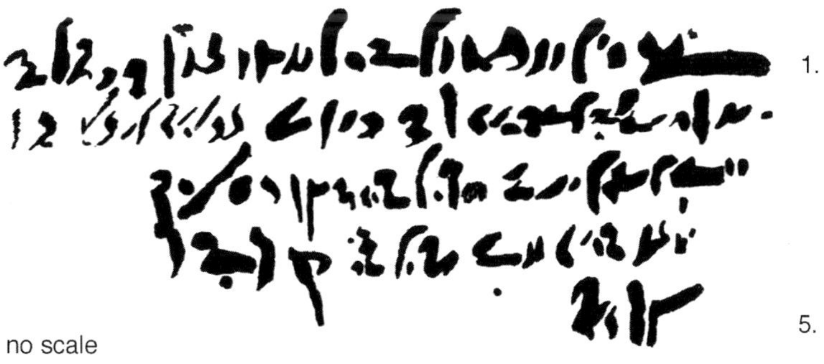

TRANSLITERATION

1. *Wsỉr pꜣ hb Wsỉr pꜣ bỉk nꜣ ntr.w*
2. *n pꜣ ꜥ.wy ḥtp tr=w tỉ.t ꜥnḫ (n) Ḥr-m-ḥb sꜣ Ḏ-ḥr(?)*

TRANSLATION

1. Osiris the ibis (and) Osiris the falcon (and) all the gods of.
2. the place of rest give life (to) *Ḥr-m-ḥb*, son of *Ḏ-ḥr*(?),

3. *pꜣ wr Ḏḥwty pꜣ ṯ ntr.w nꜣ rmt.w tꜣ ml*	3. the great one of Thoth, the taker of the gods, (and to) the men of the harbor,
4. *irm nꜣy=w pꜣ ṯ ntr.w (n) wꜥ sp*	4. together with the ones of the taker of gods (at) one time.
5. *sḫ ḥ.t-sp 5.t*	5. Written in regnal year 5.

Commentary
(Spiegelberg #8, pl. 26; Vleeming, *Graffiti*, 130 [#1492])

Line 2
(a) Spiegelberg reads *pꜣ Ḥr ...* at the end of the line. This type of votive "giving life" inscription is not common in this corpus of graffiti.

Line 3
(a) Spiegelberg read *ꜥl*, but this is clearly the same designation as found elsewhere in the corpus, "the men of the harbor" (graff. 19, 5 and 34, 3), Vleeming, *Graffiti*, 130, reads *ql*, "shrine."

Line 4
(a) We follow Vleeming, *Graffiti*, 130, who reads at the end *(n) wꜥ sp* "in one time." We had also considered *ḥry Nw.t*, "chief of Thebes" (*CDD Ḥ*, 20), but now think this unlikely. *Wꜥ sp* is a rather common phrase in this corpus:

34, 3: *pꜣ ṯ nꜣ ntr.w ꜥꜣ n nꜣ rmt.w (n) tꜣ mr.t n*	*wꜥ sp*
62, 3–5: *pꜣ wr Ḏḥwty pꜣ ṯ ntr.w ꜥꜣ Nw.t iw=f i-ir pꜣ ṯ ntr.w ꜥꜣ Nw.t*	*wꜥ sp*
69, 2: *pꜣ wr Ḏḥwty irm nꜣy=w pꜣ ṯ ntr.w*	*wꜥ sp*
74, 4: *pꜣ wr Ḏḥwty pꜣ ṯ ntr.w nꜣ rmt.w tꜣ ml irm nꜣy=w pꜣ ṯ ntr.w*	*wꜥ sp*
80, 1–2: *Wsir pꜣ hb Wsir pꜣ bik nꜣ ntr.w pꜣ ꜥ.wy n ḥtp n pꜣ hb n*	*wꜥ sp*
81, 2–4: *Wsir pꜣ hb Wsir pꜣ bik nꜣ ntr.w n pꜣ ꜥ.wy n ḥtp n pꜣ hb n*	*wꜥ sp*

Ḥry Nw.t is, on the contrary, infrequently found. An example of the title is in P. Berlin P. 13566, recto, x+21, rendered "Vorsteher von Theben," K.-Th. Zauzich, *Papyri von der Insel Elephantine*, Demotische Papyri aus den staatlichen Museen zu Berlin Preussischer Kulturbesitz 3 (Berlin: Akademie, 1993). We know of no comprehensive discussion of this title, which is rendered as "Thebarch" by J. Manning, *Land and Power in Ptolemaic Egypt: The Structure of Land Tenure* (Cambridge: Cambridge University Press, 2003), 138. See also the significant remarks of G. Vittmann, *Der demotische Papyrus Rylands 9*, Ägypten und Altes Testament 38 (Wiesbaden: Harrassowitz, 1998), 2:507–8.

75. Graffito Spiegelberg #9 (Plate 70b)

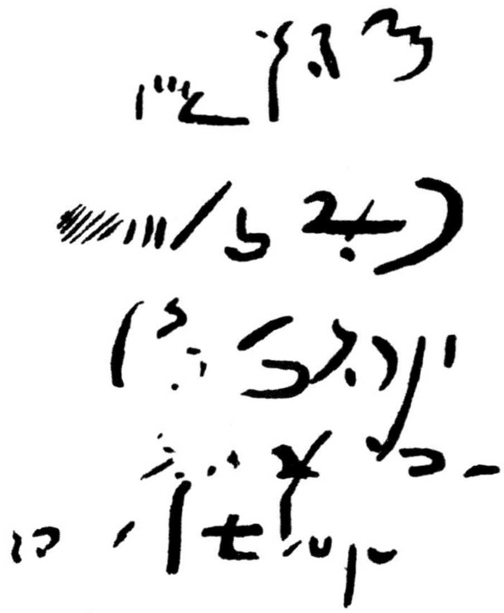

1.

5.

no scale

Transliteration

1. *wn-nꜣ.w ... [...]*
2. *wn ẖry ... [...]*
3. *ỉw=f mḥ ... [...]*
4. *n ...*
5. *sẖ Pꜣ-šr-Mn sꜣ ⸢Ḏḥwty⸣-[sḏm]*

Translation

1. A ... [...]
2. was opened below ... [...]
3. it being full ... [...]
4. ...
5. Has written *Pꜣ-šr-Mn*, son of ⸢*Ḏḥwty*⸣*-[sḏm]*

Commentary

(Spiegelberg #9, pl. 26; Vleeming, *Graffiti*, 126 [#1486])

Line 1

(a) This is presumably a word for a "chamber" or similar. The text seems to describe or commemorate the opening of a chamber for the burial of the sacred animals. Vleeming, *Graffiti*, 126, reads *wn ....* Perhaps restore or understand *ʿ.wy ḥtp*, that is, "A place of rest was opened below." One might transliterate *wn-nꜣ.w wʿ ...*, but then the *wn-nꜣ.w* would be written very strangely.

Line 3

(a) Understand possibly word for "mummies," "equipment," or "goods" after *mḥ*.

Line 5

(a) Spiegelberg aptly suggests [*Ḏḥwty-sḏm*] at the end of the line. This individual is probably the *Pꜣ-šr-Mn*, son of *Ḏḥwty-sḏm*, the "great one of Thoth," frequently appearing in these graffiti.

76. Graffito Spiegelberg #10 (Plate 71)

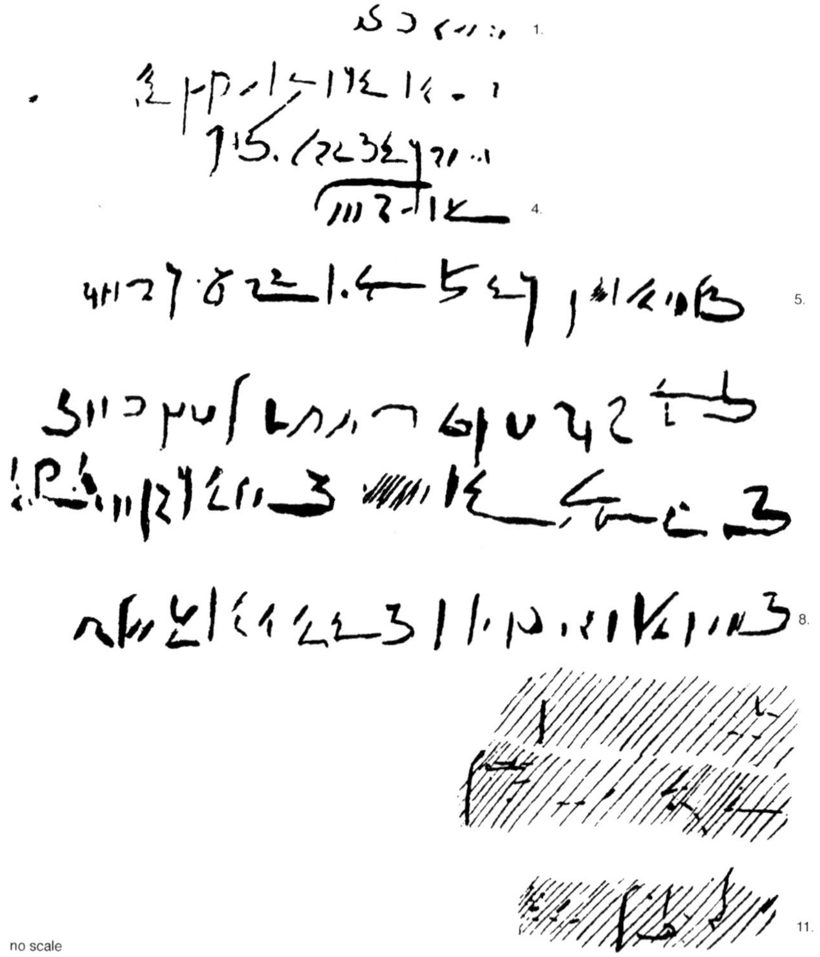

Transliteration	Translation
1. *[...] ... [...]*	1. [...] ... [...]
2. *[...] ... rn.w(?) ... r ḥry r ỉrpy [...]*	2. [...] ... names(?) ... up to the divine chapel [...]
3. *[...] ... st mqḥ n mt(?) [...]*	3. [...] ... they mourn in a thing(?) [...]
4. *[...] ỉy r nꜣy myt(?) [...]*	4. [...] to come to these paths(?) [...]
5. *šꜥ-tw=w sẖ(?) st wḫꜣ qs(.t) n sf*	5. until they are recorded(?). They desire burial with resin
6. *wtḥ ꜥnḫ(?) r-hb=w pꜣ rmt nt ỉ.ỉr(?)*	6. (of) anointing ("refined resin"?), (and the) bouquet(?) which they sent. As for the man who will(?)
7. *tm(?) rẖ(?) pḥ r-bn-nꜣy šꜥ-tw nꜣ ỉyẖ.w ...*	7. not(?) be able(?) to reach here until the things ...
8. *my tỉ s nꜣ sẖ.w(?) ... [...]*	8. let the scribes(?) give it ... [...]
9. *[...] ... [...]*	9. [...] ... [...]
10. *[...] ... [...]*	10. [...] ... [...]
11. *[...] ... [...]*	11. [...] ... [...]

Commentary
(Spiegelberg #10, pl. 27; Vleeming, *Graffiti*, 131 [#1493] without translation)

Line 2
(a) One might naturally read *tỉ* before *rn.w.*
(b) Instead of *rn.w*, one may transliterate *bn-pw=w.*

Line 3
(a) *mqḥ*, "Trauer," *Glossar*, 183, is a technical term in this corpus (see p. 47). It seems to denote the mourning performed for the sacred animal mummies.
(b) *mt* is but one possibility.

Line 4
(a) We had first considered *ỉn=y* after *nꜣy*, but now think that this may be a writing of *myt*, "path." The end of the word, is, to be sure, extremely uncertain.

Line 5
(a) Does the writer refer here to the recording of the sacred animal mummies before interment? We tentatively suggest *šʿ-tw=w*, but the suffix *w* may not be written. In line 7, *šʿ-tw* has the man with hand determinative, but that does not seem possible in this line.
(b) Graffito 54, 7 also warns the cult workers to use resin in the burial process. *Sf wtḥ* is perhaps "refined resin."

Line 6
(a) The transliteration of the line after *wtḥ* and before *pꜣ rmṯ* is highly conjectural. *ʿnḫ*, "der Blumenstrauss," *Glossar*, 64, is a suggestion. However, we do not know any evidence for flowers playing a role in the ibis cult.
(b) *ỉ-ỉr* is difficult grammatically. The reading *ỉr* is not absolutely secure. Perhaps transliterate *nt ỉw=f (r) ỉr* ?

Line 7
(a) Similarly, the interpretation of the groups before *pḥ* as *tm rḫ* is a mere guess on the basis of possible sense. We are dependent here on Spiegelberg's hand-copy, almost certainly made under difficult conditions; one wonders whether *ỉr-rḫ* may have originally been written. Still, of course, this would also be grammatically difficult to explain. The entire sentence is obscure.
(b) The line appears to continue to deal with the materials employed for the embalming of the sacred birds.
(c) Here *šʿ-tw* clearly has the man with hand to mouth determinative.

Line 8
(a) We cannot offer any satisfying transliteration of the end of this line.

77. Graffito Spiegelberg #11 (Plate 72)

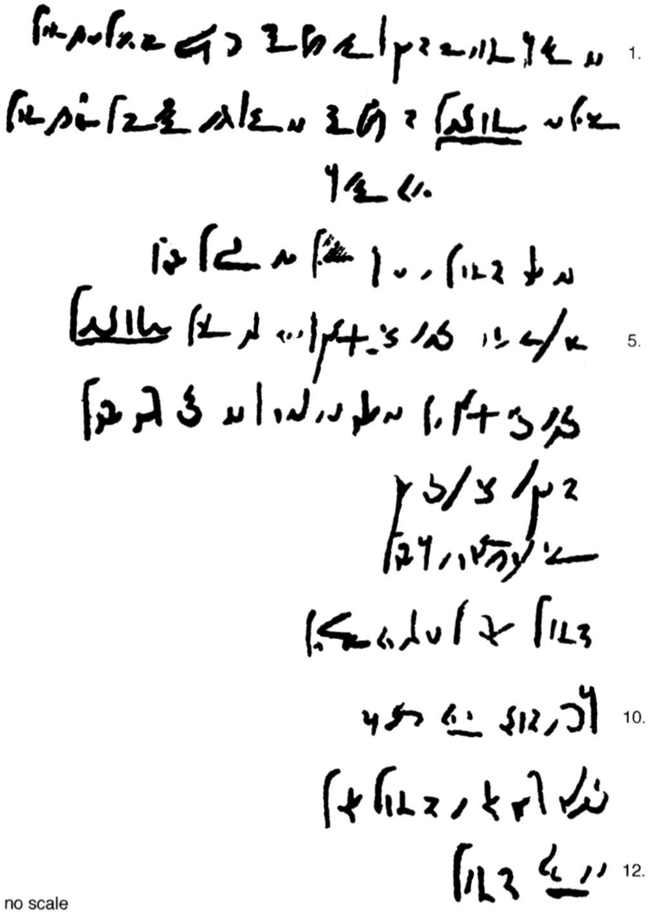

no scale

TRANSLITERATION

1. *pꜣ rn nfr nꜣ rmt.w ṯ ntr.w m-bꜣḥ Wsỉr pꜣ hb*
2. *Wsỉr pꜣ bik nꜣ ntr.w pꜣ ʿ.wy ḥtp pꜣ hb*
3. *pꜣy=w rn*
4. *Pꜣ-šr-Ḫnsw sꜣ Pꜣ-tỉ-Wsỉr pꜣ wr Ḏḥwty*
5. *Grt(?) (sꜣ) Ḥr-wn-nfr(?) ... Wsỉr bik*
6. *Ḥr-wn-nfr(?) (sꜣ) Pꜣ-šr-... pꜣ mr šn Ḏḥwty*
7. *nꜣ rmt.w wrṯ(?)*
8. *Plth sꜣ Pa-Ḏḥwty*
9. *Ḫnsw-Ḏḥwty (sꜣ) Pꜣ-šr-ʿ-pḥ.ty*
10. *Pa-nꜣ ʿntꜣy*
11. *Ḥr-Mw.t(?) sꜣ Ḫnsw-Ḏḥwty*
12. *Pꜣ-šr-n-Ḫnsw*

TRANSLATION

1. The good name of the men who take the gods before Osiris the ibis
2. (and) Osiris the falcon (and) the gods of the place of rest of the ibis.
3. Their name(s):
4. *Pꜣ-šr-Ḫnsw*, son of *Pꜣ-tỉ-Wsỉr*, the great one of Thoth,
5. *Grt*(?), (son of) *Ḥr-wn-nfr*(?), ... Osiris falcon,
6. *Ḥr-wn-nfr(?)* (son of) *Pꜣ-šr-...* the lesonis of Thoth,
7. the men of (the) cage(?):
8. *Plth*, son of *Pa-Ḏḥwty*,
9. *Ḫnsw-Ḏḥwty*, (son of) *Pꜣ-šr-ʿꜣ-pḥ.ty*,
10. *Pa-nꜣ*, the perfumer,
11. *Ḥr-Mw.t*(?), son of *Ḫnsw-Ḏḥwty*,
12. *Pꜣ-šr-n-Ḫnsw*.

Commentary
(Spiegelberg #11, pl. 27; Vleeming, *Graffiti*, 131–33 [#1494])

Line 1
(a) The *rn nfr* inscription is written on behalf of all these individuals.
(b) Presumably *nꜣ rmt.w ṯ ntr.w* is a compound phrase, denoting all those who carry out the cult activity of the sacred animal mummies. Or is "the men of (the) taker of the gods" to be understood.

Line 4
(a) Vleeming, *Graffiti*, 131, reads *Pꜣ-di͗-⌜Mn⌝*.

Line 5
(a) *Grt* is reasonable, comparing *Glṯ̂ꜣ*, *Demot. Nb.*, 1041. Still, it is hardly secure. Could this in fact be merely *gl-šr*?
(b) Compare *Ḥr-wn-nfr*, *Demot. Nb.*, 794–95. The reading is not certain; Vleeming, *Graffiti*, 131, *Ḥr-.....* The last element is reminiscent of *d̲.t*, "eternity."
(c) P. Dils, "Les *tꜣ̂j (nꜣ) ntr.w* ou θεαγοί: Fonction religieuse et place dans la vie civile," *BIFAO* 95 (1995): 156, suggests *pꜣ wr bi͗k*, at the end of this line, following H. Sottas, "Le Thiase d'Ombos," *Revue Archéologique* 13 (1921): 36. While the reading is appealing, we find this *pꜣ wr* difficult to see in Spiegelberg's copy. Vleeming reads *Ḥr-... pꜣ wr-Bi͗k*. *Wsi͗r pꜣ bi͗k* is virtually always accompanied by *Wsi͗r pꜣ hb*, but there is no trace of the latter in this hand-copy of Spiegelberg.

Line 6
(a) Vleeming, *Graffiti*, 131, reads *Pꜣ-šr-Pꜣ-ẖrṯ̂*.
(b) There are not many attestations of a "lesonis of Thoth," but see, for example, J. Berlandini, "D'un percnoptère et de sa relation à Isis, au scarabée et à la tête divine," in *"Parcourir l'éternité": Hommages à Jean Yoyotte*, ed. C. Zivie-Coche and I. Guermeur, 2 vols., Bibliothèque de l'École des hautes études, sciences religieuses 156 (Turnhout: Brepols, 2012), 125; A. Burkhardt, *Ägypter und Meroiten im Dodekaschoinos: Untersuchungen zur Typologie und Bedeutung der demotischen Graffiti*, Meroitica 8 (Berlin: Akademie, 1985) 100; Kessler, *Die heiligen Tiere und der König*, 195; T. Eide et al., *Fontes Historiae Nubiorum: Textual Sources for the History of the Middle Nile Region between the Eighth Century BC and the Sixth Century AD, Vol. 3; From the First to the Sixth Century AD* (Bergen: University of Bergen, 1998), 987; L. Török, *Between Two Worlds: The Frontier Region between Ancient Nubia and Egypt, 3700 BC–AD 500*, Probleme der Ägyptologie 29 (Leiden: Brill, 2009), 456; G. Lefebvre, *Le Tombeau de Petosiris, 1: Description* (Cairo: Imprimerie de l'institut français d'archéologie orientale, 1924), 55 and 80.

Line 7
(a) *Wrṯ̂* has been the subject of discussion. The word, which has the plant or wood determinative, has been understood as "Käfig," *Glossar*, 95. More specifically, some have suggested "aviary" on the basis of this context, den Brinker, Muhs, and Vleeming, *Berichtigungsliste*, 519. Vleeming, *Graffiti*, 133, writes: "The noun is probably to be connected with the *wlṯ.w* known from the cult of the sacred ram of Amun," citing C. Martin, "A Demotic Land Lease from Philadelphia: P. BM 10560," *JEA* 72 (1986): 167, n. 3.
(b) We understand "the men of the cage(?)" to be the heading for the following list of five individuals. Of course, it is also possible that these "men of the cage(?)" belong still to the group of men designated as those who "take the gods" in line 1.

Line 8

(a) Vleeming, *Graffiti*, 133–35, reads *Pltn*, Platon, but is not *n* difficult?

Line 10

(a) *Glossar*, 65, has only *ʿnṱ*, "Räucherwerk." For *ʿnty*, "perfumer," see J. Moje, *Demotische Epigraphik aus Dandara: Die demotischen Grabstelen*, Internet-Beiträge zur Ägyptologie und Sudanarchäologie 9 (London: Golden House, 2008), 31–32. *ʿnṱ* has generally been identified with myrrh or frankincense and can be used in mummification, Ikram and Dodson, *Mummy*, 106.

Line 11

(a) The otherwise unattested name *Ḥr-mw.t* is not certain. The second element also resembles *tny.t*, "Teil," *Glossar*, 638. Vleeming, *Graffiti*, 133, reads *Ḥr-sꜣ-Ꞽs.t(?)*.

78. Graffito Spiegelberg #12 (Plate 73a)

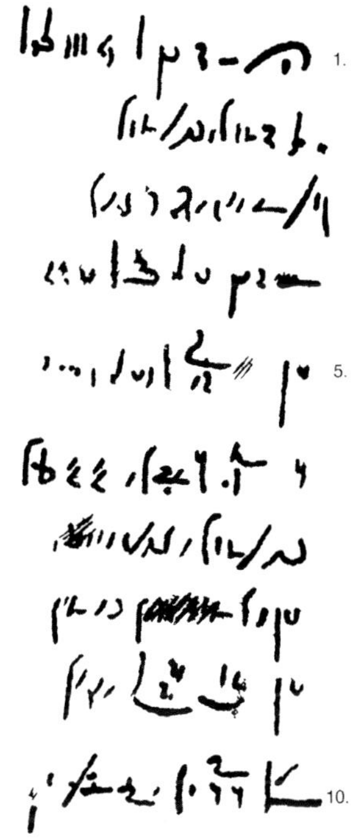

no scale

Transliteration

1. *sp n nꜣ rmt.w ꜥy.w*
2. *Pꜣ-šr-Ḫnsw sꜣ Hr*
3. *Pa-rt sꜣ Tny.t-Ḫnsw(?)*
4. *... Pꜣ-šr-...*
5. *sẖ [Pꜣy]-kꜣ(?) sꜣ Pꜣ-šr-...*
6. *Pa-Wsr sꜣ Twt*
7. *Hr sꜣ Ḥr-ỉw(?)*
8. *sẖ ʾImn-... (sꜣ) Hr*
9. *sẖ W...*
10. *Ns-Ḫmn-ỉw sꜣ Hkl(?)*

Translation

1. The remainder of the great people:
2. *Pꜣ-šr-Ḫnsw*, son of *Hr*,
3. *Pa-rt*, son of *Tny.t-Ḫnsw(?)*,
4. *... Pꜣ-šr-...*,
5. the scribe, *[Pꜣy] kꜣ(?)*, son of *Pꜣ-šr-...*,
6. *Pa-Wsr*, son of *Twt*,
7. *Hr*, son of *Ḥr-ỉw(?)*,
8. the scribe *ʾImn-...* (son of) *Hr*,
9. the scribe *W...*,
10. *Ns-Ḫmn-ỉw*, son of *Hkl(?)*.

Commentary

(Spiegelberg #12, pl. 27; Vleeming, *Graffiti*, 133–34 [#1495])

Line 1

(a) *rmt.w ꜥy.w* is a richly nuanced designation in demotic texts; its precise force in the graffiti is unclear.[204] The "great people" are presumably important locals or members of the cult. This graffito may be a continuation of graff. 77.

Line 5

(a) Perhaps *kꜣ*, "Stier," *Glossar*, 555–56. Vleeming, *Graffiti*, 133, reads ⸢*Pꜣ-*<*ʾI*>*gš*⸣.

204 On *rmt ꜥy.w* in the ibis texts, Ray, *Archive of Ḥor*, 12.

Line 6
(a) For *Pa-Wsr*, see *Demot. Nb.*, 361.

Line 7
(a) Perhaps rather *Ḥr-ꜥw(?)*, see *Demot. Nb.*, 792.

79. Graffito Spiegelberg #13 (Plate 70c)

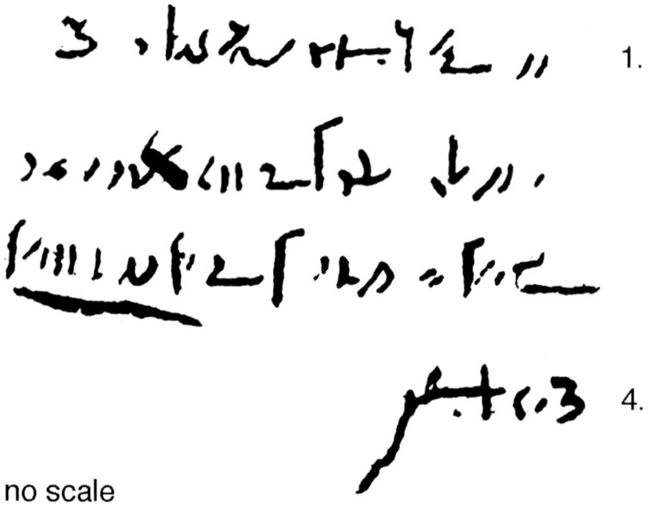

Transliteration	Translation
1. *pꜣ rn nfr Sṯꜣ=w⸢-tꜣ-wty⸣*	1. The good name of *Sṯꜣ=w⸢-tꜣ-wty⸣*,
2. *sꜣ Pꜣ-šr-Ḏḥwty mn ty ⸢m-bꜣḥ⸣*	2. son of *Pꜣ-šr-Ḏḥwty*, remains here ⸢before⸣
3. *Wsỉr pꜣ hb Wsỉr pꜣ bỉk*	3. Osiris the ibis (and) Osiris the falcon
4. *šꜥ ḏ.t*	4. forever.

Commentary
(Spiegelberg #13, pl. 27; Vleeming, *Graffiti*, 134 [#1496])

80. Graffito Spiegelberg #14 (Plate 73b)

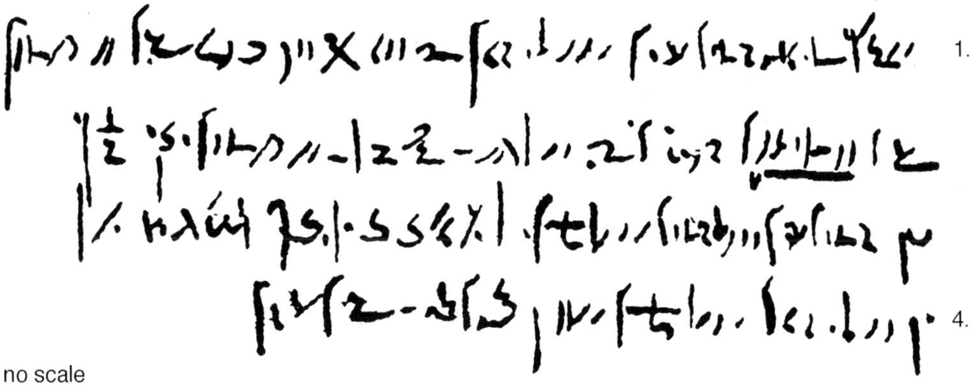

no scale

Transliteration

1. *pꜣ rn nfr Ḫnsw-Ḏḥwty sꜣ Pꜣ-šr-Ḫnsw mn ty m-bꜣḥ Wsỉr pꜣ hb*
2. *Wsỉr pꜣ bỉk nꜣ ntr.w pꜣ ʿ.wy n ḥtp n pꜣ hb n wʿ sp*
3. *sẖ Ḫnsw-Ḏḥwty sꜣ Pꜣ-šr-Ḫnsw sꜣ Pꜣ-tỉ-Mn n ḥ.t-sp 36 ỉr ỉr ḥ.t-sp 25 ỉbt 3 šmw sw 11*
4. *sẖ Pꜣ-šr-Ḫnsw sꜣ Pꜣ-tỉ-Mn pꜣy=y ỉṱ* ⸢*pꜣ wr Ḏḥwty*⸣

Translation

1. The good name of *Ḫnsw-Ḏḥwty*, son of *Pꜣ-šr-Ḫnsw*, remains here before Osiris the ibis
2. (and) Osiris the falcon (and) the gods of the place of rest of the ibis at one time.
3. Has written *Ḫnsw-Ḏḥwty*, son of *Pꜣ-šr-Ḫnsw*, son of *Pꜣ-tỉ-Mn*, in regnal year 36, which makes regnal year 25, third month of summer, day 11.
4. Has written *Pꜣ-šr-Ḫnsw*, son of *Pꜣ-tỉ-Mn*, my father, ⸢the great one of Thoth⸣.

Commentary

(Spiegelberg #14; Vleeming, *Graffiti*, 134–35 [#1497]; Chauveau, "Un été 145," 129–32)

Line 1

(a) We follow Chauveau, "Un été 145," 130, who suggested *Pꜣ-šr-Ḫnsw*, despite the odd writing or copy of *Ḫnsw*. Spiegelberg's original transliteration was *Pꜣ-šr-n-tꜣ-ỉḥ.t* here and in line 4 as well as in graff. 81. Vleeming, *Graffiti*, 134, also reads *Pꜣ-šr-Ḫnsw*. If one considers the information recorded in graff. 80 and 81, it becomes clear that only the reading *Pꜣ-šr-Ḫnsw* results in a coherent genealogy for the family of the *wr Ḏḥwty Pꜣ-šr-Ḫnsw*; the reading *Pꜣ-šr-n-tꜣ-ỉḥ.t* eliminates any connection between graff. 80 and 81. See the genealogy presented on p. 66.

Line 3

(a) Chauveau dates this text to August 4, 145 BCE; Vleeming, *Graffiti*, 134 (reign of Ptolemy VI and Ptolemy VII). As we have already remarked, "day 11" is by far the most common day recorded in this corpus.

Line 4

(a) Again, Vleeming, *Graffiti*, 134, reads *Pꜣ-šr-Ḫnsw*, as Chauveau.
(b) We follow the transliteration of Vleeming at the end of the line, *pꜣ wr Ḏḥwty*, even if the copy is not absolutely clear. It yields excellent sense.

81. Graffito Spiegelberg #15 (Plate 73c)

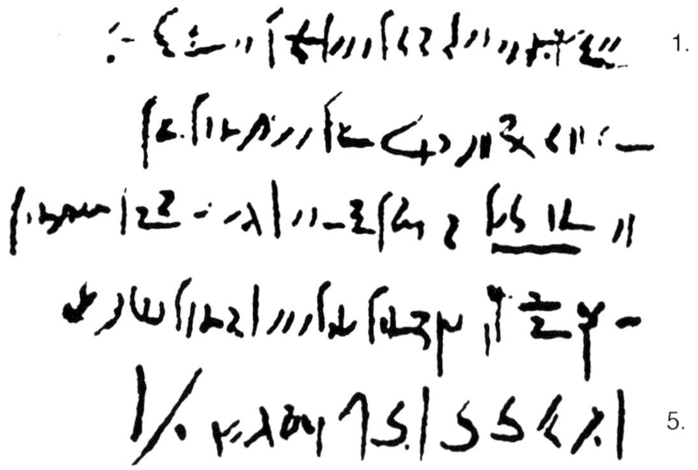

no scale

Transliteration

1. *pꜣ rn nfr Pꜣ-šr-Ḫnsw sꜣ Pꜣ-tỉ-Mn ⸢pꜣ wr Ḏḥwty⸣*
2. *mn ty m-bꜣḥ Wsỉr pꜣ hb Wsỉr*
3. *pꜣ bỉk nꜣ ntr.w n pꜣ ꜥ.wy n ḥtp n pꜣ hb*
4. *n wꜥ sp sẖ Ḫnsw-Ḏḥwty sꜣ Pꜣ-šr-Ḫnsw pꜣy=f šr*
5. *ḥ.t-sp 36 ỉr ỉr ḥ.t-sp 25 ỉbt 3 šmw sw 11*

Translation

1. The good name of *Pꜣ-šr-Ḫnsw*, son of *Pꜣ-tỉ-Mn*, ⸢the great one of Thoth,⸣
2. remains here before Osiris the ibis (and) Osiris
3. the falcon (and) the gods of the place of rest of the ibis
4. at one time. Has written *Ḫnsw-Ḏḥwty*, son of *Pꜣ-šr-Ḫnsw*, his child.
5. Regnal year 36, which makes regnal year 25, third month of summer, day 11.

Commentary

(Spiegelberg #15; Vleeming, *Graffiti*, 235 [#1498]; Chauveau, "Un été 145," 129–32)

Line 1

(a) We follow Chauveau's reading of *Pꜣ-šr-Ḫnsw* (adopted also by Vleeming, *Graffiti*, 135); Spiegelberg transliterated *Pꜣ-šr-tꜣ-ỉḥ.t*. See note (a) on graff. 80, 1.

Line 4

(a) One expects naturally *Pꜣ-šr-Ḫnsw* as graff. 80, 3. Perhaps Spiegelberg's hand-copy is misleading or there is damage to the sign for šr.

Line 5

(a) Chauveau dates this text to August 4, 145 BCE (reign of Ptolemy VI and Ptolemy VII); Vleeming, *Graffiti*, 135.

82. Graffito Spiegelberg #16 (Plate 74a)

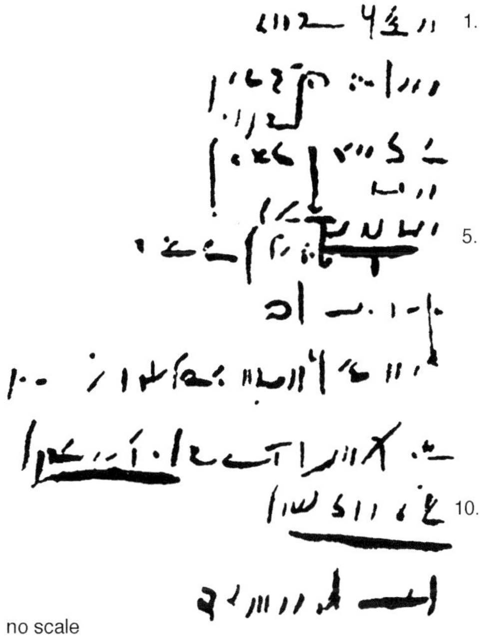

no scale

Transliteration	Translation
1. *pꜣ rn mn ...*	1. The name remains ...
2. *sꜣ Pꜣ-ti͗-... -Ḫnsw*	2. son of *Pꜣ-ti͗-... -Ḫnsw*
3. *... gm ...*	3. ... to find ...
4. ...	4. ...
5. ...	5. ...
6. ...	6. ...
7. *sẖ n ḥ.t-sp ...*	7. Written in regnal year ...
8. *n pꜣ rn pꜣ ʿ.wy ḥtp* ⌜*Ḏḥwty*⌝ ...	8. in/as the name of the place of rest of ⌜Thoth⌝ ...
9. *mn ty m-bꜣḥ ...*	9. remains here before ...
10. ...	10. ...
11. ...	11. ...

Commentary

(Spiegelberg #16, pl. 27; Vleeming, *Graffiti*, 135–36 [#1499] without continuous transliteration or translation)

Line 2

(a) Vleeming, *Graffiti*, 136, quotes a suggestion of Clarysse, *Pꜣ-ti͗-ʾIs.t sꜣ Pꜣ-ti͗-Ḫnsw.*

Line 3

(a) One may propose *ti͗.t gm i͗ry*, "to cause that a companion finds," but this yields little apparent sense in the context.

Line 11

(a) Perhaps a date, *ḥ.t-sp 7 ...?*

83. Graffito Spiegelberg #17 (Plate 74b)

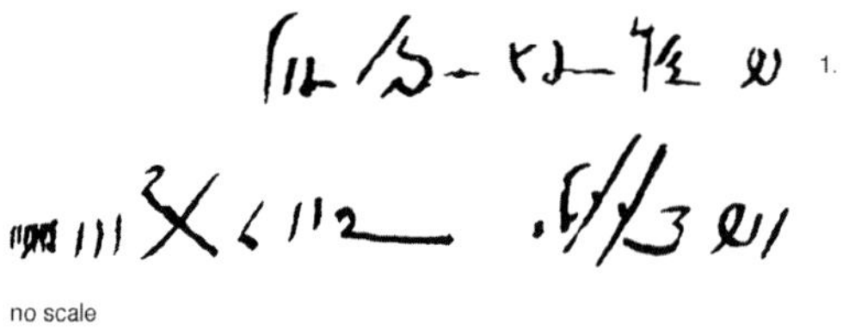

Transliteration
1. *pꜣ rn nfr n Hr*
2. *sꜣ Pꜣ-šll mn ty*

Translation
1. The good name of *Hr*,
2. son of *Pꜣ-šll*, remains here.

Commentary
(Spiegelberg #17, pl. 27; Vleeming, *Graffiti*, 136 [#1500])

Line 2
(a) For *Pꜣ-šll*, see *Demot. Nb.*, 276. An alternative reading is *Pꜣ-mll*, *Demot. Nb.*, 190. The name *Pꜣ-mrl* appears in graff. 34, 1 and 45, 5.

84. Graffito Spiegelberg #18 (Plate 74c)

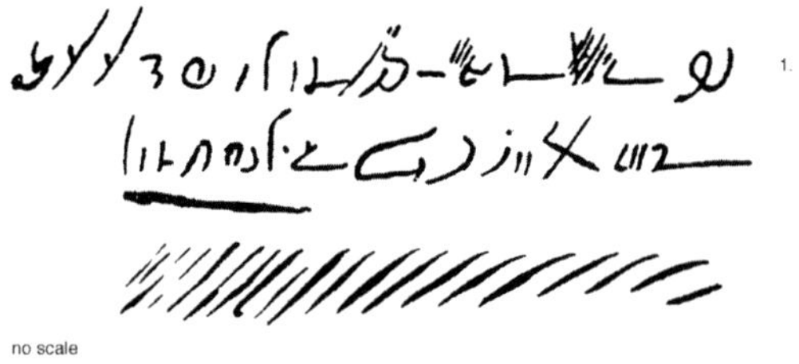

Transliteration
1. *pꜣ rn nfr n Hr sꜣ Pꜣ-šll*
2. *mn ty m-bꜣḥ Wsỉr pꜣ hb*
3. *[Wsỉr pꜣ bỉk ...]*

Translation
1. The good name of *Hr*, son of *Pꜣ-šll*,
2. remains here before Osiris the ibis
3. [(and) Osiris the falcon ...]

Commentary
(Spiegelberg #18, pl. 27; Vleeming, *Graffiti*, 136 [#1501])

Line 1
(a) An alternative reading is *Pꜣ-mll*, *Demot. Nb.*, 190; see graff. 83, 2 note (a).

Line 2
(a) The *hb* seems to have a *k* as in *bỉk*.

Line 3
(a) Probably restore *Wsỉr pꜣ bỉk*, “Osiris, the falcon.”

85. Graffito Spiegelberg #19 (Plate 75)

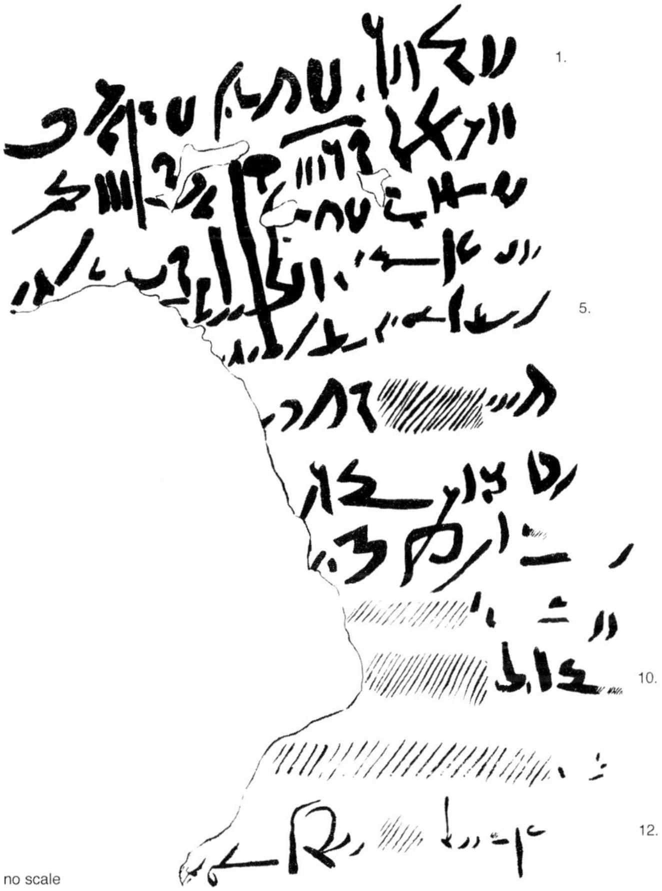

TRANSLITERATION

1. *pꜣ h̭ṱ n pꜣ hb pꜣ sẖ nb nt*
2. *ỉw=f (r) ꜥš nꜣy sẖ(.w) my ỉr=f*
3. *pꜣ bꜣk (n) pꜣ hb tꜣ ꜣtr*
4. *ỉrm Pꜣ-tỉ-Ỉs.t(?) ỉ-ỉr Pꜣ-šr-⌜M⌝[n]*
5. *sꜣ Ḏḥwty-sḏm r-ẖry [...]*
6. *⌜pr⌝(?) ... ⌜hh⌝ [...]*
7. *r ḥr=f bn-pw=f [wrr]*
8. *r ỉy r-ḥry šꜥ [...]*
9. *ỉ-ỉr ... [...]*
10. *bn-pw m[t ...]*
11. *... [...]*
12. *sẖ Pꜣ-šr-[Mn] sꜣ Ḏḥwty-sḏm [pꜣ wr Ḏḥwty]*

TRANSLATION

1. The inspiration of the ibis (for) every scribe who
2. will read these writings. Let him do
3. the work (of) the ibis in the chapel
4. with *Pꜣ-tỉ-Ỉs.t(?)*. *Pꜣ-šr-⌜M⌝[n,]*
5. son of *Ḏḥwty-sḏm*, was below [...]
6. Came out(?) ... ⌜fire⌝ [...]
7. to his face. He did not [delay]
8. to come up until [...]
9. ... [...]
10. No[thing ...]
11. ... [...]
12. Has written *Pꜣ-šr-[Mn]*, son of *Ḏḥwty-sḏm*, [the great one of Thoth].

Commentary
(Spiegelberg #19, pl. 29; Vleeming, *Graffiti*, 127–29 [#1489]; Kessler, *Die Heiligen Tiere und der König*, 161)

Line 1
(a) *ḫyṯ*, "rasen," "Verzückung," *Glossar*, 350; *CDD Ḫ*, 23–26, s.v. *ḫyṯ*; see, for example, Ray, *Texts from the Baboon and Falcon* Galleries, 114; R. Ritner, "An Eternal Curse upon the Reader of These Lines," in *Ancient Egyptian Demonology: Studies on the Boundaries between the Demonic and the Divine in Egyptian Magic*, ed. P. Kousoulis, OLA 175 (Leuven: Peeters, Departement Oosterse Studies, 2011), 21. Clearly, this is both an inspirational text and a narrative of events that have occurred in the tomb-chapel.

Line 3
(a) "The ibis in the *ꜣtr.t*-chapel," Kessler, *Die Heiligen Tiere und der König*, 159–60, quoting a translation of Zauzich.

Line 4
(a) The graffito seems to describe *Pꜣ-šr-Mn*'s situation and behavior during a fire. This fire (or several different fires?) is mentioned several times in the corpus: graff. 71, 2, 5 and 86, 3.

Line 6
(a) We had first read *hyn.w*, but think now that *prj*, "herauskommen," *Glossar*, 134, which also fits the traces, is preferable. *Prj* is used in connection with fire, *Glossar*, 135.
(b) *hh*, "Flamme," *Glossar*, 281, is a reasonable transliteration, but hardly certain.

Line 7
(a) *wrr/ḥrr*, *Glossar*, 325–26, yields good sense here.

Line 12
(a) This is certainly the best known of the "great ones of Thoth" in this corpus.

86. Graffito Spiegelberg #24 (Plate 76a)

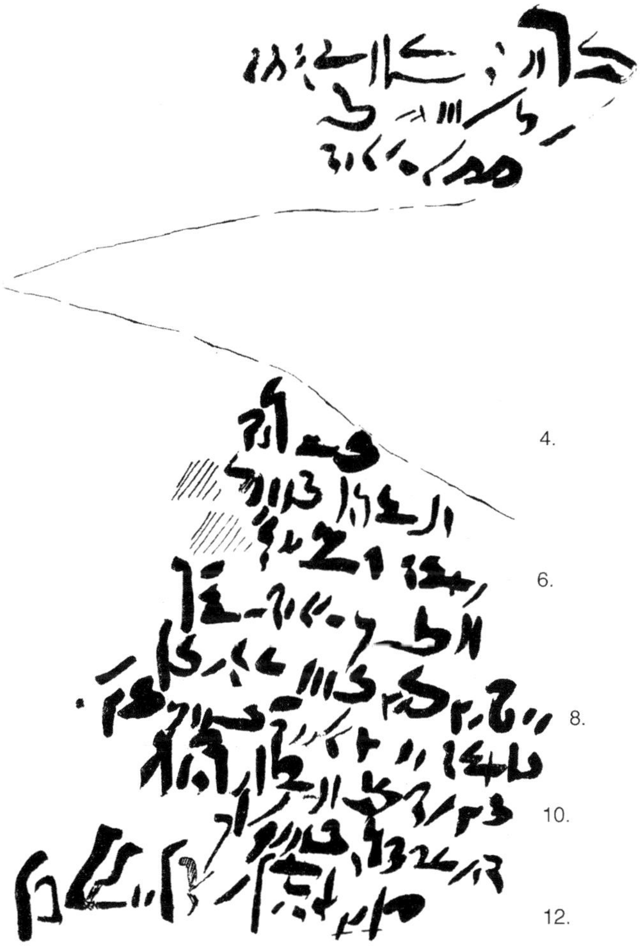

TRANSLITERATION	TRANSLATION
1. *tꜣy ḫ.t(?) tbtꜣ*	1. This area(?) of ceremony
2. *r-ḫry ḫpr*	2. below. There happened
3. *hh n-im=s*	3. a fire therein.
Presumably numerous lines lost	Presumably numerous lines lost
x+4. *ir=n ḥꜣ=s(?)*	x+4. We were before it(?),
x+5. *iw bn-pw=w <gm> myt*	x+5. without <finding> a path
x+6. *r-r=s nꜣ-ꜥšꜣ pꜣ(?) ḫr[ḫr(?) ...]*	x+6. to it. Abundant was the(?) de[struction(?) ...]
x+7. *iw ḫpr=f n-im=s n rn*	x+7. that happened in it because of
x+8. *pꜣ tm gm myt r-ir=w r*	x+8. the not finding the path that they made
x+9. *ḥr r-r=s pꜣ rmt nb pꜣ tꜣ nt iw=f (r) gm*⌉	x+9. before it. As for any man who will find a
x+10. *nkt r ti.t wbꜣ=w r ḫ.ṯ=w r*	x+10. thing to give with regard to them ... according
x+11. *tꜣy=f gm my ti=f*	x+11. to his power, let him give (it).
x+12. *sḫ Pꜣ-šr-Mn sꜣ Ḏḥwty<-sḏm> pꜣ wr Ḏḥwty*	x+12. Has written *Pꜣ-šr-Mn*, son of *Ḏḥwty*<-*sḏm*>, the great one of Thoth.

Commentary
(Spiegelberg #24 [pl. 28]; Vleeming, *Graffiti*, 124–25 [#1485]; Kessler, *Die Heiligen Tiere und der König*, 161).

Line 1
(a) We understand *h̲.t* to be either a variant of *ḫt*, “Quadrat,” *Glossar*, 371, or a form of *h̲.t*, “Leib,” *Glossar*, 373–74. However, the transliteration is extremely uncertain. One might also read *ḥꜣ.t*, “beginning, front, ” *Glossar*, 287. If so, could we translate “this front of the ceremony (area)?”
(b) *tbtꜣ*, “ceremony,”is *CDD T*, 159, s.v. *tbty*. The compound appears to designate a section of the tomb where the work of the cult is done. *Tbtꜣ* appears to end with the house determinative.

Line 3
(a) *n-ꞽm=s* would refer back to the compound in line 1.

Line x+4
Vleeming, *Graffiti*, 125, reads *[wḥ]m<=w> h̲ꜣ(.t)* “<They> [repea]ted a storey.” He suggests that this might refer to “a new construction intended to replace the storey that had been lost or damaged.” However, does this make sense in the context? He also compares the phrase in the associated inscription *wḥm=w qs.t* “They repeated a burial.” Perhaps the simplest restoration is *[ꞽ-]ꞽr=n ḥꜣ.t=s* “We are/were before it (the fire).” *ḥ* would then be *ḥꜣ(.t)*, “vor,” *Glossar*, 287 (or *ḥꜣ*, “hinter,” *Glossar*, 286?).

Line x+5
(a) We restore the same idiom *gm myt* as in line 8.

Line x+6
(a) *nꜣ-ʿšꜣ* fits the traces well. Vleeming, *Graffiti*, 125, reads *ḥp(?)* ... “Hiding(?).”
(b) *h̭rh̭r*, “Zerstörung,” *Glossar*, 367 yields excellent sense.

Line x+8
(a) Apparently, the cult workers were not able to fight this fire effectively.

Line x+9
(a) While there are a few problems of reading and translation, these last lines seem to encourage others to be as effectively active as possible in the service of the ibis and falcon in case of emergency. Vleeming, *Graffiti*, 125, transliterates *pꜣ rmt nb (n) pꜣ tꜣ nti ꞽw=f ꞽr wʿ/nk.t r dꞽ.t wbꜣ r-h̲.ṱ=w/tꜣy=f gm my ꞽr.w* <s> *n=f*, “Each person whosoever who will make a/thing to give toward them accordingly/his might may they do <it> for him.”
(b) *gm* seems preferable to *ꞽr wʿ*, even if it is written somewhat differently from the certain example in x+8.

Line x+10
(a) One might also consider a passive translation, “As for any man in the world who will find a thing to be given.”
(b) We understand the suffix pronoun *w* of *wbꜣ* to refer to the animal mummies.
(c) We refrain from offering a translation of *h̲.t=w*. This is one of several possible readings, of course, but none seems to yield convincing sense.

Line x+11
(a) *gm*, “Kraft,” *Glossar*, 580.

87. Graffito Spiegelberg #25 (Plate 76b)

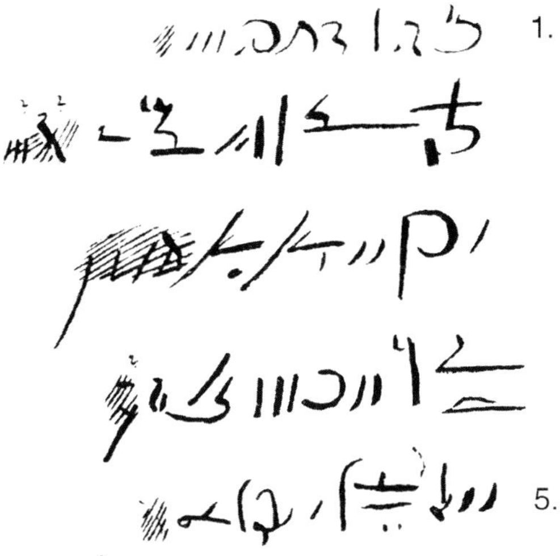

no scale

Transliteration
1. *wn-nꜣ.w nꜣ hny*
2. *k.t ʿ.wy ḥtp ty(?)*
3. *r-ḥry pꜣ trtr …*
4. *pt(?) pꜣ nt ỉw=w (r) ḏ.ṯ̭=f*
5. *Pꜣ-šr-Mn sꜣ Ḏḥwty-sḏm*

Translation
1. The jars were
2. in another place of rest here(?)
3. above the stairs …
4. What(?) is that which they will say it?
5. *Pꜣ-šr-Mn*, son of *Ḏḥwty-sḏm.*

Commentary
(Spiegelberg #25, pl. 28; Vleeming, *Graffiti*, 126–27 [#1488])

Line 1
(a) *hn*, "Krug," *Glossar*, 277, yields better sense than "some" after *nꜣ*. These jars probably contained supplies rather than the sacred birds themselves.

Line 2
(a) While Spiegelberg's *ẖʿ*, "erscheinen," *Glossar*, 350–51, is not impossible, we think that something must be missing. *k.t*, "eine andere," *Glossar*, 559, for *ky* is more likely, compare *Glossar*, 568 (second line from the bottom of the Ptolemaic examples) seems preferable.

Line 4
(a) On the basis of Spiegelberg's copy one might also read *nt ỉw=w ḏ s n=f*, "which they will say it to him."

Line 5
(a) We first read *qt*, but now think *pt* a more attractive alternative. This would be old *ptr/pt*, "Fragewort, wer, was?" *Wb.* 1:506, 2–8. The force of the question is unclear. Is *Pꜣ-šr-Mn* making a point about the placement of the jars, which were perhaps filled with flammable materials and had a role in causing the fire mentioned in graff. 85 and 86?

88. Graffito Spiegelberg #26 (Plate 76c)

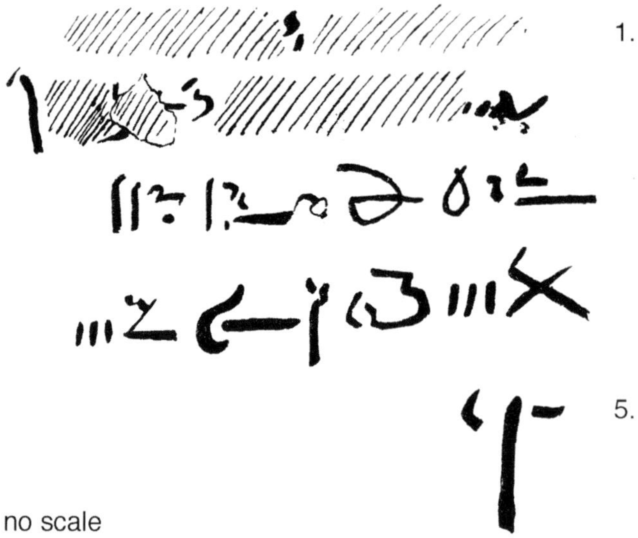

Transliteration	Translation
1. ...	1. ...
2. ... *ḏ* ...	2. ... to say ...
3. *qs(.t) m-ỉr tỉ.t ḥtp ntr*	3. burial. Do not let a god rest
4. *ty šʿ wʿ wš ʿšꜣy*	4. here for a long time.
5. *sẖ*	5. Written.

Commentary

(Spiegelberg #26, pl. 28; Vleeming, *Graffiti*, 137 [#1502] with transliteration and translation of only lines 4 and 5)

Line 3

(a) This is clearly an instructional text in which the cult workers are warned not to let the mummified animals remain in this location for too long a time.

Line 4

(a) Does *šʿ* here mean "for," compare *šʿ* "in, zu," *Glossar*, 488. Again, the point would be that the ibis mummies must be buried quickly.

(b) *wš* is a common variant for *wrš*, "die Zeit," *Glossar*, 95.

APPENDIX B

89–93 RECENTLY DISCOVERED GRAFFITI IN THE TOMB OF HERY (TT 12)

The following graffiti were recovered after cleaning during the 2019 campaign.[205]

89. Graffito TT 12/9 (Plate 48)

Location: Main corridor, N-wall

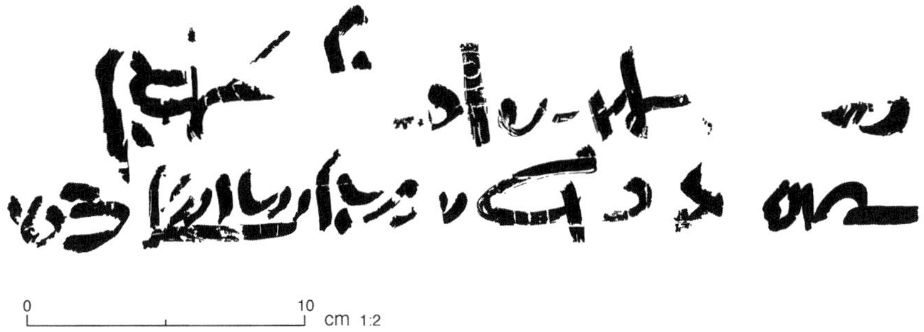

1.
2.

TRANSLITERATION

1. ⸢*pꜣ*⸣ *[rn] nfr n Pꜣ-ti͗-*⸢*hb(?)*⸣ *[sꜣ]* ⸢*Ns*⸣*-Mn*

2. *mn ty m-bꜣḥ pꜣ hb pꜣ bi͗k šꜥ [ḏ.t]*

TRANSLATION

1. ⸢The⸣ good [name] of *Pꜣ-ti͗-*⸢*hb(?)*,⸣ [son of] ⸢*Ns*⸣*-Mn*,

2. remains here before the ibis (and) the falcon for[ever].

Commentary

Line 1

(a) The reading *Pꜣ-ti-hb* seems plausible, but we have no other example.

90. Graffito TT 12/10 (Plate 48)

Location: Main corridor, N-wall

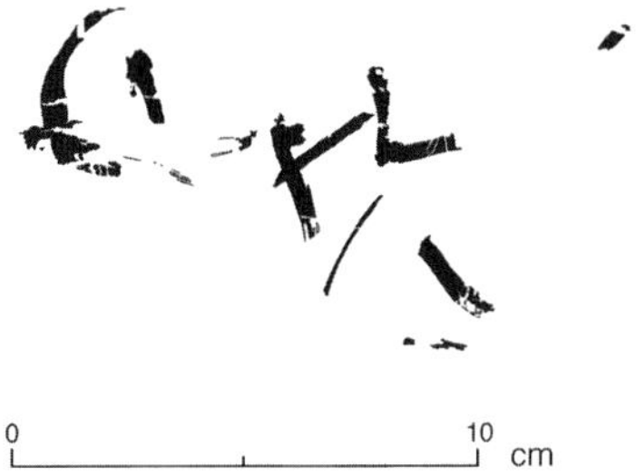

1.
2.

[205] For an illustration of the conservator Maite Béjar cleaning the deposits covering these graffiti in 2019, see: https://proyectodjehuty.com/17-febrero-2019/.

Transliteration
1. *[...] ... ⌜Ḏḥwty-⌝[...]*
2. *[...] ... [...]*

Translation
1. [...] ... ⌜*Ḏḥwty*-⌝[...]
2. [...] ... [...]

Commentary

Line 1
(a) *Ḏḥwty* is presumably part of a personal name.

91. Graffito TT 12/11 (Plate 49a)

Location: Main corridor, N-wall

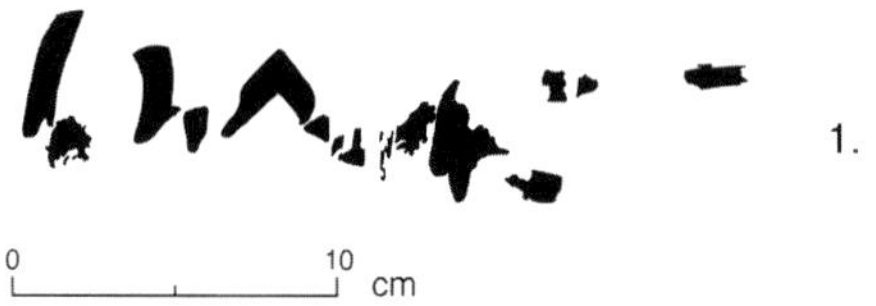

Transliteration
1. ... ⌜...⌝ *hb(?)*

Translation
1. ... ⌜...⌝ *hb(?)*

Commentary

(a) *hb* seems possible, but is hardly secure.

92. Graffito TT 12/12 (Plate 49b)

Location: Main corridor, N-wall

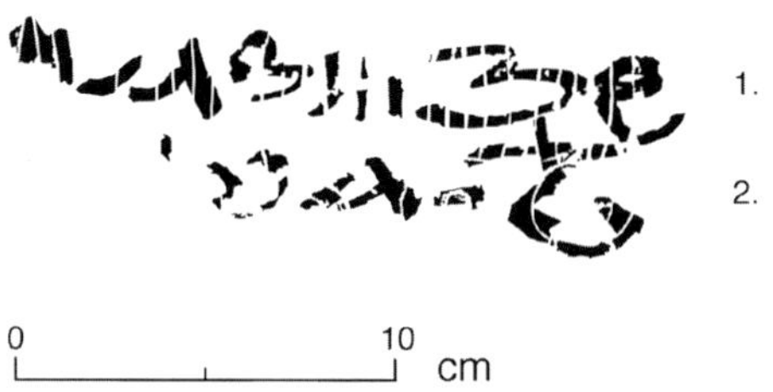

Transliteration
1. *pꜣ šym ⌜pꜣy⌝(?)*
2. *ꜥꜣ n pr ⌜mḥṱ⌝ [...]*

Translation
1. ⌜This is⌝(?) the great corridor
2. of the ⌜north⌝ [...]

Commentary

Line 1

(a) This is evidently a directional text labeling the corridor in which it is written; see *CDD Š*, 19, s.v. *šym*, "n.m. 'row (of connected rooms), corridor, ambulatory.'"

(b) We propose that the sign after the house determinative is the copula *pꜣy*, *Glossar*, 128. However, the reading is uncertain.

Line 2

(a) For *pr mḥ̭t*, "northern," *Glossar*, 175. "Great corridor of the north" is an apt description of this section of the tomb.

APPENDIX C

ADDITIONAL DEMOTIC MATERIAL FOUND BY THE SPANISH MISSION AT DRA ABU EL-NAGAꜥ

A. OSTRACA

Ostracon 1= O. DAN 2066 (Plate 77a)

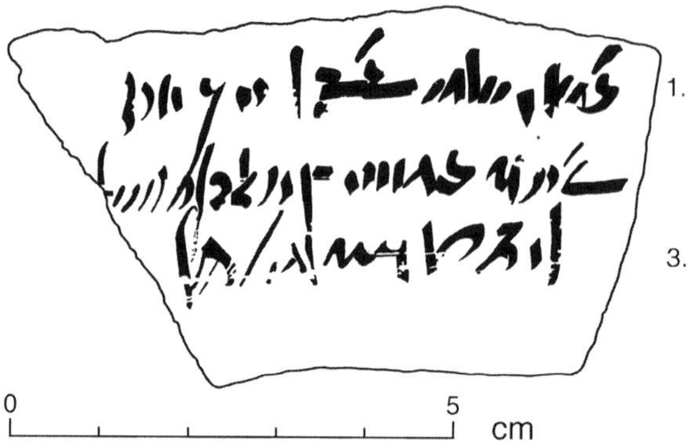

Tag: Register No.: 2066
Sector 10 sur (S-SW of TT 11 courtyard)
UE: 1000/5–Y
Found: 27.1.2014
Pottery ostracon 7.2 x 4 cm
Date: ca. 252/251 BCE(?)
Content: Receipt for price of oil issued to an individual involved in the ibis and falcon cult.

TRANSLITERATION

1. *Ḏ-ḥr pꜣ ꜥ.wy ḥtp ḥt ¼ swn*
2. *nḥḥ ỉbt 2 pr.t sw 6(?) sẖ Pꜣ-šr-ʾImn (sꜣ) Pꜣ-tỉ-Ḥr-pꜣ-Rꜥ(?) (n)*
3. *ḥ.t-sp 34 ỉbt 4 pr.t sw 17*

TRANSLATION

1. *Ḏ-ḥr* (of) the place of rest, silver-kite ¼ price (of)
2. oil, second month of winter, day 6(?). Has written *Pꜣ-šr-ʾImn*, (son of) *Pꜣ-tỉ-Ḥr-pꜣ-Rꜥ(?)* (in)
3. regnal year 34, fourth month of winter, day 17.

Commentary

Line 1

(a) The personal name *Ḏ-ḥr* and *pꜣ ꜥ.wy ḥtp* are probably in a direct genitive relationship. The persons named in these oil price receipts are sometimes identified or qualified in some fashion, for example, "Tabis, the wife of Esminis," B. Muhs, *Receipts, Scribes, and Collectors in Early Ptolemaic Thebes (O. Taxes 2)*, Studia Demotica 8 (Leuven: Peeters, 2011), 122. However, we do not have a parallel to the kind of identification found in this ostracon. Brian Muhs has kindly sent us detailed notes on this ostracon (email of June 6, 2019), and we quote: "I wonder if this *Ḏ-ḥr* could be identified with the 'Ibis-herder' (*ibioboskos*) Teos son of Patemis who purchases (with Zminis his brother) an ibiotapheion in Thebes in Year 30 of Ptolemy II, known from three bilingual receipts for the purchase, published as *UPZ* 2, nos. 153–155."

(b) We had first considered reading *ỉw=f-ʿw*, as a personal name, but Karl-Theodor Zauzich's suggestion *ḥt ¼ swn* is certainly correct. He refers us to the "price of oil receipts," in Muhs, *Receipts*, 114–15. For another possible example of *ḥḏ ¼*, see Muhs, *Receipts*, 74, 122. On oil payment receipts, see further Muhs, *Tax Receipts, Taxpayers, and Taxes in Early Ptolemaic Thebes*, OIP 126 (Chicago: Oriental Institute of the University of Chicago, 2005), 73–79.

Line 2

(a) We think *pr.t* more probable than *šmw*. *Sw 6* is also not secure, comparing *Glossar*, 708. In an email (July 15, 2019), Muhs writes: "Receipts for the price of oil frequently qualify the phrase *swn nḥḥ*, 'price of oil,' with a following month name, which is usually either the same month mentioned in the date formula, most often the preceding month, or rarely two months earlier as here, see Muhs, *Tax Receipts, Scribes, and Collectors in Early Ptolemaic Thebes*, pp. 76–78. The day of the month is given in only one other example, O. BM 19518, published in [S. Wångstedt, "Demotische Quittungen über Ölsteuer,"] *Orientalia Suecana* 29 [1980], p. 7–8 (no. 2)."

(b) A *Pꜣ-šr-ỉmn* appears as an official for the oil receipts in year 34 of Ptolemy II, in Muhs, *Tax Receipts*, 76, citing O. BM EA 5713, published by Wångstedt, "Demotische Quittungen über Ölsteuer," 10. A secure identification of this scribe depends on the reading of the patronym, which, following a suggestion of Muhs, we have rendered as *Pꜣ-tỉ-Ḥr-pꜣ-Rʿ(?)*. We had first transliterated *Pꜣ-ḥtr* (*Demot. Nb.*, 206-7). Again, Muhs has offered valuable remarks concerning the possible identity of this scribe, although quite rightly emphasizing the palaeographical difficulties of the patronym (email of June 6, 2019). We quote here his comments: "I would read *Pꜣ-šr-ỉmn (sꜣ) Pꜣ-tỉ-ḥr-pꜣ-Rʿ(?)*. A scribe of that name with very similar palaeography is attested on a Theban receipt for the price of oil from Year 35 of Ptolemy II, O. BM 5754, published by Wångstedt in *Orientalia Suecana* 29, p. 10–11 (nos. 6). He also appears on O. OIM E19504, published by [F.] Scalf and [J.] Jay ["Oriental Institute Demotic Ostraca Online (OIDOO): Merging Text Publication and Research Tools,"] in *The Acts of the Tenth International Congress of Demotic Studies*, [ed. M. Depauw and Y. Broux, OLA 231 (Leuven: Peeters),] p. 251 (there read *Pꜣ-šr-ỉmn-ỉpy*). A scribe *Pꜣ-šr-ỉmn*, possibly the same man, signs a Theban receipt for the price of oil from Year 34 of Ptolemy II, O. BM 5713, published by Wångstedt in *Orientalia Suecana* 29, p. 10 (no. 5). The reading of the patronym is ambiguous in the ostraca, but it is less so in the papyri, where he may also have been Witness 15 on P. Phil. 15, dated to Year 26 of Ptolemy II; Witness 3 on P. Phil. 17, dated to Year 6 of Ptolemy III; Witness 13 on P. Phil. 21, dated to Year 11 of Ptolemy III; Witness 10 on P. BM Andrews 35, dated to Year 24 of Ptolemy III; and Witness 1 on P. BM Reich 10073, dated to Year 5 of Ptolemy IV; see Muhs, *Receipts, Scribes and Collectors in Early Ptolemaic Thebes*, p. 236 (Scribe 38)." Muhs's identification of the scribe in this ostracon is extremely attractive, although we confess to being puzzled by the difficulties in reading the name of the patronym, and the discrepancy between the writings in the ostraca and the writings in the papyri.

Line 3

(a) Given the reference to the "place of rest," there is a clear connection with the corpus of graffiti texts. However, while the graffiti appear to date almost entirely to the second century BCE, such Theban oil payment receipts are early Ptolemaic; one wonders whether regnal year 34 may refer here to Ptolemy II, that is, 252/251 BCE (P. Pestman, *Chronologie égyptienne d'après les textes démotiques [332 av. J.-C. - 453 ap. J.-C.]*, PLBat 15 [Leiden: Brill, 1967], 25). Of course, if the above-mentioned *Pꜣ-šr-ỉmn*, (son of) *Pꜣ-tỉ-Ḥr-pꜣ-Rʿ(?)*, is the scribe of the ostracon, a date in the reign of Ptolemy II is basically confirmed. Otherwise, the date is to be attributed to either Ptolemy VI (148/149 BCE) or Ptolemy VIII (137/136 BCE), which is more in line with the date of the graffiti.

An active ibis and falcon cult may well have existed at Dra Abu el-Naga^{c} already by the Thirtieth Dynasty, so a date for this ostracon of 252/251 BCE is perfectly plausible.[206]

Ostracon 2= O. DAN 2067 (Plate 77b)

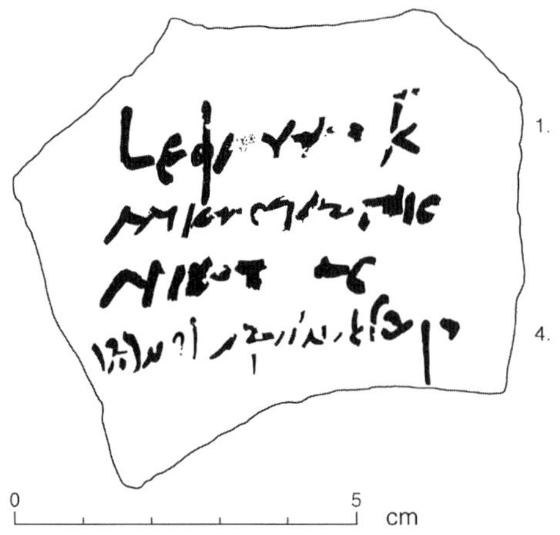

Tag: Register No.: 2067
Sector 10 sur (S-SW of TT 11 courtyard)
UE: 1000/5-Y
Found: 27.1.2014
Pottery ostracon 7.3 x 5.3 cm
Date: Year 5 of an unnamed king, perhaps Ptolemy III (244–243 BCE) or Ptolemy IV (218–217 BCE) (suggestion of Muhs)
Content: Receipt for payment of salt-tax.

Transliteration	Translation
1. (ετους) ε Φαμενωθ κ	1. (Year): 5, Phamenouth, day 20
2. αλικης Τανουβις	2. (for) the salt-tax, Tanoubis(?),
3. Λιβιου (οβ.) (ἡμιωβ.)	3. (daughter) of Libios, 1 ½ obols.
4. *sẖ Ḏḥwty-ms sȝ Ḥr-sȝ-ʾIs.t qt 1 ½ ḥt ḥmȝ*	4. Has written *Ḏḥwty-ms*, the son of *Ḥr-sȝ-ʾIs.t*: *1 ½* kite salt-tax.

Comment

Line 1

(a) We quote once more Muhs (email of June 6, 2019): "Year 5 cannot refer to Ptolemy II, since the salt-tax was not introduced until his Year 22, so it could either refer to Ptolemy III or IV." This ostracon, which was found outside of the tombs, seems to be earlier than the graffiti published in this volume, since the salt-tax is basically a third century BCE institution. On the salt-tax, see, for

[206] See, e.g., Kessler, *Die Heiligen Tiere und der König*, 165; A. von den Driesch et al., "Mummified, Deified, and Buried at Hermopolis Magna: The Sacred Birds from Tuna El-Gebel, Middle Egypt," *Ägypten und Levante/Egypt and the Levant* 15 (2005): 203; Kessler and Nur el-Din, "Tuna al-Gebel," 124. In comparison to Saqqara or Tuna el-Gebel, the early history of the ibis-falcon cult at Thebes is relatively obscure.

example, Muhs, *Receipts,* 21–86; Muhs, *Tax Receipts*, 41–51. In general, see Clarysse and Thompson, *Counting the People in Hellenistic Egypt* 2:36–89.

(b) In an email (July 15, 2019), Muhs writes: "There are possibly traces of a horizontal stroke above the *kappa*, perhaps to denote that it was being used as a numeral."

Line 2

(a) Muhs (email of July 15, 2019): "I would hesitantly suggest αλικης Ταvουβις, '(for) the salt tax, Tanoubis.' The sign(s) after *tau* and *alpha* seem unusually diagonal for *nu* and *omicron*, but alternatives provide names unattested in F. Preisigke, *Namenbuch* (Heidelberg: Selbstverlag, 1922)."

Line 3

(a) Muhs (email of July 15, 2019): "I would tentatively read Λιβιου (oβ.) (ἡμιωβ.), '(daughter) of Libios, 1 ½ obols.' There is an unusual initial uptick on the obol-sign."

Line 4

(a) Just possibly read as an alternative *r ḥ.t-sp 5 ḥt ḥmꜣ* "with regard to/for regnal year 5, salt-tax," as in the Greek date. As Muhs has observed, there is a problem in the amount given here, since, as he writes (email of June 6, 2019): "1 ½ kite is not a standard rate for the salt-tax, though it could represent a payment for multiple people, or for multiple taxes."

Ostracon 3= O. DAN 5051 (Plate 78)

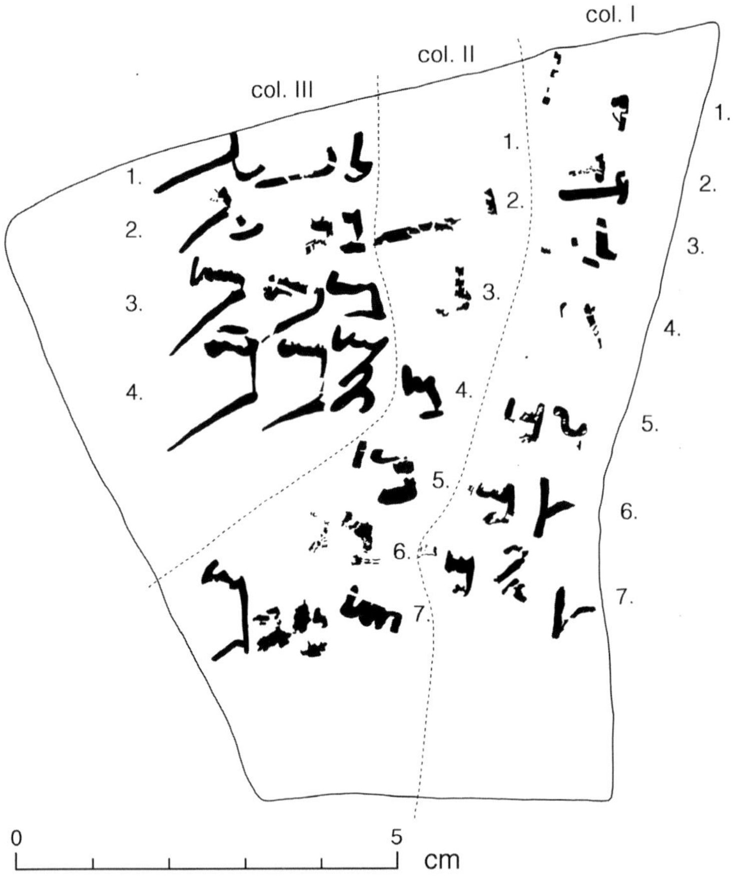

Tag: Register No.: 5051
Sector 10 sur (S-SW of TT 11 courtyard)
UE: 1019/5–Y
Found: 3.2.2015
Pottery ostracon 9.8 x 9.9 cm
Date: Ptolemaic
Content: This list of numbers is probably a school-text, although that is still a much-debated genre.[207] The placement of the numerals does seem to be systematic, and in part sequential, but the precise division of columns is not certain. One first tries to organize the numbers into consecutive lines, but, while this works in part, it simply does not for the entire text. We have consequently divided the numbers into three columns, but this too is hardly secure. The difficulty in understanding this text is exacerbated by its poor preservation; one may supply a question mark behind almost every reading. We hope that a mathematically inclined scholar will provide a more satisfactory interpretation.

[207] There do not seem to be any certain mathematical school texts; see, e.g., K. Davis, "Conceptions of Language: Egyptian Perspectives on Writing and Grammar in the Late Period and Greco-Roman Period" (PhD diss., Johns Hopkins University, 2016), 130 and 138; A. Bahé, "An Egyptian Perspective: Demotic Ostraca from Deir el-Bahari in the British Museum," in *Current Research in Egyptology 2013: Proceedings of the Fourteenth Annual Symposium, University of Cambridge, United Kingdom, March 19–22, 2013*, ed. K. Accetta et al. (Oxford: Oxbow, 2014), 16.

Transliteration / Translation

	Column I	Column II	Column III		
1.	⌜...⌝	[...]	1000, 100	...	100
2.	110	⌜100⌝	2000, 200	...	200
3.	⌜...⌝	⌜1000⌝	4000, 400		1/400
4.	⌜...⌝	⌜3000⌝	6000, 600		1/600
5.	20000, 3000	⌜4000⌝			
6.	... 4000	⌜5000⌝			
7.	..., 60000, 5000	⌜7000 ...⌝, 300			

Commentary

Column I

Line 1

(a) There is possibly a slanted stroke preserved from a previous line, now lost.

Line 5

(a) Compare 20000 in *CDD Numbers*, 263.

Line 6

(a) Lines 6 and 7 seem to have the same initial sign. It resembles, of course, "4," but this yields little sense.

Line 7

(a) "60000" is a tentative transliteration, *Glossar*, 703; *CDD Numbers*, 264.

Column II

Line 2

(a) "100" seems to be awkward here, given that the following numbers are thousands. Still, it is hard to avoid that reading.

Line 6

(a) "5000" would seem here to be written as a combination of "3000" plus "2000," The "2000" is barely visible.

Line 7

(a) Similarly, "7000," seems to be written as "4000" plus "3000." This is followed by an unread group, but it does seem that the line concludes with "300."

Column III

Line 1

(a) There seems to be a short slanted stroke, not an *r*, before the final "100." We cannot explain this sign.

Line 2

(a) Again, there seems to be an unexplained stroke before the final "200."

Line 4

(a) The supralinear stroke above the final "600" is almost certainly a discoloration in the surface. It does not seem likely that we are dealing here with the fraction 1/600.

Ostracon 4= O. DAN 9028 (Plate 77c)

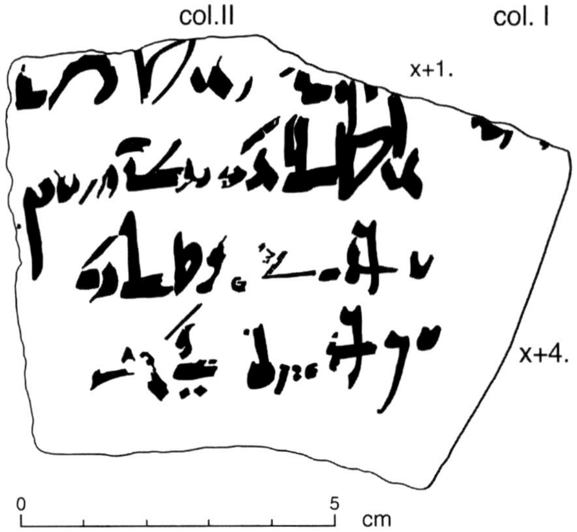

Tag: Register No.: 9028
Sector 10 sur (S-SW of TT 11 courtyard)
UE: 1001/3-X
Found: 30.1.2016
Pottery ostracon 9.0 x 6.4 cm
Date: Ptolemaic
Content: We can make little of this "mathematical" text. It may also be a scribal exercise, but possibly has a practical character.

Transliteration	Translation
Column I	Column I
x+1. *[...]* ⌜...⌝	x+1. [...] ⌜...⌝
Column II	Column II
x+1. ⌜...⌝ ... *r 94 sp 40*	x+1. ⌜...⌝ ... makes 94 remainder 40
x+2. *94 ... pꜣ rꜣ pꜣ rmt(?)*	x+2. 94 ... the number, the man(?)
x+3. *pꜣ ꜥḥꜥ 60 ... 23 ...*	x+3. the height 60 ... 23 ...
x+4. *pꜣ ¼(?) ꜥḥꜥ ... 97(?)*	x+4. The ¼(?) of height ... 97(?)

Comment

Column II

Line x+2

(a) After "94" there is perhaps a complex fraction, comparing, for example, *CDD Numbers*, 304 (= P. Cairo 89127= vso, C/18= R. Parker, *Demotic Mathematical Papyri*, Brown Egyptological Studies 7 [Providence: Brown University Press, 1972], pl. 1). A similar group appears to be written at the end of line x+3.

(b) We suggest *rꜣ*, "number, amount, area," *Glossar*, 240, rather than *wn/ ỉry-ꜥꜣ*; for *rꜣ*, see Parker, *Demotic Mathematical Papyri*, 81.

(c) Instead of *pꜣ rmt* (which hardly yields sense), read possibly *pꜣ 21*, "the 21," an admittedly awkward phrase. Compare the writings of "21," in *CDD Numbers*, 83.

Line x+3

(a) For "60," see *Glossar*, 61.

(b) There seems to be a word between "60" and "23." Could this be *r*?

(c) The final group appears very similar to that after "94," at the beginning of line x+2. Could this be *ḏy*, "diameter, height," *CDD Ḏ*, 14 s.v. *ḏy*?

Line x+4

(a) Instead of *pꜣ ¼* read perhaps *pꜣy=f*.

(b) Before "97," a group incorporating "6" appears to be written.

Ostracon 5= O. DAN 5222 (Plate 79a)

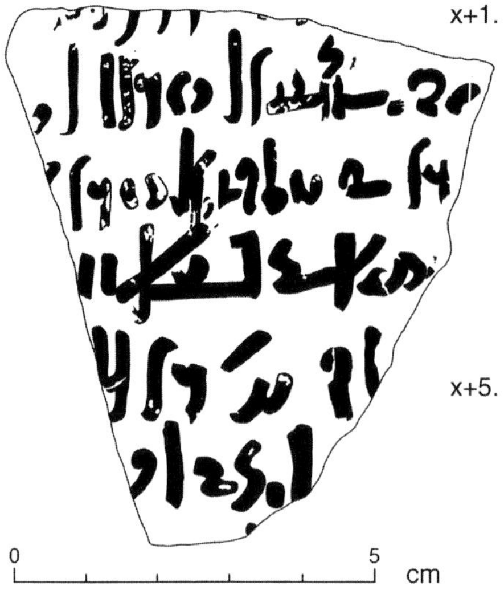

Tag: Register No.: 5222
Sector 10 sur (S-SW of TT 11 courtyard)
UE: 1033/4w
Found: 21.1.2016
Pottery ostracon 6.7 x 7.2 cm
Date: Ptolemaic
Content: Document concerned with the delivery of wheat to various individuals.

Transliteration	Translation
x+1. *[...]⸢... rtb sw⸣ [...] ⸢rtb⸣ [sw ...]*	x+1. [...]⸢...artaba wheat⸣ [...] ⸢artaba⸣ [wheat ...]
x+2. *[...] r 50(?) n ꜥbb rtb sw 1 ⸢...⸣[...]*	x+2. [...] amounts to 50(?) for(?) *ꜥbb*, artaba wheat 1 ⸢...⸣[...]
x+3. *[...rtb] sw 8 Pꜣ-šr-Ḫ̮nsw rtb sw ⸢6(?)⸣[...]*	x+3. [... artaba] wheat 8 *Pꜣ-šr-Ḫ̮nsw*, artaba wheat ⸢6(?)⸣ [...]
x+4. *[...] hrw tn 200 sw 16 [...]*	x+4. [...] day at the rate of 200, day 16 [...]
x+5. *[... rtb sw] 1 $^{1}/_{2}$ Ḥr (rtb) sw 2 [...]*	x+5. [... artaba wheat] 1 $^{1}/_{2}$ *Ḥr*, (artaba) wheat 2 [...]
x+6. *[...] ḥ.t-sp 28 ı͗bt 1 ⸢ꜣ⸣[ḫ.t ...]*	x+6. [...] Regnal year 28, first month of inun[dation season ...]
x+7. *[...] ...*	x+7. [...] ...

Comment

Line x+1

(a) The long vertical line of *rtb* descends into line x+2.

Line x+2

(a) Perhaps read rather *sw 5(?)* at the beginning of the line.
(b) The transliteration *ꜥbb* (with the divine determinative), "der Flügelskarabäus," Leitz, *LGG* 2:89; "winged beetle, falcon," Wilson, *Lexikon*, 148–49, seems secure. This may be a personal name, but we have no other examples.

Line x+6
(a) "Regnal year" 28 may possibly be that of Ptolemy VI (154/153 BCE) or Ptolemy VIII (143/142 BCE).

B. MUMMY BANDAGES

So far only two mummy bandages inscribed in demotic have been found among the numerous animal and human mummies recovered in the tombs.[208]

Mummy Bandage 1 (Plate 79b)[209]

no scale

Tag: Register No.: none
UE 260 (= funerary space at the bottom of shaft UE 82F, i.e., west/ritual south shaft in transverse hall of tomb -399-)
Found: 31.1.2007
Date: Ptolemaic

TRANSLITERATION	TRANSLATION
1. *Nfr-ḥtp tỉ ꜥnḫ (n) Pꜣ-ꜥw sꜣ Ḥr-Mn*	1. *Nfr-ḥtp* gives life (to) *Pꜣ-ꜥw*, son of *Ḥr-Mn*.

Commentary

Line 1
(a) Neferhotep is a typical epithet of Khonsu, for example, *CDD N*, 80, s.v. *Nfr-ḥtp*, although it can naturally also designate other deities, Leitz, *LGG* 4:218–19.
(b) *Pꜣ-ꜥw* is a secure reading, but the name does not appear to be attested in *Demot. Nb.*
(c) *Ḥr-Mn* is not in *Demot. Nb.*, but is in Ranke, *PN* 1:248.

[208] On 25.1.2018 a linen fragment (a shroud?) with a Greek inscription was found in level UE 278 in UE 276 (the same location as mummy bandage 2) and assigned the Register No. 6846. It will be published at a later date.

[209] The demotic inscription is well illustrated in the online excavation diary for January 27, 2015: https://proyecto-djehuty.com/27-enero-2015/. On the discovery of this inscription on January 31, 2007: https://proyectodjehuty.com/31-enero-2007/. We have not had the opportunity to examine the object in person.

Mummy Bandage 2 (Plate 80)

The name of a young girl is written on her mummy wrapping at the height of her chest.

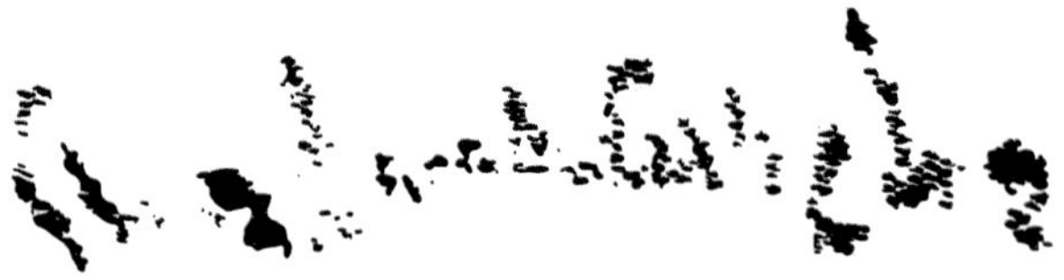

Tag: Register No.: 6815
  Eastern Galleries (UE 276)[210]
  UE 278
  Found: 23.1.2018
Date: Ptolemaic or Early Roman

TRANSLITERATION
1. *Tꜣ-šr.t-⸢Ḫnsw(?) ta(?) Pꜣ-šr-Ḫnsw(?)⸣*

TRANSLATION
1. *Tꜣ-šr.t-⸢Ḫnsw(?)*, the daughter(?) of *Pꜣ-šr-Ḫnsw(?)*⸣

210 UE 276 is part of the Eastern Galleries. UE 276 is the south (ritual east) section of the corridor and UE 278 is the filling level (stratum) in which the mummy was found (pers. comm. F. Bosch-Puche).

APPENDIX D

CONDITION OF THE INDIVIDUAL GRAFFITI

We offer general comments on the condition of the graffiti, largely based on our personal observations, supplemented by those of Bosch-Puche and Ikram. These remarks do not therefore have the scientific authority of a technical scientific conservation report. They are only intended to convey an impression of the state of the graffiti.

Graff. #	Location	Condition
1–40	TT 11, main corridor	The graffiti were written directly on the original New Kingdom wall surface. The New Kingdom reliefs had already severely suffered from erosion before the graffiti were written in the second century BCE. Graffiti 4, 6, 9, and 14, located toward the upper section of the wall, survived relatively undamaged. The remaining graffiti were all covered by a very hard layer of clay concretions. These graffiti only became visible after the conservators had completed their efforts. Before this conservation even DStretch could not bring out any traces; one saw only faint hints of a graffito, and sometimes not even that. At some point in the past, a substantial fire at the beginning to the main corridor severely burned the limestone walls by the entrance.
1	TT 11, S-wall	This graffito was especially impacted by the above-mentioned fire. The upper section of the graffito responded better to cleaning than the lower section.
2	TT 11, S-wall	The graffito was not impacted by the fire as badly as graff. 1, but still could not be completely cleaned
3	TT 11, S-wall	Severely burned, cleaning not possible.
9	TT 11, S-wall	The beginning of this graffito was written on a *Flickstein* which has fallen from the wall and is now lost.
25	TT 11, S-wall	The graffito was written directly on the surface of a badly damaged section where a part of the wall had fallen out. This clearly indicates that the walls of the tomb were already in a poor state when the graffiti were inscribed.

Graff. #	Location	Condition
28	TT 11, N-wall	This section next to the entrance where graff. 28 is located was severely burned (as seen in graff. 1). Consequently parts of the limestone wall flaked off. It was only then, after the fire, that graff. 28 was inscribed upon this new "clean" surface. The graffiti opposite graff. 28 on the south wall were severely burned by the fire; therefore, they must have been written before the fire.
29	TT 11, N-wall	The graffito was written on a large flaked-off surface of the wall (now partially filled in with cement to accommodate well-preserved fragments found outside the tomb). This area seems unaffected by fire, as was the case also with graff. 28.
41–42	TT 11, N-doorjamb	The surface of the northern doorway had mostly flaked off already before the graffiti were added. Fragments of its original decoration have been found outside the tomb.
43	TT 11, N-doorjamb	The very top of the doorway with the graffito was still intact.
44	TT 11, chapel, E-wall	The lower left corner of the graffito has been destroyed by antiquity hunters who have looted decorated surface.
45	tomb –399–, underground	This graffito was written on an uneven surface covered with a thin layer of mud/whitewash. Both the inscription and the surface were later slightly blackened by smoke.
46	tomb –399–, underground	This graffito is written on a smooth surface (natural joint) with some concretions.
47	passage between TT 12 and tomb –399–	This graffito is situated in a later, roughly cut out passage between TT 12 and tomb –399–. It was written on an irregular wall segment, on a thin layer of mud/whitewash. This passage was blocked up during the conservation work, so the inscription is now concealed.
48–51, 89–92	TT 12, main corridor	The graffiti were written directly on the New Kingdom wall decoration, often on a thin layer of mud/whitewash. These decorated walls and therefore the graffiti, have suffered severely from vandalism. There is less damage from fire or erosion than in TT 11.

Graff. #	Location	Condition
48	TT 12, S-wall	Graffito 48 is located next to the later added passage where graff. 47 was written. The construction of this passage may have resulted in a loss of part of the text of the graffito. It is possible that the passage was enlarged at a later date further affecting it. When Spiegelberg copied the inscription, there was more of it preserved.
49	TT 12, S-wall	Graffito 49 has also suffered from antiquity hunters. When Spiegelberg copied the inscription, it was still intact.
51	TT 12, N-wall	The area around graff. 51 was badly destroyed. Only one small fragment (very light in color) was in situ. Additional fragments, the surfaces of which are darkened by soot, have been found in debris. These have been placed back on the wall.
89–92	TT 12, N-wall	This area was covered with a very smooth hard layer of clay concretions that completely hid the graffiti.
52	TT 12, chapel	Written on an unfinished surface and covered with some later concretions.
53–55, 57		The walls of the Eastern Galleries were blackened with soot before the graffiti were added. In the more protected areas toward the back there are some lighter patches on the wall. In contrast, the walls in the entrance and the main axis are almost completely black. In some cases, such as graff. 53 and 55, the walls may have been cleaned before the graffiti were inscribed. One observes that the first sign formed with the freshly dipped brush is quite prominent, but each succeeding sign rapidly becomes fainter. The blackened surface is surely not well suited for these red ochre inscriptions. In most cases smoke and soot from later fires also blackened the texts already on the walls.
53	UE 212, W-wall	Written on a smooth surface covered with light colored plaster or wash. Since there does not seem to be any trace of fire, the surface was either cleaned very thoroughly or the burned surface was plastered over. In any case, this is the only graffito that does not display any sign of fire. In contrast, however, the neighboring graff. 54 is blackened by fire.

Graff. #	Location	Condition
54	UE 212, N-wall	The right side of graff. 54 is darkened by black soot, but the left side is distinctly lighter, either that part of the inscription was not affected or some signs were rewritten.
55	UE 270, W-wall	Written on a thick layer of light pinkish plaster or wash that smoothed out the very rough stone surface. Toward the bottom of the graffito there are remains of dark patches. The red ink is clearly written on top of these darker patches. The whole area was probably first black from soot, and then cleaned. However, the workmen did not do a thorough job, and left several dark patches at the bottom.
56	UE 276, E-wall of connection to an unexcavated chamber below the tomb of Ay	Graffito 56 is clearly covered by a thick layer of black soot and the ink is almost invisible. This graffito was probably also written on a blackened surface, but certainty is impossible.
57	UE 276, N-wall	Graffito 57 is written for the most part on top of a thick layer of black soot, only the left bottom section is distinctly lighter.
58	UE 277, NE-corner, connecting to UE 325	Graffito 58 is written on the NE-corner of the main axis of the Eastern Galleries, almost at ground level. The stone is extremely rough and uneven, and a thin layer of mud/whitewash was applied as a preparation. The stone surface displays some soot, but not as much as in the area toward the entrance of the tomb.
59	UE 277, NW-corner, connecting to UE 325	The limestone on which graff. 59 was written has largely fallen away. The small area of preserved surface is black with a few lighter patches. It is located opposite graff. 58, but inscribed at the top of the wall.
60	UE 277, S-wall	Graffito 60 was written on an uneven surface. Although located deeper in the tomb, the surface is quite black from soot; the red ink has a rather "washed out" appearance.

Graff. #	Location	Condition
61	no UE, unexcavated chamber below the tomb of Ay	Graffito 61 must also have been written on top of the soot-blackened surface. The inscription is located on the lower part of the wall in an unexcavated chamber of a tomb below the tomb of Ay. This unexcavated tomb is still full of debris. It seems that most of the soot was "abraded" away over time. The red ink is now still very visible on the black surface, but in the area where the black is gone, the red ink is very faded. One wonders whether the red ochre ink has seeped through the soot into the limestone, the resulting "stains" retaining the shape of the original Demotic signs.
62	Upper Gallery, chamber F (above entrance to chamber H)	The entire surface of the Upper Gallery is pitch black, except for the area of graff. 62. Originally it seems that this area was also blackened, but, before the graffito was added, the surface was cleaned of soot. Inspection of the area of graff. 62 suggests that there was mud/whitewash underneath the blackened surface. The extent of this mud/whitewash is unclear. Graffito 62 stands out quite dramatically; the writer doubtless intended the inscription to be the focal point of the space. There is some later blackening by soot, but only on the right end of the graffito. It seems that most of the graffito, which was written above the doorway to a small chamber, was somehow protected from a later fire. Perhaps the inscription was walled-up when the space was sealed.
63 64d	Upper Gallery, chamber G	In contrast to the case of graff. 62, the surface of graff. 63–64 was not cleaned. They are written directly on the black surface. These graffiti are now virtually invisible, since smoke and soot from later fires also further blackened the walls.
65–88	unknown	Since the location of "The Great Tomb of the Ibis and Hawks" is unknown, nothing can be said regarding the condition of these graffiti.

APPENDIX E

CONCORDANCE OF GRAFFITI NUMBERS EMPLOYED IN THIS VOLUME WITH THOSE IN THE EDITIONS OF SPIEGELBERG AND VLEEMING

Graff.	Spiegelberg[211]	Vleeming[212]
1	Spiegelberg 23	#1470
6	Spiegelberg 22	#1469
7	Spiegelberg 21	#1468
9	Spiegelberg 20	#1467
14	Spiegelberg 27	#1471
48	Spiegelberg 29	#1473
49	Spiegelberg 28	#1472
50	Spiegelberg 30	#1474
65	Spiegelberg 31	#1475
66	Spiegelberg 32	#1476
67	Spiegelberg 1	#1480
68	Spiegelberg 2	##1481–1482
69	Spiegelberg 3	#1483
70	Spiegelberg 4	#1487
71	Spiegelberg 5	#1484
72	Spiegelberg 6	#1490
73	Spiegelberg 7	#1491
74	Spiegelberg 8	#1492
75	Spiegelberg 9	#1486
76	Spiegelberg 10	#1493
77	Spiegelberg 11	#1494
78	Spiegelberg 12	#1495
79	Spiegelberg 13	#1496

Graff.	Spiegelberg[211]	Vleeming[212]
80	Spiegelberg 14	#1497
81	Spiegelberg 15	#1498
82	Spiegelberg 16	#1499
83	Spiegelberg 17	#1500
84	Spiegelberg 18	#1501
85	Spiegelberg 19	#1489
86	Spiegelberg 24	#1485
87	Spiegelberg 25	#1488
88	Spiegelberg 26	#1502

211 Northampton, Spiegelberg, and Newberry, *Report on Some Excavations in the Theban Necropolis.*

212 Vleeming, *Graffiti.*

Glossary

SELECT VOCABULARY

ꜣlr “mourning”	39, 4
ꜣḥ=k “your body”	68, 2
ꜣtr.t “chapel”	60, 1 *ꜣtr.t r ti.t ḥtp*; 71, 1; 85, 3
ꜣtr.w “chapels”	55, 3 *ꜣtr.w nꜣ ntr.w nt mqḥ*; 57, 2 *ꜣtr.w nt ẖr nꜣ ntr.w nt mqḥ*
ỉy “to come”	54, 5; 76, 4; 85, 8
ỉyẖ.w “things”	76, 7
ỉw (circ. converter)	53, 2; 58, 2; 65, 1; 66, 2; 86, x+7
ỉw=w	54, 3 (circ.); 54, 5 (future); 87, 4 (rel. future III)
ỉw=f	4, 1 (rel. future III); 9, 4 (circ. converter); 62a, 4 (circ. converter); 65, 1 (cond.); 66, 2 (cond.); 71, 5 (circ. converter); 75, 3 (circ. converter); 85, 2 (rel. future III); 86, x+9 (rel. future III)
ỉp “reckon”	58, 3
ỉmnt; see pr ỉmnt	
ỉn “to bring”	58, 2
ỉr “to do, make, spending”	14, 3; 34, 5; 54, 6 (*ỉr=f*); 62a, 4 (*ỉ.ỉr*); 63, 5; 65, 1; 65, 4; [66, 2]; 85, 2 (*ỉr=f*)
ỉr	80, 3 *ỉr ỉr* (perf. part.); 81, 5 *ỉr ỉr* (perf. part.); 86, x+4 (2nd tense); 86, x+8 *r-ỉr=w* (rel. form)

ỉ-ỉr	60, 2 (perf. part.); 76, 6(?); 85, 4 (2nd tense); 85, 9
n ỉr(?) "to make(?)"	65, 1
ỉrpy "temple"	14, 2; 34, 4; 63, 4; 76, 2
ỉrm "together"	34, 3; 35, 8; 64b, 5; 64d, 5; 69, 2; 74, 4; 85, 4
ỉt "father"	80, 4
ꜥ.wy "place"	50 , 3
ꜥ.wy ḥtp "place of rest"	2, 4 *pꜣ hb pꜣ bỉk ... ꜥ.wy ḥtp*; 5, 8 *pꜣ hb pꜣ bỉk(?) [...] pꜣ ꜥ.wy ḥtp*; 16, 3 ...; 21, 3 *Wsỉr pꜣ hb Wsỉr pꜣ bỉk ꜥq=w n pꜣ ꜥ.wy ḥtp*; 30, 8 ...; 37a, 5 *pꜣ hb pꜣ bỉk ...ꜥ.wy ḥtp*; 49, 1 *pꜣ ꜥ.wy ḥtp mn ty m-bꜣḥ pꜣ hb pꜣ bỉk*; 50, 3 *šms.w r pꜣ ꜥ.wy (ḥtp)*; 53, 1 *ꜥ.wy ḥtp ẖry*; 66, 3 *ꜥ.wy ḥtp [ẖr] pꜣ hb [pꜣ bỉk]*; 67, 1 *ꜥ.wy ḥtp n pꜣ hb pꜣ bỉk*; 67, 2 *ꜥ.wy ḥtp (n) pꜣ hb pꜣ bỉk*; 69, 1 *pꜣ ꜥ.wy ḥtp n pꜣ hb*; 73, 4 *nꜣ ntr.w pꜣ ꜥ.wy ḥtp pꜣ hb*; 74, 2 *nꜣ ntr.w n pꜣ ꜥ.wy ḥtp*; 77, 2 *nꜣ ntr.w pꜣ ꜥ.wy ḥtp pꜣ hb*; 80, 2 *nꜣ ntr.w pꜣ ꜥ.wy ḥtp pꜣ hb*; 81, 3 *nꜣ ntr.w pꜣ ꜥ.wy ḥtp pꜣ hb*; 82, 8 *pꜣ ꜥ.wy ḥtp Ḏḥwty*; 87, 2 *k.t ꜥ.wy ḥtp*; 01, 1
ꜥ.wy.w ḥtp "places of rest"	31, 4(?); 33a, 1 *tꜣ mỉ.t r hyn.w ꜥ.wy.w ḥtp*; 44, 1–2 *tꜣ mỉ.t r nꜣ ꜥ.wy.w ḥtp r ḥry*; 65, 1–2 *ꜥ.wy.w ḥtp ẖr pꜣ hb pꜣ bỉk*
ꜥ.wy.w ẖry.w "lower chambers"	4, 3
ꜥꜣ "great"	92, 2
ꜥꜣ.t "great"	42, 2
ꜥꜣ.w "great"	78, 1 *rmt.w ꜥy.w*
ꜥnḫ "to live"	68, 1
ꜥnḫ=k "may you live"	68, 1

ꜥnḫ "life"	19, 2; 74, 2; mummy bandage 1
ꜥnḫ(?) "bouquet(?)"	76, 6
ꜥḥꜥ "height"	O4, II, x+3; O4, II, x+4
ꜥš "read"	4, 1; 85, 2
ꜥšꜣy "many, long, numerous"	14, 4; 34, 5 *ꜥšꜣ.w*; 63, 5; 75, 1(?); 88, 4
nꜣ-ꜥšꜣy "numerous"	50, 3; 86, x+6
ꜥq(?) "enter"	9, 3; 33b, 1
ꜥq=f "he caused to enter"	13, 1
ꜥq=w "they caused to enter"	14, 1 *r pꜣ ỉrpy*; 21, 3 *n pꜣ ꜥ.wy ḥtp*; 34, 4 *r [pꜣ] ỉrpy*; 63, 3 *r ỉrpy*
ꜥq=w "they entered"	71, 3
=w "they"	14, 1; 63, 3; 65, 1; 66, 2; 86, x+8
wꜥ; see also *wꜥ sp*	65, 3 Ø; 75, 1; 88, 4
wꜥ sp "all together, one time"	34, 3; 62a, 5; 64b, 6; 69, 2; 74, 4; 80, 2; 81, 4
wbꜣ (prep.) "with regard to"	86, x+10
wpy.t "work"	65, 4
wn verb of existence	42, 1; 53, 1
wn "open"	4, 4(?); 65, 3 *wn=w*; 75, 2
wn-nꜣ.w (imperf. converter)	50, 3; 75, 1; 87, 1
wrr "delay"	85, 7 Ø
wrṯ(?) "cage(?)"; see *rmt.w wrṯ(?)*	77, 7
wḥm "again"	71, 2
wḫꜣ "to desire"	65, 1; 66, 2; 76, 5

wsḫ "hall" — 55, 1 *wsḫ mḥ-1.t*

wš "time" — 88, 4

wtḥ "anointing, refined" — 76, 6

m-bꜣḥ "before" — 2, 3 Ø; 10, 3; 12, 1; 14, 6 Ø; 15, 2; 16, 2; 18, 4; 18, 6; 24, 7; 31, 3 Ø; 33a, 9; 34, 2; 35, 3; 35, 7; 35, 11 Ø; 37a, 4; 41, 4 Ø; 48, 4; 49, 1; 50, 2; 62b, 1; 67, 1; 67, 2; 73, 2; 77, 1; 79, 2; 80, 1; 81, 2; 82, 9 Ø; 84, 2; 89, 2

bꜣk "work" — 85, 3

by=k "your ba" — 68, 1

bik "falcon" — 2, 3 *pꜣ hb*; 8, 3 *pꜣ hb*; 9, 2 *pꜣ hb*; 19, 1 *Wsir pꜣ hb Wsir pꜣ bik*; 21, 2 *Wsir pꜣ hb Wsir pꜣ bik*; 34, 2 *pꜣ hb*; 35, 3 *pꜣ hb*; 35, 7 *pꜣ hb*; 37a, 4 *pꜣ hb*; 45, 3 *pꜣ hb*; 49, 2 *pꜣ hb*; 52, 1; 62b, 2 *pꜣ hb*; 65, 2 *pꜣ hb*; [66, 4]; 67, 1 *pꜣ hb*; 67, 2 *pꜣ hb*; 68, 2 *Wsir pꜣ hb Wsir pꜣ bik pꜣ ꜥḫm Wsir Twtw(?)*; 73, 3 *Wsir pꜣ hb Wsir pꜣ bik*; 74, 1 *Wsir pꜣ hb Wsir pꜣ bik*; 77, 2 *Wsir pꜣ hb Wsir pꜣ bik*; 77, 5 *Wsir*; 79, 3 *Wsir pꜣ hb Wsir pꜣ bik*; 80, 2 *Wsir pꜣ hb Wsir pꜣ bik*; 81, 3 *Wsir pꜣ hb Wsir pꜣ bik*; [84, 3 *Wsir pꜣ hb Wsir pꜣ bik*]; 89, 2 *pꜣ hb*

bik(?) "falcon" — 5, 7 *pꜣ hb* Ø; 52, 1

bw-ir=w (negative aorist) — 58, 3

bn … in "not" — 53, 3 …

bn-pw (negative past) — 85, 7 *bn-pw=f*; 85, 10; 86, x+5 *bn-pw=w*

r-bn-nꜣy "here" — 76, 7

bnr "outside" — 33a, 4 *pꜣ bnr*; 58, 6

bry "new" — 54, 4

p3 "the" — 1, 4; 2, 3; 4, 1; 6, 1; 14, 2; 18, 5; 19, 1 (2x); 19, 4; 25, 1; 28, 1; 30, 6; 31, 5; 32, 1; 34, 1; 34, 3; 39, 1; 40, 1; 41, 5; 42, 4; 43, 1; 46, 1; 49, 1; 49, 2; 50, 1; 50, 2; 52, 1, 54, 1; 54, 8; 55, 5; 57, 1; 57, 5; 58, 1; 58, 7; 61, 3; 62a, 1; 62a, 3; 62b, 3; 63, 4; 64a, 1; 64b, 1; 64b, 3; 64b, 5; 69, 1 (2x) , ; 69, 2; 74, 1 (2x) , ; 83, 1; 84, 1; 85, 1; 92, 1; O1, 1; O4, II, x+4

p3y (copula) — 57, 3

p3y (dem. pronoun) — 57, 3

p3y "this" — 53, 2

p3y=y "my" — 80, 4

p3y=f "his" — 81, 4

p3y=w "their" (poss. adjective) — 58, 6; 77, 3

pr imnt "west" — 33a, 2

pr mḥt "north(?)" — 92, 2

pr "house"; see also *pr-Imn* under place names — 7, 2 *Pr Mnṱ*; 29, 1 *Pr-Mnṱ*

pr-ḏ.t "House-of-Eternity" — 68, 3

pr(?) "came out(?)" — 85, 6

pḥ "to reach, to arrive" — 33a, 3; 53, 3; 71, 4; 76, 7

pt(?) "what(?)" — 87, 4

=f (suffix pronoun) — 86, x+7

m-ir "do not" — 4, 2; 58, 5; 88, 3

m-ir(?) "do not" — 70, 3

m3 "place" — 58, 2; 71, 4(?)

mꜣt “way, path”; see also *myt*	46, 1
my “let”	54, 6; 60, 2; 65, 3; 65, 4; 76, 8; 85, 2; 86, x+11
mi͗.t “path, way”	33a, 1; 44, 1
myt “path, way”; see also *mꜣt*	54, 1; 55, 2 *ṯ-myt*; 57, 1; 60, 3 *pꜣ(?) myt*; 65, 3; 76, 4(?); 86, x+5; 86, x+8
mw.t=f “his mother”	47, 2
mn “remains”	1, 8; 2, 2b; 7, 3; 8, 5; 8, 6; 10, 2; 10, 4; 11, 2; 11, 3; 11, 5; 11, 6 Ø; 12, 1; 13, 2; 14, 6; 15, 2; 16, 2; 18, 2; 18, 3; 18, 5; 22, 2; 24, 1; 29, 5 Ø; 31, 3; 31, 6 Ø; 31, 12; 31, 14 Ø; 33a, 9; 33a, 12; 34, 2; 35, 2; 35, 6 Ø; [37, 3]; 39, 2; 41, 3; 41, 8; 43, 2; 47, 2; 48, 4; 49, 1; 50, 2; 51, 2; 62b, 1; 64b, 4; 67, 1; 67, 2; 68, 4; 72, 2; 73, 2; 79, 2; 80, 1; 81, 2; 82, 1; 82, 9; 83, 2; 84, 2; 89, 2
mr.t “harbor”	19, 5; 34, 3; 74, 3
mḥ “to be full”	75, 3
mh̭ṱ; see pr mh̭ṱ “north(?)”	
mqḥ “mourned, sad”	55, 4 *nꜣ ntr.w nt mqḥ*; 57, 3 *nꜣ ntr.w nt mqḥ*; 76, 3
mt “thing”	54, 3(?); 60, 2 *mt.w*; 76, 3(?); 85, 10
mtw=f (independent pronoun)	55, 5
mtw=s (independent pronoun)	55, 2
mtr(?) “satisfied(?)”	54, 3

mtre "proper mode of conduct, correct" 58, 1 [gl.]; 70, 1 [gl.]

n (genitive) 19, 5 [gl.]; 64b, 2 [gl.]

n "in, from" 19, 5 [gl.]; 63, 5 [gl.]; 64b, 4 [gl.]

n (prep.) 54, 5 [gl.]; 71, 2 [gl.]; 86, 3 [gl.]; 86, x+7 [gl.]

=*n* "we" 86, x+4 [gl.]

nꜣ "the" (plural definite article) 19, 5 [gl.]; 49, 1 [gl.]; 55, 3 (2x) [gl.], [gl.]; 57, 2 [gl.]; 57, 3 [gl.]; 58, 1 [gl.]; 58, 2 [gl.]; 60, 1 [gl.]; 64d, 5 [gl.]; 73, 3 [gl.]; 76, 7 [gl.], 77, 7 [gl.]; 87, 1 [gl.]

nꜣy=w "their" 49, 7 [gl.]

nꜣy=f "his" 50, 3 [gl.]

nꜣy=w "the ones of" (poss. prefix) 34, 3 [gl.]; 64b, 5 [gl.]; 69, 2 [gl.]; 74, 4 [gl.]

nꜣy "these" (dem. adjective) 4, 1 [gl.]; 76, 4 [gl.]; 85, 2 [gl.]

nꜣy "these" (dem. pronoun) 33a, 4 [gl.]; 53, 4 [gl.]

nb "all, every, any" 4, 1 [gl.]; 39, 4 [gl.]; 51, 3 [gl.]; 54, 5 [gl.]; 58, 1 [gl.]; 65, 4 Ø; 85, 1 [gl.]; 86, x+9 [gl.]

nb "lord" 7, 2 [gl.]; 29, 4 [gl.]

nfr; see *rn nfr*

nfr(?) "well(?)" 55, 6 [gl.]

nḥḥ "oil" O1, 2 [gl.]

nḫt.t "strong" 54, 3 [gl.]; 58, 3 [gl.]

nkt "thing" 86, x+10 [gl.]

nt "which, who" 4, 1 [gl.]; 19, 4 [gl.]; 39, 4 [gl.]; 51, 3 Ø; 54, 5 [gl.]; 55, 2 [gl.]; 55, 4 [gl.]; 57, 2 [gl.]; 57, 3 [gl.]; 76, 6 [gl.]; 85, 1 [gl.]; 86, x+9 [gl.]; 87, 4 [gl.]

nṯr "god" 4, 2 [gl.]; 10, 5 [gl.] in [gl.]; 88, 3 [gl.]

ntr.w "gods"; see also *ṯ-ntr.w*	55, 3 *ꜣtr.w nꜣ ntr.w* ; 55, 6 *ḥtp nꜣ ntr.w* ; 57, 3 *nꜣ ntr.w nt mqḥ* ; 60, 2 ; 67, 1 ; 67, 2 ; 73, 3 ; 74, 1 ; 77, 2 ; 80, 2 ; 81, 3
r "into, for"	44, 1 ; 53, 3(?) ; 58, 2 ; 58, 3 ; 58, 6 ; 60, 1 ; 63, 4
r (rel. converter)	76, 6
r-r=s "to it"	54, 3 ; 60, 3 ; 86, x+6 ; 86, x+9 *r ḥr r-r=s*
r-r=f "to it/him"	70, 3
r-r=w "to them"	54, 6
rꜣ "entrance, door"	33a, 3 ; 53, 2
rꜣ "number"	O4, II, x+2
rpy "to rejuvenate"	68, 1
rpy=k "may you be rejuvenated"	68, 1
rmt "man"	4, 1 *rmt nb n pꜣ tꜣ nt ỉw=f (r) ꜥš* ; 39, 4 *rmt nb nt ꜣlr* ; 51, 3 *rmt nb* ; 54, 5 *rmt nb nt ỉw=w (r) ỉy* ; 76, 6 *rmt nt i.ir(?) tm(?) rẖ(?)* ; 86, x+9 *rmt nb pꜣ tꜣ nt ỉw=f (r) gm* ; O4, II, x+2(?)
rmt.w "people, men"	19, 5 ; 34, 3 ; 49, 7 ; 74, 3 in *rmt.w tꜣ ml* ; 77, 1 ; 77, 7 in *rmt.w wrṯ(?)* ; 78, 1 *rmt.w ꜥꜣ.w*
rn "name"	28, 1 ; 32, 1 ; 43, 1 ; 77, 3 ; 82, 1 ; 82, 8
rn "because of"	86, x+7
rn=f "his names"	24, 1
rn nfr "good name"	1, 4 ; 1, 7 ; 2, 1 Ø; 6, 1 ; 7, 1 ; 8, 1 Ø; 8, 6 ; 10, 1 ; 11, 1 Ø; 11, 3 ; 11, 4 ; 11, 6 ; 12, 1 ; 13, 2 ; 14, 5 ; 15, 1 ; 16, 1 ; 18, 1 Ø; 18, 3 ; 18, 5 ; 18, 7 ; 20, 1 ; 22, 1 ; 23, 1 ; 24, 6 ; 25, 1 ; 29, 1 ; 30, 3 ; 30, 6 ; 31, 1 ; 31, 5 ; 31, 13 ; 31, 15 ;

rn nfr "good name" (cont.) — 34, 1; 35, 1; 35, 5; 35, 10; 37a, 2; 37b, 1; 39, 1; 41, 1; 41, 5; 47, 1; 48, 1; 49, 1; 50, 1; 51, 1 Ø; 62a, 1–2; 64a, 1; 64b, 1; [67, 1]; [67, 2]; 68, 4; 72, 1; 73, 1; 77, 1; 79, 1; 80, 1; 81, 1; 83, 1; 84, 1; 89, 1

rn nfr(?) "good(?) name" — 2, 1

rn.w "names, aforesaid" — 55, 6; 76, 2(?)

rnp.t "year" — 14, 3; 33a, 3; 34, 5; 63, 5 *rnp.(w)t*

rẖ(?) "to be able(?)" — 76, 7

rtb "artabe" — O5, x+1 (2x) Ø; O5, x+2; O5, x+3 Ø; O5, x+3; O5, x+5 (2x) Ø

hyn.w "some" — 33a, 1; 53, 1; 54, 2; 54, 4

hb "to send" — 76, 6

hb "ibis" — 2, 3 *pꜣ bi͗k*; 5, 7 *pꜣ bi͗k(?)*; 8, 3 *pꜣ bi͗k* Ø; 9, 2 *pꜣ bi͗k*; 10, 3; 19, 1 *Wsi͗r pꜣ hb Wsi͗r pꜣ bi͗k*; 21, 1 *Wsi͗r pꜣ hb Wsi͗r pꜣ bi͗k*; 31, 3; 33b, 3; 34, 2 *pꜣ bi͗k*; 35, 3 *pꜣ bi͗k*; 35, 7; 37a, 4 *pꜣ bi͗k* Ø; 45, 2 *pꜣ bi͗k*; 48, 5; 49, 2 *pꜣ bi͗k*; 50, 2; 62b, 2 *pꜣ bi͗k*; 65, 2 *pꜣ bi͗k*; 66, 3 *[pꜣ bi͗k]*; 67, 1 *pꜣ bi͗k*; 67, 2 *pꜣ bi͗k*; 68, 1 *pꜣ hb pr-ꜥꜣ*; 68, 2 *Wsi͗r pꜣ hb Wsi͗r pꜣ bi͗k pꜣ ꜥẖm Wsi͗r Twtw(?)*; 69, 1; 73, 2 *Wsi͗r pꜣ hb Wsi͗r pꜣ bi͗k*; 73, 4; 74, 1 *Wsi͗r pꜣ hb Wsi͗r pꜣ bi͗k*; 77, 1 *Wsi͗r pꜣ hb Wsi͗r pꜣ bi͗k*; 77, 2; 79, 3 *Wsi͗r pꜣ hb Wsi͗r pꜣ bi͗k*; 80, 1 *Wsi͗r pꜣ hb Wsi͗r pꜣ bi͗k*; 80, 2; 81, 2 *Wsi͗r pꜣ hb Wsi͗r pꜣ bi͗k*; 81, 3; 84, 2 *Wsi͗r pꜣ hb [Wsi͗r pꜣ bi͗k]*; 85, 1; 85, 3; 89, 2 *pꜣ bi͗k*; 91, 1(?)

hny "jars"; see *ḥn.w* "jars" — 58, 2; 87, 1

hrw "day" — O5, x+4

hh "flame, fire" — 71, 2; 71, 5; 85, 6; 86, 3

ḥ.t-nṯr "divine chapel, temple"	9, 4; 14, 4; 21, 5 (?); 34, 5; 63, 5
ḥ.t-sp "regnal year"	10, 1; 13, 1; 14, 3; 14, 4; 19, 6 (2x), ; 21, 6; 24, 3; 30, 9; 31, 3; 33a, 7; 34, 2 (2x), ; 34, 6; 37a, 1; 45, 1; 47, 3; 48, 7; 62a, 1; 63, 1; 63, 6; 64b, 3 (2x), ; 64b, 4; 64b, 6; 69, 2; 74, 5; 80, 3 (2x), ; 81, 5 (2x), ; 82, 7 Ø; O1, 3; O5, x+6
ḥꜣ=s(?) "before it"	86, x+4
ḥꜣṯ(?) "heart(?)"	70, 1
ḥmꜣ "salt"	O2, 4
ḥn.w "jars"; see *hny* "jars"	54, 4 *ḥn.w bry*
ḥnꜥ "together with"	39, 3; 49, 7
ḥr=f "his face"	85, 7 *r ḥr=f*
ḥr "before"	86, x+9 *r ḥr r-r=s*
ḥr "upon"	44, 2
(r-)ḥry "up, above"	42, 3; 42, 4(?); 44, 2; 46, 1(?); 70, 2; 76, 2; 85, 8; 87, 3
ḥt "silver-deben"	O1, 1; O2, 4 *ḥt ḥmꜣ* "salt-tax"
ḥtp "rest"; see *ꜥ.wy ḥtp*	4, 2 *m-ỉr tỉ.t ḥtp nṯr ty*; 8, 4 *tỉ=f ḥtp* Ø; 9, 4 *ỉw=f ḥtp (n) ḥ.t-nṯr*; 42, 3 *qs(.t)(?) ꜥꜣ.t ḥtp ty ḥry*; 45, 2 *ḥtp pꜣ hb*; 55, 5 *ḥtp nꜣ nṯr.w*; 58, 5 *m-ỉr tỉ.t ḥtp pꜣy=w bnr*; 60, 1; 88, 3 *m-ỉr tỉ.t ḥtp nṯr ty*
ḫpr "happened"	60, 2; 65, 1; 66, 2; 71, 1; 86, 2; 86, x+7
ẖ.t "group, body"	33a, 2
ẖ.wt(?) "bodies"	71, 6
ẖ.t(?) "area(?)"	86, 1 *ẖ.t tbtꜣ*

ẖ.ṱ=w(?) (reading and meaning uncertain) — 86, x+10

ẖn "in" — 54, 4; 70, 2

r-ẖn "inside, into" — 53, 2; 57, 1

ẖr "for, contain" — 57, 2; 65, 2; [66, 3]

ẖry.w "lower"; see *ʿ.wy ẖry.w*

ẖry "below" — 53, 1; 75, 2

r-ẖry "below" — 85, 5; 86, 2

h̭rh̭r(?) "destruction(?)" — 86, x+6

h̭ṱ "inspiration" — 85, 1

s (dependent pronoun) — 76, 8

sꜣ "son of" — 18, 5; 19, 3; 31, 2; 39, 2; 42, 6; 43, 1; 57, 4; 58, 7(?); 61, 2; 64b, 2; 77, 8; 86, x+12; mummy bandage 1

m-sꜣ "after" — 14, 3; 34, 5; 63, 4

sw "wheat" — O5, x+1 (2x) Ø; O5, x+2; O5, x+3; O5, x+3; O5, x+5 Ø; O5, x+5

swn "price" — O1, 1

nꜣ-sbk "to be few" — 53, 3

sf "resin" — 54, 7; 76, 5

sp ; see *wʿ sp*

sp "remainder" — 78, 1; O4, II, x+1

sẖ "written, recorded, to write" — 4, 4; 16, 3; 21, 6; 24, 3; 33a, 4; 33a, 5; 33b, 4(?) Ø; 34, 6, 42, 5; 45, 4; 47, 3; 47, 3(?); 50, 4; 52, 6; 52, 7; 53, 4 *sẖ.w*; 54, 7; 55, 4; 56, 3; 57, 4; 58, 6; 59a, 5(?); 59c, x+1; 60, 4; 61, 2; 62b, 3;

sẖ "written, recorded, to write" (cont.)	63, 6; 64b, 6; 69, 2; 69, 3; 70, 4; 71, 10; 74, 5; 75, 5; 76, 5(?); 80, 3; 80, 4; 81, 4; 82, 7; 85, 12; 86, x+12; 88, 5; O1, 2; O2, 4
sẖ.w "writings"	4, 1; 85, 2
st (proclitic pronoun)	76, 3; 76, 5
sty "flame"	58, 4
šym "corridor, row (of connected rooms)"	92, 1
šꜥ "until, unto, up to"	5, 8; 33a, 3; 53, 4; 58, 4; 85, 8; 88, 4
šꜥ-tw "until" (terminative)	4, 3; 76, 5 *šꜥ-tw=w*; 76, 7
šꜥ ḏ.t "until eternity"	7, 3; 8, 7; 11, 4; 13, 3; 18, 2; 18, 4 Ø; 18, 6 Ø; 21, 6; 22, 2; 24, 1; 29, 5–6 Ø; 31, 12 Ø; 31, 14; 35, 4(?) Ø; 39, 2; 43, 2; 47, 3; 48, 6(?); 51, 3; 52, 6; 62b, 2; 64b, 4; 67, 1; 67, 2; 72, 2; 73, 4; 79, 4; 89, 2
šw(?) "right(?)"	54, 6
šm "to go"	70, 3
šr "child"	81, 4
qs "to bury"	54, 6
qs(.t) "burial"	42, 2(?); 71, 3; 76, 5; 88, 3
qt "Kite"	O2, 4
k.t "another"	87, 2
kꜣ.t "chapel"	54, 2
gm "power"	86, x+11

gm "to find"	82, 3 ; <86, x+5>; 86, x+8 ; 86, x+9
tꜣ "the"	19, 5 ; 33a, 1 ; 33a, 2 ; 44, 1 ; 55, 1 ; 55, 1(?)) ; 55, 2 ; 60, 1
tꜣ (dem. pronoun)	56, 3 *tꜣ(?) tꜣyl* ; 60, 3 *tꜣ tꜣy*
tꜣy=f "her"	86, x+11
tꜣ "land, world"	4, 1 ; 7, 2 ; 29, 4 ; 86, x+9
ta(?) "daughter of"	Mummy bandage 2
tꜣy "this"	54, 2 ; 55, 1 ; 56, 3 ; 60, 3 ; 71, 1 ; 86, 1
ti͗.t/ ti͗ "to give, cause, let"	4, 2 ; 4, 2 ; 19, 2 ; 55, 5 ; 58, 5 ; 60, 1 ; 74, 2 ; 76, 8 ; 86, x+10 ; 88, 3 ; mummy bandage 1
ti͗=f "he causes, he gives"	8, 3 ; 86, x+11
ty "here"	1, 8 ; 2, 2b ; 4, 2 ; 7, 3 ; 8, 6 ; 10, 2 ; 10, 4 ; 11, 2 ; 11, 3 Ø; 11, 5 ; 11, 6 ; 12, 1 ; 13, 2 ; 14, 6 ; 15, 2 , 16, 2 , 18, 2 Ø; 18, 3 Ø; 18, 6 ; 22, 2 ; 24, 1 ; 24, 7(?) Ø; 29, 5 ; 30, 5 ; 31, 3 ; 31, 6(?) Ø; 31, 12 ; 31, 14 ; 33a, 9 ; 34, 2 ; 35, 2 Ø; 35, 7 ; 37a, 3 ; 39, 2 ; 41, 3 ; 41, 8 ; 42, 3 ; 43, 2 ; 47, 2 ; 48, 4 ; 49, 1 ; 50, 2 ; 51, 2 Ø; 53, 2 ; 55, 1 ; 60, 3 ; 62b, 1 ; 64b, 4 ; 67, 1 ; 67, 2 ; 68, 4 ; 72, 2 ; 73, 2 ; 79, 2 ; 80, 1 ; 81, 2 ; 82, 9 ; 83, 2 ; 84, 2 ; 88, 4 ; 87, 2 ; 89, 2
tw; see šꜥ tw	
r-tbꜣ "on account of"	60, 2
tbtꜣ "ceremony"	86, 1 *ẖ.t tbtꜣ*
tm "not" (negative verb)	76, 7(?) ; 86, x+8
tn "at the rate of"	O5, x+4
tr "all, entirety"	64d, 5 ; 74, 2

tr.t “in the hand”	69, 1 
trt “stairs”	42, 4 ; 44, 3 ; 87, 3 *trtr* 
thm “to enter”	58, 1 
ṯ “to take”; see also *ṯ ntr.w*	54, 2 ; 60, 2 *ṯꜣy=w* 
ṯ-myt “to lead”	55, 2 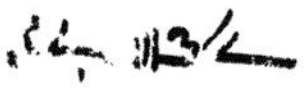
ṯ(?) “from” (prep.)	53, 2 
ḏ.t “eternity”; see *šꜥ ḏ.t*	
ḏ “to say”	87, 4 *ḏ.ṯ=f* ; 88, 2 
ḏm “offspring, generation”	33a, 2 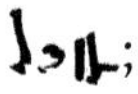; 53, 3 

Unread

…	17, 1 
…	38, 1 
…	54, 4 … *ẖn hyn.w ḥnw bry* 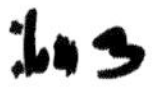
…	70, 2 
…	75, 3 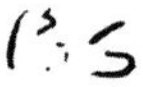
	70, 2 
…	76, 8 
…	76, 8 
…	92, 1 
…	O4, II, x+2 ; O4, II, x+3 
…	O4, II, x+4 
…	O4, II, x+4 

PERSONAL NAMES

ꜣrꜥblws, son of *Ỉy-m-ḥtp* — 69, 1 *wr Ḏḥwty* 

Ỉy-m-ḥtp, father of *ꜣrꜥblws* — 69, 1 

Ỉy-m-ḥtp, father of *Pꜣ-hb* — 11, 3 

Ỉy-m-ḥtp, father of *<Pꜣ->hb* — 73, 1 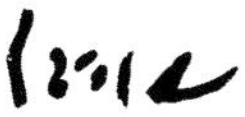

Ỉy-m-ḥtp, son of *Pꜣ-šr-pꜣ-mwt* — 8, 6 

ʾ *Ỉy-m-ḥtp*, son of *Pꜣ-šr-...* — 11, 1 

ʾ *Ỉy-m-ḥtp(?)*, father of *Pꜣ-šr-Ỉmn(?)* — 11, 4 

Ỉy-m-ḥtp(?), father of *Hr* — 22, 1 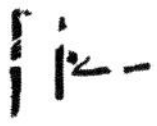

Ỉmn-ḥtp(?), son of *Pꜣ-...(?)* — 29, 2 *wr Ḏḥwty; ṯ nṯr.w Pr-Mnṯ nb tꜣ* 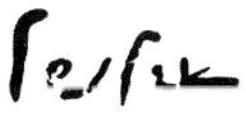

ʾ *Ỉmn-ḥtp* — 1, 2 

ʾ *Ỉmn-...*, son of *Hr* — 78, 8 *sḫ; rmt ꜥꜣ* (in list) 

ꜥbb (PN?) — 05, x+2 

ꜥnḫ-rn=f, son of *Ns-Mn* — 49, 4 *ỉry.w-ꜥꜣ pꜣ ꜥ.wy ḥtp* 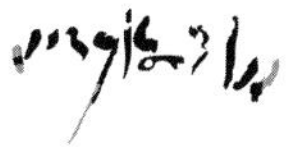

Wsỉr-wr, son of *Ḥr*, grandson of *Gl-šr*, great-grandson of *Ḥr* — 48, 2 

Wsỉr-wr, father of ...	64d, 2
W...	78, 9 *sẖ; rmt ꜥ3* (in list)
P3-ỉšwr, son of *P3-mrl*	34, 1 *wr Ḏḥwty*
P3-ꜥw, son of *Ḥr-Mn*	Mummy bandage 1
P3-m3y(?)	5, 4
P3-mrl, father of *P3-ỉšwr*	34, 1
[P3]-mrl	45, 5
P3-nfr-ỉr-ḥr, son of *Ḏ-ḥr*	49, 6 *ỉry.w-ꜥ3 p3 ꜥ.wy ḥtp*
P3-hb	1, 4 ; 52, 7
P3-hb, son of *ʾIy-m-ḥtp*	11, 3
<P3->hb, son of *ʾIy-m-ḥtp*	73, 1
P3-hb, father of *P3-...*	35, 2
P3-hb, son of *Pa-hb*	43, 1
P3-hb, father of *Pa-hb*	43, 1
P3-hb, father of *Hr*	10, 2 ; 10, 4 ; 64d, 5 ; 64d, 7
P3-hb(?)	35, 10 Ø

Pꜣ-ḥ.t-nṯr, father of *Ḫnsw-Ḏḥwty*	7, 1
Pꜣ-šr-ʾImn(?), son of *ʾIy-m-ḥtp(?)*	11, 4
Pꜣ-šr-ʾImn, son of *Pꜣ-tỉ-Ḥr-pꜣ-Rꜥ(?)*	O1, 2
Pꜣ-šr-[ʾImn], son of *Ḏḥwty-sḏm*	42, 5
Pꜣ-šr-ꜥ-pḥ.ty, father of *Ḫnsw-Ḏḥwty*	77, 9
Pꜣ-šr-pꜣ-mwt, father of *ʾIy-m-ḥtp*	8, 6
Pꜣ-šr-pꜣ-mwt, son of *Ḏḥwty-ỉw*	72, 1 *wr Ḏḥwty*
Pꜣ-šr-Mn, son of *Ḏḥwty-sḏm*	4, 4 *wr Ḏḥwty*; 54, 7 *wr Ḏḥwty*; 55, 4 *wr Ḏḥwty*; 56, 3; 57, 4 *wr Ḏḥwty*; 58, 6 *wr Ḏḥwty*; 60, 4 *wr Ḏḥwty*; 61, 2 *wr Ḏḥwty*; 70, 4; 71, 10 *wr Ḏḥwty*; 75, 5; 85, 4; 85, 12 *[wr Ḏḥwty]*; 86, x+12 *wr Ḏḥwty*; 87, 5
Pꜣ-šr-Mn, father of *Ḏḥwty-sḏm*	35, 5; 50, 1
Pꜣ-šr-Mn, father of *Pa-Wsr*, son of *Ns-Mn*	64b, 2
Pꜣ-šr-Mn, father of *Pa-Wsr(?)*	62a, 2
Pꜣ-šr-Mn(?), father of *Ḥr...*	21, 4
Pꜣ-šr-Ḫnsw	77, 12 *rmt wrṯ̭(?)* (in list); *ṯ nṯr.w* (in list)(?)

Pꜣ-šr-Ḫnsw,
father of ...
13, 2 ; O5, x+3 

Pꜣ-šr-Ḫnsw,
son of *Pꜣ-šr-...*
35, 6 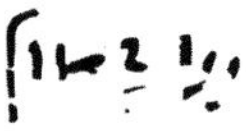

Pꜣ-šr-Ḫnsw,
son of *Pꜣ-ti͗-Wsi͗r*
77, 4 *wr Ḏḥwty; ṯ ntr.w* (in list) 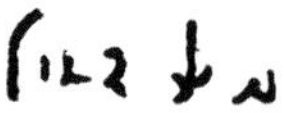

Pꜣ-šr-Ḫnsw,
son of *Pꜣ-ti͗-Mn*
69, 3 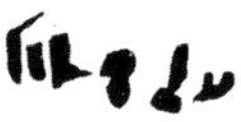

Pꜣ-šr-Ḫnsw,
son of *Pꜣ-ti͗-Mn*,
father of *Ḫnsw-Ḏḥwty*
80, 1 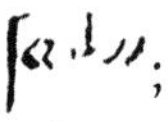; 80, 3 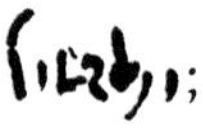; 80, 4 *wr Ḏḥwty* 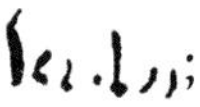; 81, 1 *wr Ḏḥwty* 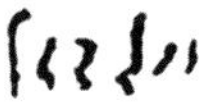

Pꜣ-šr-Ḫnsw,
son of *Ḥr*
78, 2 *rmt ꜥꜣ* (in list) 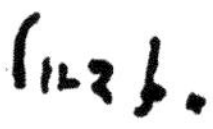

Pꜣ-šr-Ḫnsw,
father of *Ḫnsw-Ḏḥwty*
81, 4 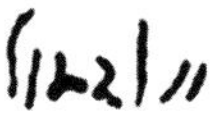

Pꜣ-šr-Ḫnsw(?),
father of *Tꜣ-šr.t-Ḫnsw(?)*
Mummy bandage 2 

Pꜣ-šr-Ḏḥwty,
father of *Sṱꜣ=w-tꜣ-wty*
79, 2 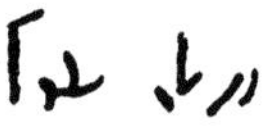

Pꜣ-šr-...,
father of *ʾIy-m-ḥtp*
11, 1 

Pꜣ-šr-...,
father of *Pꜣ-šr-Ḫnsw*
35, 6 

Pꜣ-šr-...,
father of *Ḥr-wn-nfr(?)*
77, 6 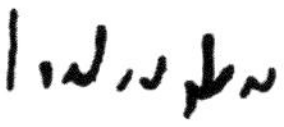

Pꜣ-šr- ...,
father of *Pꜣy-kꜣ(?)*
78, 5 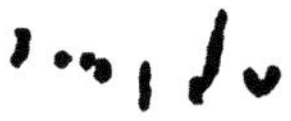

Pꜣ-šr-...,
father of *...(?)*
78, 4 *rmt ꜥꜣ* (in list) 

Pꜣ-šll,
father of *Ḥr*
83, 2 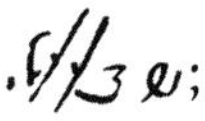; 84, 1 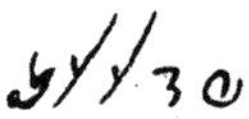

Pꜣ-tỉ-Ỉmn, 30, 7 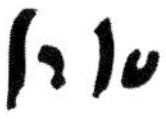
father of *Pa-ʿnḫ(?)*

Pꜣ-tỉ-Ỉs.t(?) 85, 4 

Pꜣ-tỉ-Wsỉr 1, 9 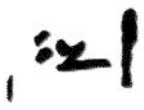

Pꜣ-tỉ-Wsỉr, 77, 4 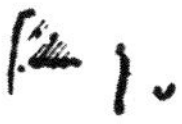
father of *Pꜣ-šr-Ḫnsw*

Pꜣ-tỉ-Mn, 69, 3 
father of *Pꜣ-šr-Ḫnsw*

Pꜣ-tỉ-Mn, 80, 3 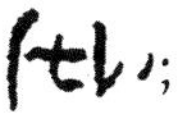; 80, 4 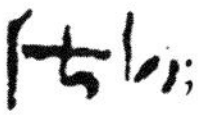; 81, 1 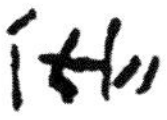
father of *Pꜣ-šr-Ḫnsw*,
grandfather of *Ḫnsw-Ḏḥwty*

Pꜣ-tỉ-Nfr-ḥtp, 64d, 4 *ỉt-ntr mr ḫꜣs.t* 
father of ...

Pꜣ-tỉ-hb(?), 89, 1 
son of *Ns-Mn*

Pꜣ-tỉ-Ḥr-pꜣ-Rʿ(?), 01, 2 
father of *Pꜣ-šr-Ỉmn*

Pꜣ-tỉ-Ḥr-pꜣ-ẖrt(?), 39, 3 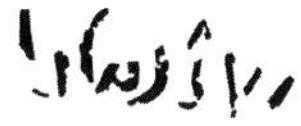
son of *Ḏḥwty-... (?)*

Pꜣ-tỉ-Ḫnsw 31, 12 

Pꜣ-tỉ-Ḫnsw-pꜣ-sḫy 24, 2 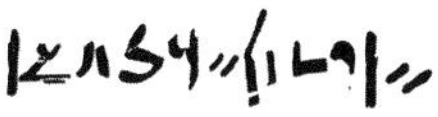

Pꜣ- tỉ-...(?), 37a, 3 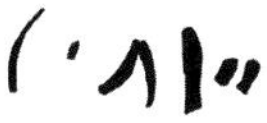
father of ...-*Ỉs.t*

Pꜣ-tỉ-..., 82, 2 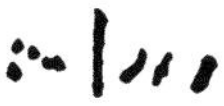
father of [...],
son(?) of ...- *Ḫnsw*

Pꜣ- tỉ-... 59a, 4 

Pꜣ-...(?), 29, 2 
father of *Ỉmn-ḥtp(?)*

Pꜣ-..., son of *Pꜣ-hb*	35, 1 ; 35, 8 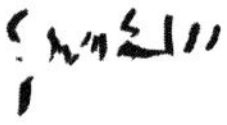
Pa-ꜥnḫ(?), son(?) of *Pꜣ-tỉ-Ỉmn*	30, 6 *wr Ḏḥwty* 
Pa-Wsr	6, 1 
Pa-Wsr, son of *Pꜣ-šr-Mn*, grandson of *Ns-Mn*	64b, 2 
Pa-Wsr(?), son of *Pꜣ-šr-Mn*	62a, 2 *wr Ḏḥwty, ṯ ntr.w, ꜥꜣ Nw.t* 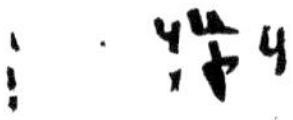
Pa-Wsr, son of *Twt*	78, 6 *rmt ꜥꜣ* (in list) 
Pa-nꜣ	77, 10 *ꜥntꜣy, rmt wrṱ(?)* (in list), *ṯ ntr.w* (in list)(?) 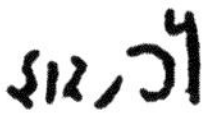
Pa-nꜣ-ḫṱ.w, father of *Mnḫ-pꜣ-Rꜥ(?)*	19, 3 
Pa-rt, son of *Tny.t-Ḫnsw(?)*	78, 3 *rmt ꜥꜣ* (in list) 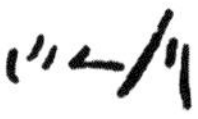
Pa-tm, son of *Ns-Mn*	49, 5 *ỉry.w-ꜥꜣ pꜣ ꜥ.wy ḥtp* 
Pa-Ḏḥwty, father of *Plth*	77, 8 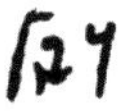
Pꜣy=f-ṯꜣw-ꜥ.wy-Ḫnsw, son of *Ns-Mn*	33a, 4 *sẖ* ; 33a, 5 *wr Ḏḥwty* ; 53, 4 *sẖ, wr Ḏḥwty* 
Pꜣy=s-nfr(?)	31, 2 
Pꜣy-kꜣ(?), son of *Pꜣ-šr-...*	78, 5 *sh, rmt ꜥꜣ* (in list) 
Plth, son of *Pa-Ḏḥwty*	77, 8 *rmt wrṱ(?)* (in list), *ṯ ntr.w* (in list)(?) 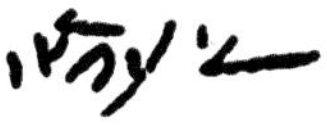

Mnḫ-pꜣ-Rꜥ(?), 19, 2 *wr Ḏḥwty*[213] 
son of *Pa-nꜣ-ḫṯ.w*

Ns-pꜣ-Rꜥ(?) 2, 1 

Ns-Mn, 49, 4 
father of *ꜥnḫ-rn=f*

Ns-Mn,
father of *Pꜣ-šr-Mn,* 64b, 2 
grandfather of *Pꜣ-Wsr*

Ns-Mn, 89, 1 
father of *Pꜣ-tỉ-hb(?)*

Ns-Mn, 49, 5 
father of *Pa-tm*

Ns-Mn, 33a, 5 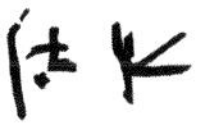; 53, 4 
father of *Pꜣy=f-ṯꜣw-ꜥ.wy-Ḫnsw*

Ns-Mn, 49, 3 
father of *Ḥr*

Ns-Mn, 41, 6 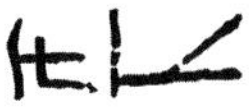
son of ...

Ns-Mn(?) 66, 1(?) 

Ns-Mn-...(?), 34, 6 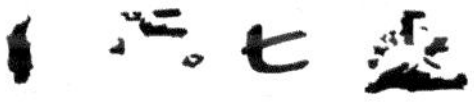
son of *Hr*

Ns-nb-ꜥy, 68, 3 
father of *Ḏḥwty-sḏm*

Ns-Ḫmn-ỉw, 78, 10 *rmt ꜥꜣ* (in list) 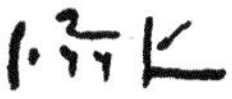
son of *Hkl(?)*

Ns(?)-..., 41, 7 
father of *Ns-Mn*

Lwꜣ, 52, 6 ; 59c, x+1 ; 62b, 3 *sḫ, ṯ ntr.w, ꜥꜣ Nw.t* 
son of *Ḥr*

[213] Followed by *n pꜣ nt ṯ nꜣ ntr.w n nꜣ rmt.w tꜣ mr.t* "(and) to the one who takes the gods (and) to the men of the harbor."

Hr	12, 1; 16, 1; 34, 6
Hr, son of *ʾIy-m-ḥtp(?)*	22, 1
Hr, father of *ʾImn-...*	78, 8
Hr, son of *Pꜣ-hb*	10, 1; 10, 4; 64d, 7
Hr..., son of *Pꜣ-šr-Mn(?)*	21, 4
Hr, father of *Pꜣ-šr-Ḫnsw*	78, 2
Hr, son of *Pꜣ-šll*	83, 1; 84, 1
Hr, father of *Ns-Mn-...(?)*	34, 6
Hr, son of *Ḥr-ỉw(?)*	78, 7 *rmt ꜥꜣ* (in list)
Hr, son of *Ḫnsw-Ḏḥwty*	39, 1
Hr, son of *...(?)*	18, 5 *wr Ḏḥwty*
Hrgls	14, 5
Hkl(?), father of *Ns-Ḫmn-ỉw*	78, 10
Ḥr	O5, x+5
Ḥr, father of *Lwꜣ*	52, 7; 59c, x+1 Ø; 62b, 3
Ḥr, son of *Ns-Mn*	49, 3 *ỉry.w-ꜥꜣ pꜣ ꜥ.wy ḥtp*

Ḥr, son of *Gl-šr*, father of *Wsỉr-wr*, grandson of *Ḥr*	48, 2 
Ḥr, father of *Gl-šr*, grandfather of *Ḥr*, great-grandfather of *Wsỉr-wr*	48, 3 
Ḥr-ỉw(?), father of *Hr*	78, 7 
Ḥr-wn-nfr(?), (son of) *Pꜣ-šr-...*	77, 6 *mr šn Ḏḥwty*, *ṯ ntr.w* (in list) 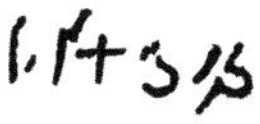
Ḥr-wn-nfr(?), father of *Grt(?)*	77, 5 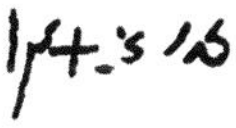
Ḥr-pa-ʾIs.t, son of *Sylws*	68, 4 
Ḥr-m-ḥb, son of *Ḏ-ḥr(?)*	74, 2 *wr Ḏḥwty*, *ṯ ntr.w* 
Ḥr-Mw.t(?), son of *Ḫnsw-Ḏḥwty*	77, 11 *rmt wrṱ(?)* (in list), *ṯ ntr.w* (in list)(?) 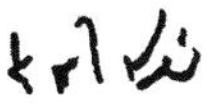
Ḥr-Mn, father of *Pꜣ-ꜥw*	Mummy bandage 1 
Ḥr-sꜣ-ʾIs.t, father of *Ḏḥwty-ms*	O2, 4 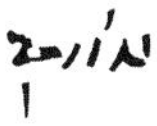
Ḥr-Ḏḥwty(?), father of ...	41, 2 
Ḫnsw-Ḏḥwty, son of *Pꜣ-ḥ.t-ntr*	7, 1 *wr Ḏḥwty* 
Ḫnsw-Ḏḥwty, son of *Pꜣ-šr-ꜥ-pḥ.ty*	77, 9 *rmt wrṱ(?)* (in list), *ṯ ntr.w* (in list)(?) 

Ḫnsw-Ḏḥwty, son of *Pꜣ-šr-Ḫnsw*, grandson of *Pꜣ-ti͗-Mn* — 80, 3 

Ḫnsw-Ḏḥwty, son of *Pꜣ-šr-Ḫnsw* — 80, 1 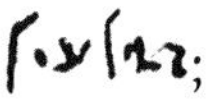; 81, 4 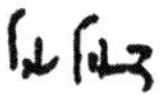

Ḫnsw-Ḏḥwty, father of *Hr* — 39, 2 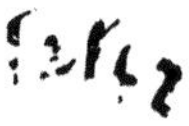

Ḫnsw-Ḏḥwty, father of *Ḥr-Mw.t(?)* — 77, 11 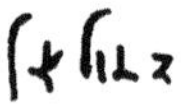

Ḫnsw-... — 12, 1 ; 25, 2 

Sylws, father of *Ḥr-pa-ʾIs.t* — 68, 4 

Sṯꜣ=w-tꜣ-wty, son of *Pꜣ-šr-Ḏḥwty* — 79, 1 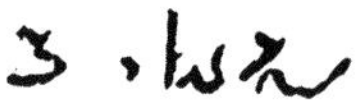

Grt(?), son of *Ḥr-wn-nfr(?)* — 77, 5 *ṯ ntr.w* (in list) 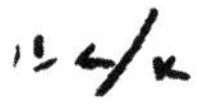

Gl-šr, son of *Ḥr*, father of *Ḥr*, grandfather of *Wsi͗r-wr* — 48, 3 

Tꜣ-šr.t-Ḫnsw(?), daughter of *Pꜣ-šr-Ḫnsw(?)* — Mummy bandage 2 

Tꜣy-lwꜣ(?), mother of ... — 47, 2 

Twt, father of *Pa-Wsr.t* — 78, 6 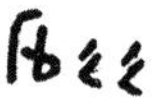

Twtw(?) — 68, 2 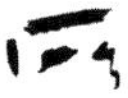

Tny.t-Ḫnsw(?), father of *Pa-rt* — 78, 3 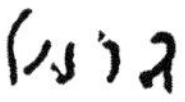

Ḏ-ḥr — 01, 1 *pꜣ ꜥ.wj ḥtp* 

Ḏ-ḥr, father of *P3-nfr-ỉr-ḥr* — 49, 6

Ḏ-ḥr(?), father of *Ḥr-m-ḥb* — 74, 2

Ḏ-ḥr-m-ḥb — 1, 1

Ḏw-ʿḥy — 1, 3

Ḏḥwty-ỉw, father of *P3-šr-p3-mwt* — 72, 1

Ḏḥwty-ms, son of *Ḥr-s3-ʾIs.t* — O2, 4

Ḏḥwty-sḏm, father of *P3-šr-[ʾImn]* — 42, 6

Ḏḥwty-sḏm, son of *P3-šr-Mn* — 35, 5; 50, 1

Ḏḥwty-sḏm, father of *P3-šr-Mn* — 4, 5; 54, 7; 55, 4; 56, 3; 57, 4; 58, 7; 60, 4; 61, 2; 70, 4; 71, 10; 75, 5 Ø; 85, 5; 85, 12; 86, x+12 *Ḏḥwty*<*-sḏm*>; 87, 5

Ḏḥwty-sḏm, son of *Ns-nb-ʿy* — 68, 3 *sẖ pr-ḏ.t*

Ḏḥwty-[...] — 90, 1 Ø

Ḏḥwty-...(?), father of *P3-tỉ-Ḥr-p3-ẖrt(?)* — 39, 3

..., son of *Wsỉr-wr* — 64d, 2 *ỉt-ntr*

...-ʾIs.t, son of *P3-tỉ-...* — 37a, 2

...-Ḫnsw, father(?) of *Pꜣ-tỉ-...*	82, 2 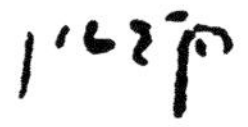
..., son of *Pꜣ-šr-Ḫnsw*	13, 2 
..., son of *Pꜣ-šr-...(?)*	78, 4 
..., son of *Pꜣ-tỉ-Nfr-ḥtp*	64d, 4 
..., father of *Hr*	18, 5  perhaps *ꜥꜣ(?)*
..., son of *Tꜣy-lwꜣ(?)*	47, 2 Ø
...	9, 1 *wr Ḏḥwty* 
...	64d, 1 *ỉt-ntr* Ø
...	45, 3–4 *wr Ḏḥwty* Ø

TITLES

iry.w-ꜥꜣ pꜣ ꜥ.wy ḥtp "pastophoroi of the place of rest" — 49, 1

it-ntr "god's-father" — 64d, 1; 64d, 2; 64d, 4 *mr ẖꜣs.t*

ꜥꜣ n nꜣ rmt.w n tꜣ mr.t "great one of the men of the harbor" — 34, 3

ꜥꜣ Nw.t "great one of Thebes" — 62a, 4 *t ntr.w*; 62a, 5 *t ntr.w*; 62b, 4 *t ntr.w*

ꜥntꜣy "perfumer" — 77, 10

wꜥb.w "priests" — 64d, 3 *rt nꜣ wꜥb.w*

wr Ḏḥwty "the great one of Thoth" — 4, 6; 7, 2; 8, 5; 9, 1; 18, 5; 19, 3–4; 29, 3; 30, 7; 33a, 6; 34, 1; 45, 4; 53, 5; 54, 8; 55, 5; 57, 5; 58, 7; 60, 5; 61, 3; 62a, 3; 64b, 3; 67, 1; 69, 2; 71, 11; 72, 2; 74, 3; 77, 4; 80, 4; 81, 1; [85, 12]; 86, x+12

bꜣk.w "servants" — 50, 4; 64d, 5 *mr ẖꜣs.t*

pr-ꜥꜣ "pharaoh" — 68, 1

mr ẖꜣs.t "overseer of the necropolis" — 64d, 4 *irm nꜣ bꜣk.w*; 67, 2

mr šn Ḏḥwty "lesonis of Thoth" — 77, 6

rmt.w ꜥy.w "great people" — 78, 1

rmt.w wrṯ(?) "men of (the) cage(?)" — 77, 7

rmt.w tꜣ mr.t "men of the harbor" — 19, 5; 34, 3 *ꜥꜣ n nꜣ rmt.w n tꜣ mr.t*; 74, 3

rt "representative"	64d, 3 *rt nꜣ wꜥb.w*
ḥry(?) "chief"	70, 2
sẖ "scribe"	33a, 4 ; 34, 6 ; 53, 4 ; 62b, 3 ; 64d, 5 ; 76, 8(?); 78, 5 ; 78, 8 ; 78, 9 ; 85, 1
sẖ pr-ḏ.t "scribe of the House-of-Eternity"	68, 3
sẖ.w "scribes"	76, 8(?)
skrṯ(?) Greek title(?)	64d, 6
šms.w "servants"	50, 3
ṯ ntr.w/ ṯ nꜣ ntr.w "taker of the gods"	19, 4 ; 34, 3 ; 62a, 3 ; 62a, 4–5 ; 62b, 4 ; 64b, 5 ; 69, 2 ; 74, 3 ; 74, 4 ; 77, 1
ṯ ntr.w Pr-Mnṯ nb tꜣ "taker of the gods (in) the House-of-Montu, lord of the land"	7, 2 ; 29, 3–4
ṯ ... "taker(?) ..."	31, 11

DEITIES

ꜥẖm "falcon"	68, 2 *Wsir*
Wsir "Osiris"	19, 1 *pꜣ hb* ; 19, 1 *pꜣ bik* ; 21, 1 *pꜣ hb* ; 21, 2 *pꜣ bik* ; 68, 2 *pꜣ hb* ; 68, 2 *pꜣ bik* ; 68, 2 *pꜣ ꜥẖm* ; 68, 2 *Twtw(?)* ; 68, 3 *Ḥr nb Sẖm* ; 73, 2 *pꜣ hb* ; 73, 3 *pꜣ bik* ; 74, 1 *pꜣ hb* ; 74, 1 *pꜣ bik* ; 77, 1 *pꜣ hb* ; 77, 2 *pꜣ bik* ; 77, 5 *bik* ; 79, 3 *pꜣ hb* ; 79, 3 *pꜣ bik* ; 80, 1 *pꜣ hb* ; 80, 2 *pꜣ bik* ; 81, 2 *pꜣ hb* ; 81, 2 *pꜣ bik* ; 84, 2 *pꜣ hb*

bỉk; see *bỉk* "falcon"

Mnṯ "Montu" — 7, 2 *Pr-Mnṯ nb tꜣ*; 29, 4 *Pr-Mnṯ nb tꜣ*

nb Sḫm "lord of Letopolis" — 68, 3

nb tꜣ "lord of the land" — 7, 2; 29, 4

Nfr-ḥtp (epithet of Khonsu) — Mummy bandage 1

hb; see *hb* "ibis"

Ḥr "Horus" — 68, 3 *Wsỉr Ḥr nb Sḫm*

ḫnṯ Wsr(.t) "foremost of Thebes" — 14, 1–2 *Ḏḥwty*; 34, 4 *Ḏḥwty*; 63, 3 *Ḏḥwty*

Twtw(?) "Tutu" — 68, 2 *Wsỉr Twtw(?)*

Ḏḥwty "Thoth"; see also title *wr Ḏḥwty* — 9, 3; 12, 1; 13, 1; 14, 1 *ḫnṯ Wsr.t*; 14, 6 Ø; 18, 4; 18, 6; 24, 6; 24, 7; 33a, 9; 34, 4 *ḫnṯ Wsr.t*; 34, 5; 62b, 1; 63, 3 *ḫnṯ Wsr.t*; 67, 1; 67, 2; 77, 6; 82, 8

PLACE NAMES

Pr-ỉmn "House-of-Amun" — 64d, 6

Pr-Mnṯ "House-of-Montu" — 7, 2; 29, 4

Nw.t "Thebes" — 62a, 4 *ꜥꜣ Nw.t*; 62a, 5 *ꜥꜣ Nw.t*; 62b, 4 *ꜥꜣ Nw.t*

Wsr(.t) "Thebes" — 14, 2; 34, 4; 63, 3 *Ḏḥwty ḫnṯ Wsr(.t)*

Sḫm "Letopolis" — 68, 3 *Wsỉr Ḥr nb Sḫm*

NUMERALS

mḥ-1.t	55, 1
mḥ-3.t	33a, 2
1	O5, x+2
1 1/2	O2, 4 ; O5, x+5
2	O5, x+5
2.t	47, 3
5.t	31, 3 ; 69, 2 ; 74, 5
6	O5, x+3(?) Ø
7	62a, 1
7.t	64b, 3
8	64b, 3 ; O5, x+3
9	14, 3 ; 14, 4 ; 33a, 7 ; 64b, 6
9.t	13, 1 ; 30, 9(?) ; 34, 2 ; 63, 1 ; 63, 6 ; 64b, 4
10.t	24, 3(?) Ø; 34, 2 ; 34, 6(?) ; 37a, 1
11.t	10, 1
20	45, 1
20.t	19, 6
21.t	19, 6
21.t(?)	21, 6
23	O4, II, x+3
25	80, 3 ; 81, 5
28	O5, x+6

34	O1, 3
36	80, 3 ; 81, 5
40	O4, II, x+1
50	O5, x+2(?)
60	O4, II, x+3
94	O4, II, x+1 ; O4, II, x+2
97	O4, II, x+4(?)
100	O3, II, 2(?) ; O3, III, 1 ; O3, III, 1
110	O3, I, 2(?)
200	O3, III, 2 ; O3, III, 2 ; O5, x+4
300	O3, II, 7
400	O3, III, 3
600	O3, III, 4
1000	O3, II, 3(?) ; O3, III, 1
2000	O3, III, 2
3000	O3, I, 5(?) ; O3, II, 4(?)
4000	O3, I, 6(?) ; O3, II, 5(?) ; O3, III, 3
5000	O3, II, 6(?) ; O3, I, 7(?)
6000	O3, III, 4
7000	O3, III, 7(?)
20000	O3, I, 5
60000	O3, I, 7

$^{1}/_{4}$ O1, 1 ; O4, II, x4(?)

$^{1}/_{400}$ O3, III, 3

$^{1}/_{600}$ O3, III, 4

DATES

ỉbt 1 "first month" O5, x+6

ỉbt 2 "second month" O1, 2

ỉbt 3 "third month" 14, 4 ; 21, 7 ; 33, 7(?) Ø; 34, 7(?) ; 45, 6(?) ; 47, 3 ; 63, 1 ; 80, 3 ; 81, 5

ỉbt 4 "fourth month" 14, 3 ; 24, 3 ; 37a, 1 ; 45, 1 ; 62a, 1 ; 63, 6 ; 64b, 6 ; O1, 3

ꜣḫ.t "inundation" O5, x+6

pr.t "winter" 14, 3 ; 34, 7 ; 21, 7(?) Ø; 24, 3 ; 45, 1 ; 62a, 1 ; 63, 1 ; 63, 6 ; 64b, 6 ; O1, 2 ; O1, 3

šmw "summer" 80, 3 ; 81, 5

sw 6 "day 6" O1, 2(?)

sw 11 "day 11" 14, 4 ; 21, 7 ; 24, 3 ; 37a, 1 ; 45, 1 ; 62a, 1 ; 63, 5 ; 64b, 6 ; 80, 3 ; 81, 5

sw 16 "day 16" O5, x+4(?)

sw 17 "day 17" O1, 3

sw 19 "day 19" 14, 3 ; 63, 2

GREEK PERSONAL NAMES

Τανουβις O2, 2
Λιβιος O2, 3

BIBLIOGRAPHY

Amir, M. el-. *A Family Archive from Thebes: Demotic Papyri in the Philadelphia and Cairo Museums from the Ptolemaic Period*. Cairo: General Organisation for Government Printing Offices, 1959.

Andrews, C. A. R. *Ptolemaic Legal Texts from the Theban Area*. Catalogue of Demotic Papyri in the British Museum 4. London: British Museum, 1990.

Arlt, C. *Deine Seele möge leben für immer und ewig: Die demotischen Mumienschilder im British Museum*. Studia Demotica 10. Leuven: Peeters, 2011.

Arnold, Di. *Gräber des Alten und Mittleren Reiches in El-Tarif*. Archäologische Veröffentlichungen 17. Mainz: von Zabern, 1976.

———. *Grabung im Asasif 1963–1970: Das Grab des Jnjjtj.f; Die Architectur*. Archäologische Veröffentlichungen 4. Mainz: von Zabern, 1971.

Aston, D. *Elephantine XIX: Pottery from the Late New Kingdom to the Early Ptolemaic Period*. Archäologische Veröffentlichungen 95. Mainz: von Zabern, 1999.

Bahé, A. "An Egyptian Perspective: Demotic Ostraca from Deir el-Bahari in the British Museum." Pages 11–21 in *Current Research in Egyptology 2013: Proceedings of the Fourteenth Annual Symposium, University of Cambridge, United Kingdom, March 19–22, 2013*. Edited by K. Accetta, R. Fellinger, P. Lourenço Gonçalves, S. Musselwhite, and W. P. van Pelt. Oxford: Oxbow, 2014.

Berlandini, J. "D'un percnoptère et de sa relation à Isis, au scarabée et à la tête divine." Pages 83–133 in *"Parcourir l'éternité": Hommages à Jean Yoyotte*. Edited by C. Zivie-Coche and I. Guermeur. 2 vols. Bibliothèque de l'École des Hautes Études, Sciences religieuses 156. Turnhout: Brepols, 2012.

Bietak, M. "La Belle Fête de la vallée: L'Asasif revisité." Pages 135–64 in *"Parcourir l'éternité": Hommages à Jean Yoyotte*. Edited by C. Zivie-Coche and I. Guermeur. 2 vols. Bibliothèque de l'École des Hautes Études, Sciences religieuses 156. Turnhout: Brepols, 2012.

Birch, S. *Select Papyri in the Hieratic Character from the Collections of the British Museum, Vol. 2*. London: Woodfall & Kinder, 1860.

Borghouts, J. "Month." *LÄ* 4:cols. 200–204.

Borrego, F. "Inscripciones e imágenes sobre textiles de la dinastía XXII de Dra Abu el-Naga (Proyecto Djehuty)." *Trabajos de Egiptología/Papers on Ancient Egypt* 10. In press.

———. "New Evidence on the King's Son Intefmose from Dra Abu el-Naga: A Preliminary Report." Pages 53–58 in *Proceedings of the XI International Congress of Egyptologists, Florence Egyptian Museum, Florence, 23–30 August 2015*. Edited by G. Rosati and M. Guidotti. Archaeopress Egyptology 19. Oxford: Archaeopress, 2017.

Brinker, A. den, B. Muhs, and S. Vleeming, eds. *A Berichtigungsliste of Demotic Documents: Ostrakon Editions and Various Publications*. 2 vols. Studia Demotica 7. Leuven: Peeters, 2005.

Brovarski, E. "A Coffin from Farshût in the Museum of Fine Arts, Boston." Pages 37–69 in *Ancient Egyptian and Mediterranean Studies in Memory of William A. Ward*. Edited by L. Lesko. Providence: Department of Egyptology, Brown University, 1998.

———. "Coffin of Menkabu." Pages 99–100 in *Mummies & Magic: The Funerary Arts of Ancient Egypt*. Edited by S. D'Auria, P. Lacovara, and C. Roehrig. Boston: Museum of Fine Arts, 1988.

Brunner-Traut, E. "Spitzmaus und Ichneumon als Tiere des Sonnengottes." *Göttinger Vorträge vom Ägyptologischen Kolloquium der Akademie vom 25. und 26. August 1964. Nachrichten von der Akademie der Wissenschaften in Göttingen: Philologisch-Historische Klasse* 1965.7 (1965): 123–63.

Burkhardt, A. Ägypter und Meroiten im Dodekaschoinos*: Untersuchungen zur Typologie und Bedeutung der demotischen Graffiti*. Meroitica 8. Berlin: Akademie, 1985.

Cauville, S. "La Chapelle de Thot-Ibis à Dendera édifiée sous Ptolémée Ier par Hor, scribe d'Amon-Re." *BIFAO* 89 (1989): 43–66.

Cenival, F. de. *Les associations religieuses en Égypte d'après les documents démotiques*. 2 vols. BdE 46. Cairo: Institut français d'archéologie orientale, 1972.

———. "Deux papyrus inédits de Lille avec une révision du P. dém. Lille 31." *Enchoria* 7 (1977): 1–49.

Černý, J. *Egyptian Stelae in the Bankes Collection*. Oxford: Oxford University Press, 1958.

Charron, A. "Les animaux et le sacré dans l'Égypte tardive: Fonctions et signification." PhD diss., EPHE, 1996.

———. "Les animaux sacrés à l'époque ptolémaïque." Pages 173–214 in *La mort n'est pas une fin: Pratiques funéraires en Égypte d'Alexandre à Cléopâtre; Catalogue de l'exposition, 28 septembre 2002 > 5 janvier 2003, Musée de l'Arles antique*. Edited by A. Charron. Arles: Musée de l'Arles antique, 2002.

———. "Les musaraignes d'Abou Rawash." *Égypte Afrique et Orient* 66 (2012): 3–14.

———. "Massacres d'animaux à la Basse Epoque."*RdÉ* 41 (1990): 209–13.

Chauveau, M. "Un été 145: Post-scriptum." *BIFAO* 91 (1991): 129–34.

Clarysse W., and D. Thompson. *Counting the People in Hellenistic Egypt*: *Population Registers (P. Count)*. 2 vols. Cambridge: Cambridge University Press, 2006.

Colin, F. "Un jeu de déterminatifs en démotique." *RdE* 65 (2014): 179–84.

Dack, E. van ʾt et al. *The Judean-Syrian-Egyptian Conflict of 103–101 B.C.: A Multilingual Dossier concerning a "War of Sceptres."* Collectanea Hellenistica 1. Brussels: Publikatie van het comité klassieke studies, subcomité hellenisme koninklijke Academie voor Wettenschappen, Letteren en schone Kunsten van Belgié, 1989.

Davies, S. "The Organization, Administration and Functioning of the Sacred Animal Cults at North Saqqara as Revealed by the Demotic Papyri from the Site." Pages 77–84 in *Acts of the Seventh International Conference of Demotic Studies: Copenhagen, 23–27 August 1999*. Edited by K. Ryholt. CNI 27. Copenhagen: Carsten Niebuhr Institute of Ancient Near Eastern Studies, 2002.

Davis, K. "Conceptions of Language: Egyptian Perspectives on Writing and Grammar in the Late Period and Greco-Roman Period." PhD diss., Johns Hopkins University, 2016.

Depauw, M. *The Archive of Teos and Thabis from Early Ptolemaic Thebes: P. Brux. Dem. Inv. E. 8252–8256*. MRE 8. Brepols: Fondation Égyptologique Reine Élisabeth, 2000.

Depuydt, L. "Demotic Script and Demotic Grammar (II): Dummy Prepositions Preceding Infinitives." *Enchoria* 27 (2001): 3–35.

Devauchelle, D. "Les serments à la porte de Djémé." *RdE* 48 (1997): 260–63.

Díaz-Iglesias Llanos, L. "Glimpses of the First Owners of a Reused Burial: Fragments of a Shroud with Book of the Dead Spells from Dra Abu el-Naga North." *BIFAO* 118 (2018): 83–126.

Diego Espinel, A. "Killing the Nubian: A Study on a Neglected Ritual Depicted in Two Theban Tombs and Its Possible Relationship to Execration Rituals." In *A Closer Look at Execration Figures*. Edited by C. Kühne and J. Quack. ZÄS Beiheft. Berlin: de Gruyter, in press.

———. "Practical Issues with the Epigraphic Restoration of a Biographical Inscription in the Tomb of Djehuty (TT 11), Dra Abu el-Naga." Pages 448–63 in *The Oxford Handbook of Egyptian Epigraphy and Palaeography*. Edited by D. Laboury and V. Davies. Oxford: Oxford University Press, 2020.

Dils, P. "Les *ṯꜣj (nꜣ) ntr.w* ou θεαγοί: Fonction religieuse et place dans la vie civile." *BIFAO* 95 (1995): 153–71.

Dousa, T., F. Gaudard, and J. Johnson. "P. Berlin 6848: A Roman Period Inventory." Pages 139–222 in *Res Severa Verum Gaudium: Festschrift für Karl-Theodor Zauzich zum 65. Geburtstag am 8. Juni 2004*. Edited by F. Hoffmann and H.-J. Thissen. Studia Demotica 6. Leuven: Peeters, 2004.

Driesch, A. von den, D. Kessler, F. Steinmann, V. Berteaux, and J. Peters. "Mummified, Deified, and Buried at Hermopolis Magna: The Sacred Birds from Tuna El-Gebel, Middle Egypt." *Ägypten und Levante/Egypt and the Levant* 15 (2005): 203–44.

Dziobek, E. "The Architectural Development of Theban Tombs in the Early Eighteenth Dynasty." Pages 69–79 in *Problems and Priorities in Egyptian Archaeology*. Edited by J. Assmann and G. Burkard. London: Kegan Paul, 1987.

Eide, T. et al. *Fontes Historiae Nubiorum: Textual Sources for the History of the Middle Nile Region between the Eighth Century BC and the Sixth Century AD, Vol. 3; From the First to the Sixth Century AD*. Bergen: University of Bergen, 1998.

El-Enany, K. "Le saint thébain Montouhotep-Nebhépetrê." *BIFAO* 103 (2003): 167–90.

Fahmy, A., J. M. Galán, and R. Hamdy. "A Deposit of Floral and Vegetative Bouquets at Dra Abu el-Naga (TT 11)." *BIFAO* 110 (2010): 73–89.

Farid, A. *Fünf demotische Stelen aus Berlin, Chicago, Durham, London und Oxford mit zwei demotischen Türinschriften aus Paris und einer Bibliographie der demotischen Inschriften*. Berlin: Achet, 1995.

Fitzenreiter, M. ed. *Tierkulte im pharaonischen Ägypten und im Kulturvergleich*. Internet-Beiträge zur Ägyptologie und Sudanarchäologie 4. Berlin: Golden House, 2005.

Flossmann-Schütze, M. C. "Études sur le cadre de vie d'une association religieuse dans l'Égypte gréco-romaine: L'exemple de Touna el-Gebel." Pages 203–8 in *Proceedings of the XI International Congress of Egyptologists, Florence Egyptian Museum, Florence, 23–30 August 2015*. Edited by G. Rosati and M. Cristina Guidotti. Archaeopress Egyptology 19. Oxford: Archaeopress, 2017.

Franke, D. "Die Stele des Jayseneb aus der Schachtanlage K01.12." Pages 73–83 in *Die Pyramidenanlage des Königs Nub-Cheper-Re Intef in Dra Abu el-Naga': Ein Vorbericht*. Edited by D. Polz and A. Seiler. SDAIK 24. Mainz: von Zabern, 2003.

Galán, J. M. "11th Dynasty Burials below Djehuty's Courtyard (TT 11) in Dra Abu el-Naga." *BES* 19 (2015): 331–46.

———. "Ahmose(-Sapair) in Dra Abu el-Naga North." *JEA* 103 (2018): 179–201.

———. "Early Investigations in the Tomb-Chapel of Djehuty (TT 11)." Pages 155–81 in *Sitting beside Lepsius: Studies in Honour of Jaromir Malek at the Griffith Institute*. Edited by D. Magee, J. Bourriau, and S. Quirke. OLA 185. Leuven: Peeters, 2009.

———. "Excavations at the Courtyard of the Tomb of Djehuty (TT 11)." Pages 207–20 in *Proceedings of the Tenth International Congress of Egyptologists: University of the Aegean, Rhodes, 22–29 May, 2008*. Edited by P. Kousoulis and N. Lazaridis. 2 vols. OLA 241. Leuven: Peeters, 2015.

———. "The Inscribed Burial Chamber of Djehuty (TT 11)." Pages 247–72 in *Creativity and Innovation in the Reign of Hatshepsut: Papers from the Theban Workshop 2010*. Edited by J. M. Galán, B. Bryan, and P. Dorman. SAOC 69. Chicago: Oriental Institute of the University of Chicago, 2014.

——— ed. Spanish Mission at Dra Abu El-Naga Tombs of Djehuty and Hery (TT 11–12). Proyecto Djehuty website: https://proyectodjehuty.com/.

———. "The Tomb-Chapel of Hery (TT 12) in Context." In *Mural Decoration in the Theban New Kingdom Necropolis*. Edited by B. Bryan and P. Dorman. SAOC. Chicago: Oriental Institute of the University of Chicago, in press.

———. "The Tombs of Djehuty and Hery (TT 11–12) at Dra Abu el-Naga." Pages 777–87 in *Proceedings of the Ninth International Congress of Egyptologists: Grenoble, 6–12 Septembre 2004*. Edited by J. Goyon and C. Cardin. 2 vols. OLA 150. Leuven: Peeters, 2007.

Galán, J. M., and Z. Barahona. "Looking at a Robbed 17th Dynasty Funerary Shaft." In *Second Intermediate Period Assemblages: The Building Blocks of Local Relative Sequences of Material Culture*. Edited by B. Bader. Vienna: Österreichischen Akademie der Wissenschaften, in press.

Galán, J. M., and D. García. "Twelfth Dynasty Funerary Gardens in Thebes." *EA* 54 (2019): 4–8.

Galán, J. M., and A. Jiménez-Higueras. "Three Burials of the Seventeenth Dynasty in Dra Abu el-Naga." Pages 101–19 in *The World of Middle Kingdom Egypt (2000–1550 BC): Contributions on Archaeology, Art, Religion, and Written Sources*. Edited by G. Miniaci and W. Grajetzki. Middle Kingdom Studies 1. London: Golden House, 2015.

Galán, J. M., and G. Menéndez. "The Funerary Banquet of Hery (TT 12) Robbed and Restored." *JEA* 97 (2011): 143–66.

Geisbusch, J. "Digging Diary 2016." *EA* 49 (2016): 34–36.

Germer, R., H. Kischkewitz, and M. Lüning. "Pseudo-Mumien der ägyptischen Sammlung Berlin." *SAK* 21 (1994): 81–94.

Graefe, E. *Das Grab des Ibi, Obervermögensverwalters der Gottesgemahlin des Amun (Thebanisches Grab Nr. 36): Beschreibung und Rekonstruktionsversuche des Oberbaus Funde aus dem Oberbau*. Brussels: Fondation Égyptologique Reine Élisabeth, 1990.

Gregorio, E de. "Votive Pottery Deposits Found by the Spanish Mission at Dra Abu el-Naga." Pages 166–71 in *Proceedings of the XI International Congress of Egyptologists, Florence Egyptian Museum, Florence, 23–30 August 2015*. Edited by G. Rosati and M. Cristina Guidotti. Archaeopress Egyptology 19. Oxford: Archaeopress, 2017.

Griffith, F. L. *Stories of the High Priests of Memphis: The Sethon of Herodotus and the Demotic Tales of Khamuas*. Oxford: Clarendon, 1900.

Grimaldi, D. M., and P. Meehan. "The Transformation of Theban Tomb 39 (TT 39): A Contribution from a Conservation Viewpoint in Terms of Its History after Dynastic Occupation." Pages 247–253 in *Proceedings of the XI International Congress of Egyptologists, Florence Egyptian Museum, Florence, 23–30 August 2015*. Edited by G. Rosati, and M. C. Guidotti. Archaeopress Egyptology 19. Oxford: Archaeopress, 2017.

Grimm, A., D. Kessler, and H. Meyer. *Der Obelisk des Antinoos: Eine kommentierte Edition*. Munich: Fink, 1994.

Grunert, S. *Thebanische Kaufverträge des 3. und 2. Jahrhunderts v. u. Z.* Demotische Papyri aus den staatlichen Museen zu Berlin 2. Berlin: Akademie, 1981.

Harvey, S. "Report on Abydos, Ahmose and Tetisheri Project, 2006–2007 Season." *ASAE* 82 (2008): 143–55.

Hoffmann, F., and J. Quack, "Pastophoros." Pages 127–55 in *A Good Scribe and an Exceedingly Wise Man: Studies in Honour of W. J. Tait*. Edited by A. Dodson, J. Johnston, and W. Monkhouse. GHP Egyptology 21. London: Golden House, 2014.

Hoffmeier, J. *"Sacred" in the Vocabulary of Ancient Egypt: The Term DSR with Special Reference to Dynasties I–XX*. OBO 59. Fribourg: Universitätsverlag; Göttingen: Vandenhoeck & Ruprecht, 1985.

Ikram, S. "Animals in a Ritual Context at Abydos: A Synopsis." Pages 417–32 in *The Archaeology and Art of Ancient Egypt: Essays in Honor of David B. O'Connor*. Edited by Z. Hawass and J. Richards. SASAE 36. Cairo: Conseil Suprême des Antiquités de l'Egypte, 2007.

———. "Divine Creatures: Animal Mummies." Pages 1–15 in *Divine Creatures: Animal Mummies in Ancient Egypt*. Edited by S. Ikram. Rev. ed. Cairo: American University in Cairo Press, 2015.

———, ed. *Divine Creatures: Animal Mummies in Ancient Egypt*. Rev. ed. Cairo: American University in Cairo Press, 2015.

———. "A Monument in Miniature: The Eternal Resting Place of a Shrew." Pages 335–40 in *Structure and Significance: Thoughts on Ancient Egyptian Architecture*. Edited by P. Jánosi. Österreichische Akademie der Wissenschaften, Denkschriften der Gesamtakademie 33. Untersuchungen der Zweigstelle Kairo des Österreichischen Archäologischen Institutes 25. Vienna: Österreichischen Akademie der Wissenschaften, 2005.

———. "Shedding New Light on Old Corpses: Developments in the Field of Animal Mummy Studies." Pages 179–91 in *Creatures of Earth, Water and Sky: Essays on Animals in Ancient Egypt and Nubia*. Edited by S. Porcier, S. Ikram, and S. Pasquali. Leiden: Sidestone Press, 2019.

———. "Speculations on the Role of Animal Cults in the Economy of Ancient Egypt." Pages 211–28 in *Apprivoiser le sauvage/Taming the Wild*. Edited by M. Massiera, B. Mathieu, and F. Rouffet. CENIM 11. Montpellier: Université Paul Valéry Montpellier 3, 2015.

Ikram, S., and A. Dodson, *The Mummy in Ancient Egypt: Equipping the Dead for Eternity*. London: Thames & Hudson, 1998.

Ikram, S., and N. Iskander. *Catalogue Général of Egyptian Antiquities in the Cairo Museum: Nos. 24048–24056; 29504–29903 (Selected); 51084 51101; 61089; Non-Human Mummies*. Cairo: Supreme Council of Antiquities, 2002.

Ikram, S., and M. López-Grande. "Three Embalming Caches from Dra Abu el-Naga." *BIFAO* 111 (2011): 205–28.

Ikram, S., and M. Spitzer. "The Cult of Horus and Thoth: A Study of Egyptian Animal Cults in Theban Tombs 11, 12, and -399-." In *Archaeozoology of Southwest Asia and Adjacent Areas XIII: Proceedings of the Thirteenth International Symposium, University of Cyprus, Nicosia, Cyprus, June 7–10*. Edited by J. Daujat, A. Hadjikoumis, and R. Berthon. Atlanta: Lockwood Press, in press.

Jasnow, R., J. G. Manning, K. Yamahana, and M. Krutzsch. *The Demotic and Hieratic Papyri in the Suzuki Collection of Tokai University*. Atlanta: Lockwood Press, 2016.

Jenkins, M. "The 'Temple of Thot' on the West Bank at Luxor." *KMT* 21.4 (2010–2011): 50–61.

Kampp, F. *Die thebanische Nekropole: Zum Wandel des Grabgedankens von der XVIII. Bis zur XX. Dynastie; Teil 2*. Theben 13. Mainz: von Zabern, 1996.

———. "The Theban Necropolis: An Overview of Topography and Tomb Development from the Middle Kingdom to the Ramesside Period." Pages 2–10 in *The Theban Necropolis: Past, Present and Future*. Edited by N. Strudwick and J. Taylor. London: British Museum Press, 2003.

Kessler, D. *Die heiligen Tiere und der König, Teil I: Beiträge zu Organisation, Kult und Theologie der spätzeitlichen Tierfriedhöfe*. Ägypten und Altes Testament 16. Wiesbaden: Harrassowitz, 1989.

———. *Die Oberbauten des Ibiotapheion von Tuna el-Gebel*. Tuna el-Gebel 3. Vaterstetten: Brose, 2011.

———. "Ibis-Vögel mit Eigennamen: Tiere des Festes und des Orakels." Pages 261–72 in *Honi soit qui mal y pense: Studien zum pharaonischen, griechisch-römischen und spätantiken Ägypten zu Ehren von Heinz-Josef Thissen*. Edited by H. Knuf, C. Leitz, and D. von Recklinghausen. OLA 194. Leuven: Peeters, 2010.

———. "Spitzmaus und Ichneumon im Tierfriedhof von Tuna el-Gebel." *Bulletin of the Egyptian Museum* 4 (2007): 71–82.

———. "Tierkult." *LÄ* 6:cols. 571–87.

Kessler, D., and Abd el H. Nur el-Din. "Tuna al-Gebel: Millions of Ibises and Other Animals." Pages 120–63 in *Divine Creatures: Animal Mummies in Ancient Egypt*. Edited by S. Ikram. Rev. ed. Cairo: American University in Cairo Press, 2015.

Klotz, D. *Caesar in the City of Amun: Egyptian Temple Construction and Theology in Roman Thebes*. MRE 15. Turnhout: Brepols, 2012.

Lansing, A. "The Egyptian Expedition 1918–1920: I, Excavations at Thebes 1918–19." *BMMA* 15 (1920): 4–12.

Laskowska-Kusztal, E. *Le sanctuaire ptolémaïque de Deir el-Bahari*. Deir el-Bahari 3. Warsaw: PWN-Éditions scientifiques de Pologne, 1984.

Lauffray, J. *La chapelle d'Achôris à Karnak, Vol. 1: Les fouilles, l'architecture, le mobilier et l'anastylose*. Paris: Éditions Recherche sur les Civilisations, 1995.

Lefebvre, G. *Le Tombeau de Petosiris, 1: Description*. Cairo: Institut français d'archéologie orientale, 1924.

Lecuyot, G., and G. Pierrat-Bonnefois. "Corpus de la céramique de Tôd: Fouilles 1980–1983 et 1990." *Cahiers de la céramique égyptienne* 7 (2004): 145–209.

López-Grande, M., and E. de Gregorio. "Pottery Vases from a Deposit with Flower Bouquets Found at Dra Abu el-Naga." Pages 305–18 in *Proceedings of the Tenth International Congress of Egyptologists: University of the Aegean, Rhodes. 22-29 May, 2008*. Edited by P. Kousoulis and N. Lazaridis. 2 vols. OLA 241. Leuven: Peeters, 2015.

———. "Two Funerary Pottery Deposits at Dra Abu el-Naga." *Memnonia* 18 (2007): 145–56.

Luiselli, M. "Personal Piety." In *UCLA Encyclopedia of Egyptology*. Edited by J. Dieleman and W. Wendrich. Los Angeles. https://uee.cdh.ucla.edu/articles/personal_piety_(modern_theories_related_to).

McKnight, L., A. David, D. Brothwell, and J. Adams. "The Pseudo-Mummies from Bolton Museum and Art Gallery, Great Britain." Pages 687–90 in *Mummies and Science—World Mummies Research: Proceedings of the VI World Congress on Mummy Studies; Teguise, Lanzarote, February 20th to 24th, 2007*. Edited by P. Atoche Peña, C. Rodríguez Martín, and M. Ramírez Rodríguez. Santa Cruz de Tenerife: Academia Canaria de la Historia, 2008.

Manniche, L. "A Report on Work Carried Out at Dra^{c} Abu el-Naga^{c}." *ASAE* 72 (1992–1993): 49–52.

Manning, J. *Land and Power in Ptolemaic Egypt: The Structure of Land Tenure*. Cambridge: Cambridge University Press, 2003.

Mariette, A. *Itinéraire des invités aux fêtes d'Inauguration du Canal de Suez qui séjournent au Caire et Font le voyage du Nil, publié par Ordre de S. A. Le Khédive*. Cairo: Mourès, 1869.

Martin, C. "A Demotic Land Lease from Philadelphia: P. BM 10560." *JEA* 72 (1986): 159–73.

Masson, A. "Persian and Ptolemaic Ceramics from Karnak: Change and Continuity." *Cahiers de la céramique égyptienne* 9 (2011): 269–310.

Meyer, M. de, and J. Serrano. "Cattle Feet in Funerary Rituals: a Diachronic View Combining Archaeology and Iconography." Pages 402–7 in *Old Kingdom Art and Archaeology 7: Proceedings of the International Conference; Università degli studi di Milano 3–7 July 2017*. Edited by P. Piacentini and A. delli Castelli. 2 vols. Egyptian & Egyptological Documents, Archives, Libraries 6. Milan: Pontremoli, 2019.

Miniaci, G. "The Necropolis of Dra Abu el-Naga." Pages 14–33 in *Seven Seasons at Dra Abu el-Naga: The Tomb of Huy (TT 14); Preliminary Results*. Edited by M. Betrò, P. del Vesco, and G. Miniaci. Progetti: Documenti per l'archeologia egiziana 3. Pisa: Plus, Pisa University Press, 2009.

———. *Rishi Coffins and the Funerary Culture of Second Intermediate Period Egypt*. GHP Egyptology 17. London: Golden House, 2011.

Moje, J. *Demotische Epigraphik aus Dandara: Die demotischen Grabstelen*. Internet-Beiträge zur Ägyptologie und Sudanarchäologie 9. London: Golden House, 2008.

Muhs, B. *Receipts, Scribes, and Collectors in Early Ptolemaic Thebes (O. Taxes 2)*. Studia Demotica 8. Leuven: Peeters, 2011.

———. *Tax Receipts, Taxpayers, and Taxes in Early Ptolemaic Thebes*. OIP 126. Chicago: Oriental Institute of the University of Chicago, 2005.

Nicholson, P. "The Sacred Animal Necropolis at North Saqqara, the Cults and Their Catacombs." Pages 44–71 in *Divine Creatures: Animal Mummies in Ancient Egypt*. Edited by S. Ikram. Rev. ed. Cairo: American University in Cairo Press, 2015.

Northampton, W. G. Marquis of, W. Spiegelberg, and P. Newberry. *Report on Some Excavations in the Theban Necropolis during the Winter of 1898–9*. London: Constable, 1908.

Parker, R. *Demotic Mathematical Papyri*. Brown Egyptological Studies 7. Providence: Brown University Press, 1972.

Peet, T. E. *The Great Tomb-Robberies of the Twentieth Egyptian Dynasty: Being a Critical Study, with Translations and Commentaries, of the Papyri in Which These are Recorded*. Oxford: Clarendon, 1930.

Pestman, P. *Chronologie égyptienne d'après les textes démotiques (332 av. J.-C.–453 ap. J.-C.)*. PLBat 15. Leiden: Brill, 1967.

———. *Recueil de textes démotiques et bilingues*. 3 vols. Leiden: Brill, 1977.

Petrie, W. M. F., and J. H. Walker. *Qurneh*. British School of Archaeology in Egypt 16. London: School of Archaeology; Quaritch, 1909.

Polz, D. *Der Beginn des Neuen Reiches: Zur Vorgeschichte einer Zeitenwende*. SDAIK 31. Berlin: de Gruyter, 2007.

———. ed. *Für die Ewigkeit geschaffen: Die Särge des Imeni und der Geheset*. Mainz: von Zabern, 2007.

———. "New Archaeological Data from Dra' Abu el-Naga and Their Historical Implications." Pages 343–53 in *The Second Intermediate Period (Thirteenth–Seventeenth Dynasties): Current Research, Future Prospects*. Edited by M. Marée. OLA 192. Leuven: Peeters, 2010.

Polz, D. et al. "Bericht über die 6., 7. und 8. Grabungskampagne in der Nekropole von Dra' Abu el-Naga/Theben-West." *MDAIK* 55 (1999): 370–402.

Polz, D., U. Rummel, I. Eichner, and T. Beckh. "Topographical Archaeology in Dra' Abu el-Naga: Three Thousand Years of Cultural History." *MDAIK* 68 (2012): 115–34.

Polz, D., and A. Seiler. *Die Pyramidenanlage des Königs Nub-Cheper-Re Intef in Dra Abu el-Naga: Ein Vorbericht*. SDAIK 24. Mainz: von Zabern, 2003.

Prada, L., and P. D. Wordsworth. "Evolving Epigraphic Standards in the Field: Documenting Late Period and Graeco-Roman Egyptian Graffiti through Photogrammetry at Elkab." Pages 76–93 in *The Materiality of Texts from Ancient Egypt: New Approaches to the Study of Textual Material from the Early Pharaonic to the Late Antique Period*. Edited by F. Hoogendijk, and S. van Gompel. PLBat 35. Leiden: Brill, 2018.

Preisigke, F. *Namenbuch*. Heidelberg: Self-published, 1922.

Preisigke, F., and W. Spiegelberg. *Die Prinz-Joachim-Ostraka: Griechische und demotische Beisetzungsurkunden für Ibis-und Falkenmumien aus Ombos*. Schriften der Wissenschaftlichen Gesellschaft in Strassburg 19. Strassburg: Trübner, 1914.

Quack, J. "Eine weise Stimme der Autorität (Papyrus Amherst Eg. XLIII.1 rt.): Mit Anhängen über Abrechnungen (Papyrus Amherst Eg. XLIII.1 vs. und XLIII.2)." Pages 303–18 in *Illuminating Osiris: Egyptological Studies in Honor of Mark Smith*. Edited by R. Jasnow and G. Widmer. Material and Visual Culture of Ancient Egypt 2. Atlanta: Lockwood Press, 2017.

Quegebaeur, J. "La Désignation 'porteur(s) des dieux' et le culte des dieux-crocodiles dans les textes des époques tardives." Pages 161–76 in *Mélanges Adolphe Gutbub*. Montpellier: Publication de la Recherche–Université de Montpellier, 1984.

Ragazzoli, C. *La grotte des scribes à Deir el-Bahari: La tombe MMA 504 et ses graffiti*. MIFAO 135. Cairo: Institut français d'archéologie orientale, 2017.

———. "Lire, inscrire et survivre en Égypte ancienne: Les inscriptions de visiteurs du Nouvel Empire." Pages 290–311 in *Les Lieux de Savoir, II: Les mains de l'intellect*. Edited by C. Jacob. Paris: Albin Michel, 2011.

———. "The Scribes' Cave: Graffiti and the Production of Social Space in Ancient Egypt circa 1500 BC." Pages 23–36 in *Scribbling through History: Graffiti, Places and People from Antiquity to Modernity*. Edited by C. Ragazzoli, Ö. Harmanşah, C. Salvador, and E. Frood. London: Bloomsbury, 2018.

Ray, J. *The Archive of Ḥor*. EES Texts from Excavations 2. London: Egypt Exploration Society, 1976.

———. *Texts from the Baboon and Falcon Galleries: Demotic, Hieroglyphic and Greek Inscriptions from the Sacred Animal Necropolis, North Saqqara*. EES Texts from Excavations 15. London: Egypt Exploration Society, 2011.

Ritner, R. "An Eternal Curse upon the Reader of These Lines." Pages 3–24 in *Ancient Egyptian Demonology: Studies on the Boundaries between the Demonic and the Divine in Egyptian Magic*. Edited by P. Kousoulis. OLA 175. Leuven: Peeters, Departement Oosterse Studies, 2011.

Rouvière, L. "Le culte des canidés dans la région de Hardaï/Cynopolis: Enquête épigraphique et archéologique." Pages 109–28 in *Géographie et archéologie de la religion égyptienne: Espaces cultuels et pratiques locales*. Edited by C. Cassier. CENIM 17. Montpellier: Université Paul Valéry, 2017.

Rummel, U. "Gräber, Feste, Prozessionen: Der Ritualraum Theben-West in der Ramessidenzeit." Pages 207–32 in *Nekropolen: Grab—Bild—Ritual; Beiträge des zweiten Münchner Arbeitskreises Junge Aegyptologie (MAJA 2), 2. Bis 4.12.2011*. Edited by G. Neunert, K. Gabler, and A. Verbovsek. Wiesbaden: Harrassowitz, 2013.

———. "Ramesside Tomb-Temples at Dra Abu el-Naga." *EA* 42 (2013): 14–17.

———. "Ritual Space and Symbol of Power: Monumental Tomb Architecture in Thebes at the End of the New Kingdom." Pages 249–75 in *The Ramesside Period in Egypt: Studies into Cultural and Historical Processes of the 19th and 20th Dynasties; Proceedings of the International Symposium Held in Heidelberg, 5th to 7th June, 2015*. Edited by S. Kubisch and U. Rummel. SDAIK 41. Berlin: de Gruyter, 2018.

Scalf, F. "Resurrecting an Ibis Cult: Demotic Votive Texts from the Oriental Institute Museum of the University of Chicago." Pages 361–88 in *Mélanges offerts à Ola el-Aguizy*. Edited by F. Haikal. BdE 164. Cairo: Institut français d'archéologie orientale, 2015.

Scalf, F., and J. Jay. "Oriental Institute Demotic Ostraca Online (OIDOO): Merging Text Publication and Research Tools." Pages 243–61 in *Acts of the Tenth International Congress of Demotic Studies Leuven, 26–30 August 2008*. Edited by M. Depauw and Y. Broux. OLA 231. Leuven: Peeters.

Schentuleit, M. *Aus der Buchhaltung des Weinmagazins im Edfu-Tempel: Der demotische P. Carlsberg 409*. Carlsberg Papyri 9. CNI Publications 32. Copenhagen: Museum Tusculanum Press, 2006.

Schreiber, G. *Late Dynastic and Ptolemaic Painted Pottery from Thebes (4th–2nd c. BC)*. Dissertationes Pannonicae 3.6. Budapest: Eötvös Lorand University, 2003.

Serrano, J. "The Ritual of 'Encircling the Tomb' in the Funerary Monument of Djehuty (TT 11)." *ZÄS* 146 (2019): 209–23.

Smith, H. "The Saqqara Papyri: Oracle Questions, Pleas and Letters." Pages 367–75 in *Acts of the Seventh International Conference of Demotic Studies: Copenhagen, 23–27 August 1999*. Edited by K. Ryholt. CNI Publications 27. Copenhagen: Museum Tusculanum Press, 2002.

Smith, H., C. Andrews, and S. Davies. *The Sacred Animal Necropolis at North Saqqara: The Mother of Apis Inscriptions*. EES Texts from Excavations 14. London: Egypt Exploration Society, 2011.

Smith, H., and W. Tait, *Saqqara Demotic Papyri I*. EES Texts from Excavations 7. London: Egypt Exploration Society, 1983.

Smith, M. *The Mortuary Texts of Papyrus British Museum 10507*. Catalogue of Demotic Papyri in the British Museum 3. London: British Museum Publications, 1987.

———. *Traversing Eternity: Texts for the Afterlife from Ptolemaic and Roman Egypt*. Oxford: Oxford University Press, 2009.

Soliman, R. *Old and Middle Kingdom Theban Tombs*. London: Golden House, 2009.

Sottas, H. "Le Thiase d'Ombos." *Revue Archéologique* 13 (1921): 24–36.

Steinmann, F. "Ein ptolemäerzeitlicher Gefäßtyp in Tuna el-Gebel." Pages 477–93 in *Kleine Götter-Große Götter: Festschrift für Dieter Kessler zum 65. Geburtstag*. Edited by M. Flossmann-Schütze, M. Goecke-Bauer, F. Hoffmann, A. Hutterer, K. Schlüter, A. Schütze, and M. Ullmann. Tuna el-Gebel 4. Vaterstetten: Bose, 2013.

Strudwick, N. "Some Aspects of the Archaeology of the Theban Necropolis in the Ptolemaic and Roman Periods." Pages 167–88 in *The Theban Necropolis: Past, Present and Future*. Edited by N. Strudwick and J. H. Taylor. London: British Museum Press, 2003.

Strudwick, N., and H. Strudwick. *Thebes in Egypt: A Guide to the Tombs and Temples of Ancient Egypt*. London: British Museum Press, 1999.

Thissen, H.-J. *Die demotischen Graffiti von Medinet Habu: Zeugnisse zu Tempel und Kult im ptolemäischen Ägypten*. Demotische Studien 10. Sommerhausen: Gisela Zauzich Verlag, 1989.

———. "Zu den demotischen Graffiti von Medinet Habu." *Enchoria* 2 (1972): 37–54.

Thomas, E. "The Royal Necropoleis of Thebes." PhD diss., Princeton University, 1966.

Thomas, S. "The *Pastophorion* Revisited: Owners and Users of 'Priests Houses' in Ptolemaic Pathyris and Elsewhere in Egypt." *JEA* 100 (2014): 111–32.

Török, L. *Between Two Worlds: The Frontier Region between Ancient Nubia and Egypt, 3700 BC–AD 500*. Probleme der Ägyptologie 29. Leiden: Brill, 2009.

Traunecker, C. "Le temple de Qasr el-Agouz dans la nécropole thébaine, ou Ptolémées et savants thébains." *Bulletin de la Société Française d'Égyptologie* 174 (2009): 29–69.

Ullman, M. "Thebes: Origins of a Ritual Landscape." Pages 3–26 in *Sacred Space and Sacred Function in Ancient Thebes*. Edited by P. Dorman and B. Bryan. SAOC 61. Chicago: Oriental Institute of the University of Chicago, 2007.

Vandorpe, K. "City of Many a Gate, Harbour for Many a Rebel: Historical and Topographical Outline of Gręco-Roman Thebes." Pages 203–39 in *Hundred-Gated Thebes: Acts of a Colloquium on Thebes and the Theban Area in the Graeco-Roman Period*. Edited by S. Vleeming. PLBat 27. Leiden: Brill, 1995.

Vinson, S. *The Nile Boatman at Work*. MÄS 48. Munich: von Zabern, 1998.

Vittmann, G. *Der demotische Papyrus Rylands 9*. 2 vols. Ägypten und Altes Testament 38. Wiesbaden: Harrassowitz, 1998.

———. "Ein thebanischer Verpfründungsvertrag aus der Zeit Ptolemaios' III. Euergetes: P. Marseille 298+299." *Enchoria* 10 (1980): 127–39.

Vleeming, S. *Demotic and Greek-Demotic Mummy Labels and Other Short Texts Gathered from Many Publications (Short Texts II 278–1200)*. 2 vols. Studia Demotica 9. Leuven: Peeters, 2011.

———. *Demotic Graffiti and Other Short Texts Gathered from Many Publications (Short Texts III 1201–2350)*. Studia Demotica 12. Leuven: Peeters, 2015.

———. "The Office of a Choachyte in the Theban Area." Pages 241—55 in *Hundred-Gated Thebes: Acts of a Colloquium on Thebes and the Theban Area in the Graeco-Roman Period*. Edited by S. Vleeming. PLBat 27. Leiden: Brill, 1995.

———. *Some Coins of Artaxerxes and Other Short Texts in the Demotic Script Found on Various Objects and Gathered from Many Publications*. Studia Demotica 5. Leuven: Peeters, 2001.

Volokhine, Y. "Le dieu Thot au Qasr el-Agouz *Ḏd-ḥr-pꜣ-hb, Ḏḥwty-stm*." *BIFAO* 102 (2002): 405–23.

Wahid El-Din, S. M. "The Chief of the Necropolis Tax." Pages 639–49 in *Res Severa Verum Gaudium: Festschrift für Karl-Theodor Zauzich zum 65. Geburtstag am 8. Juni 2004*. Edited by F. Hoffmann and H.-J. Thissen. Studia Demotica 6. Leuven: Peeters 2004.

Wångstedt, S. "Demotische Quittungen über Ölsteuer." *Orientalia Suecana* 29 (1980): 5–26.

Wasef, S. "Ancient Egyptian Sacred Ibis Mummies: Evolutionary Mitogenomics Resolves the History of Ancient Farming." PhD diss., Griffith University, 2016.

——— et al. "Radiocarbon Dating of Sacred Ibis Mummies from Ancient Egypt." *Journal of Archaeological Science: Reports* 4 (2015): 355–61. DOI: 10.1016/j.jasrep.2015.09.020.

Winlock, H. "The Tombs of the Kings of the Seventeenth Dynasty at Thebes." *JEA* 10 (1924): 217–77.

Wodzińska, A. *A Manual of Egyptian Pottery, Vol. 4: Ptolemaic Period–Modern*. AERA Field Manual Series 1. Boston: Ancient Egypt Research Associates, 2010.

Woodman, N., and S. Ikram. "Ancient Egyptian Mummified Shrews (Eulipotyphla: Soricidae) and Mice (Rodentia: Muridae) from the Spanish Mission to Dra Abu el-Naga', Luxor, and Their Implications for Environmental Change in the Nile Valley during the Past Two Millennia." *Quaternary Research* 100 (2021): 21–31.

Woodman, N., C. Koch, and R. Hutterer. "Rediscovery of the Type Series of the Sacred Shrew, *Sorex religiosus* I: Geoffroy Saint-Hilaire, 1826, with Additional Notes on Mummified Shrews of Ancient Egypt (Mammalia: Soricidae)." *Zootaxa* 4341 (2017): 1–24. DOI: 10.11646/zootaxa.4341.1.1.

Woodman, N., A. T. Wilken, and S. Ikram. "See How They Ran: Morphological and Functional Aspects of Skeletons from Ancient Egyptian Shrew Mummies (Eulipotyphla: Soricidae: Crocidurinae)." *Journal of Mammalogy* 100 (2019): 1199–210. DOI: 10.1093/jmammal/gyz091.

Zaghloul, El-Hussein Omar M. "Frühdemotische Urkunden aus Hermupolis." *Bulletin of the Center of Papyrological Studies* 2 (1985): 1–120.

Zauzich, K.-Th. "Differenzierende Schreibungen bei differierender Wortbedeutung." Pages 109–13 in *Aspects of Demotic Lexicography: Acts of the Second International Conference for Demotic Studies, Leiden, 19–21 September 1984*. Edited by S. Vleeming. Studia Demotica 1. Leuven: Peeters, 1987.

———. *Papyri von der Insel Elephantine*. Demotische Papyri aus den staatlichen Museen zu Berlin Preussischer Kulturbesitz 3. Berlin: Akademie, 1993.

GENERAL INDEX

Note: subjects covered in the glossaries are only selectively included in this index.

adult (birds), 22
advice (to cult work readers of graffiti), 46
Ahhotep, 4, 8
Ahmes-Nefertari, 1, 11, 14
Ahmose-Sapair, 9
alteration, 3, 19 (of tomb)
Amenhotep (son of Ramessesnakht), 14, 15
Amenhotep I, 1, 3, 4, 10, 11, 12 (deified), 14
Amenhotep III, 3
amphora(e), 30
Amun/Amun-Ra, 4, 11, 12, 13, 14, 15, 58, 147
animal cult(s), 13, 14, 17, 31, 32, 34, 37, 40, 41, 42, 44, 74, 111, 119
animal mummy/mummies, 12, 13, 14, 17, 18, 19, 20, 25, 29, 32, 34, 37 (difficulty of distinguishing between sacred and votive), 43, 55, 74, 107, 117, 145, 147, 158
antiquity hunter(s), 39, 176, 177
Anubis, 10
architectural term(s), 48
"area(?) of ceremony," 52, 57, 157
Armant, 76, 92,
arrow(s), 6
ash(es), 20, 33
Assasif, 11
aviary, 147
Ay (overseer of the weavers), 4 (tomb of), 11, 13, 14, 18, 19, 30, 31, 32, 37, 51, 120, 126, 179

ba, 17
baboon, 18
bag (linen), 12
Baki (overseer of the cattle of Amun), 4, 11, 13, 18, 19, 30, 31, 37, 51
bandage(s) (mummy), 6, 12, 23, 25, 37, 58, 173–74
bitumen, 26
body (part), 27
bone(s), 6, 18, 20, 22, 25, 26, 27, 29, 31, 32, 33
botanical remains, 7, 9
bouquet offering, 47
Bouriant, Urbain, 10
box(es), 11 (for infant burial), 12 (canopic), 123
bracelet(s), 30
breeding installation(s) (for sacred ibis), 81
bronze, 30
Bubasteion, 18
bundle(s), 20, 23, 25, 26, 27, 30
burial (collective), 97 (of ibis and falcon mummies)

cage (men of the), 59, 60, 62, 63, 146, 147
canine cults, 40
canine mummies, 30
canopic box, 12
canopic jars, 12
carbonized mummies, 26
cartonnage, 12, 23 (masks), 25, 32 (masks), 33 (masks)
cartouche (royal), 6, 10
cat, 29
catacomb(s), 13, 18, 19, 27, 30, 31, 34
cattle, 4, 11, 18
ceiling, 6, 12, 13, 32, 33
cement, 176
ceremony, 158
cession-document, 65
chapel(s), 2, 4, 7, 8, 9, 10, 11, 12, 13, 14, 15, 17, 18, 19, 30, 31, 32, 33, 34, 39, 40, 48, 49, 50, 52, 53, 54, 55, 56, 57, 81, 82, 86, 98, 104, 105, 106, 114, 117, 118, 119, 121, 125, 129, 139, 144, 155, 156, 176, 177
Charron, Alain, 17
Chauveau, Michael, 38, 45, 151, 152
"chief" (as title?), 63
"chief of Thebes," 142

cloth, 23 (nest), 25 (large square)
coffin(s), 1, 3, 4, 6, 8, 9, 10, 11 (anthropomorphic of woman), 12 (anthropomorphic), 41 (Berlin), 123
color(s), 13, 23 (of linen wrappings), 177
combustion (spontaneous), 35
commemoration (of exploits), 48, 57
commemorative (graffiti), 46, 57
concentration (of graffiti), 50
condition, 37 (under which Spiegelberg copied graffiti), 175–79 (of graffiti)
conduct (proper), 122
conflagration, 27
connection(s) (between tombs), 13, 18, 19, 20, 22, 30, 31, 178
conservation (program), 39
conservator, 40, 98, 113, 161, 175
container, 27 (large Ptolemaic), 28, 30, 123
Coptic (date), 32
corridor, 4, 6, 7, 11, 12, 13, 19, 20, 31, 32, 50, 51, 53, 71, 72, 73, 74, 75, 163, 174, 175 and passim
crocodile (remains), 33
cult, 9 (posthumous), 10 (royal), 13, 14, 15, 17, 41 (animal) and passim
curse, 48 (formula), 156
cutter (vibrating), 40 (for conservation)

Dahshur, 3
daiu-linen, 9
damnatio memoriae, 13
date(s) (double), 44
dating (of graffiti), 42–45
debris, 6, 10, 12, 13, 27, 31, 32, 33, 46, 113, 132, 177, 179
decoration, 3, 4, 13, 19, 27 (painted plant), 28, 39 (original in tomb -399-), 176
degradation (of walls), 19
Deir el-Bahari, 4, 11, 14, 15, 65
deities (mentioned in graffiti), 58–59
delivery, 97 (of sacred mummies), 172 (of wheat)
desmostachya bipinnata, 30
deposit, 6 (of mummies), 9 (pottery), 10 (of offering vessels), 12 (mummification), 13, 15, 18, 22 (bone), 27 (secondary), 29 (Ptolemaic), 30, 31, 32, 33, 57, 108
dereliction (of duty), 48 (concerns regarding)
destruction, 29 (of content of tomb chamber), 30 (of walls), 57 (of mummy deposits)
detritus (used for "false mummies"), 26
directional/utilitarian (graffiti), 31, 39, 45, 46, 48, 49, 50, 97, 105, 106, 108, 115, 119, 120, 121, 125, 133, 162
diversity (of mummies), 23
divine chapel, 53, 54, 55, 56, 81, 82, 98, 129, 144
Djehuty Project, 17
Djehuty (tomb of), passim
dockworker(s), 59, 86
dog(s), 18, 29, 30
doorjamb(s), 31, 176
doorway(s), 27, 50, 104, 105,106, 128, 176, 179
double tomb complex, 11, 14
Dra Abu el-Naga^c, passim
drawing(s), 39 (subjective nature of graffiti)
dump, 32 (for human mummies)
dye(s), 23

eagle(s), 22, 25
Eastern Gallery/Galleries, 30–32 and passim
egg, 27 (ibis)
eggshell(s), 29, 30
Eighteenth Dynasty, 3, 4, 7, 9, 10, 11, 13, 15
El-Tarif, 1, 7
eleventh day of the week, 45
Eleventh–Twelfth Dynasty, 1, 3, 4, 6, 10, 15
embalming material(s), 118, 123, 145
entrance, 6, 7, 8, 9, 11, 13, 14, 19, 20, 30, 31, 32, 33, 48, 49, 50, 52, 98, 115, 127, 175, 176, 177, 178, 179
entrance hall, 31, 33
environment, 22, 44 (physical), 48 (of cult personnel), 122
erosion (of walls), 19, 39, 40, 175, 176
ex-voto(s), 17

faience necklace(s), 4, 8
fake (mummies), 27
falcon(s), 6, 18, 22, 27, 29, 30, 40 and passim
"false mummies," 27
Farshut Road, 3
feather(s), 24, 26, 27
"feeder (of the hawk)," 41, 58

figure (mummy-form), 9
fill, 32 (animal mummies as)
fire, 12, 19, 20, 23, 26, 27, 29, 30, 31, 32, 33, 34, 40, 48, 50, 53, 57, 123, 125, 139, 140, 156, 157, 158, 159, 175–77, 179
"First Hall," 50, 51, 52, 53, 118, 120
fledgling(s), 22
Flickstein, 175
flower(s), 7, 145
"foremost of Thebes," 17 (designation of individual sacred bird of Thoth?), 54, 56, 58, 82, 98, 99, 129
fox, 29
fraction, 170, 171 (complex)
fracture(s), 22 (of bird leg-bones)
frankincense, 148
fringed (pieces of linen), 25
funerary chamber, 31 (twin)
funerary shaft(s), 6, 8, 9, 10, 11, 12, 13, 14, 31
fur, 27

garden, 7, 8, 10, 11, 12
genealogy, 65, 66, 110, 151
German Archaeological Institute, 1, 6, 8
girl (mummy of), 174
Giza, 3
goat, 29
god's father(s), 12, 60, 61, 62, 63, 131
gold, 25
"good name" (graffiti), 45, 55 (*rn nfr*), 60, 64 and passim
graffiti (demotic), passim
grave (mass), 6
"great one of Thebes," 59, 60, 61, 63, 64, 125, 127, 207
"great one(s) of Thoth," 41–42, 47, 55, 57, 59, 60, 61, 62, 63, 64, 65 and passim
"great people," 62, 149
"Great Tomb of the Ibis and Hawks," 19, 34, 37, 38, 39, 40, and passim
"Great Revolt of the Egyptians," 35
Greek (inscription), 173

habitation, 32
halfa grass (mats), 30

harbor, 59, 60 (men of the), 61, 62, 64, 85, 86, 98, 99, 142
Hathor, 10, 15
Hatshepsut, 3, 4, 10, 11
hawk(s), 19, 22 and passim
hem(s), 25
herringbone (pattern of mummy bandaging), 24, 32
Hery (tomb of), 4, 7 and passim
hieroglyphic inscription(s), 29
hieroglyphs (Ptolemaic), 51
High Priest of Amun, 14
historical background (of graffiti), 40–42
hole(s), 12 (in floor to accommodate canopic box)
Ḥor archive, 48
Horus, 6, 23, 58 (as Lord of Letopolis), 59, 63, 136
"House-of-Amun," 58, 131
"House of Eternity," 56, 63, 136
"House-of-Montu," 58, 61, 64, 75, 92
human (burial), 32
human (mummies), 27, 30, 32, 173
human (remains), 29
hymn(s), 46
hypogeum, 18

Ibi (TT 36), 27
ibiotapheion, 164
ibis, 14 (on stand) and passim
ibis-herder, 164
imperata cylindrica, 30
incantation, 27
industrial space, 30
infant (burials), 10, 11
infections (among birds), 22
ink, 118, 178 (red), 179
instruction(s) (to cult worker reader), 31, 46, 122, 160
Intef (king), 8
Intefmose (king's son), 8, 9, 10
"intermediate tomb" (Kampp designation of no. –399–), 18, 19
interment, 17, 19, 29, 30, 49, 53, 56, 80, 82, 87, 97, 99, 107, 145
invocation(s) (to the ibis), 46
Isis, 29 (bust of Greek/Hellenized)

jar(s), 12 ("sausage type"), 27 (Ptolemaic globular four-handled), 28, 29, 32, 117, 118, 123, 159
juvenile (birds), 22, 30

ka (royal), 14
Kamose, 8
Kampp, Friederike, 4, 18
Kares, 10
Karnak Temple, 1, 14
Kenres, 10
key(s), 59 (to the "place of rest")
Kheperkara (Sesostris I), 10
Khokha, 11
Khonsu, 58, 173
Khonsu Neferhotep, 58
King's son, 8, 9, 10
kite(s) (bird), 22

lamp(s), 30, 32, 35, 122, 123
landscape, 3, 7, 8
lesonis, 12, 59, 62, 146, 147
Letopolis, 46, 58, 59, 63, 136
libation tray(s), 6
light(ing), 37 (conditions of Spiegelberg's work in tomb), 123 (oil for)
limestone, 6, 9, 11, 175, 176, 178, 179
linen, 6, 9, 12, 23, 25 (reused), 123, 173
linen bandages, 12
linen shroud, 6
lintel, 6, 31
Lisht, 3

Mariette, Auguste, 1, 8
markings (physical), 82 (to identify sacred animals)
marl clay vessel(s), 6
mask(s), 23, 32, 33
mastabas (Old Kingdom), 3
mat(s), 6 (reed), 30 (halfa grass)
mathematical school-texts, 168, 170
Medamud, 58
Medinet Habu, 42, 45, 58, 81, 136
Meidum bowl, 8
Men-iset, 1
Middle Kingdom, 3, 6, 7, 8, 10, 11, 12, 31, 120 (tomb), 126
Montu, 58 and passim
Montuhotep II Nebhepetra, 10, 14, 15
mourn(ing)/mourned, 47, 50, 52, 53, 103, 118, 120, 144, 145
movement (of animal mummies through tomb), 47
mud, 4 (libation tray), 7, 8, 13, 23, 26, 30, 176, 178, 179
mud-brick, 1, 8, 9, 10, 12, 13, 14, 18, 19, 20, 21, 30, 31, 33, 34
mummification deposit(s), 12
mummification materials, 26
mummification process, 47
mummy/mummies, 6, 13, 14, 17, 18, 19, 20 (carbonised), 22 and passim
mummy bandage(s), 37, 58, 173–74
mummy-brace(s), 12
mummy bundle(s), 25
mummy case(s), 12
mummy-form, 9
mummy (votive), 17
muna, 30
myrrh, 148

natron, 12
Neb, 9, 10 (*rishi*-coffin of)
Nebhepetra, 10, 15
necklace, 4, 8
Neferhotep, 58, 173 (as epithet of Khonsu)
nest, 23
New Kingdom, 12, 14, 18, 19, 30, 46, 47, 120, 126, 133 (tombs), 175, 176
Newberry, Percy, 8, 9
Nubia(n), 6
Nubkheperra Intef, 8, 9
numeral(s) (in school-text), 168

oath(s) (temple), 58
obelisk, 8, 9
ochre (red), 18, 37, 51, 177, 179
offering chapel(s), 8, 9, 10, 11, 12
offering formula(s), 4, 6
offering ritual, 4
offering table, 7

offering vessel(s), 10
offspring, 49, 50, 56, 57 (sacred ibises and falcons as), 96, 97, 115
oil(s), 26, 45 (price of oil receipt), 65, 123, 164, 165
Old Kingdom, 3, 8
oracular (implications), 42
organization, 45 (of cult personnel), 56 (of ibis and falcon cult)
Osiris, 12, 14, 40, 45, 46, 54, 55, 56, 57, 60, 63, 64 and passim
Osorkon I (king), 12
ostracon/ostraca, 44, 45, 51 (hieratic), 65, 164–73
overseer of the cattle of Amun, 4, 11
overseer of the double granary, 4
overseer of the necropolis, 60, 62, 63, 66, 131, 132, 135
overseer of the treasury, 4
overseer of (the) weavers, 4, 11, 32, 120, 126
overseer of works, 4

package(s), 22 (of mummified shrews/rodents and snakes), 23 (of mummified snakes)
packet(s) (rectangular), 23 (containing animals related to the solar cult)
paddle doll(s), 6
Papyrus Abbott, 1, 8
pastophoros/pastophoroi, 41, 55, 59, 60, 111
perfumer, 60, 146, 148
personal name(s), 65–67 and passim
personal piety, 45
Petrie, W. M. Flinders, 1
pharaoh, 46, 62, 63, 119, 136
pink(ish), 23, 178
planning (of burial of sacred birds), 46
plant (decoration), 27, 28
plaster(ed), 4, 13, 177, 178
Plegadis falcinellus, 22
pottery, 4, 6, 7, 8, 9, 12, 14, 32, 164, 166, 168, 170, 172
"Place of Rest," 54–55 and passim
pot, 32 (globular)
powder (light brown), 29
preparation, 46 (of tombs to receive animal mummies), 52 (mummy), 178
processional way, 14
profession(s), 59–64
pseudo-mummies, 27
Ptah, 10
Ptolemy, 82
Ptolemy II, 65, 164, 165, 166
Ptolemy III, 165, 166
Ptolemy IV, 165, 166
Ptolemy VI, 44, 151, 152, 165, 173
Ptolemy VIII Euergetes II, 42, 44, 151, 152, 165, 173
pyramid(s), 1, 3, 8, 9, 10, 11, 14
pyramidion, 8

Qasr el-Aguz (Temple of Thoth), 42, 56, 58, 81
Qena, 3
quarters (living), 53 (of sacred ibis)

Ra, 6
ram (sacred of Amun), 147
Ramesses II, 11, 32
Ramessesnakht, 14, 15
"Ramesside Chapel" (= inner chamber of the tomb-chapel of Hery), 32
Ramose, 11, 32
ramp, 19
raptor(s), 17, 18, 20, 22, 23, 24, 30, 31, 32, 33, 34
Re-Harakhte, 23
reburial(s) (of damaged bird mummies), 27
receipt, 44, 65 (for price of oil), 164, 165 (bilingual), 166
red, 4, 6, 13, 18, 20, 23, 26, 27,
red ochre, 18, 37, 51, 177, 179
regnal year(s), 43, 44, 54 and passim
representative(s) (of the priests), 60, 61, 62, 63, 131
resin(s)/resinous, 23, 26, 29, 47, 117, 123, 144, 145
reuse 6, 7, 10, 11, 13, 17, 25, 27, 29, 30, 32, 40, 46
revolt (of Egyptians), 35
rishi-coffin, 9, 10
robber(s) (tomb), 6, 7, 13, 30 (hole of), 31, 32 (tomb), 35
rock-cut tomb-chapels(s), 4, 6, 7, 8, 10, 11, 12, 15, 17, 30, 120
rodent(s), 22, 23, 25, 33

rope, 23
route(s) (of cult workers within tombs), 19, 32, 48, 49, 124
row(s) (of connected rooms), 53
row(s) (of mummies), 20

saff tombs, 1, 7, 8, 15 (*saff*-facade)
Saite (period), 33
sale-document, 65
salt-tax document(s), 41, 166, 167
sandstone, 10
Saqqara, 3, 18, 27, 34, 41, 117, 123, 166
scarab, 9
school-text, 168
scribal exercise, 170
scribe(s), 48, 63 and passim
"scribe of the House-of-Eternity," 56, 63, 136
seal impression(s), 14, 29 (clay), 31
Second Intermediate Period, 8, 12
Sekhemra-Wepmaat Intef-aa, 8
self-bow, 6
serekh, 6
servant(s), 41, 55, 61 and passim
serpent(s), 30
service, 46 (graffiti type), 45, 46, 158
Sesostris I, 10
Setne II, 119
Seventeenth Dynasty, 1, 6, 8, 9, 10, 12, 14, 15
shabti(s), 9, 11
Sheikh Abd el-Qurna, 11
shrew(s), 18, 22, 23, 25, 29, 30, 31, 33, 34
shroud, 6, 12, 23, 30, 173
signposts (graffiti as), 48
Siosiris, 119
smoke, 176, 177, 179
snake(s), 18, 22, 23, 25, 29, 31, 33, 34
Sobekemsaef II (king), 8, 9, 10
solar cult, 23
soot, 32, 177, 178, 179
Spanish Mission, passim
speos (of Hathor), 15
Spiegelberg, Wilhelm, 8, 9, 19, 34, 37, 38, 39, 40, 42, 43, 44, 52, 66, 109, 110, 111, 113, 133, 135, 137, 138, 142, 143, 145, 147, 151, 152, 159, 177, 180
squeeze(s), 109 (of Spiegelberg)
stair(s), 18, 19, 49, 50, 51, 105, 106, 133, 159
staircase(s), 7, 13, 18, 19, 20, 21, 30, 31, 32, 33, 43, 46, 49, 50, 51, 52, 106, 108
stairway, 51
stave(s), 6
stela/stelae, 8, 10, 41, 63
stevedore(s), 59, 86
stick-*shabti(s)*, 9
stone(s), 3, 10, 27, 29, 138, 178
stonemason, 138
straw, 26
string (linen), 23
Sudoku, 3
Suez Canal, 2
system (Spiegelberg's numbering), 38

"taker(s) of the gods," 59, 60, 61, 62, 63, 64 and passim
teardrop (shape of ibis mummy), 23, 30, 32, 33
temple(s), 53–54 and passim
Tetisheri (temple of, at Abydos), 30
Third Intermediate (period), 3, 33, 47
Threskiornis aethiopicus, 22
Thirteenth Dynasty, 11
Thoth, 42 (cult on West Bank of Thebes) and passim
thread, 23
Thutmose III, 4, 10
title(s), 41, 42, 59–64 and passim
Tomb –399–, 4, 7, 13, 18, 19–21, 27, 29 and passim
tomb-chapel, 4, 7, 8, 9, 11, 12 and passim
torch(es), 122, 123
tourism, 34 (eighteenth and nineteenth century)
transverse hall, 11, 12, 13, 19, 29, 30, 173
TT 11, passim
TT 12, passim
TT 141, 37
Tuna el-Gebel, 18, 27, 41, 82, 117, 166
Twelfth Dynasty, 1, 3, 4, 6, 10, 15
Twentieth Dynasty, 14
Twenty-First Dynasty, 11
Twenty-Second Dynasty, 6, 11, 12
Twenty-Sixth Dynasty, 12

underworld, 119
Upper Gallery, 32 and passim

Valley of the Kings, 3
Valley of the Queens, 3
vandalism, 176
vase(s), 4, 30, 47
vessel(s) (pottery), 4, 6, 9 (in deposit), 10, 15, 117, 122
votive, 17 (animals), 18, 37, 41, 45 (graffiti), 58, 136 (prayer), 142
vulture(s), 22

wab-priest(s), 12
Wadi Sikket Taqa el-Zeid, 3
wash, 177, 178
water, 12, 13 (eroding reliefs)
wax, 26
Western Valley, 3
wheat (delivery of), 172
whitewash, 11, 176, 177, 178, 179
wig, 23
wind (eroding reliefs and walls), 12, 13, 19
wrapping (elaborate coffered), 23, 25, 26, 174

yellow, 23

View of Dra Abu el-Nagaʿ at the northern end of the Theban necropolis, on the West Bank of Luxor, opposite to Karnak temple on the East Bank. Photograph by J. Latova.

View of the archaeological site of the Spanish Mission, February 2018. Photograph by J. Latova.

a.

b.

a.–b. Photograph and drawing of stamped mud brick with a seal impression of Thoth.
Drawing by P. Rodrígues Frade. Photograph by J. Latova.

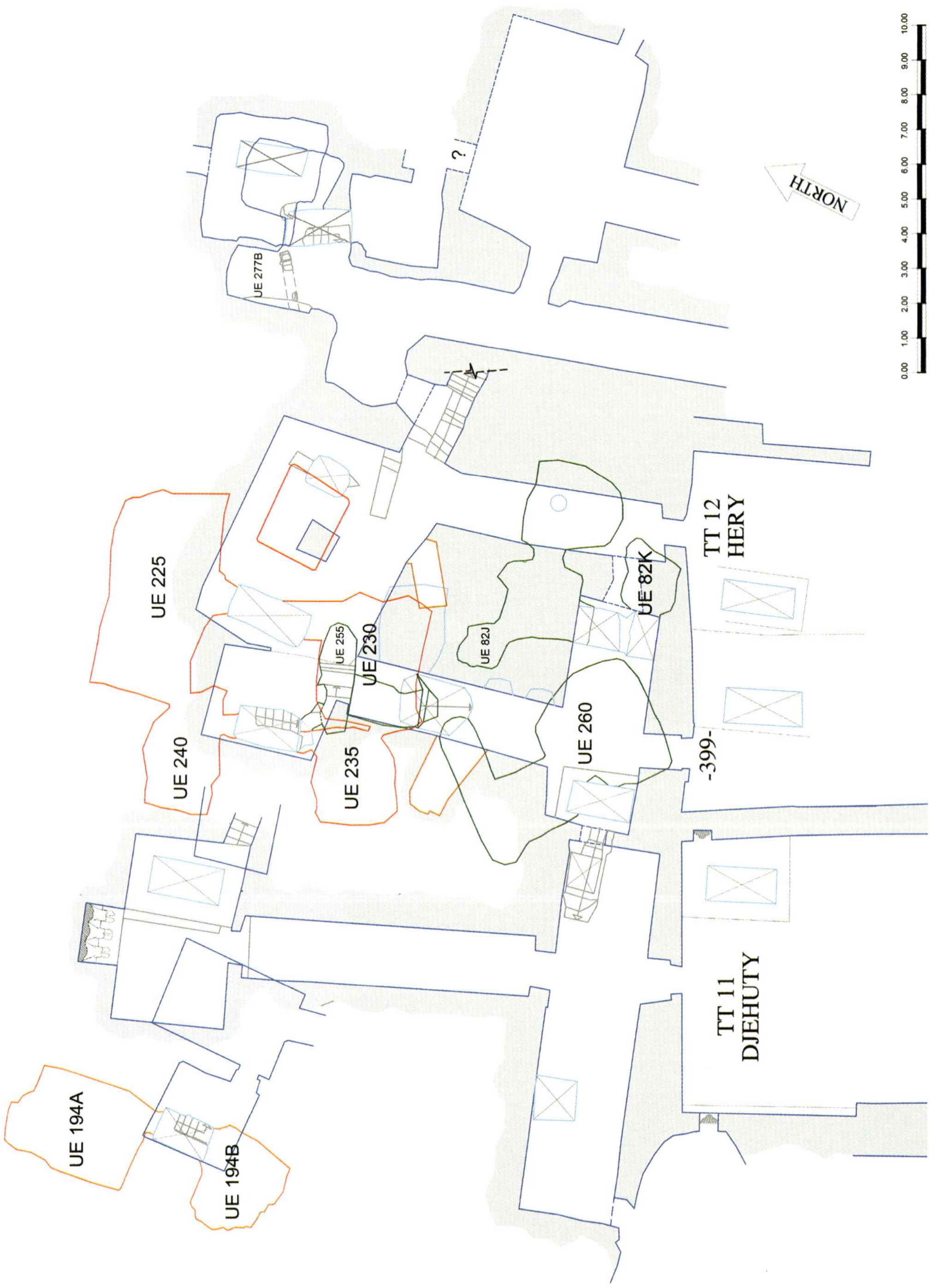

Keyplan showing location of deposits of animal mummies and bones in tomb –399–, TT 12, Eastern Galleries, and tomb above TT 11.

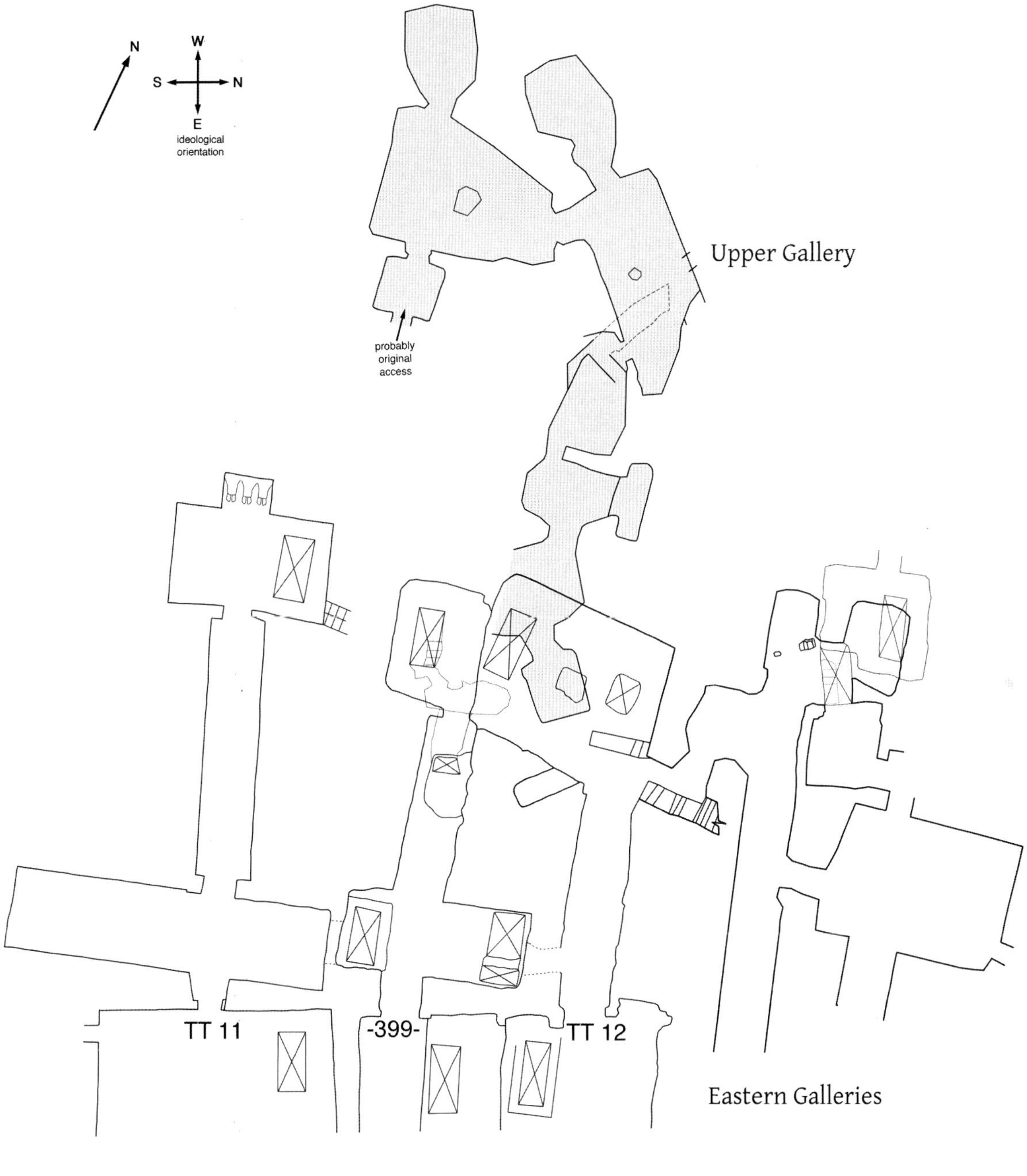

Plan of TT 11, TT 12, tomb –399–, Upper Gallery, and Eastern Galleries.

Keyplan showing location of graffiti in TT 11, TT 12, tomb -399-, and Eastern Galleries.

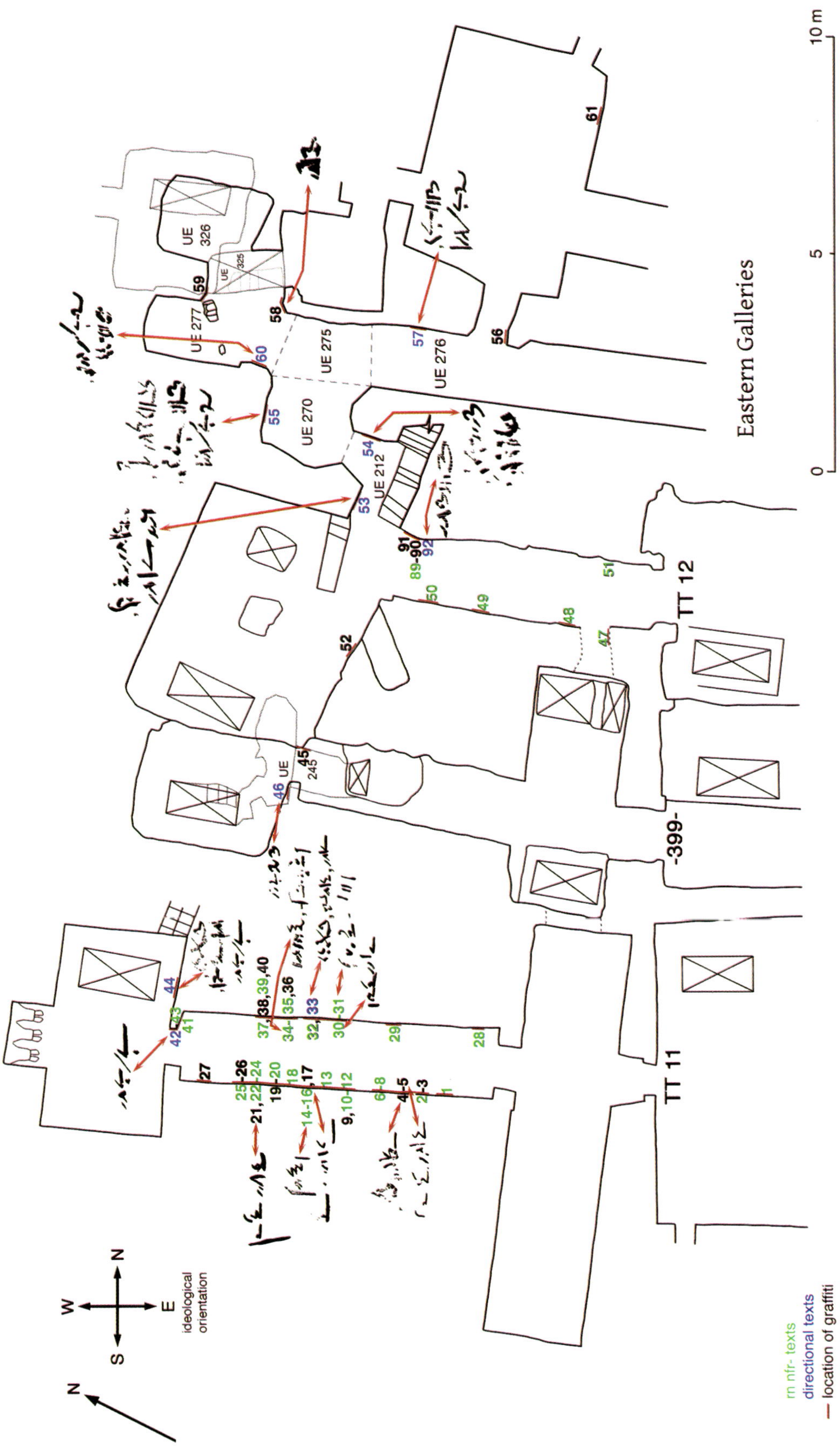

Keyplan showing location of the graffiti containing distinctive architectural and directional terms (with demotic hand-copies).

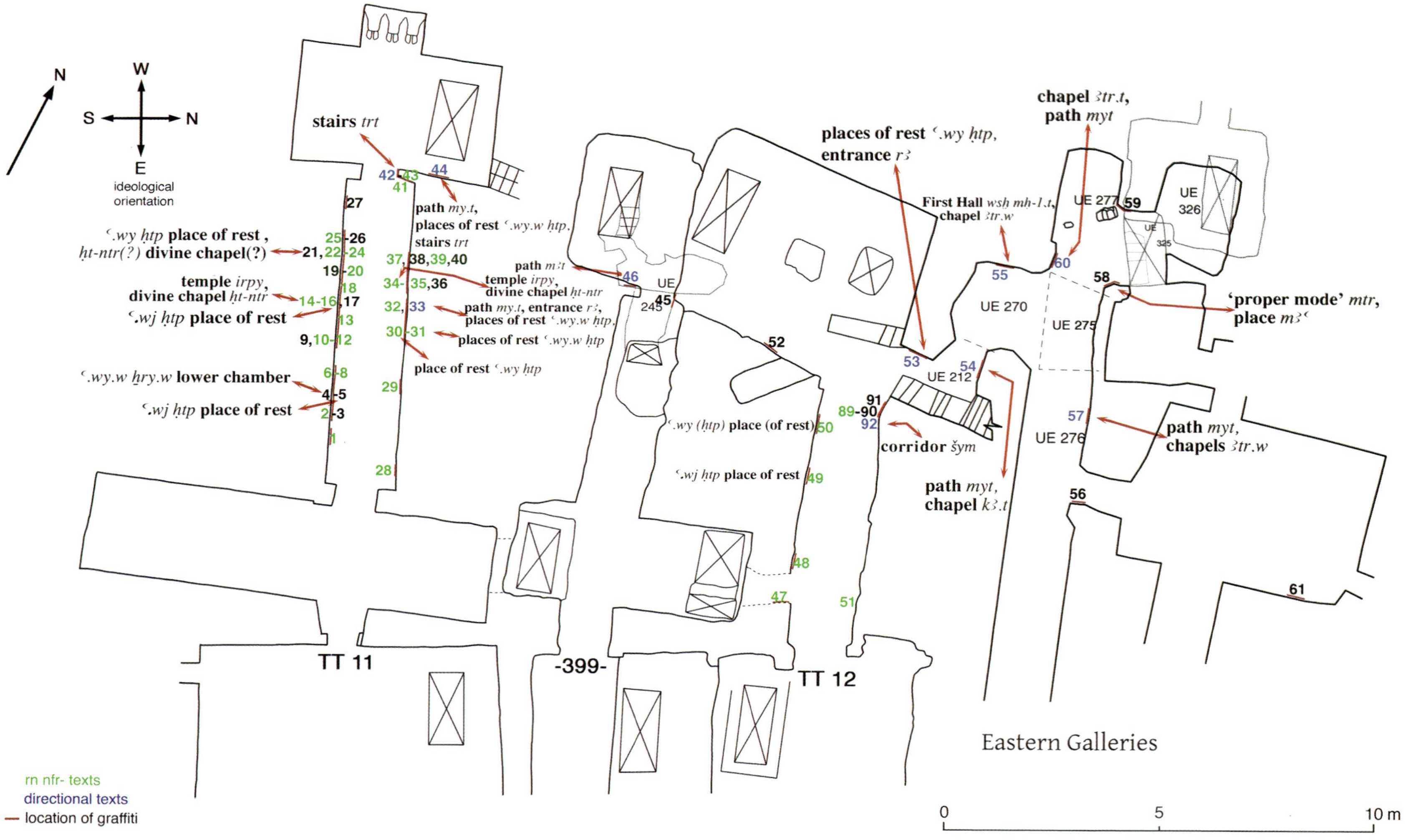

Keyplan showing location of the graffiti containing distinctive architectural and directional terms (with translation of the demotic terms in pl. 7).

Keyplan of graffiti on N-wall in the tomb of Djehuty (TT 11). Photograph courtesy of J. M. Galán.

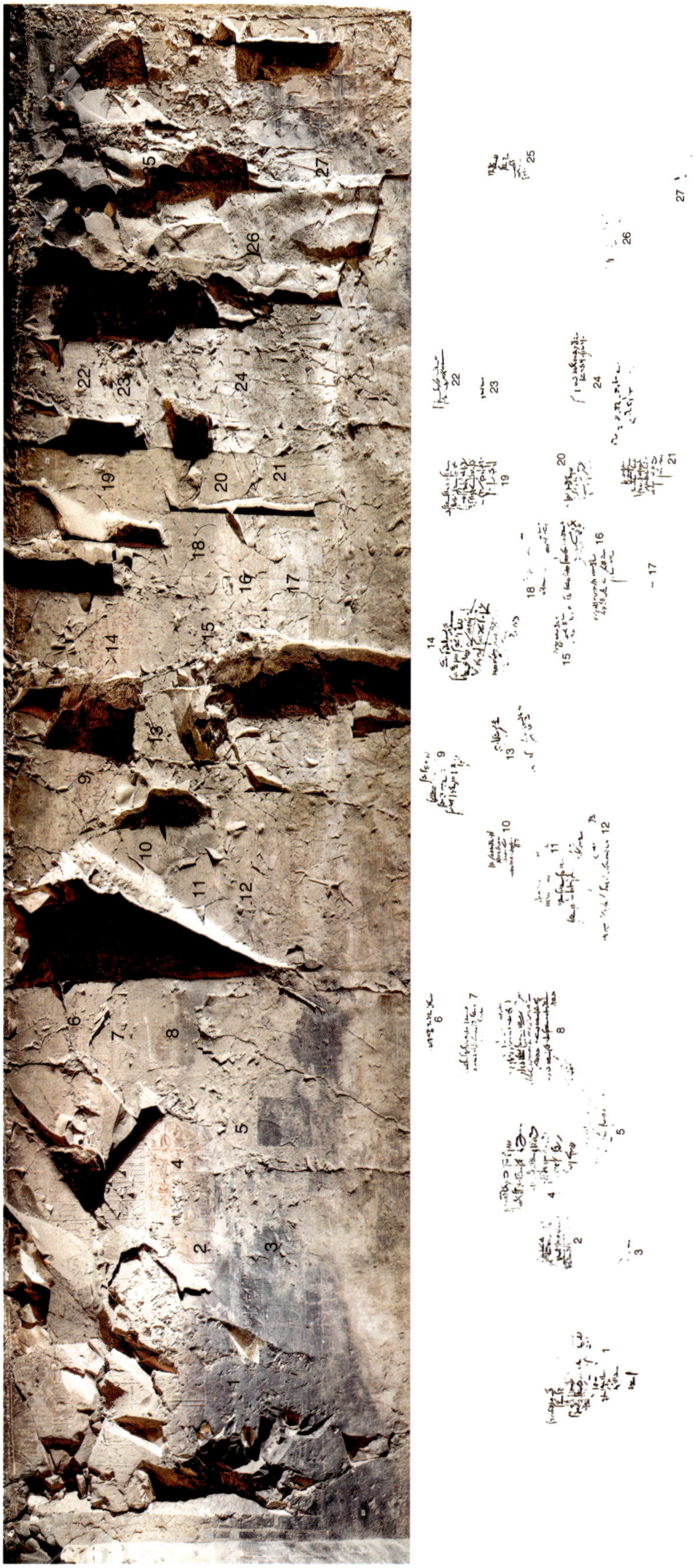

Keyplan of graffiti on S-wall in the tomb of Djehuty (TT 11). Photograph courtesy of J. M. Galán.

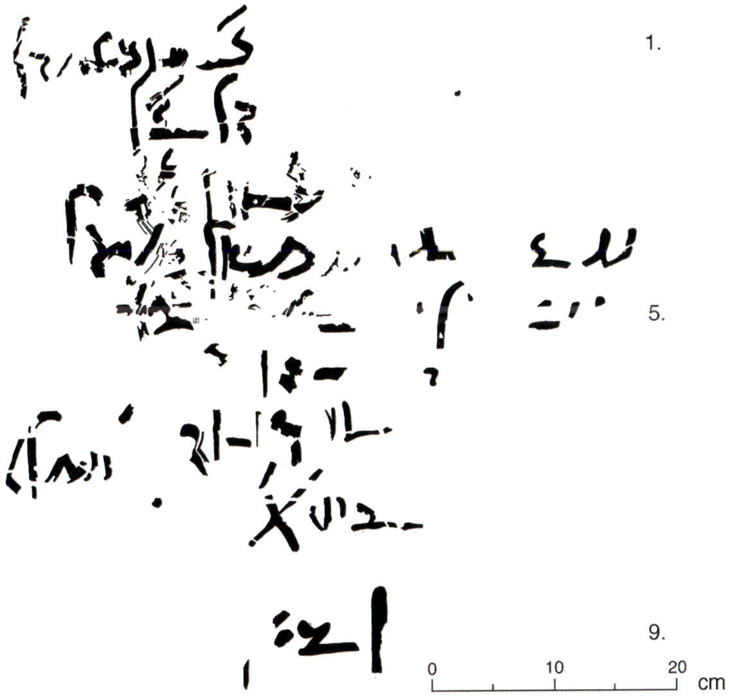

Graffito 1

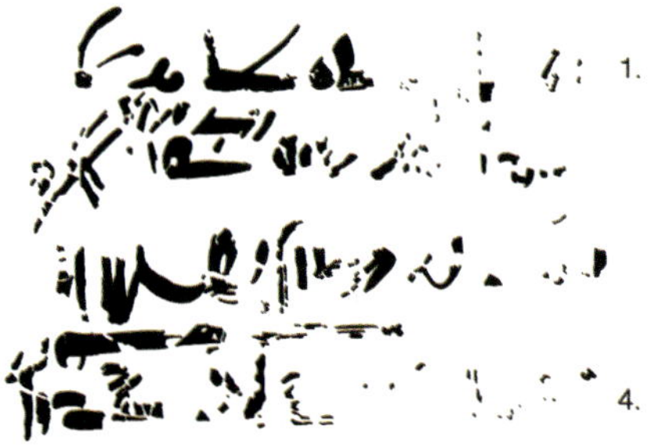

Graffito 2

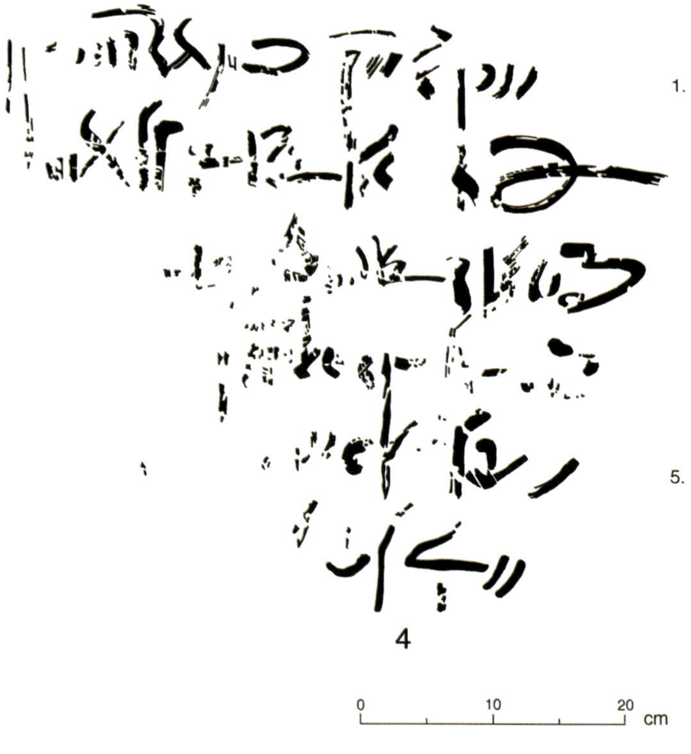

Graffito 4

a. Graffito 3

b. Graffito 5

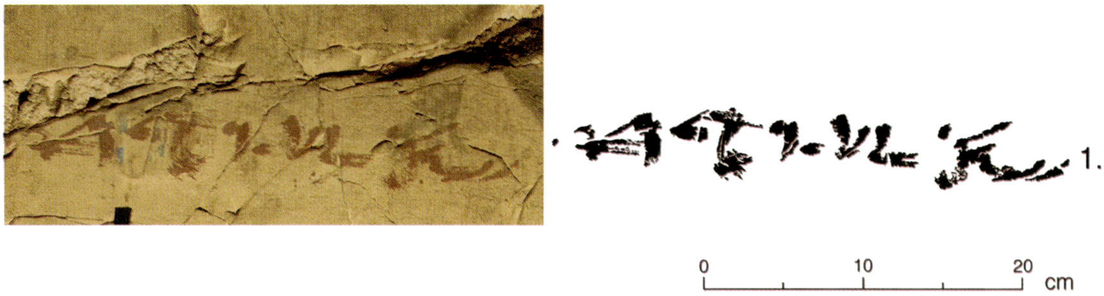

a. Graffito 6

b. Graffito 7

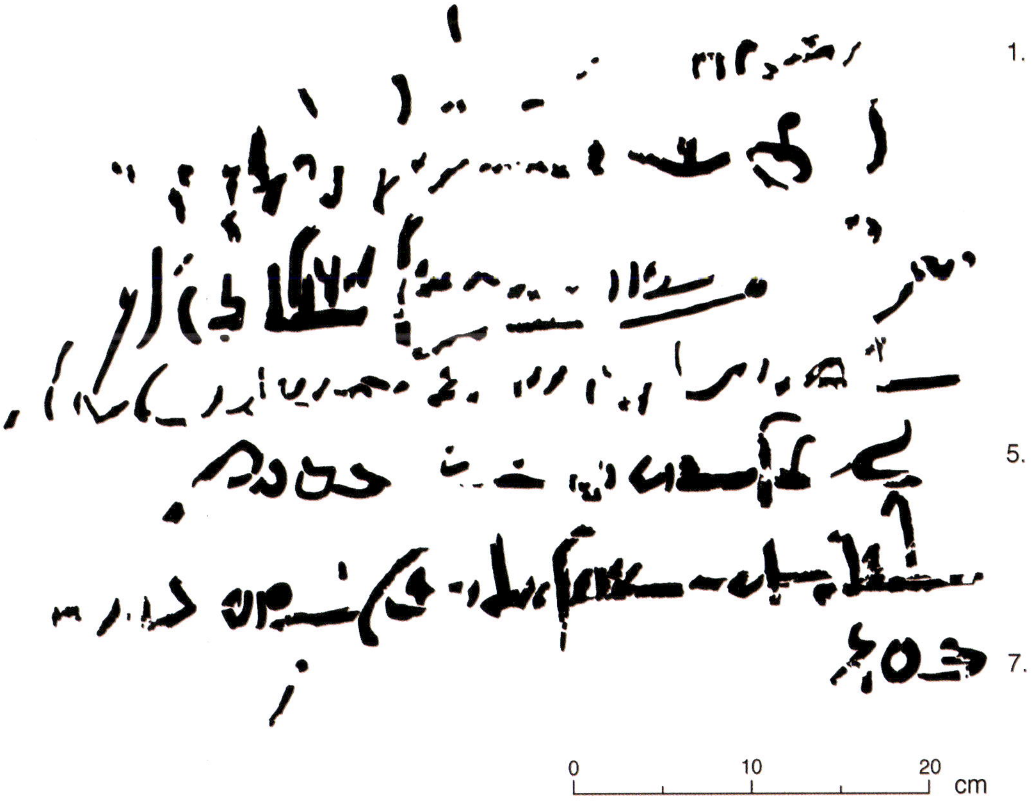

Graffito 8

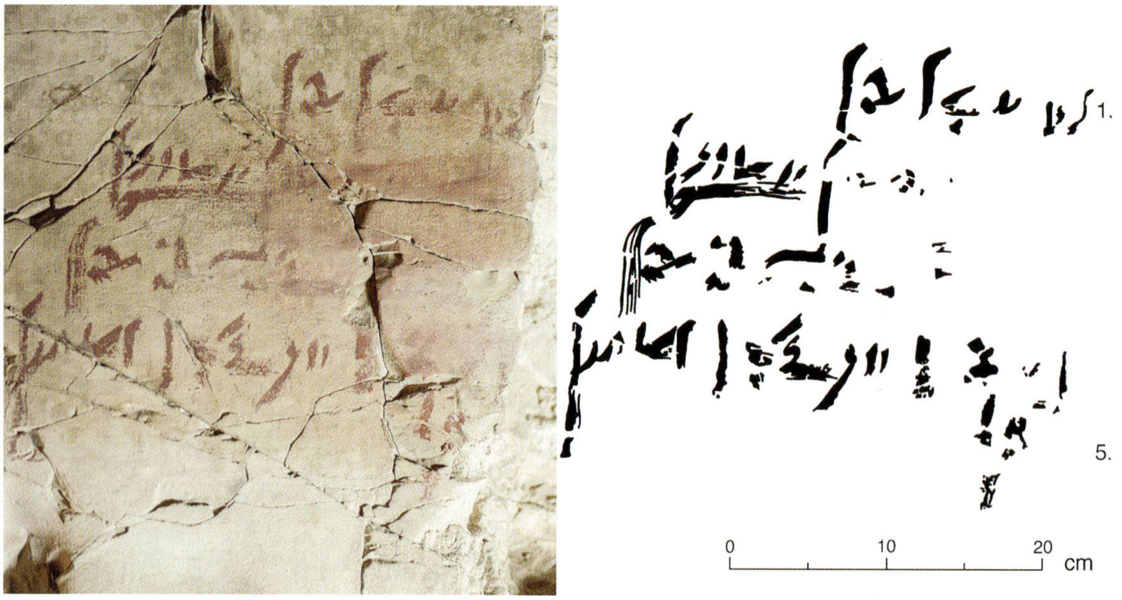

a. Graffito 9

b. Graffito 10

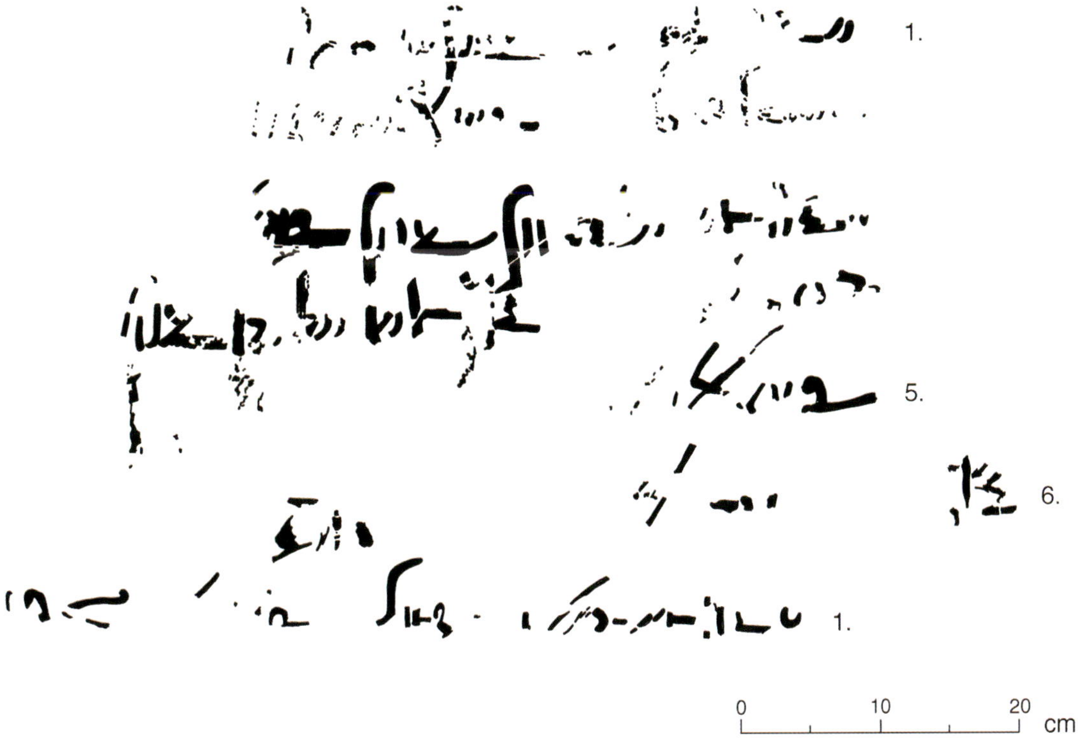

Graffiti 11 and 12

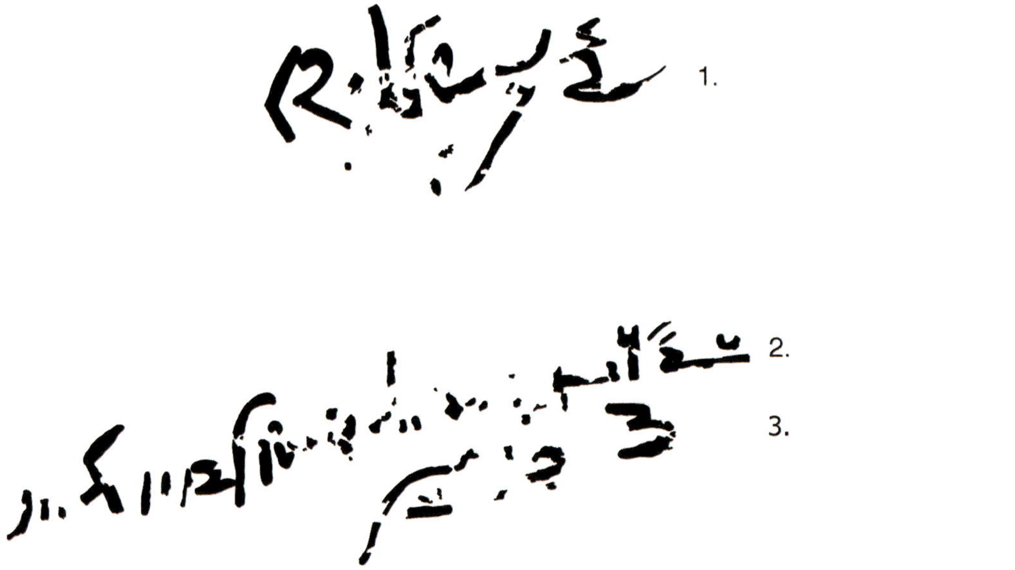

Graffito 13

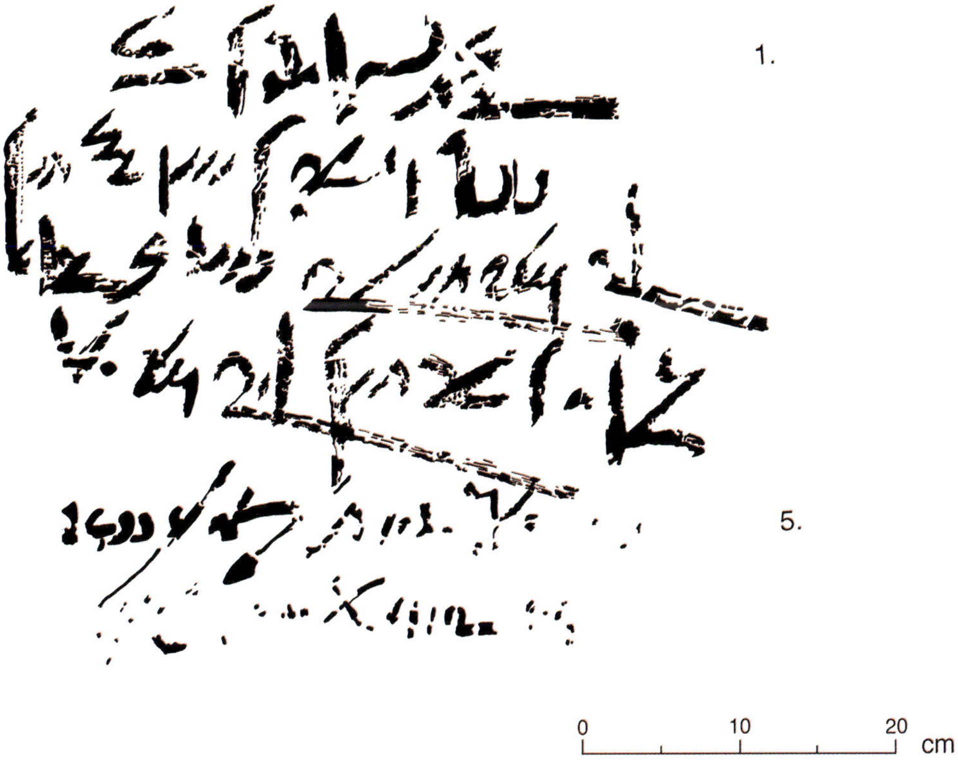

Graffito 14

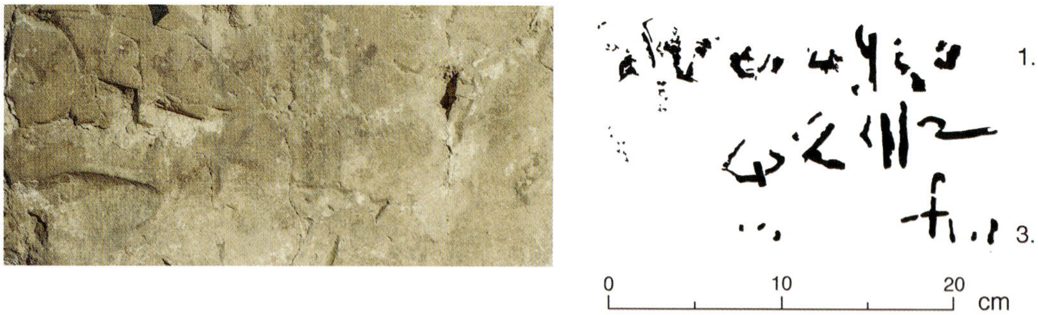

a. Graffito 15

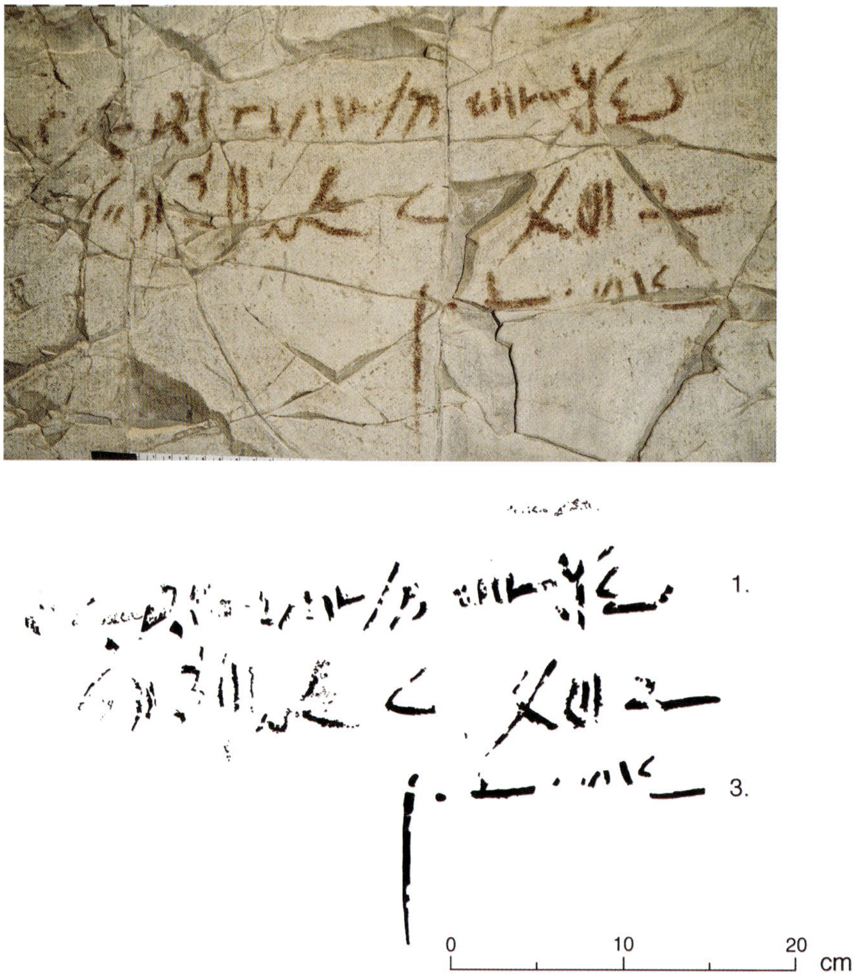

b. Graffito 16

c. Graffito 17

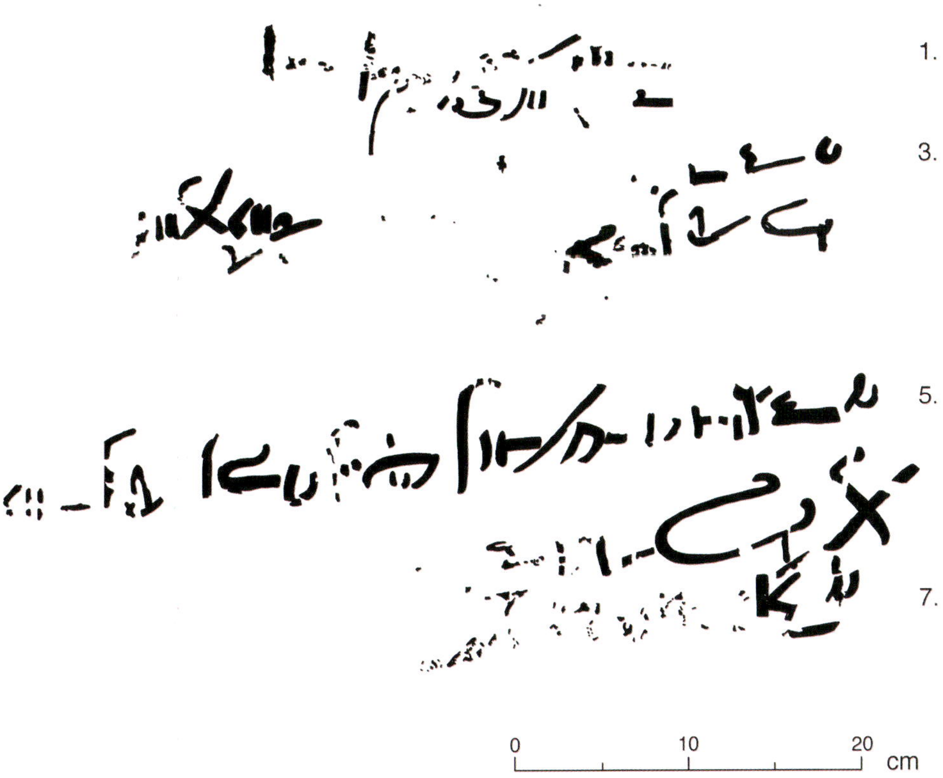

Graffito 18

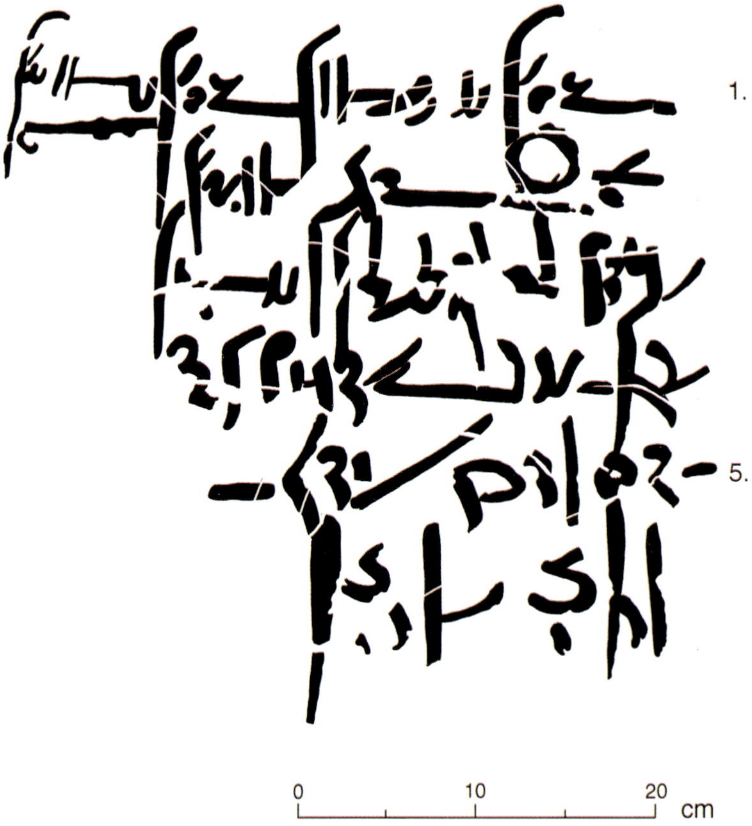

Graffito 19

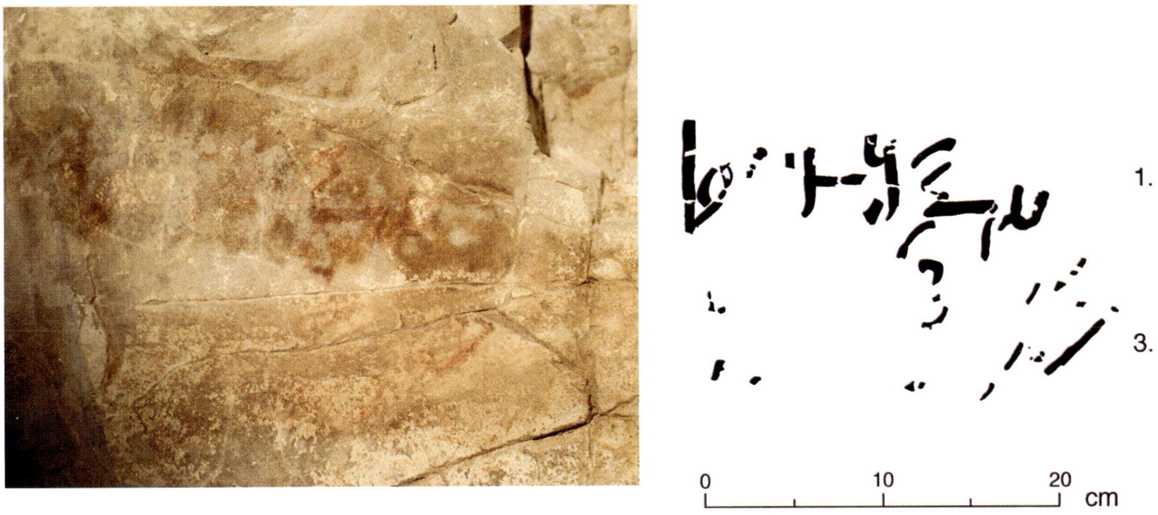

a. Graffito 20

b. Graffito 21

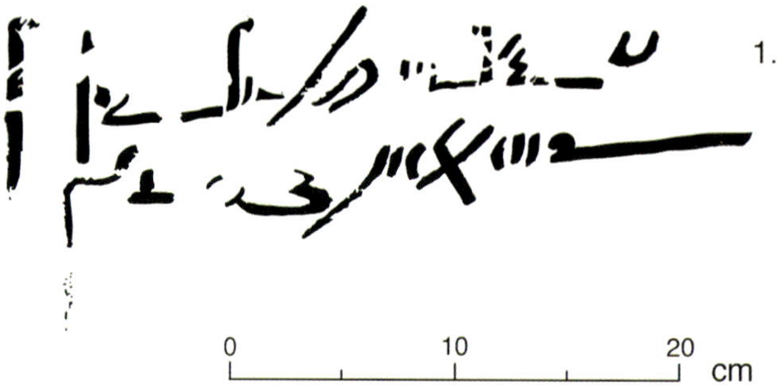

a. Graffito 22

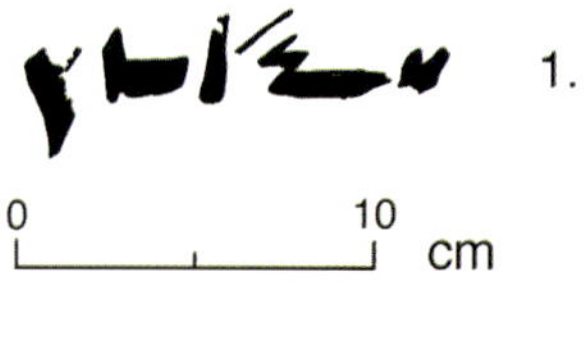

b. Graffito 23

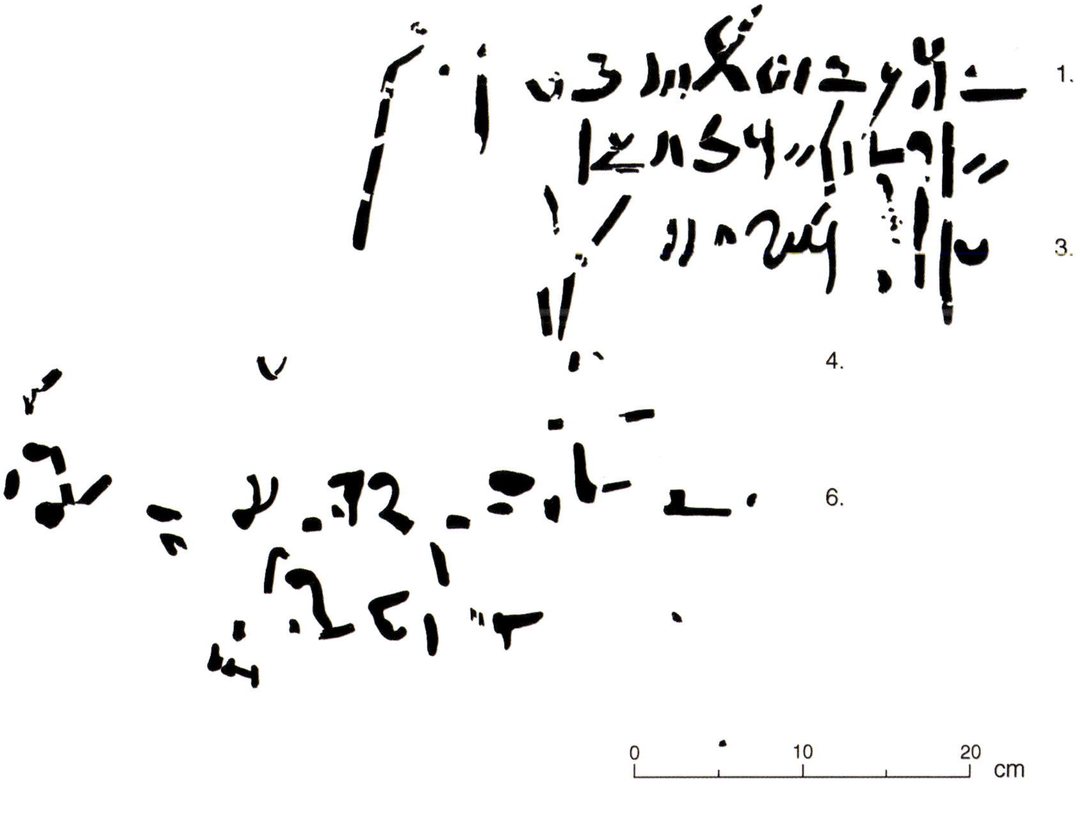

Graffito 24

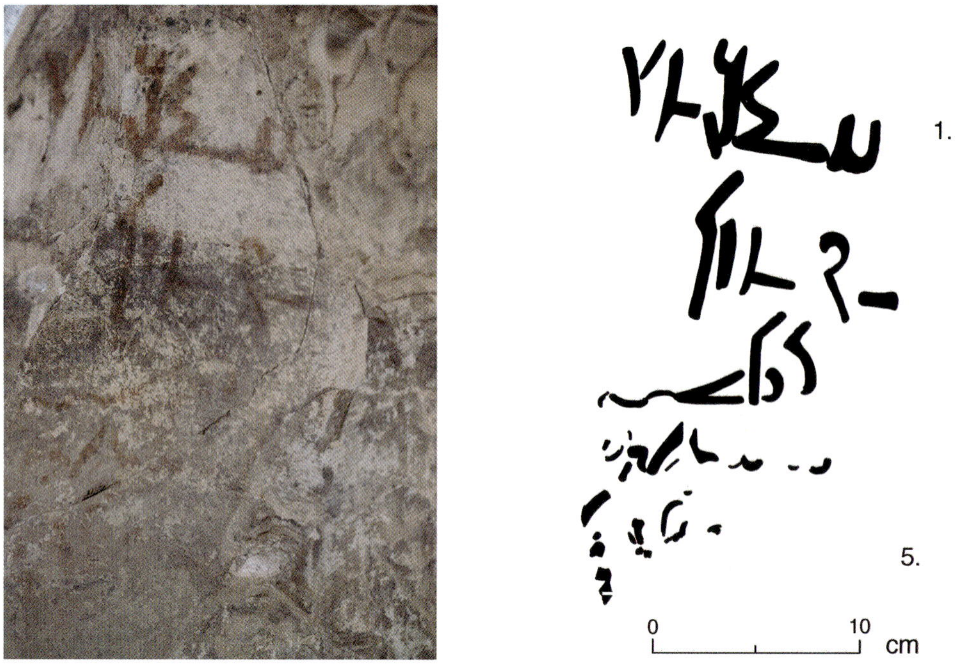

a. Graffito 25

b. Graffito 26

c. Graffito 27

a. Graffito 28

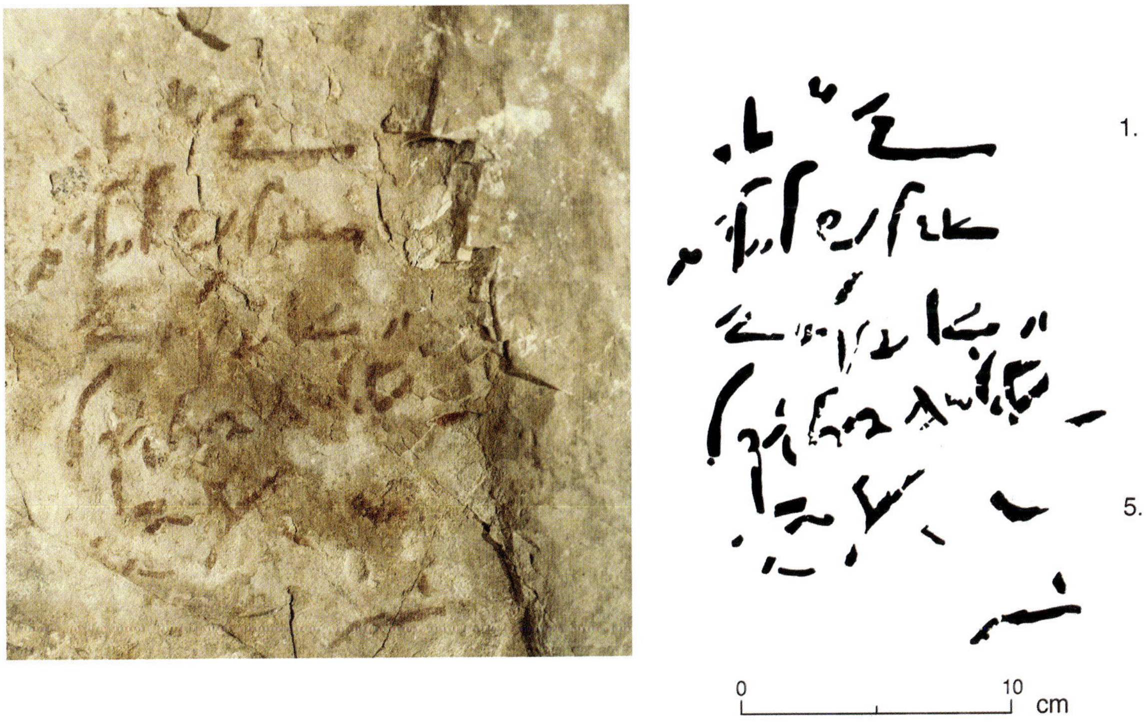

b. Graffito 29

c. Graffito 32

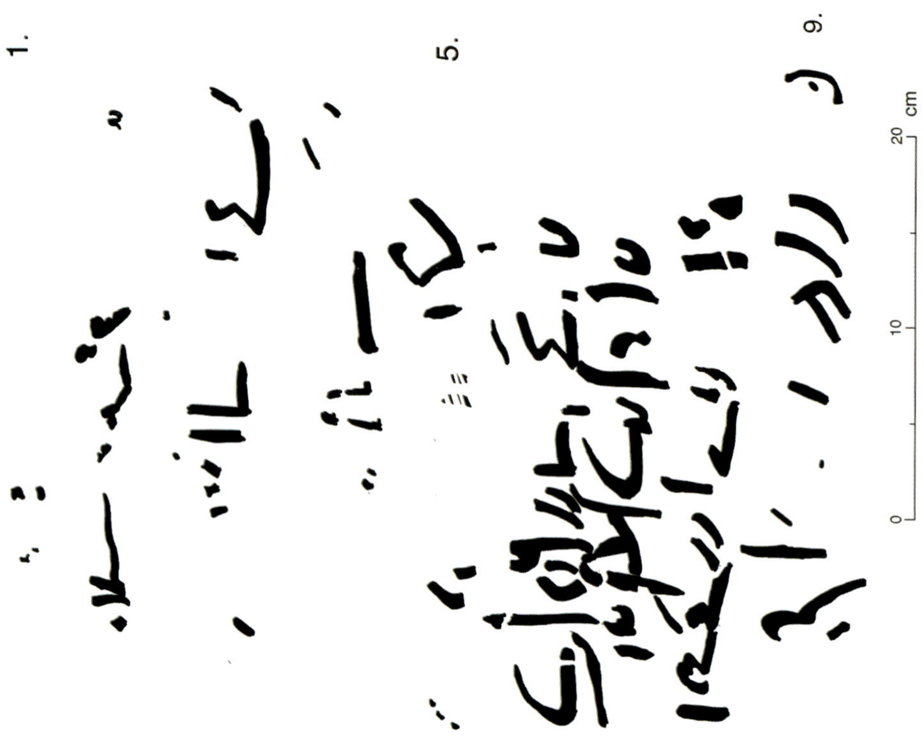

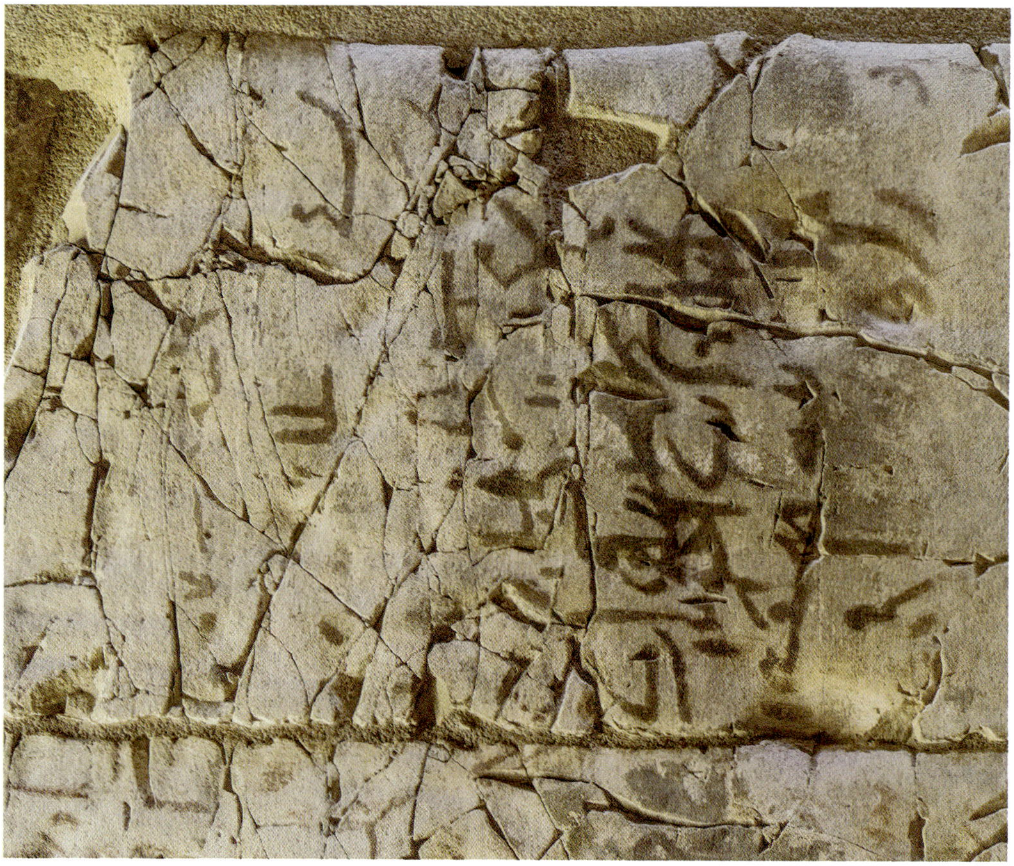

Graffito 30

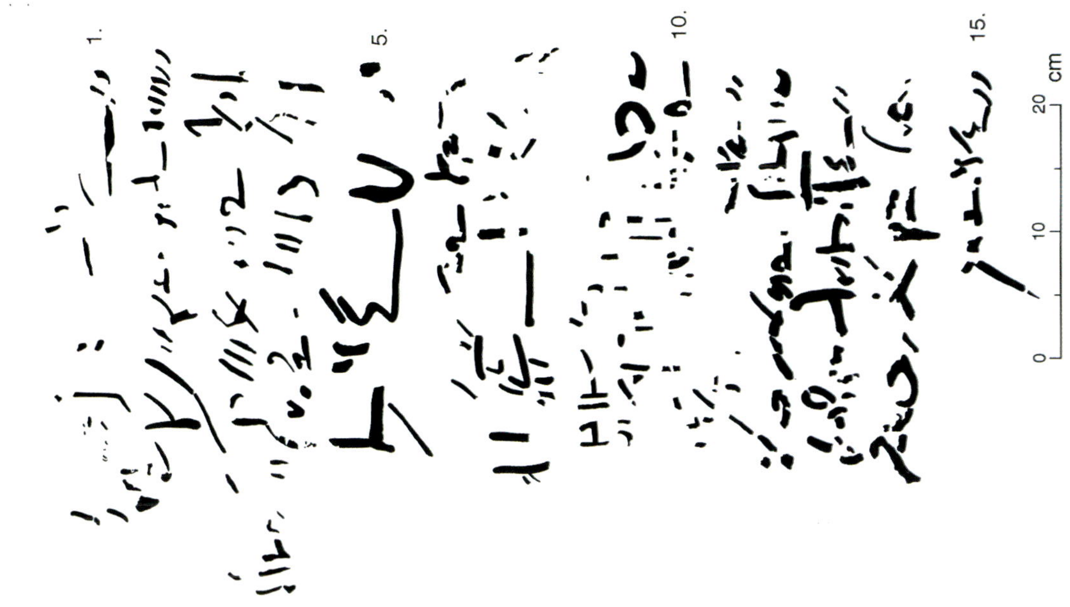

Graffito 31

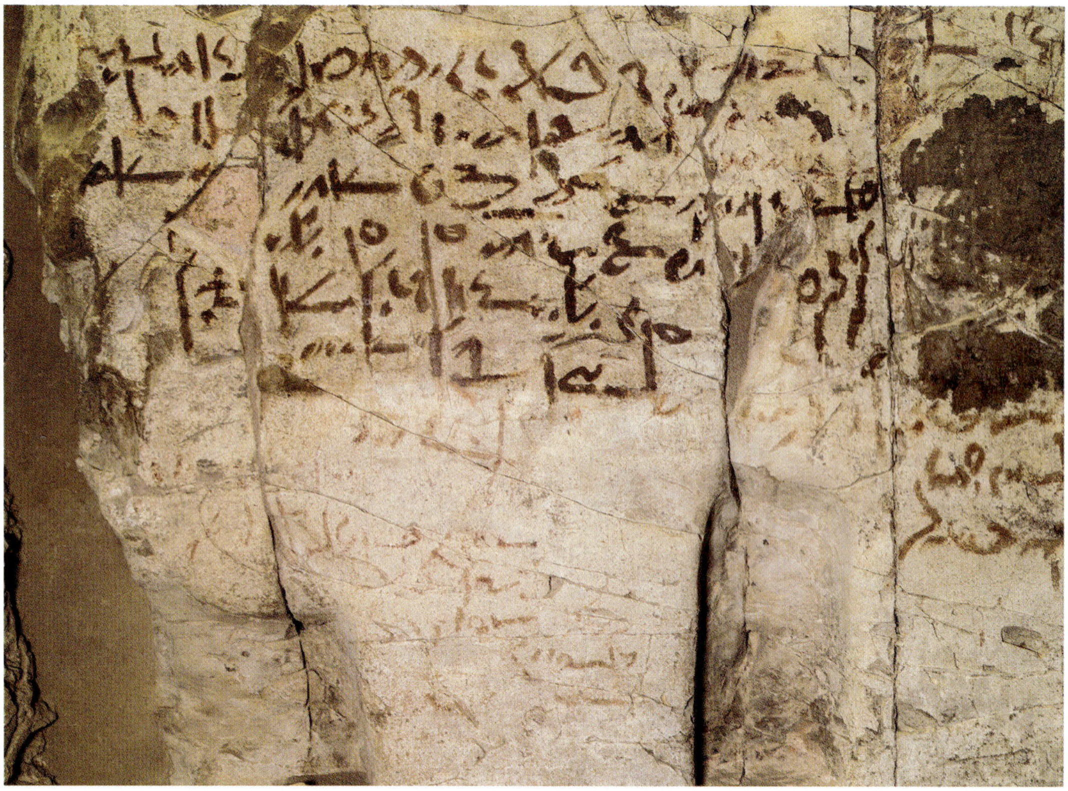

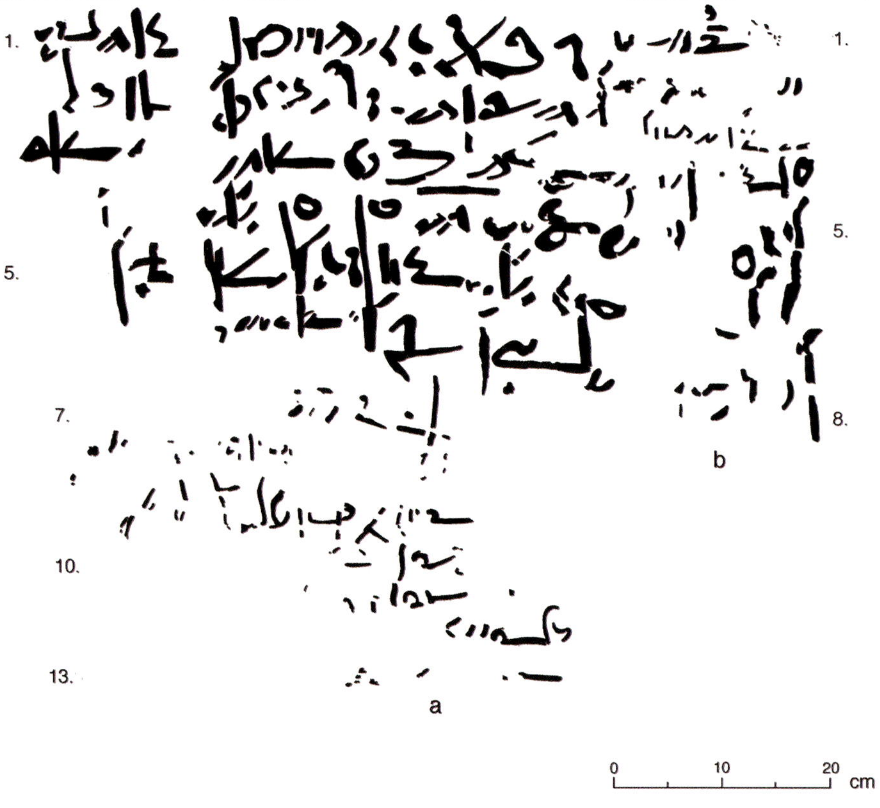

Graffito 33

Mid-cleaning

Pre-cleaning

Cleaned

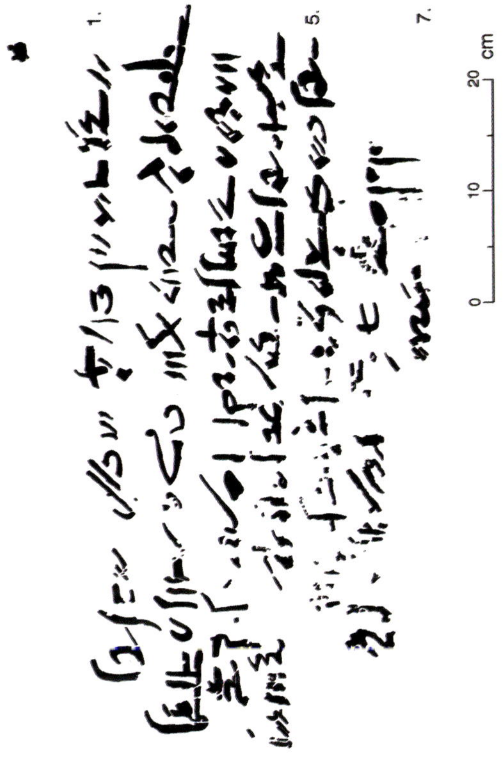

Graffito 34

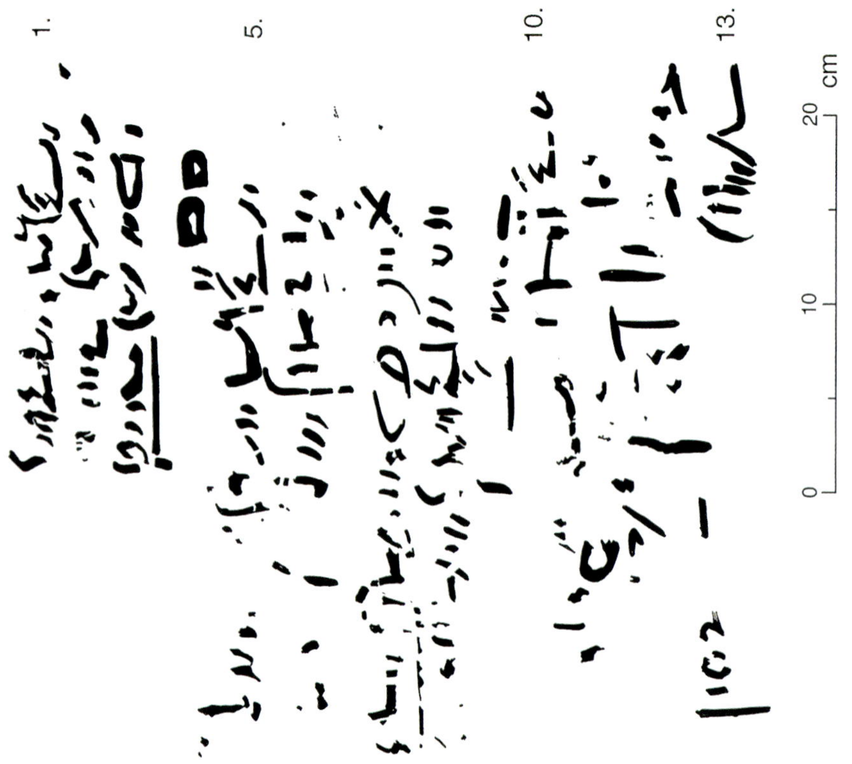

Graffito 35

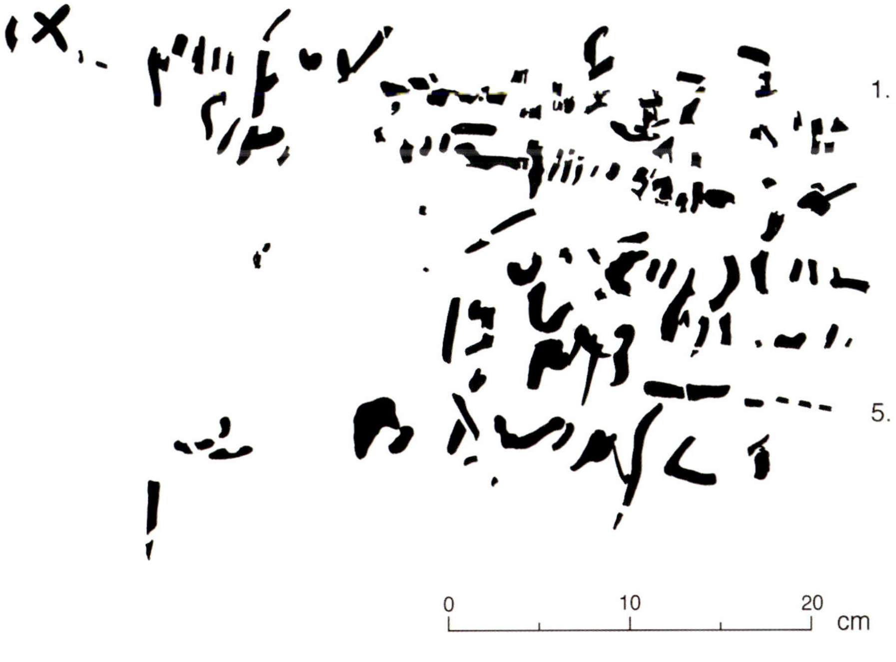

Graffito 36

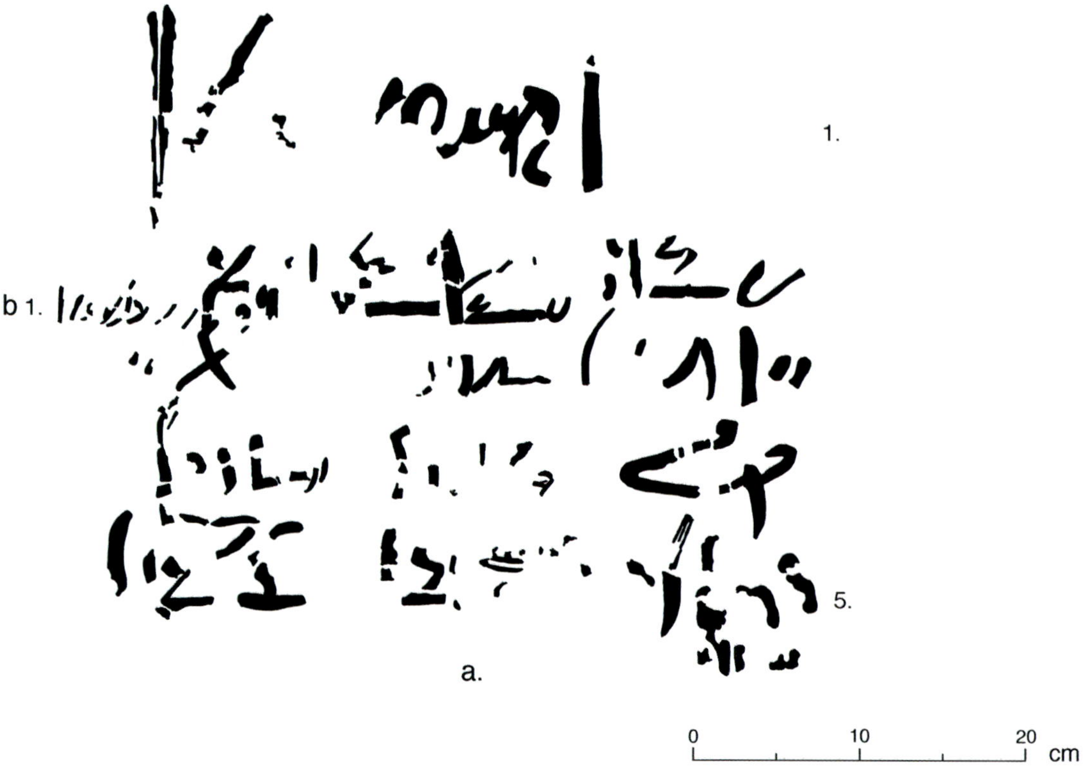

Graffito 37

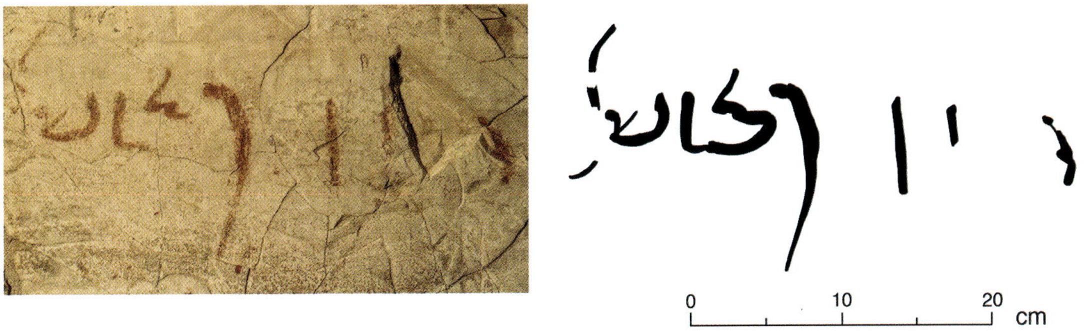

a. Graffito 38

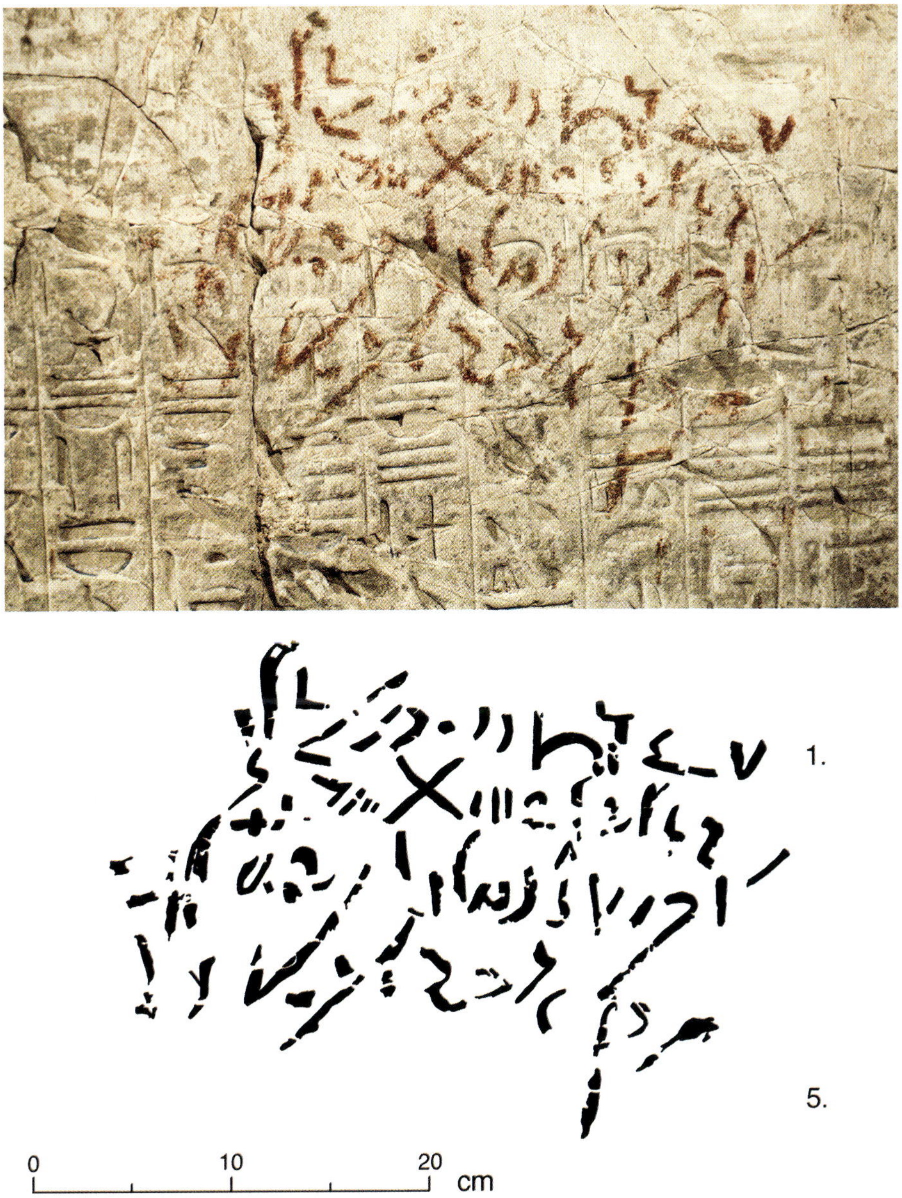

b. Graffito 39

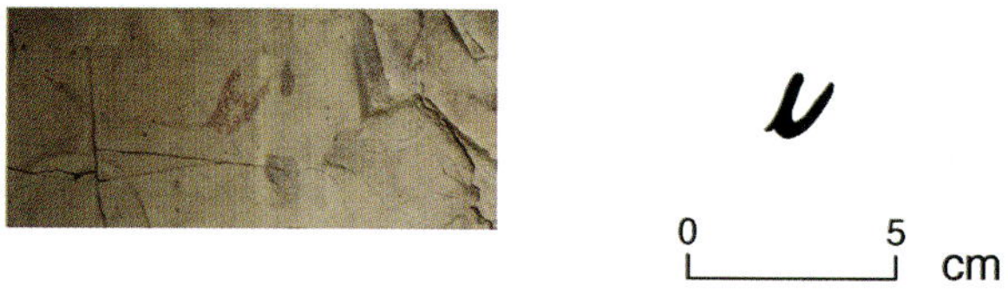

a. Graffito 40

b. Graffito 41

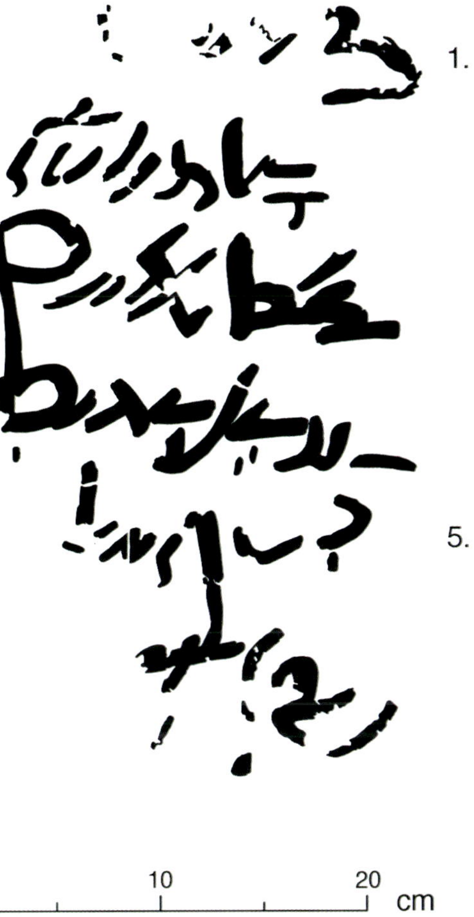

a. Graffito 42

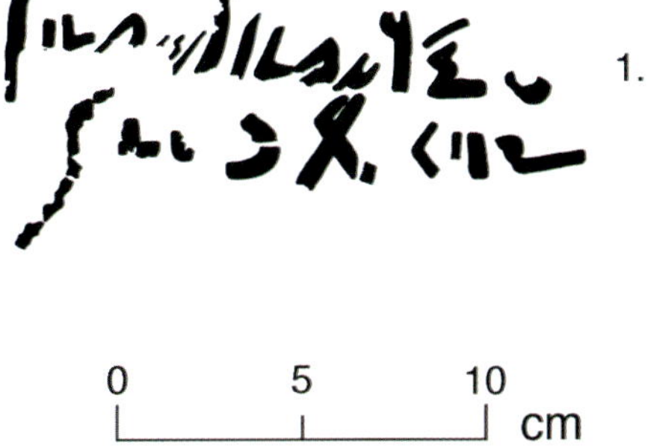

b. Graffito 43

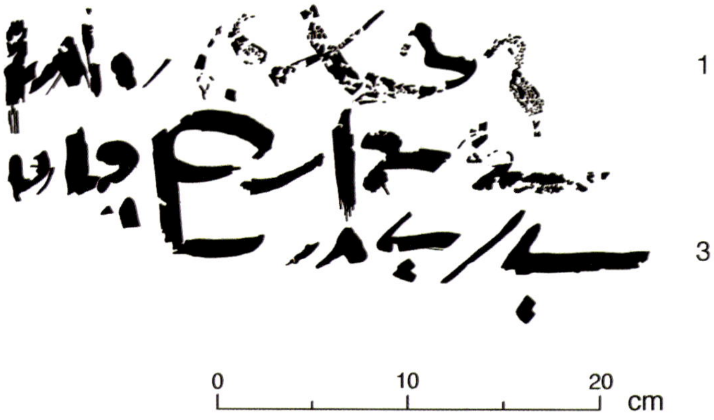

Graffito 44

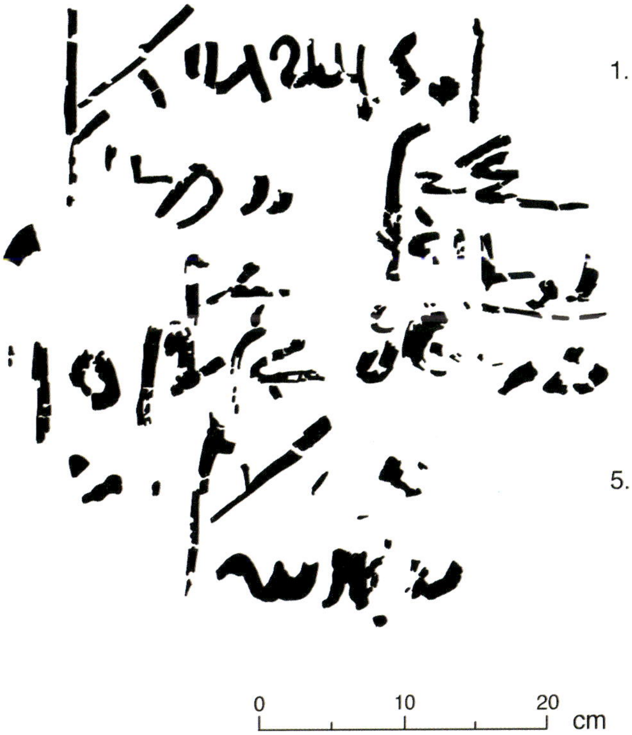

Graffito 45

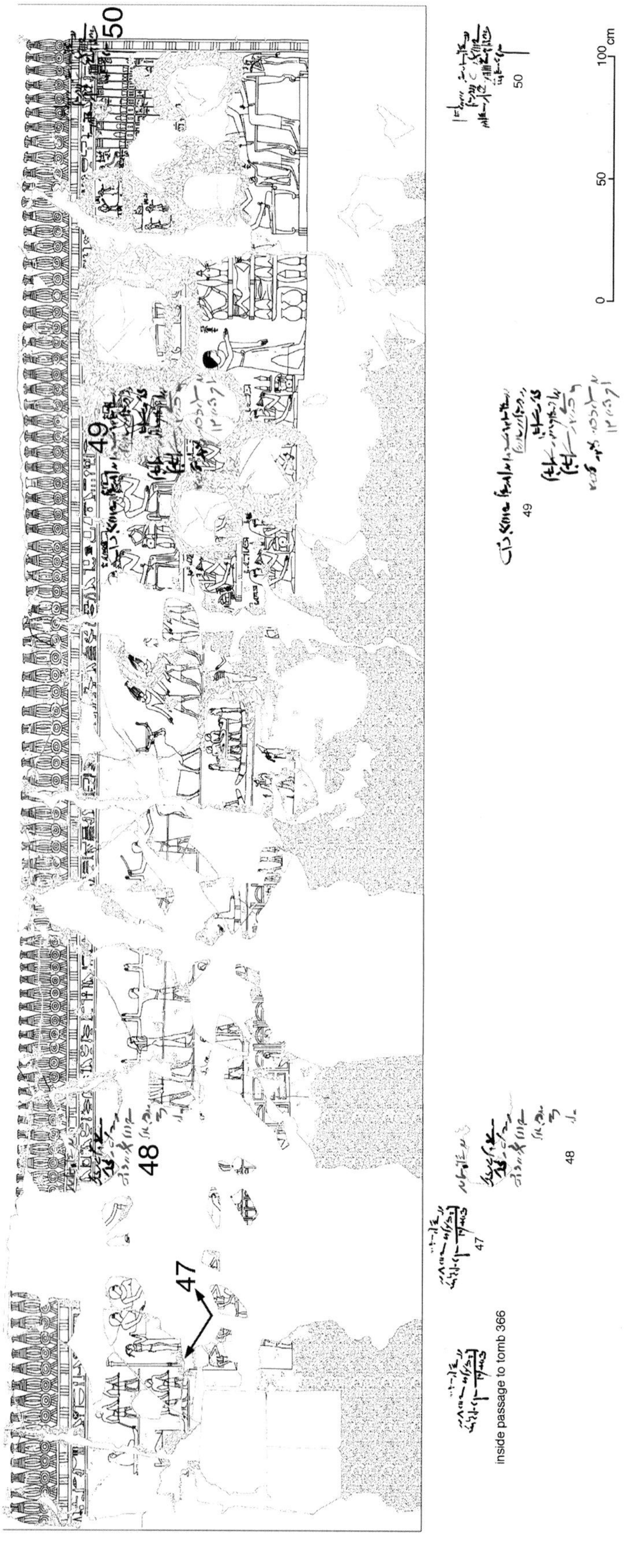

Keyplan of graffiti on S-wall in the tomb of Hery (TT 12). Drawing by G. Menéndez and J. M. Galán.

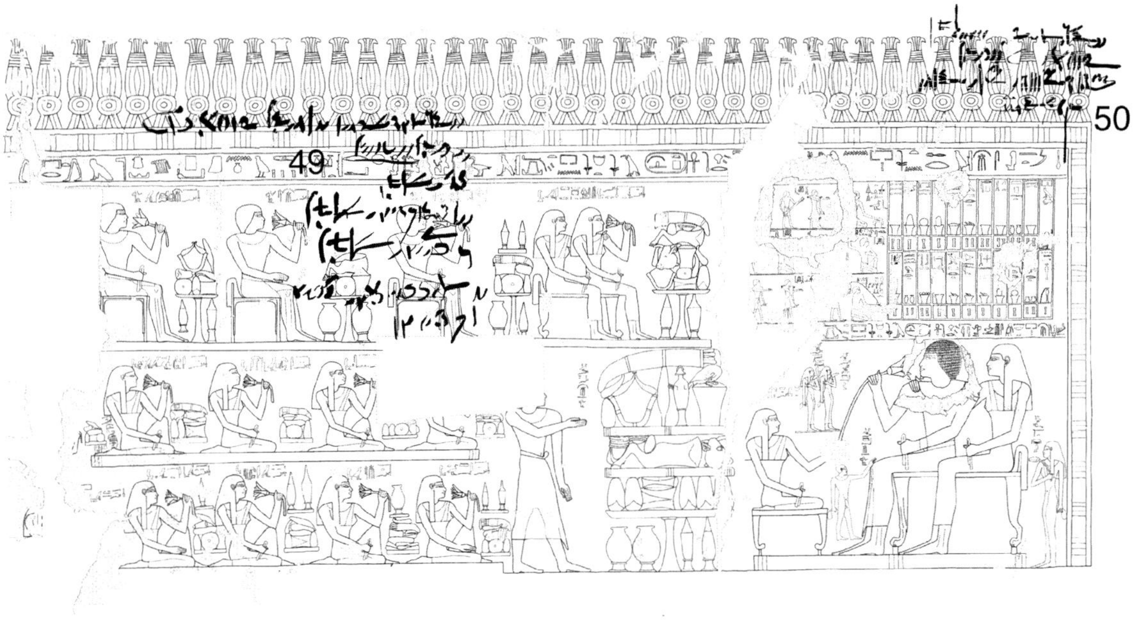

a. W-section of S-wall at the time of Spiegelberg (ca. 1896) with graffiti 49 and 50.

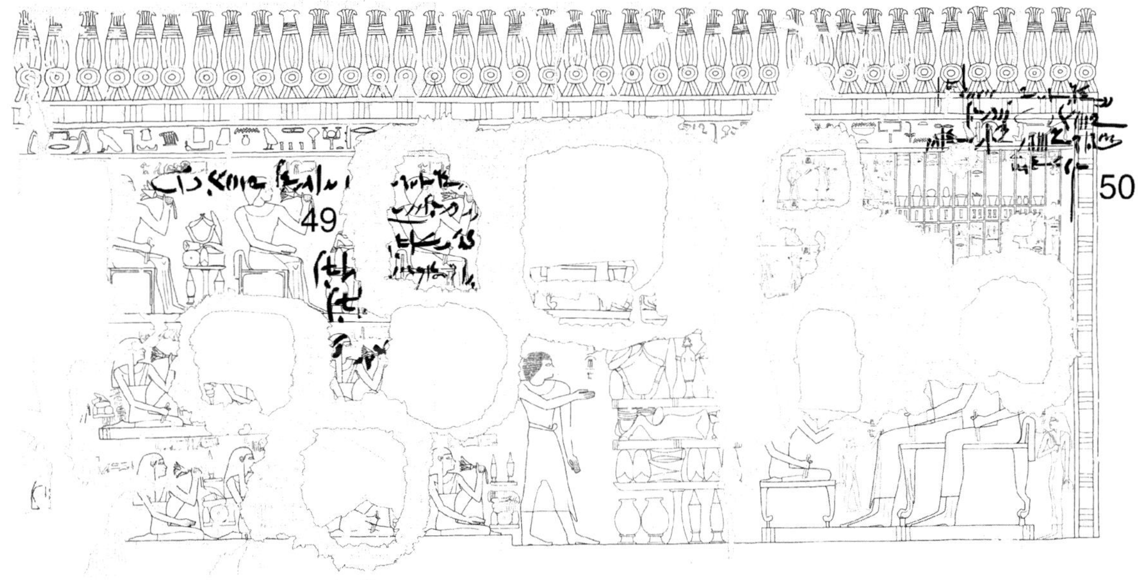

b. W-section of S-wall in present time (2019) with graffiti 49 and 50.

Detail of keyplan of graffiti on the W-section of the S-wall in the tomb of Hery (TT 12).
Drawing by G. Menéndez and J. M. Galán.

a. Graffito 46

b. Graffito 48

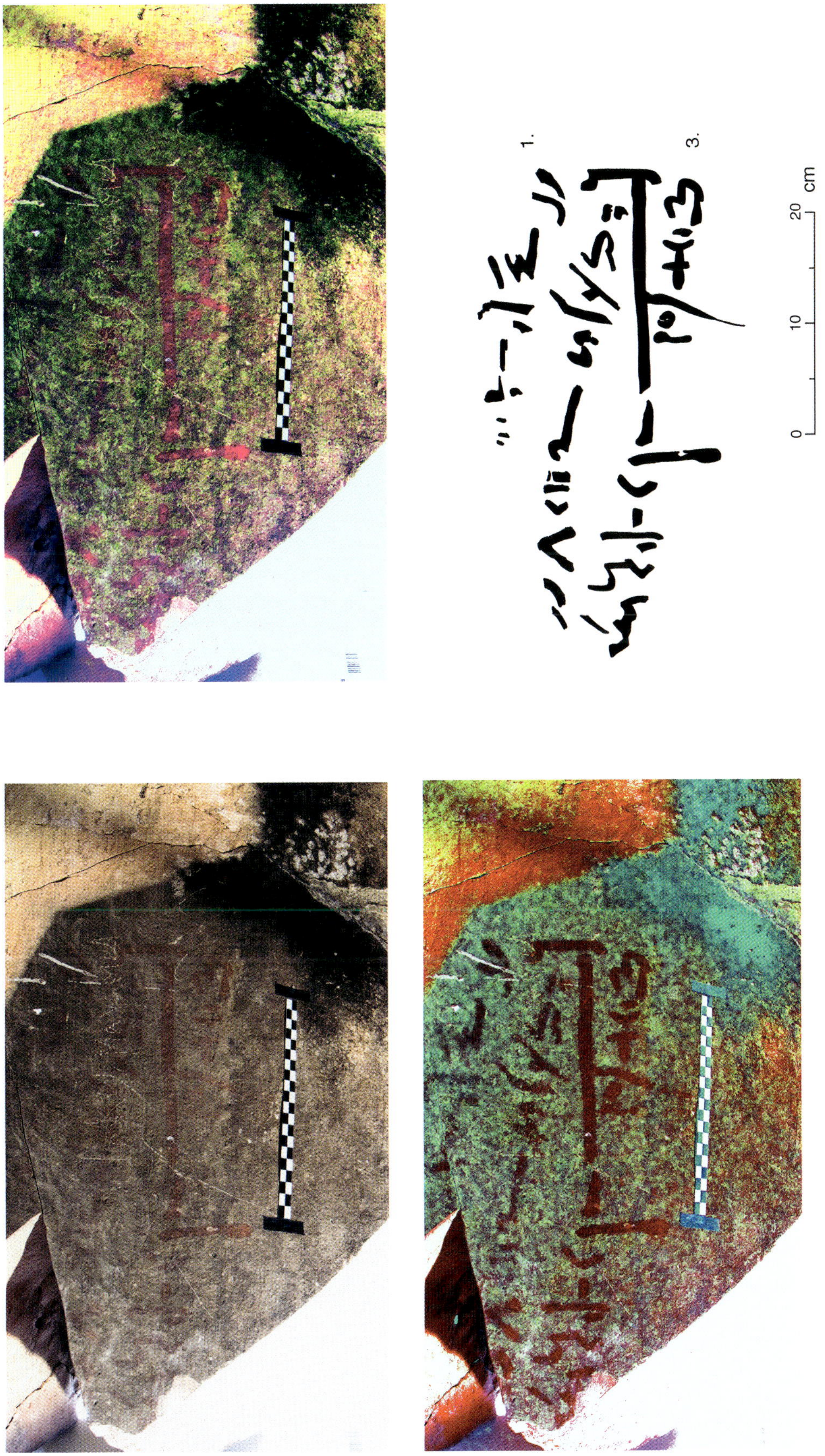

Graffito 47 (with DStretch images).

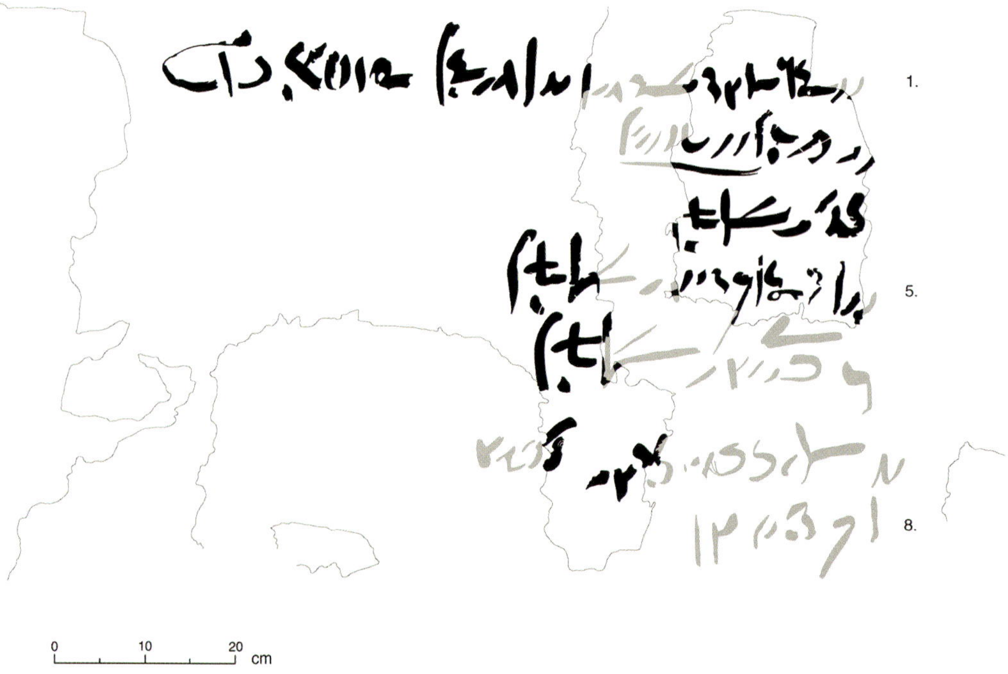

Graffito 49 in photograph and hand-copy with areas lost since the time of Spiegelberg indicated in gray.

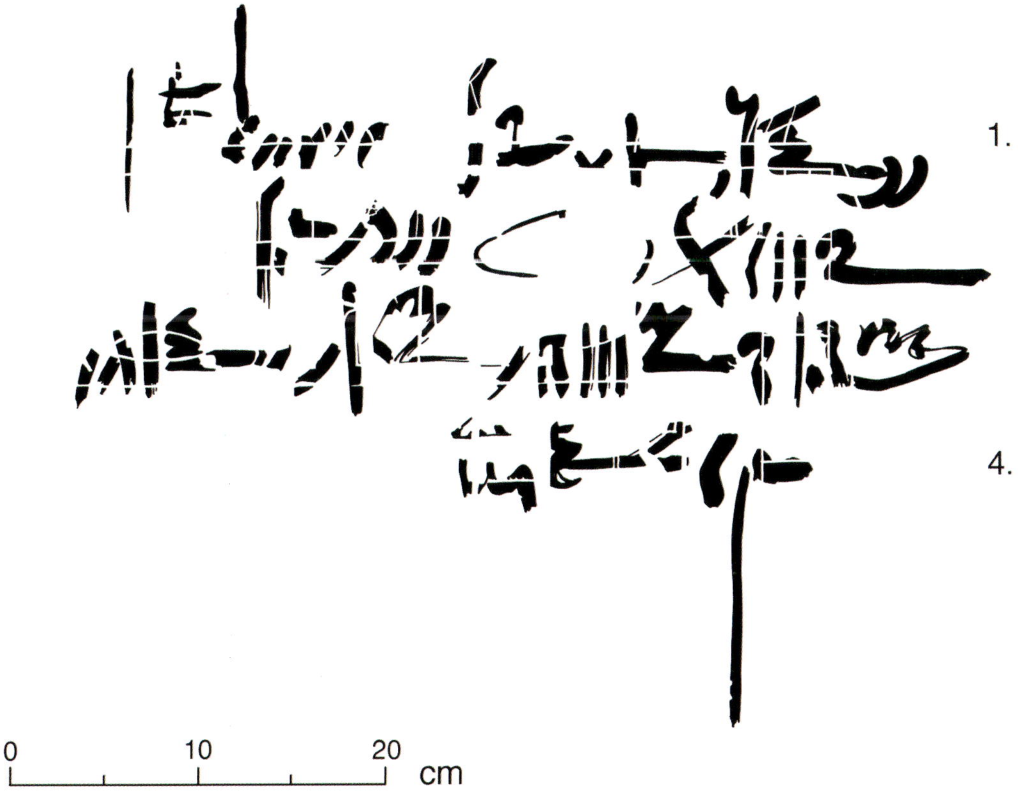

Graffito 50

Graffito 51

Graffiti 89, 90, 91, and 92 in general photograph.

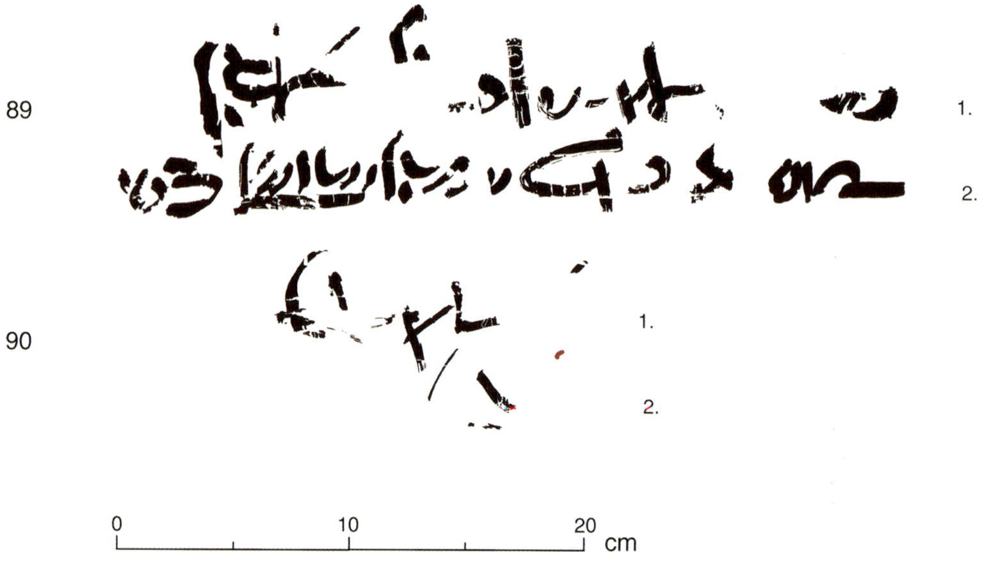

Graffiti 89 and 90

a. Graffito 91

b. Graffito 92

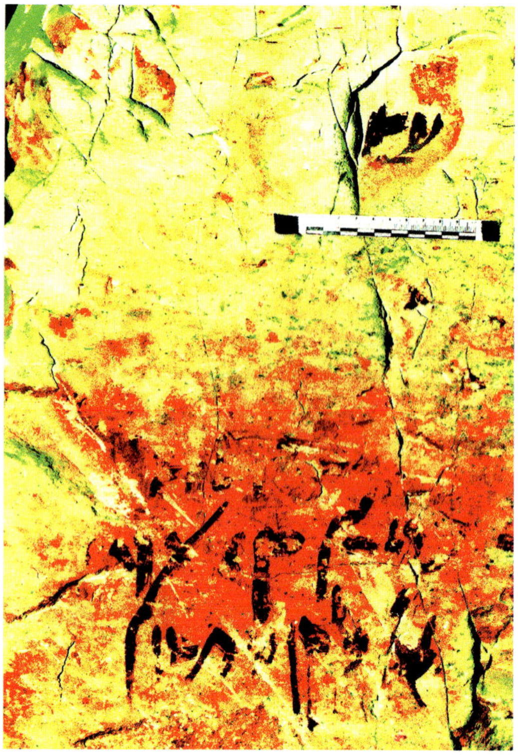

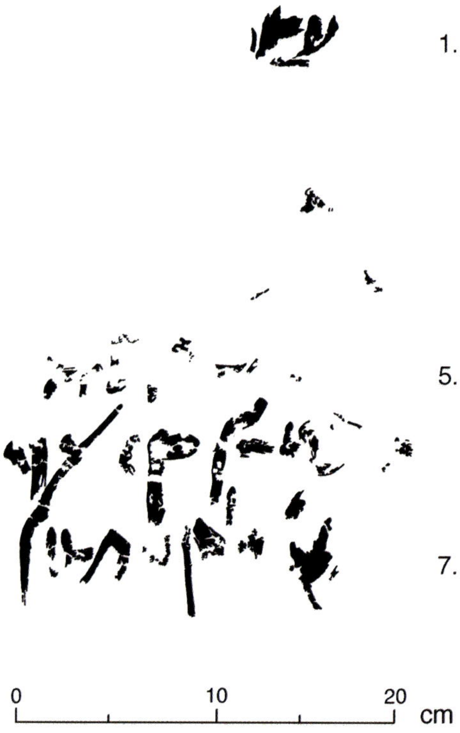

Graffito 52 (with DStretch images).

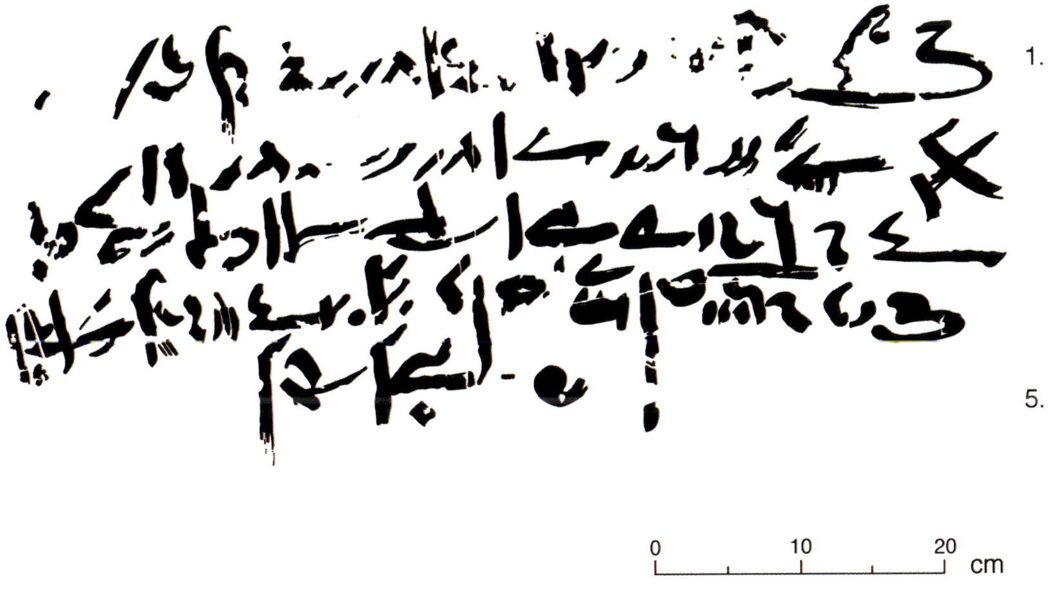

Graffito 53

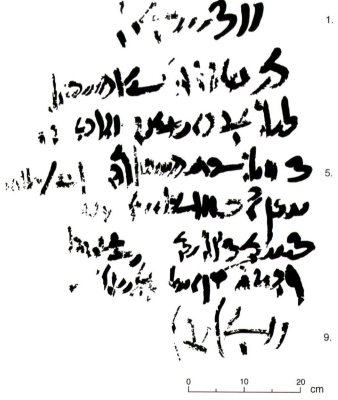

Graffito 54

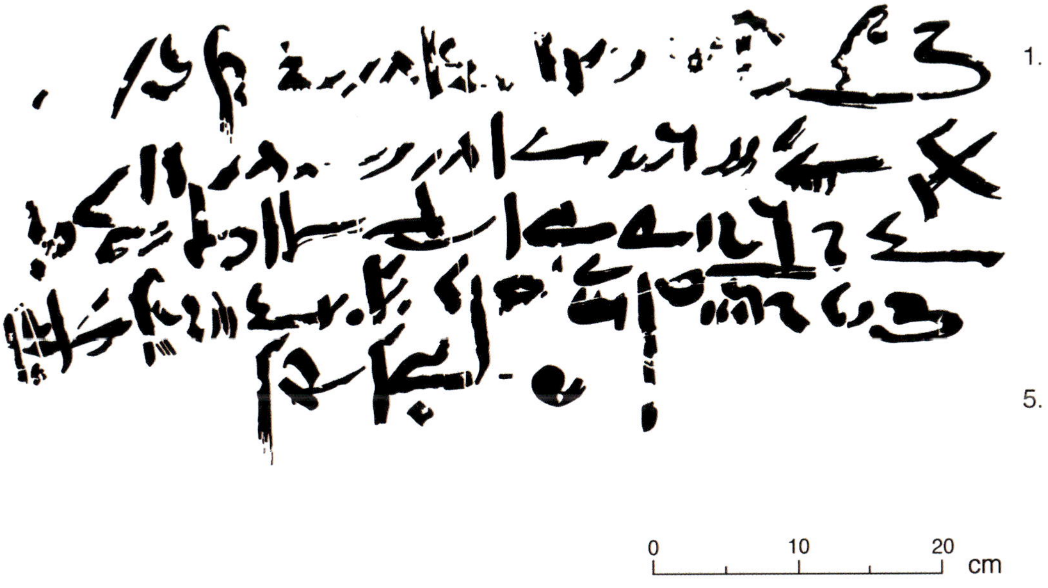

Graffito 53

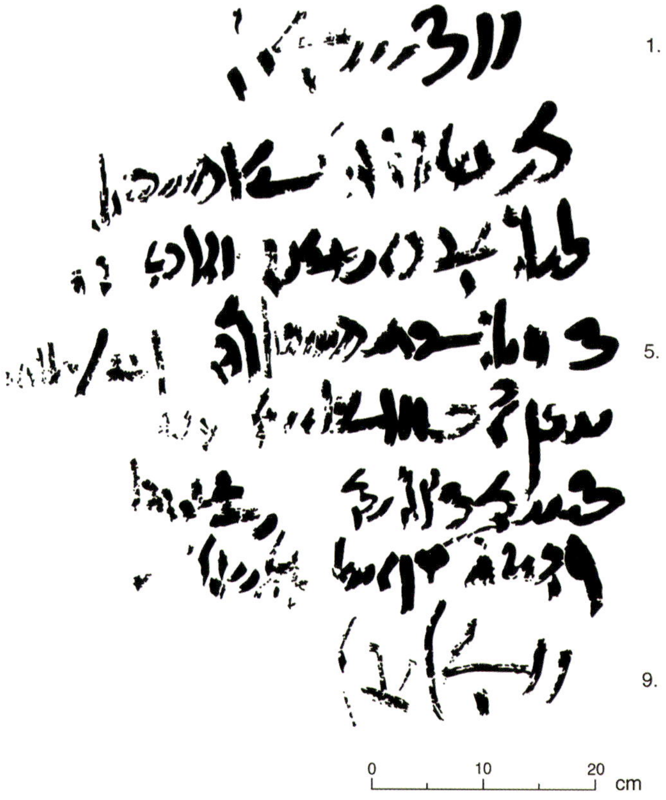

Graffito 54

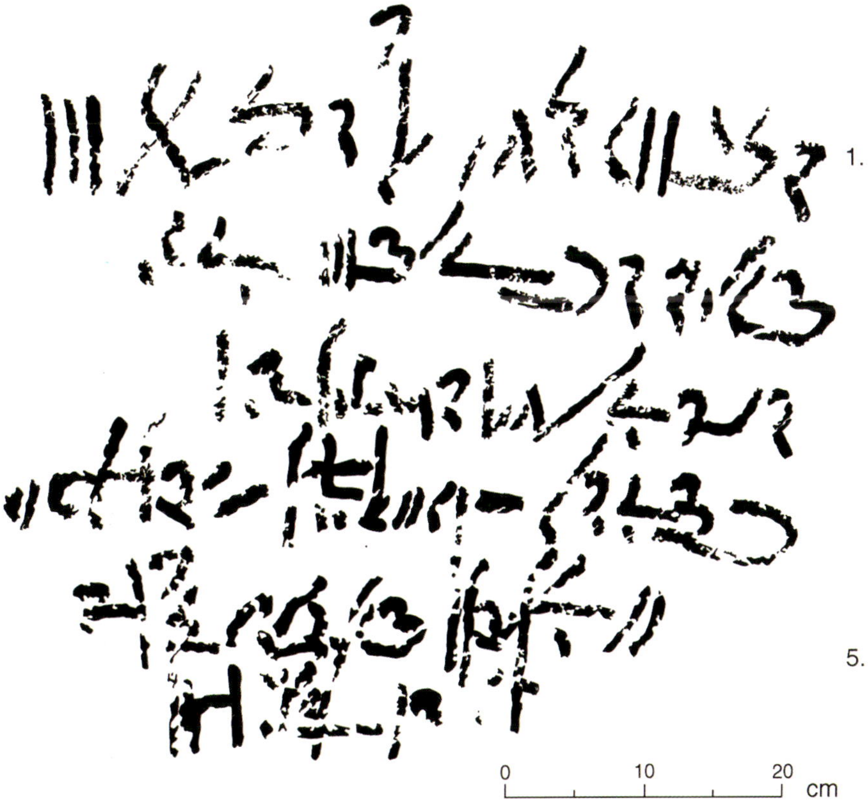

Graffito 55

Graffito 56 (with DStretch image).

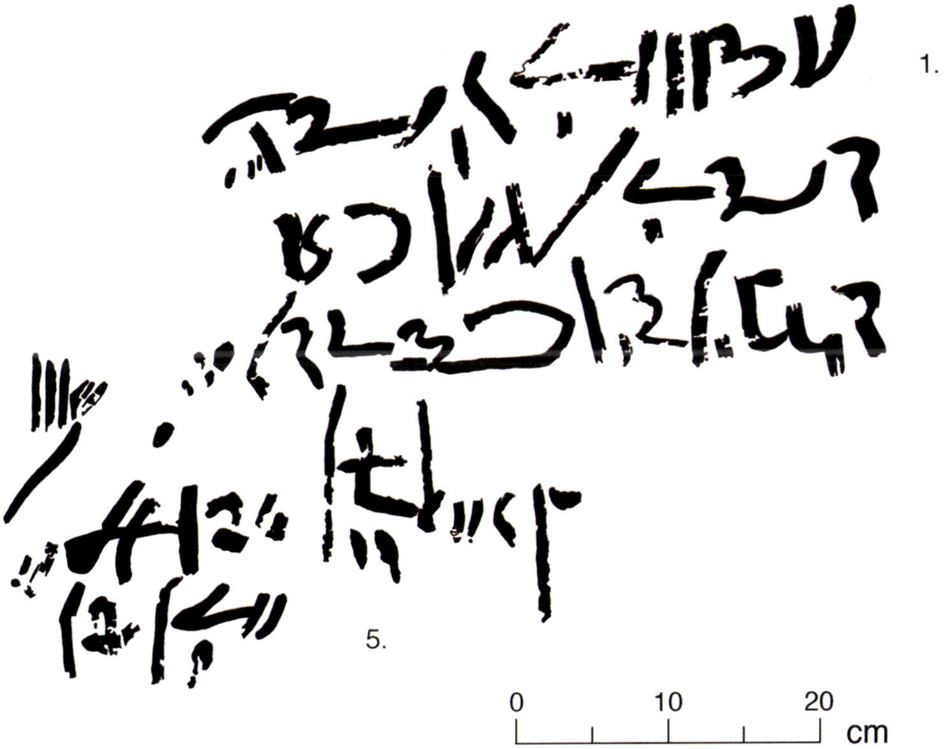

Graffito 57

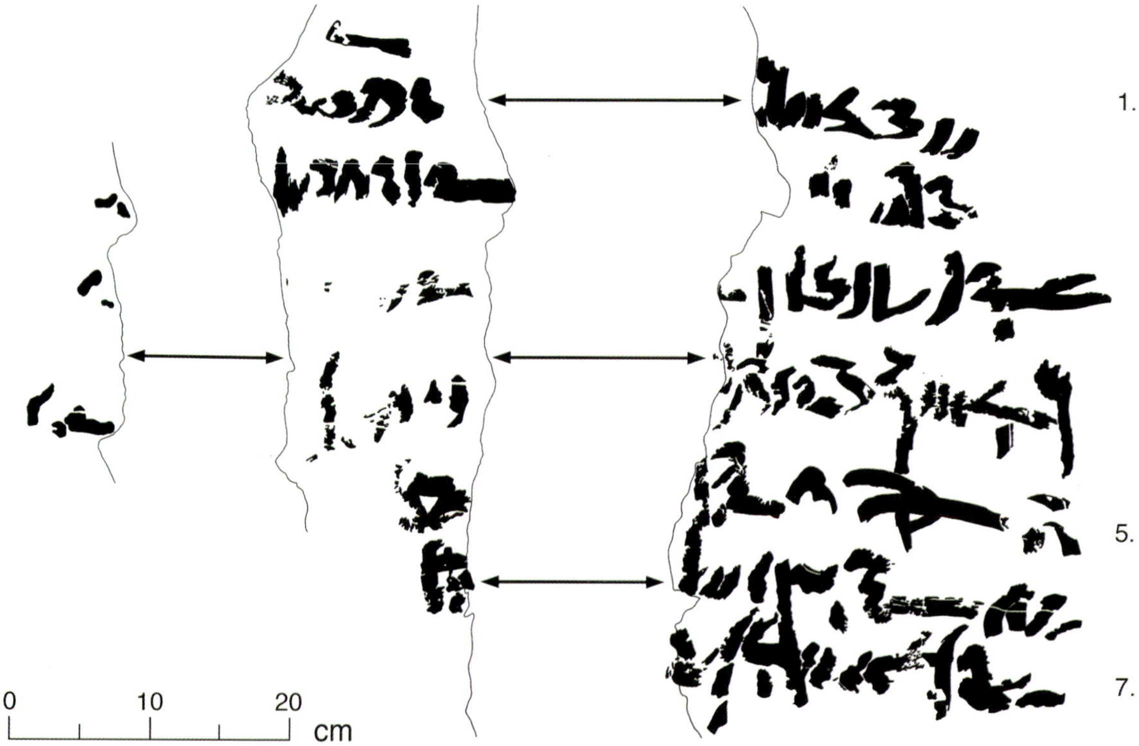

Graffito 58 (arrows indicate that the text continues around the corner or bend in the wall).

a. Graffito 59

b. Graffito 61

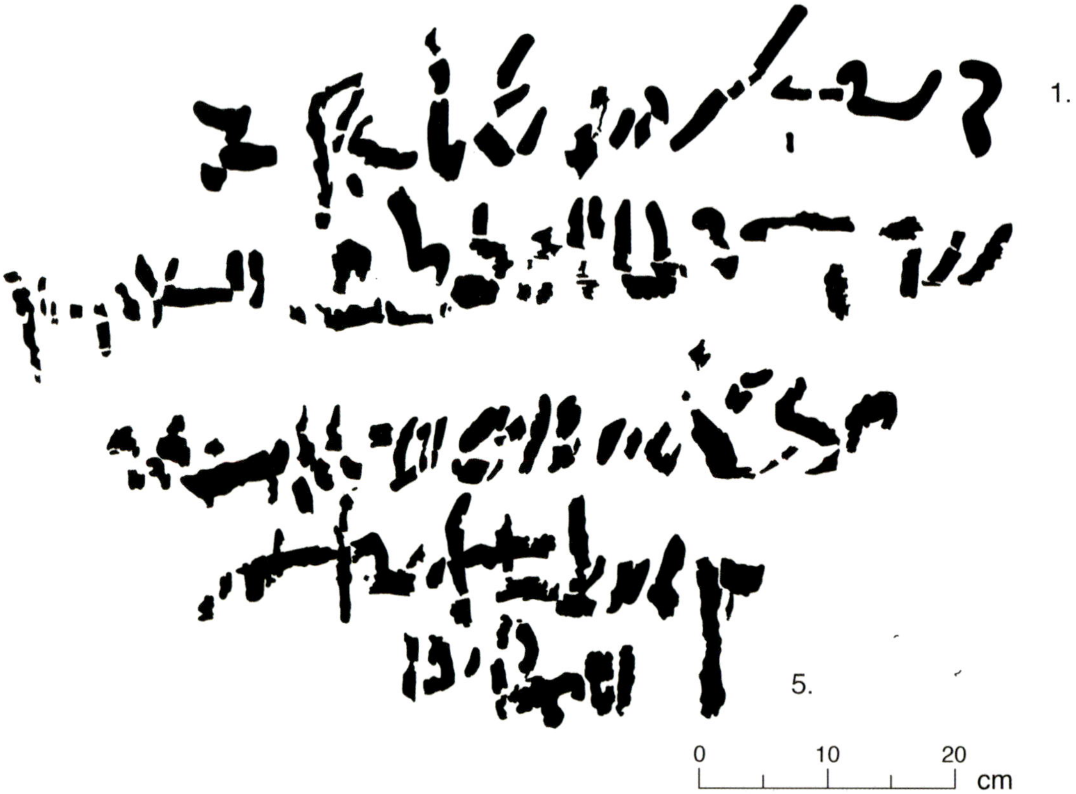

Graffito 60

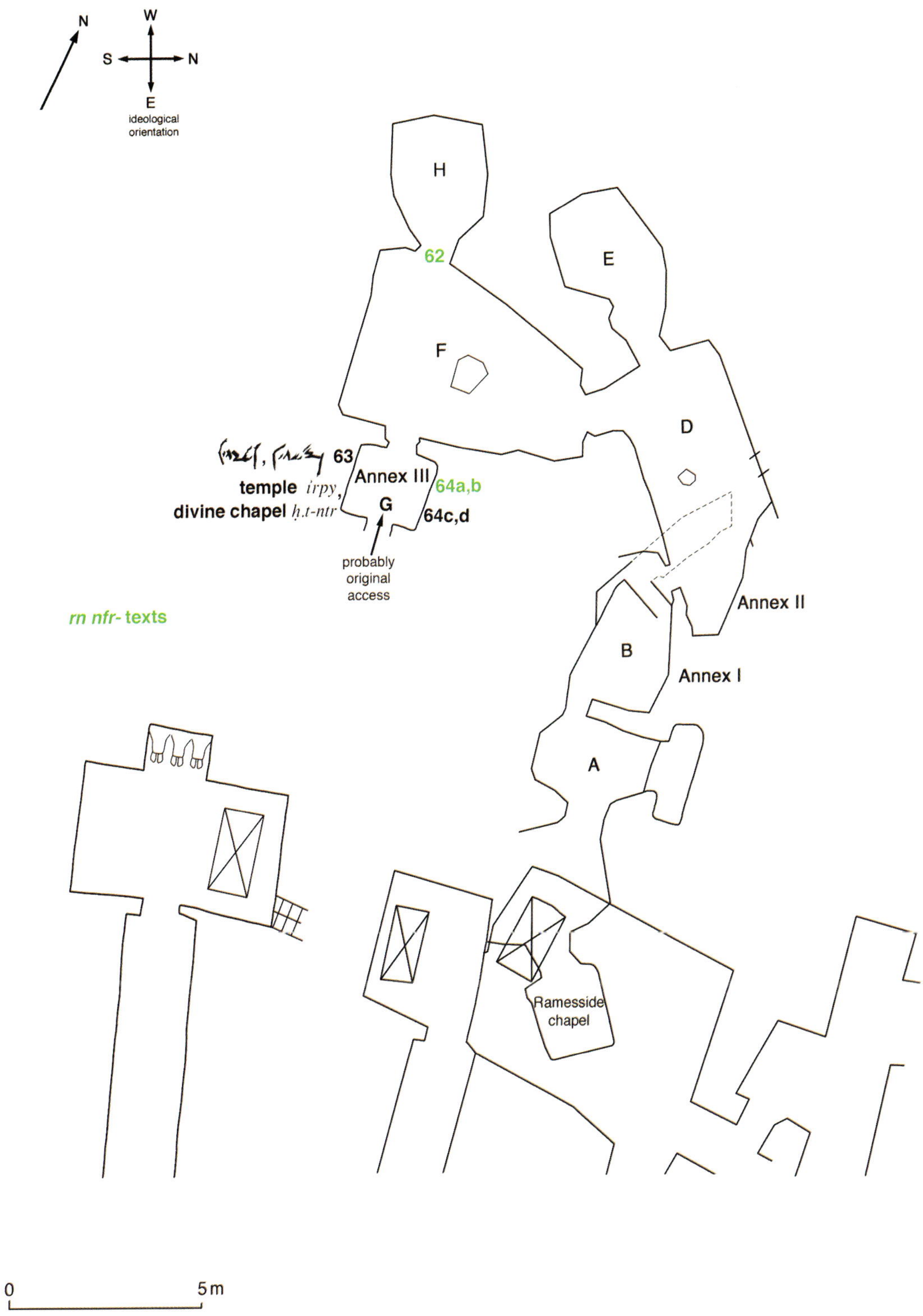

Keyplan of graffiti in Upper Gallery.

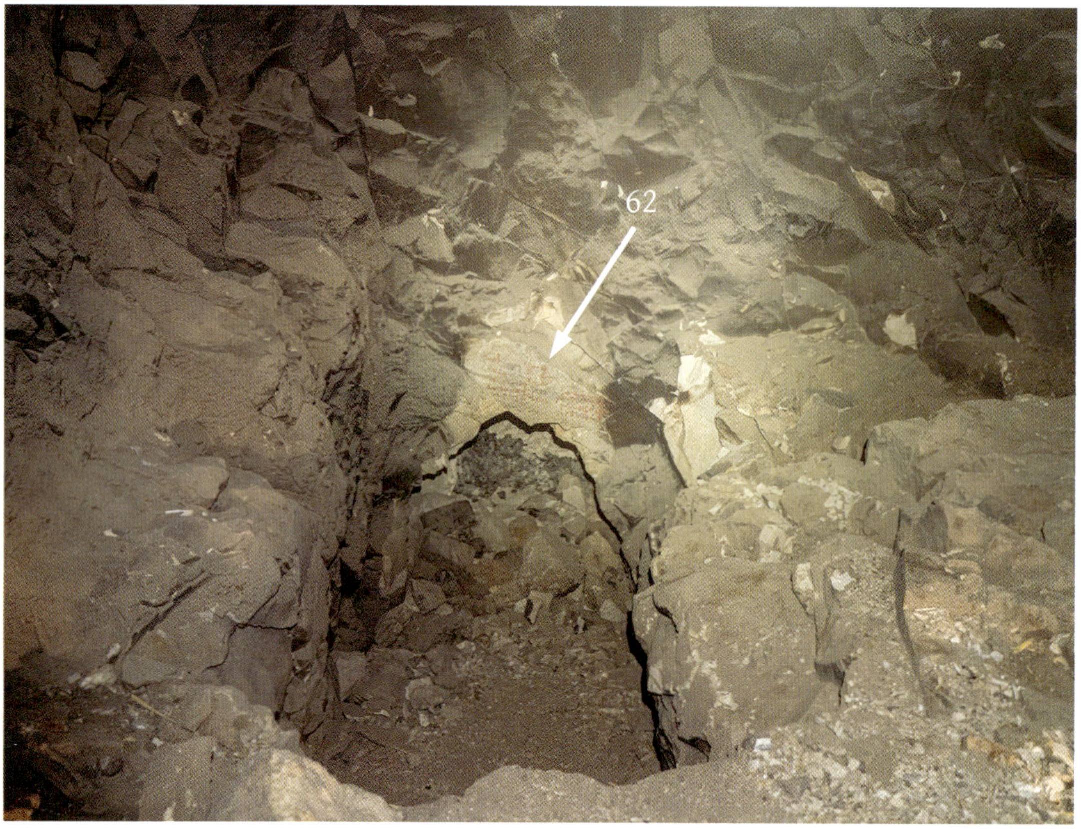

a. Entrance to chambers H in Upper Gallery with graffito 62.

b. Chamber G in Upper Gallery with graffiti 63 and 64.

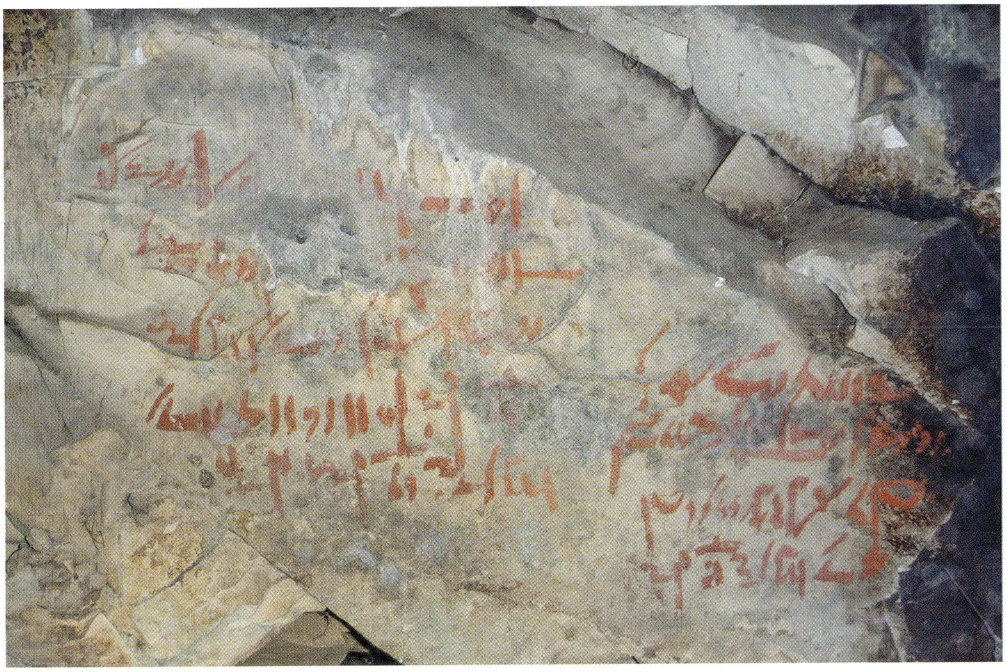

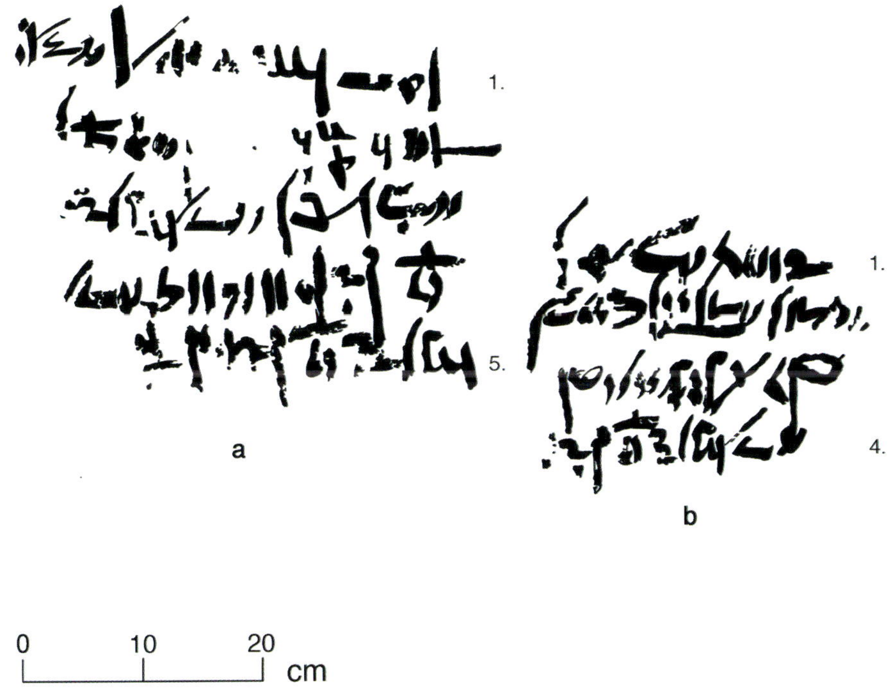

Graffito 62

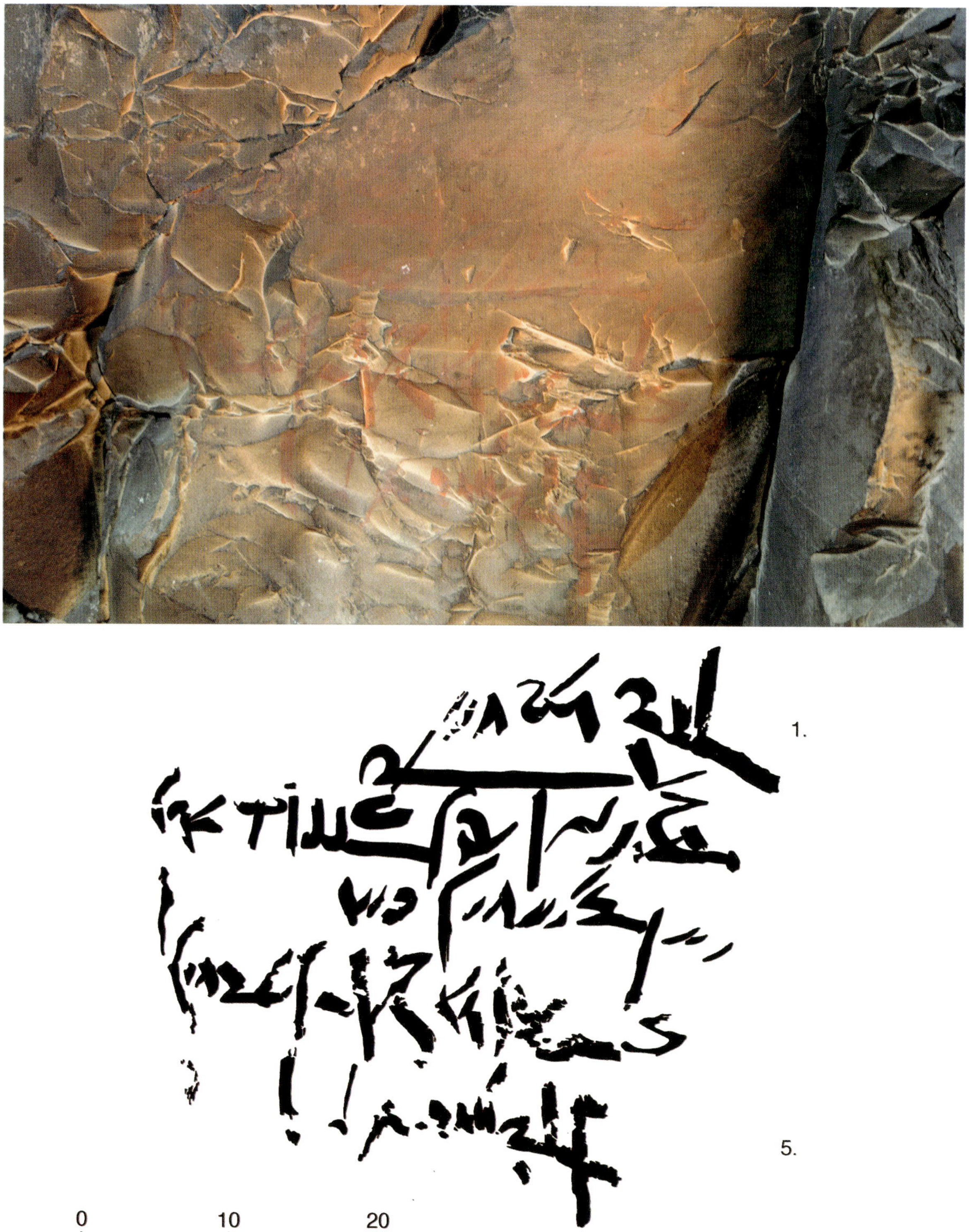

Graffito 63

Chamber G in Upper Gallery with graffiti 64a–d.

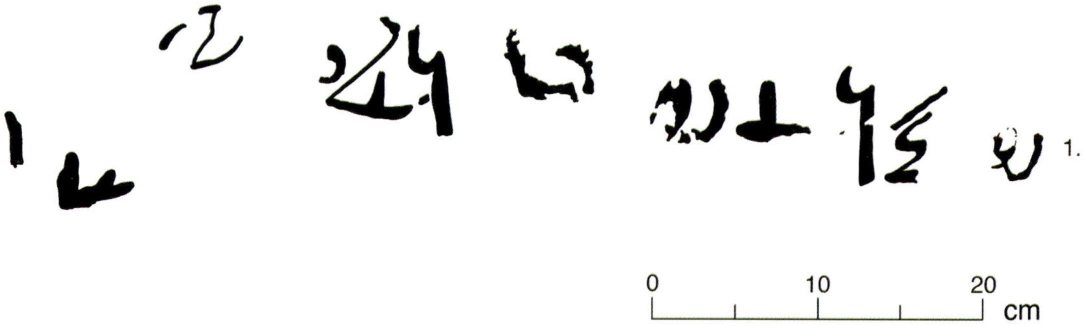

Graffito 64a (with DStretch image).

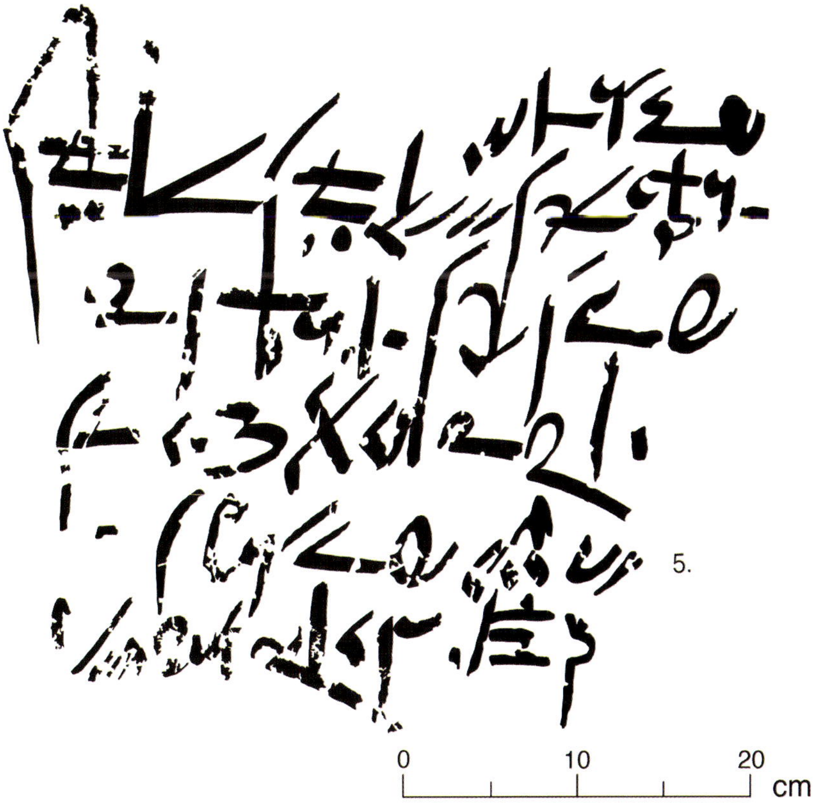

Graffito 64b (with DStretch image).

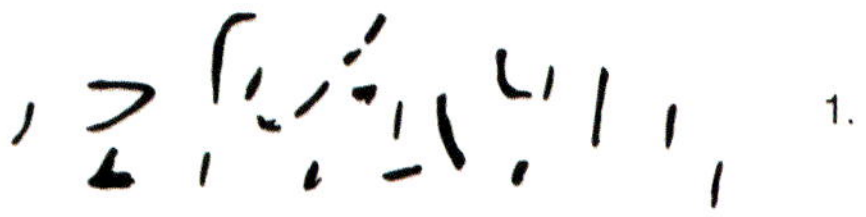

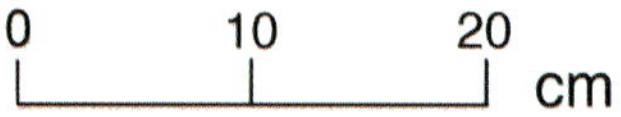

a. Graffito 64c

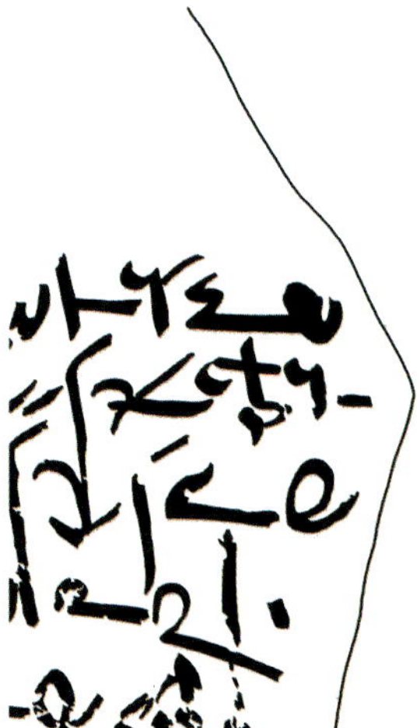

partially visible right side
of Graffito 64b

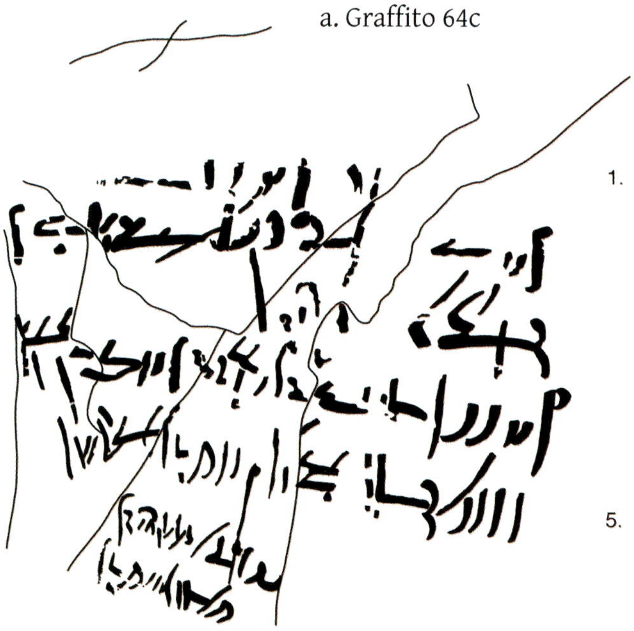

b. Graffito 64d

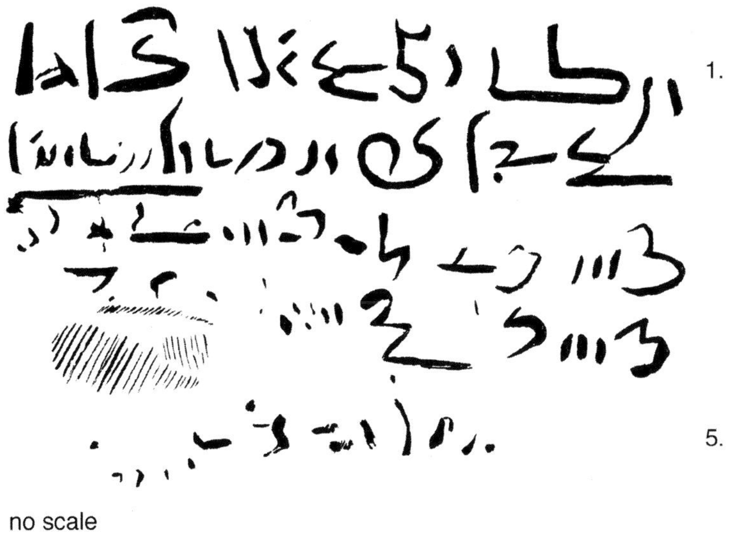

a. Graffito 65 (Spiegelberg hand-copy)

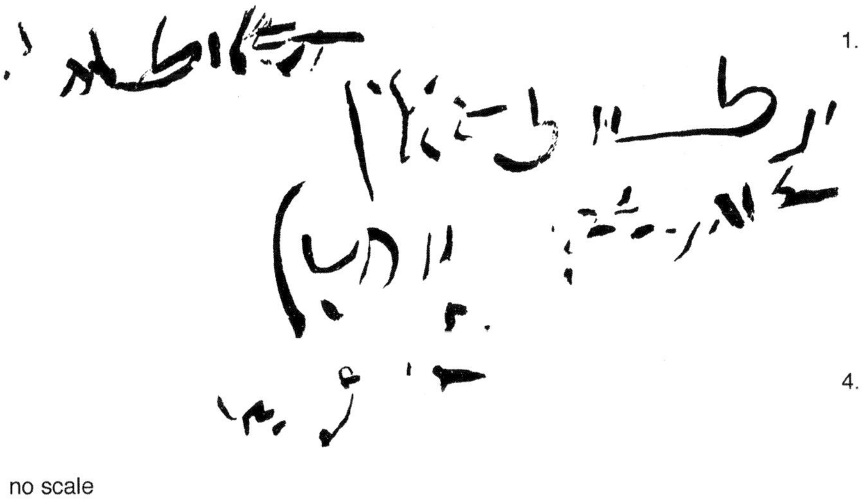

b. Graffito 66 (Spiegelberg hand-copy)

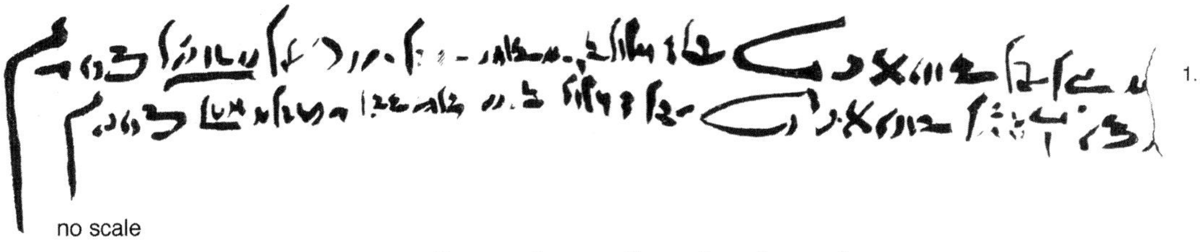

c. Graffito 67 (Spiegelberg hand-copy)

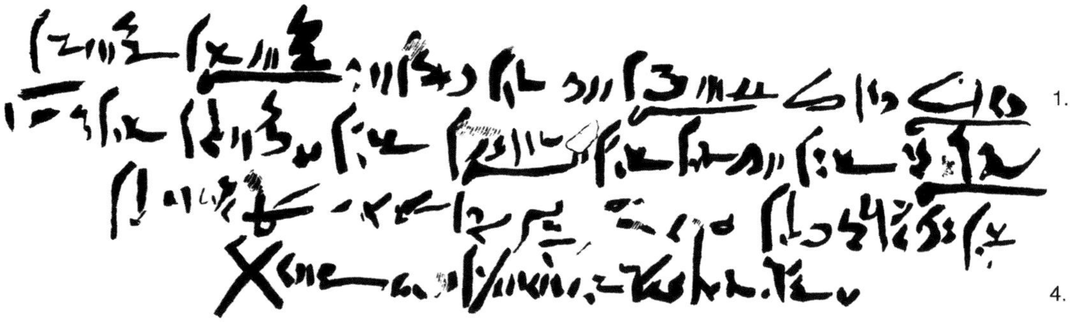

no scale

a. Graffito 68 (Spiegelberg hand-copy)

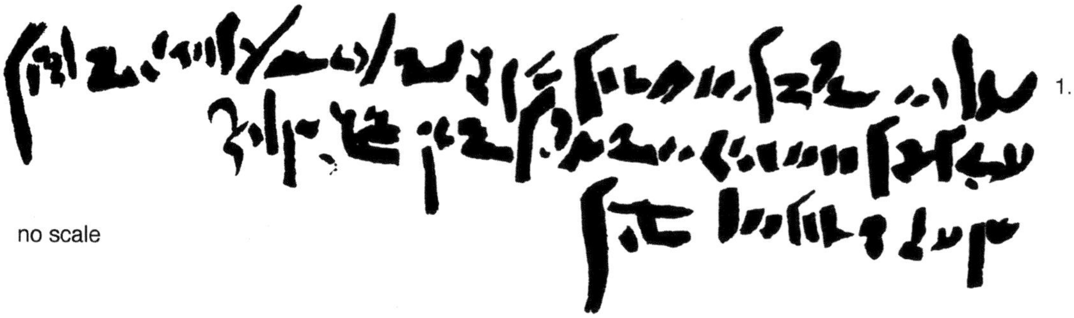

no scale

b. Graffito 69 (Spiegelberg hand-copy)

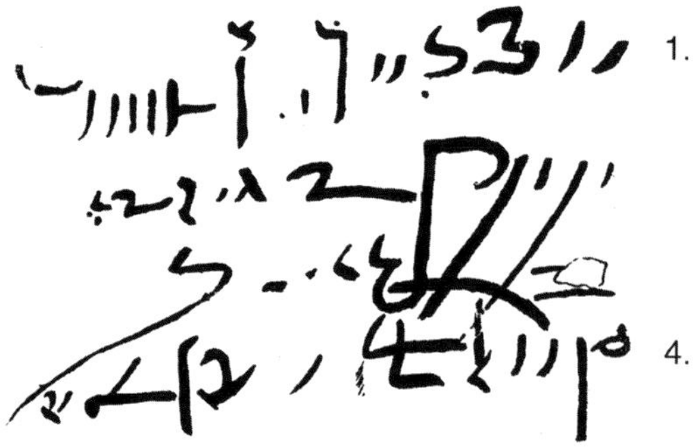

no scale

c. Graffito 70 (Spiegelberg hand-copy)

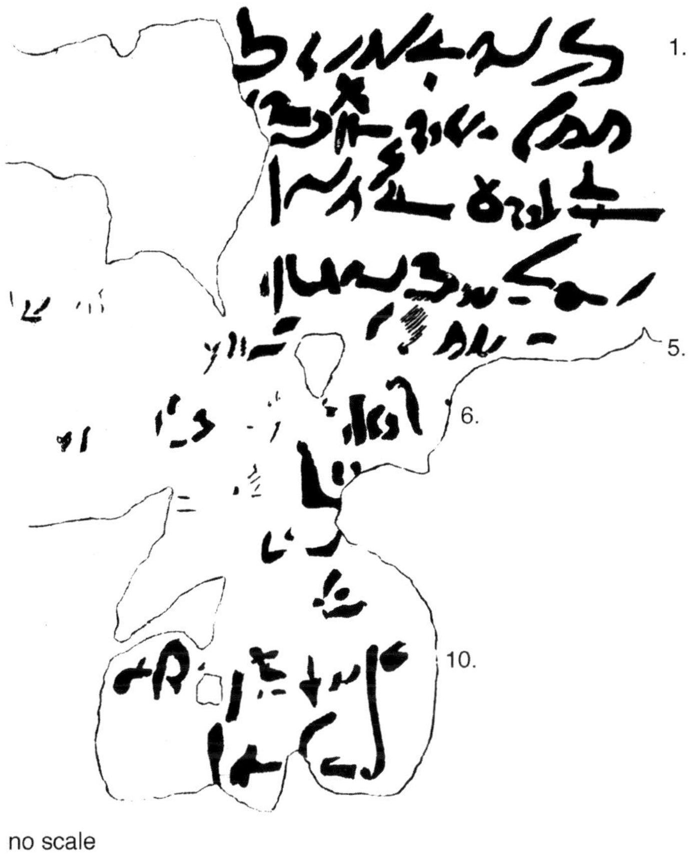

a. Graffito 71 (Spiegelberg hand-copy)

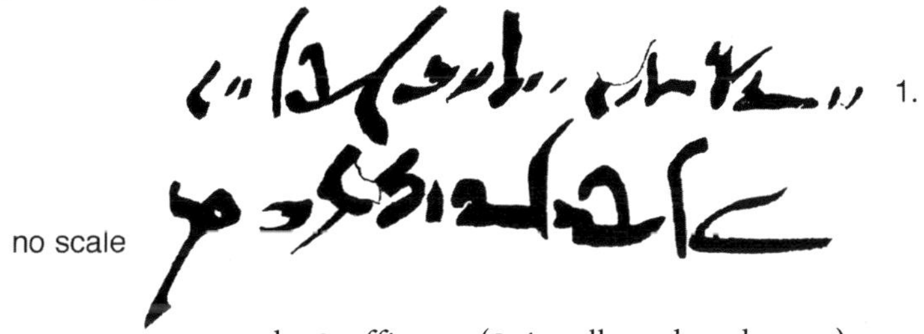

b. Graffito 72 (Spiegelberg hand-copy)

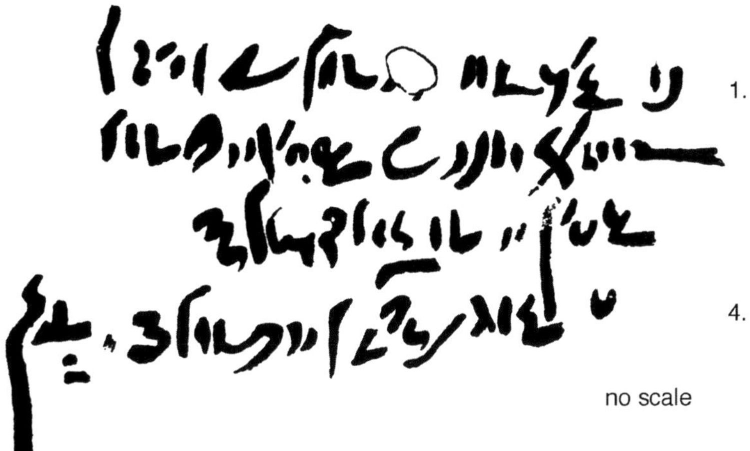

c. Graffito 73 (Spiegelberg hand-copy)

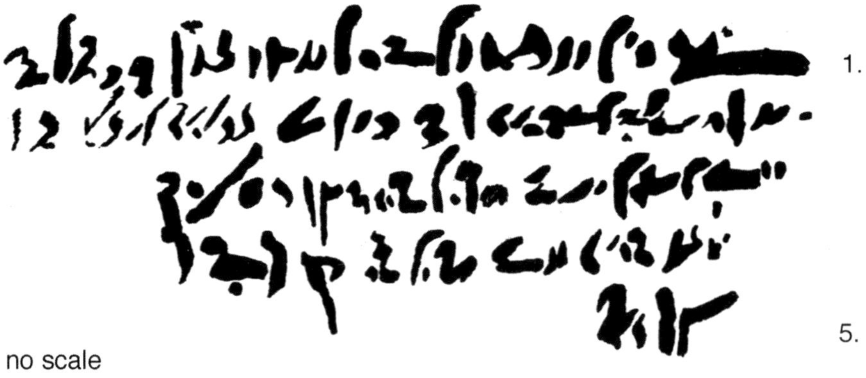

a. Graffito 74 (Spiegelberg hand-copy)

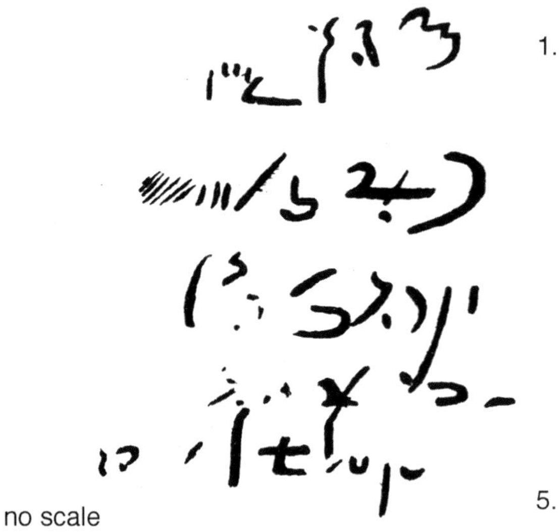

b. Graffito 75 (Spiegelberg hand-copy)

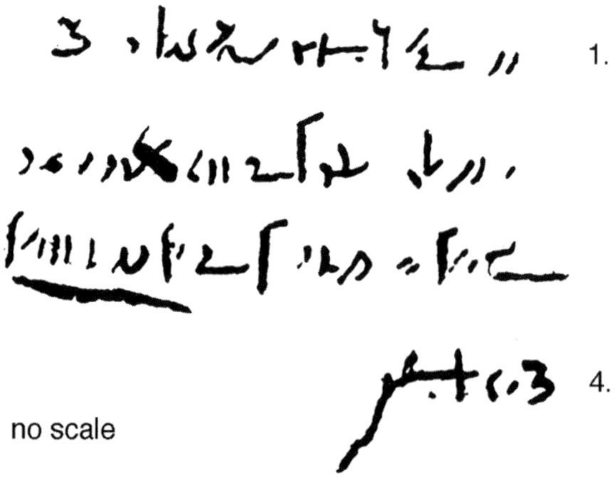

c. Graffito 79 (Spiegelberg hand-copy)

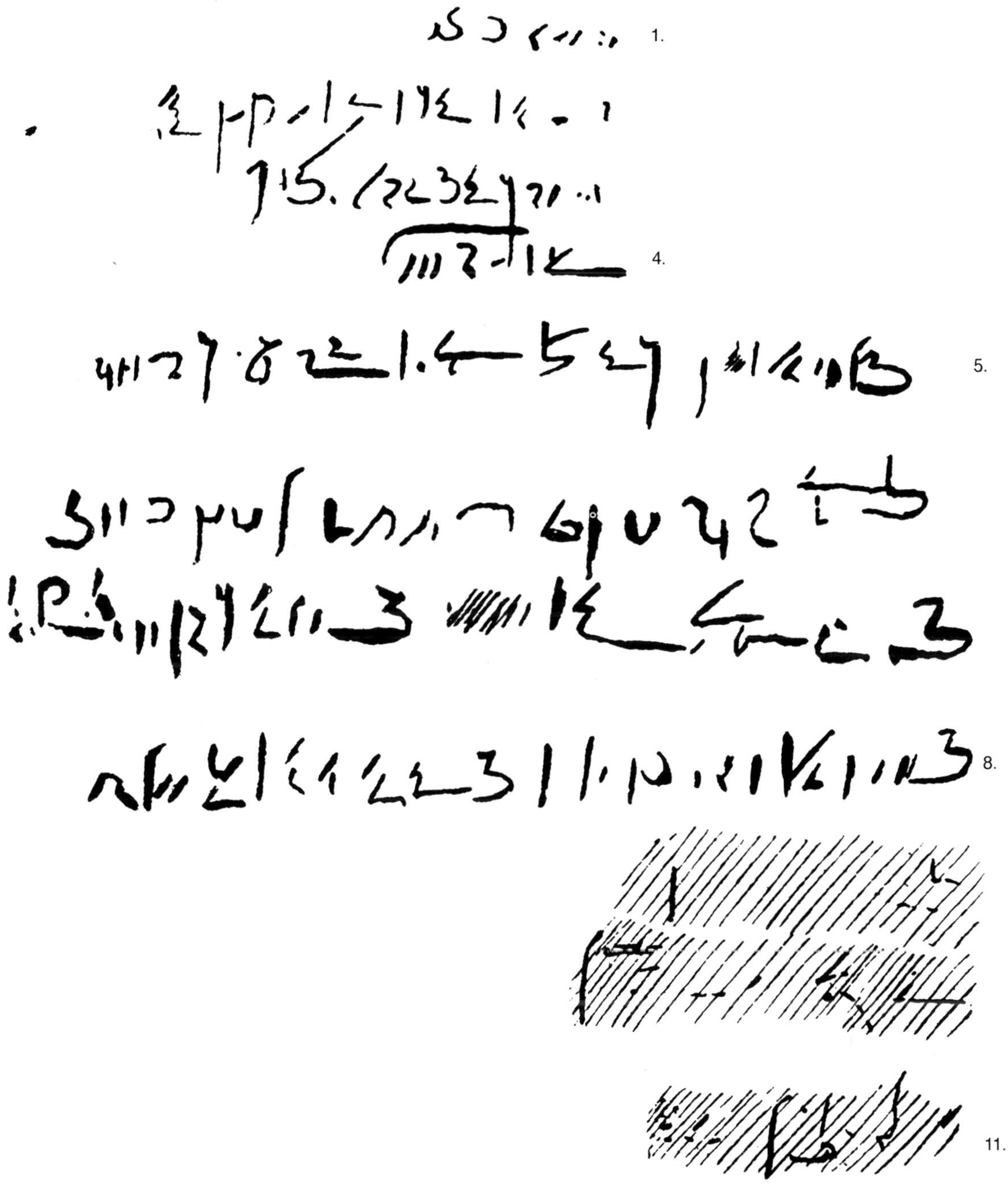

no scale

Graffito 76 (Spiegelberg hand-copy)

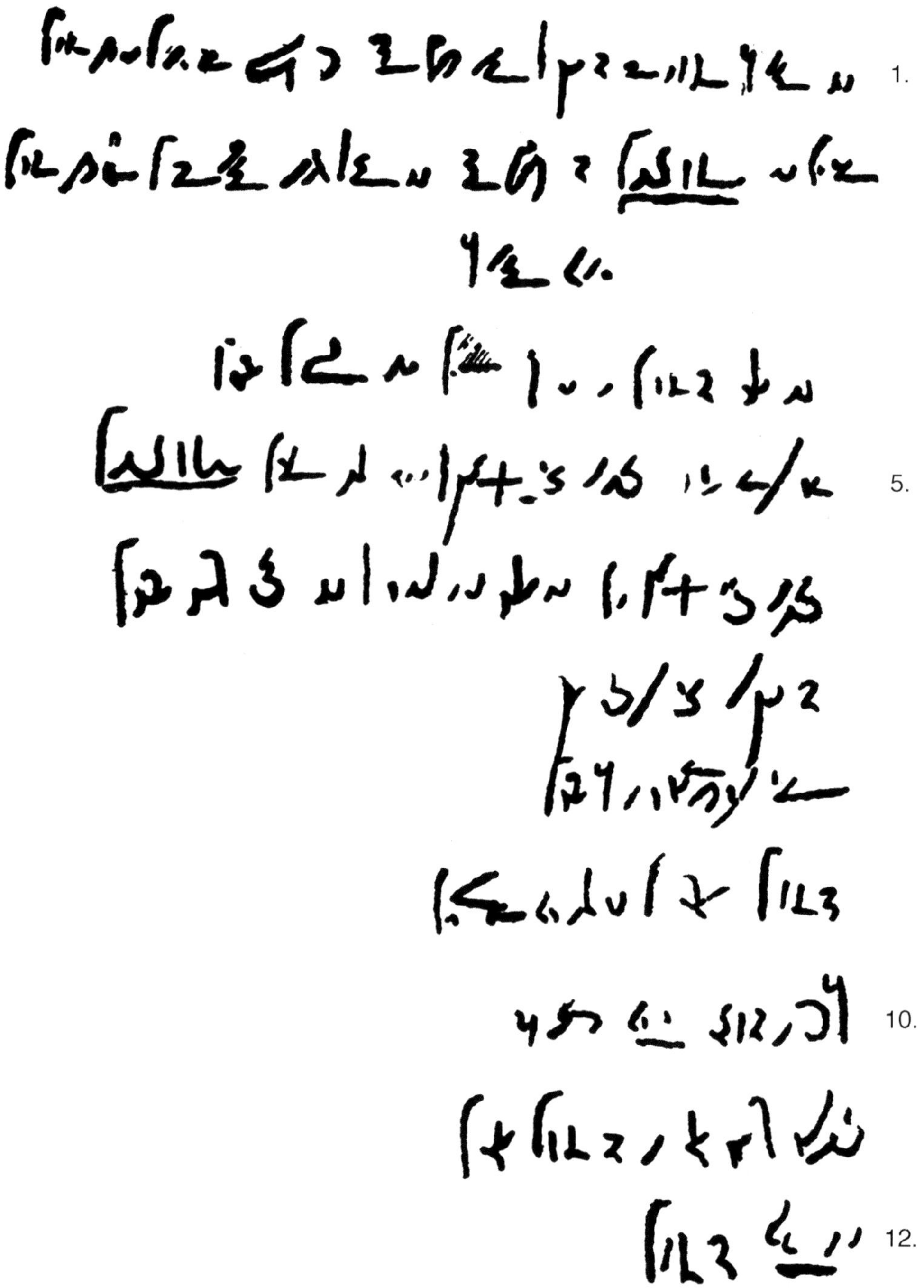

no scale

Graffito 77 (Spiegelberg hand-copy)

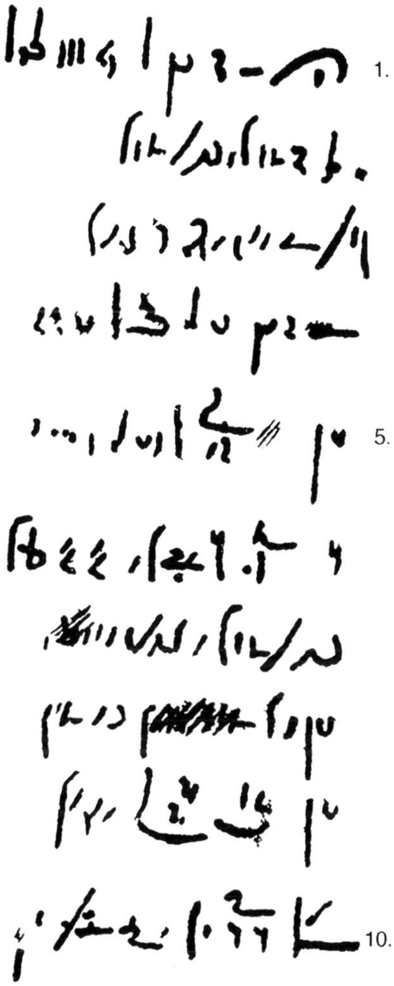

no scale

a. Graffito 78 (Spiegelberg hand-copy)

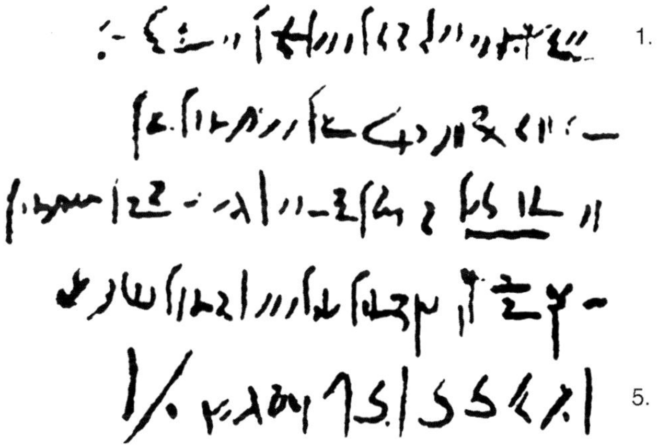

no scale

b. Graffito 80 (Spiegelberg hand-copy)

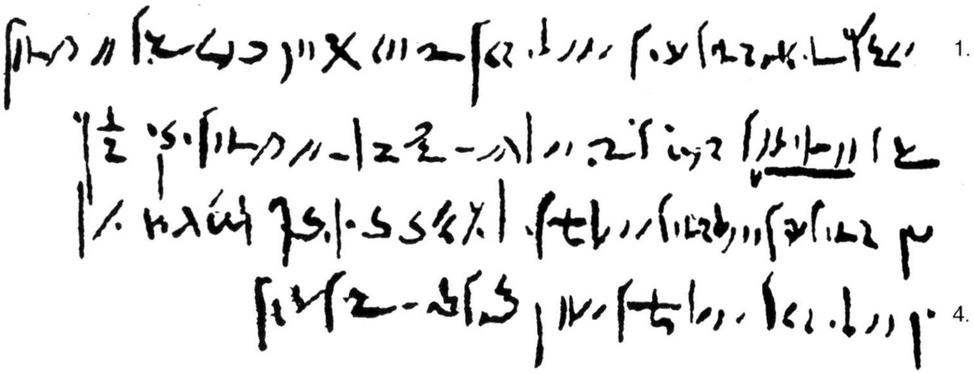

no scale

c. Graffito 81 (Spiegelberg hand-copy)

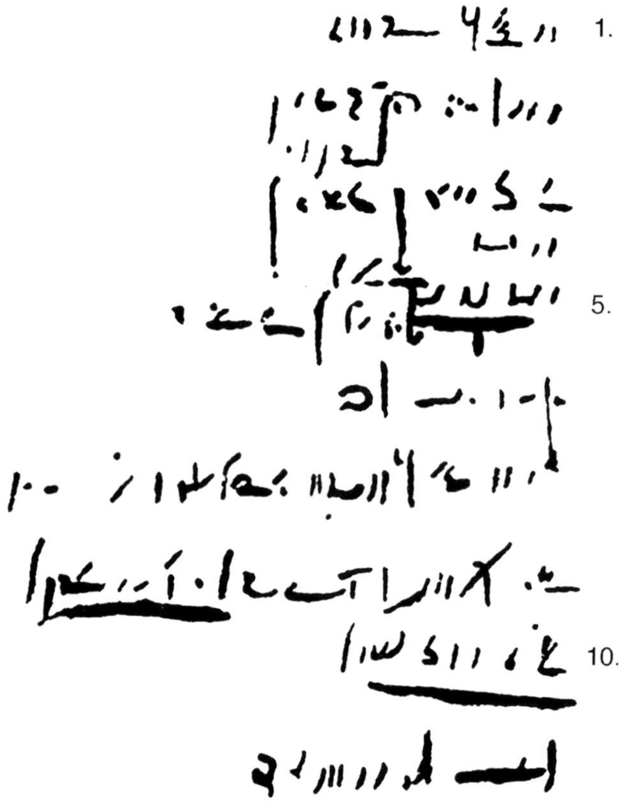

no scale

a. Graffito 82 (Spiegelberg hand-copy)

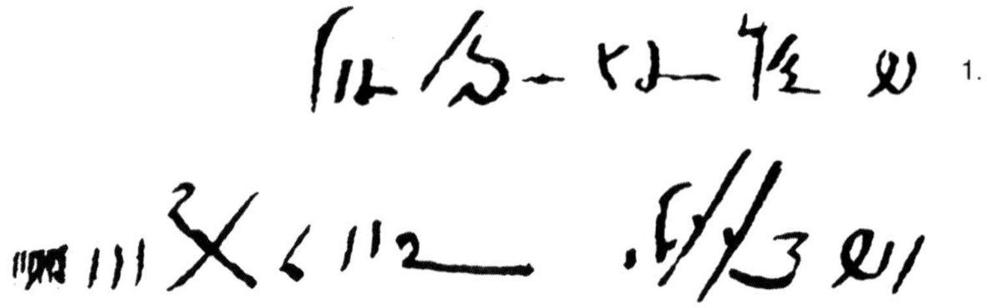

no scale

b. Graffito 83 (Spiegelberg hand-copy)

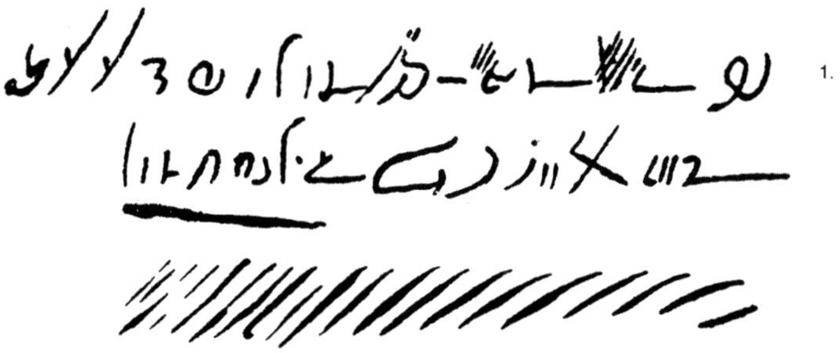

no scale

c. Graffito 84 (Spiegelberg hand-copy)

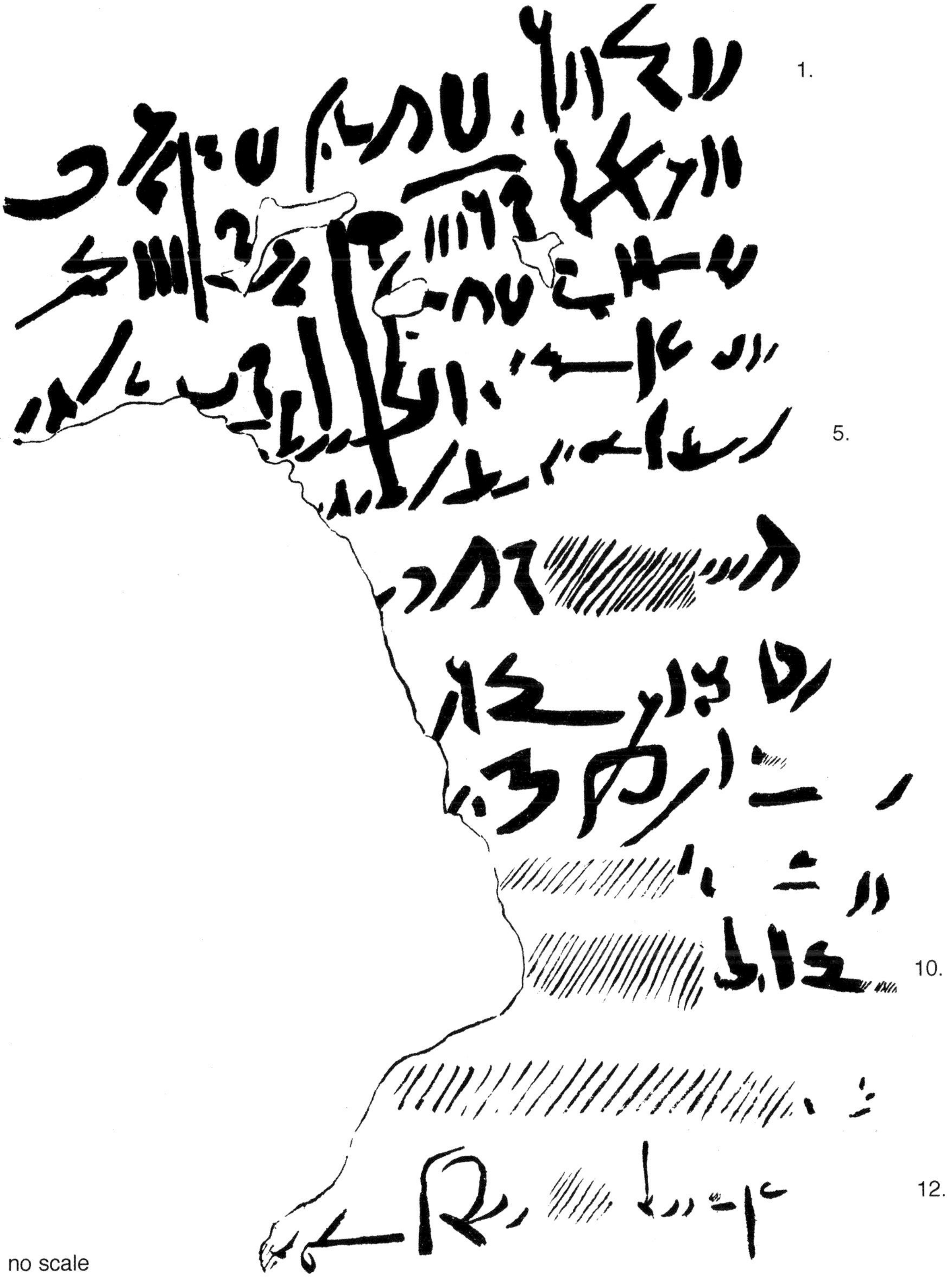

Graffito 85 (Spiegelberg hand-copy)

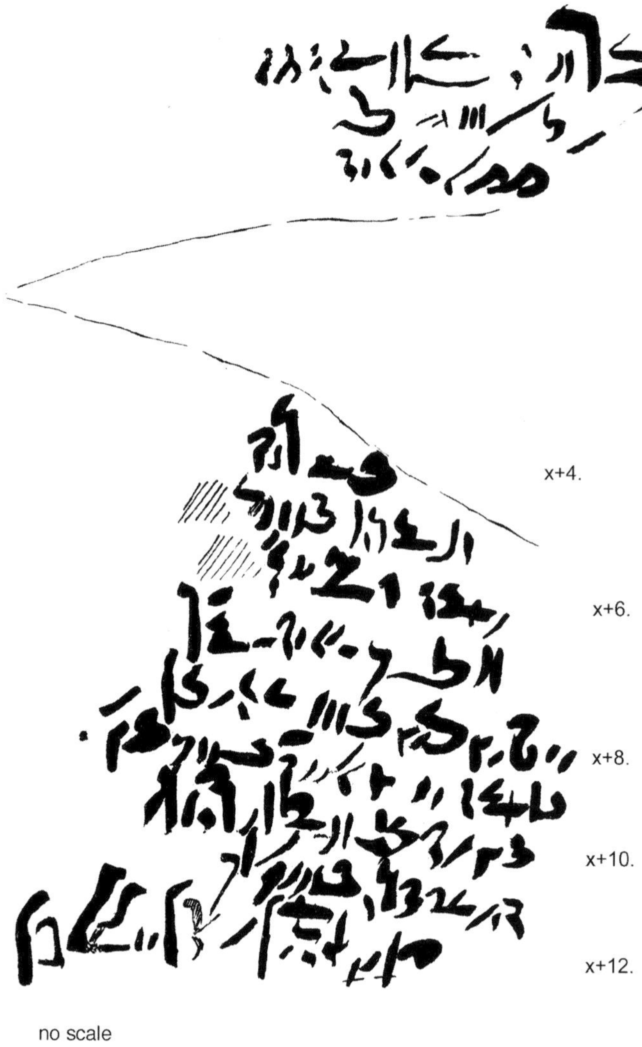

a. Graffito 86 (Spiegelberg hand-copy)

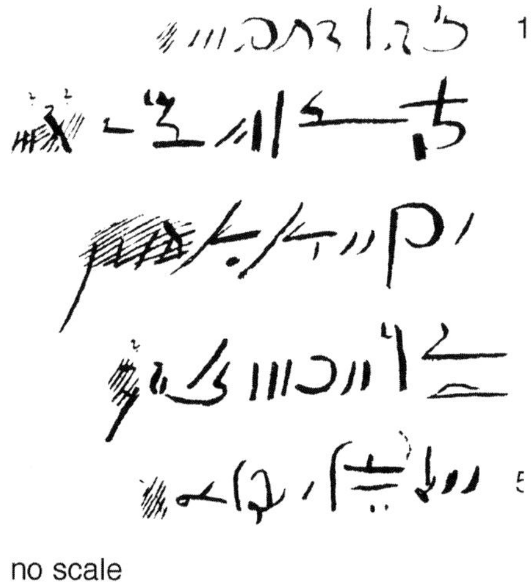

b. Graffito 87 (Spiegelberg hand-copy)

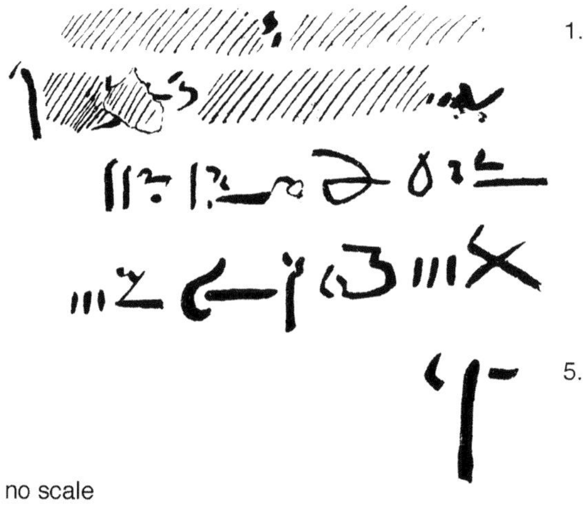

c. Graffito 88 (Spiegelberg hand-copy)

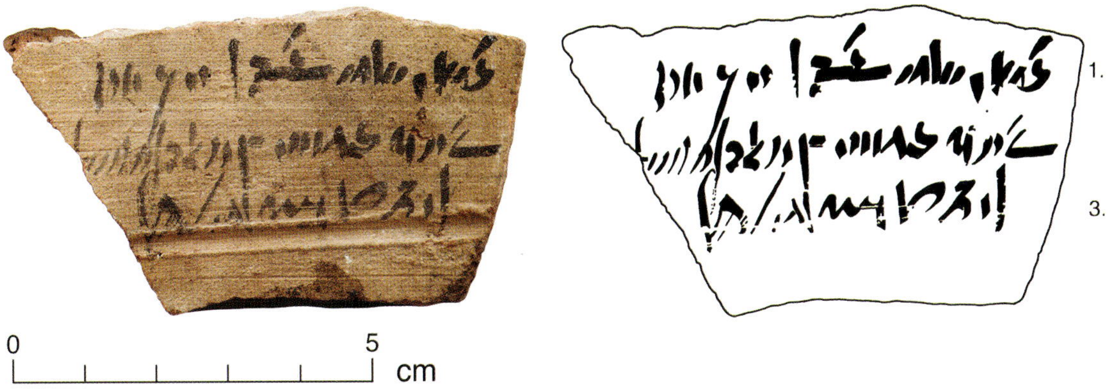

a. Ostracon 1

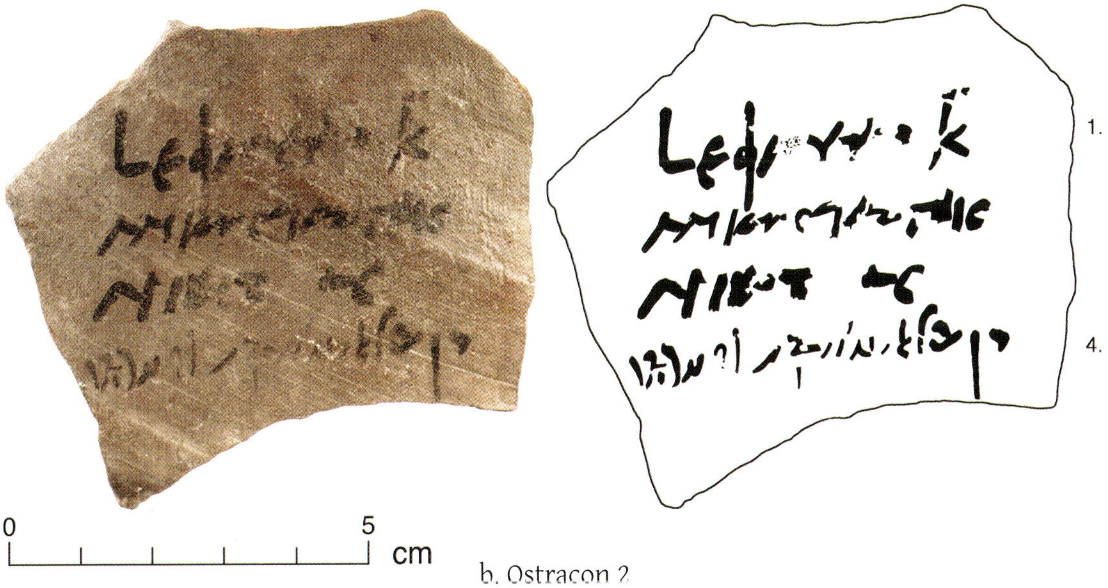

b. Ostracon 2

c. Ostracon 4

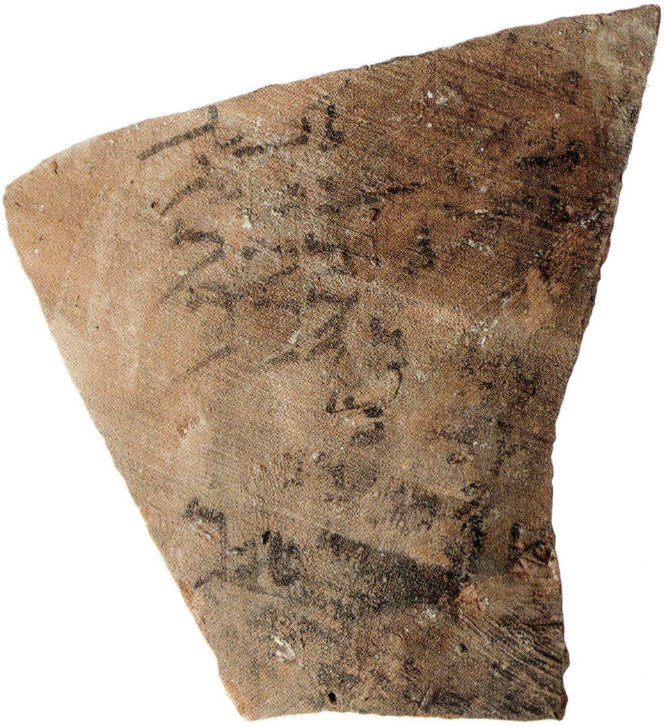

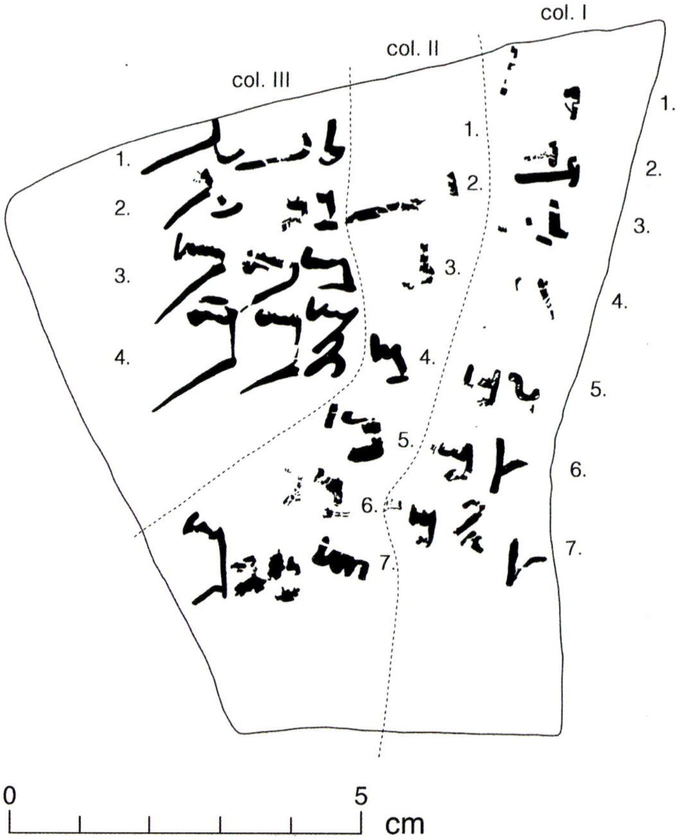

Ostracon 3

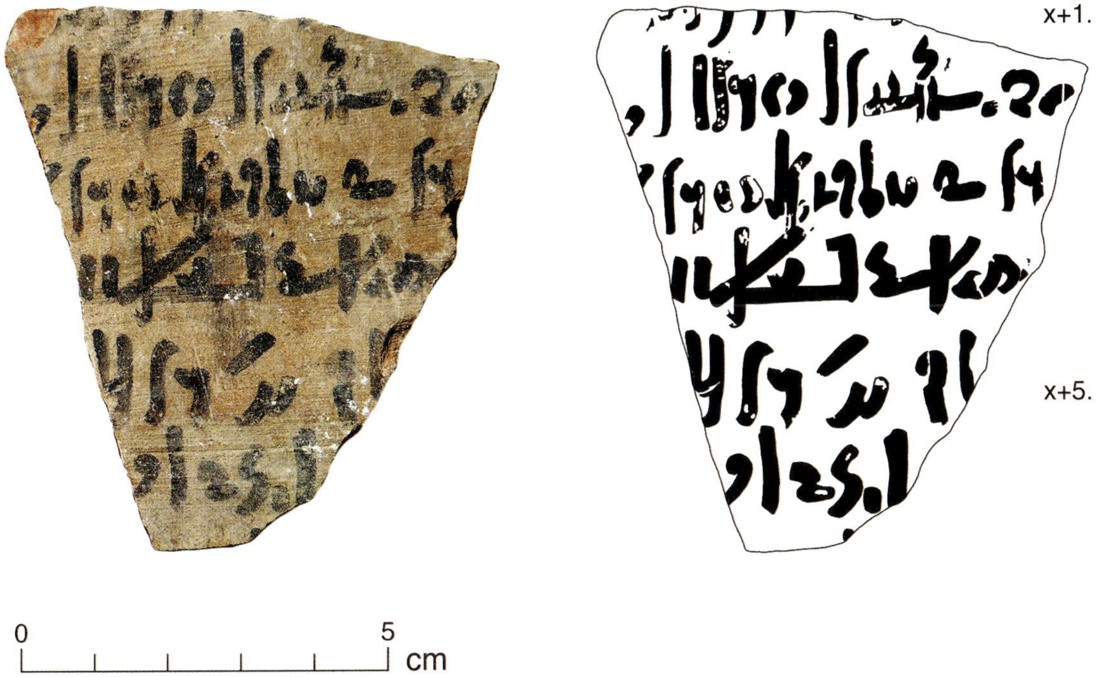

a. Ostracon 5

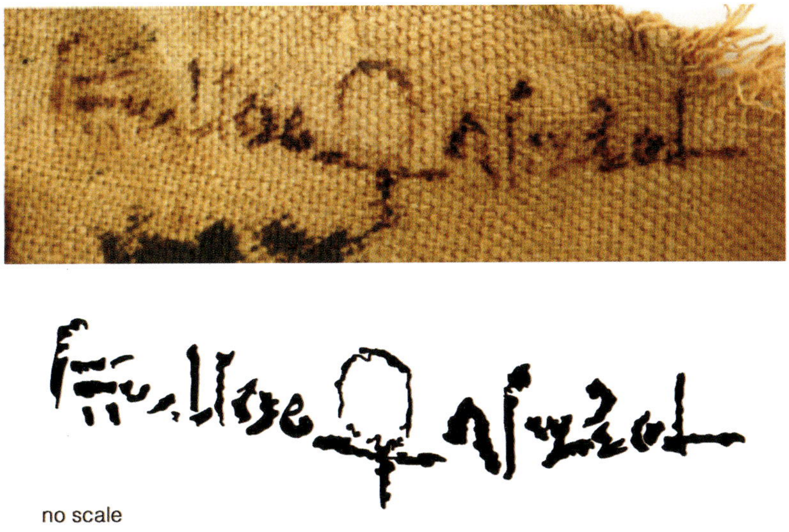

b. Mummy Bandage 1

Child mummy with Mummy Bandage 2.
a. Photograph of child mummy; b. detail of demotic inscription;
c–d. DStretch images of demotic inscription; e. hand-copy of demotic inscription.